# Arthur Ashe

# Arthur Ashe

*Tennis and Justice in the Civil Rights Era*

ERIC ALLEN HALL

Johns Hopkins University Press
*Baltimore*

© 2014 Johns Hopkins University Press
All rights reserved. Published 2014
Printed in the United States of America on acid-free paper
2  4  6  8  9  7  5  3  1

Johns Hopkins University Press
2715 North Charles Street
Baltimore, Maryland 21218-4363
www.press.jhu.edu

*Library of Congress Cataloging-in-Publication Data*
Hall, Eric Allen.
Arthur Ashe : tennis and justice in the Civil Rights era / Eric Allen Hall.
pages   cm.
Includes bibliographical references and index.
ISBN-13: 978-1-4214-1394-5 (hardcover : alk. paper)
ISBN-13: 978-1-4214-1395-2 (electronic)
ISBN-10: 1-4214-1394-9 (hardcover : alk. paper)
ISBN-10: 1-4214-1395-7 (electronic)
1. Ashe, Arthur.   2. Tennis players—United States—Biography.
3. African American tennis players—Biography.   4. Civil rights—
United States.   5. African Americans—Civil rights—History—
20th century.   I. Title.
GV994.A7H35 2014
796.342092—dc23
[B]     2013043573

A catalog record for this book is available from the British Library.

*Special discounts are available for bulk purchases of this book.*
*For more information, please contact Special Sales at 410-516-6936 or*
*specialsales@press.jhu.edu.*

Johns Hopkins University Press uses environmentally friendly book
materials, including recycled text paper that is composed of at least
30 percent post-consumer waste, whenever possible.

*For my parents,*
*Don and Cathy Hall,*
*who always encouraged me to follow my heart*

# Contents

# Acknowledgments

As a child growing up in suburban Chicago in the days before the Internet, I would entertain myself for hours by bouncing a rubber ball against the wall of my family's brick house. I imagined myself as Cubs second baseman Ryne Sandberg hitting a home run or pitcher Greg Maddux hurling a complete game. In the evenings I would peck away on a typewriter, compiling an imaginary box score from the day's imaginary game. I was completely in love with sports, and I even dreamed of a career in sports broadcasting, hoping to join the ranks of Harry Caray and Ernie Harwell. That idea didn't quite work out, but I'm still able to offer commentary on popular culture as a historian of African American history. Bill "Doc" White first encouraged me to pursue a PhD in history when I was only a freshman at Saint Joseph's College. His unwavering belief in me mattered more than he'll ever know. Bill is a great professor and an even better human being.

At Purdue University I was fortunate to work with and learn from a number of talented scholars. My major professor, Randy Roberts, encouraged this project from the beginning and treated me more like a colleague than his student. He was always available to talk about my work, yet he gave me the space that I needed to make the project my own. Nancy Gabin, despite advising many graduate students in the department, read my entire manuscript and offered support and guidance throughout my graduate career. Neil Bynum, Darren Dochuk, Jen Foray, and Mike Morrison took time away from their busy schedules to read my work and listen to my ideas. Doug Hurt provided generous funding for conference travel.

I am eternally grateful to my fellow graduate students, especially Johnny Smith. Johnny has read and offered incisive feedback on nearly every grant proposal, article, and chapter that I have ever written. My deep conversations with Johnny have sharpened my understanding of the relationship between popular culture and the black freedom movement. I am a better scholar for having met him. Jamal Ratchford, Andrew Smith, and Nate Corzine, also members of the Roberts cohort, helped me position my work within the fields of African

American and sports history. Others who contributed to this book in one way or another include Alex Olson, Sara Morris, Erin Kempker, Megan Birk, Katie Higgins, Brett Scipioni, and my adopted aunt, Gilda Abreu, who housed, fed, and entertained me during my long research trip to New York. My wonderful new colleagues at Georgia Southern University, Lisa Costello, Abby Brooks, Eric Silva, Larry Griffin, Michelle Haberland, Jon Bryant, Jeff Burson, Kathleen Comerford, and Cathy Skidmore-Hess, read portions of my manuscript and talked at length with me about my research. The Feltmans—Brian, Carrie, Naomi, and Max—have been the best friends a person could ever ask for.

This book would not have been possible without funding from the Purdue Research Foundation, the Harold Woodman Graduate Research Fund, and the Purdue Graduate Student Government. Johnathan O'Neill, chair of the Department of History at Georgia Southern, graciously provided funding for images. I am forever indebted to the archivists at the Schomburg Center for Research in Black Culture, as well as the staffs at the Library of Congress and the Interlibrary Loan offices at Purdue and Georgia Southern. Special thanks to V. P. Franklin and Dexter Blackman, who published an earlier version of chapters 1-3 in the *Journal of African American History* 96, no. 4 (Fall 2011): 474–502.

My editor at Johns Hopkins University Press, Bob Brugger, recognized this book's potential long before I did. His steady advice throughout the publishing process and his eye for the bigger picture have greatly improved the manuscript. Melissa Solarz answered many annoying e-mails and kept my stress level to a minimum. Joanne Allen saved me from many grammatical errors and is a first-rate copyeditor.

A few others deserve special recognition. Rosendo and Teresa Abreu, my wonderful in-laws, watched the dog so I could do research, attended one of my conferences, and supported me in more ways than I can detail here. My brother, Adam, has encouraged me from the time he could speak, no matter how crazy my dreams. My loving parents, Don and Cathy, always told me to follow my heart. If I lived by that rule, they said, everything else would fall into place. They were right. From the old Mazda that my father drove to work to the many luxuries my mother lived without, my parents always put their children first. And I would not be where I am today without Stuart, Sally, and the love of my life, Christina Abreu. Through good times and bad, winters in Ann Arbor and summers in Orlando, days in the archives and evenings on the couch, Christina has been right beside me. She is everything to me—my adviser, my editor, my comic relief, my workout partner, my reality check, and most importantly my best friend. She has made me who I am. *Te amo mi amor.*

# Arthur Ashe

# Introduction

The grandstands of the West Side Tennis Club in Forest Hills, New York, brimmed with excitement on September 9, 1968, the date of the first-ever U.S. Open championship match. Ever since the United States Lawn Tennis Association made the venue its home in 1915, the crowds that entered the turnstiles had watched as the best tennis players in the world—Don Budge, Jack Kramer, and Rod Laver, among others—battled each other for athletic supremacy. This match was different. Tom Okker of the Netherlands took the court that day dressed in white from head to toe, wearing white shoes, white socks, white shorts, and a white shirt, and bouncing a white ball. On the other side of the net stood a lanky, thinly muscled young man standing six foot one and weighing 155 pounds. He too wore white, but his skin was black. As Arthur Ashe Jr., a native of the segregated South, prepared to serve his first ball, the significance of the moment set in. Not since Althea Gibson's win at Wimbledon in 1957 had the tennis world witnessed such a dominating African American star. Never had men's tennis seen a black man exhibit such an overpowering serve, a lightning-quick backhand, and near-perfect mechanics. A writer for *Life* commented that Ashe "seemed a spectator to his own success," an observation of the ease with which he worked.[1]

Tom Okker had little chance. In the first set, Ashe served like Bob Gibson pitched, driving home fifteen aces with a degree of pinpoint control that kept the quick-footed Okker constantly on the run. Okker excelled at longer points, but Ashe's serve-and-volley game ensured that Okker "didn't get enough tennis." The final set saw an exasperated Okker return one serve wide, another long, and a third into the net. Through five sets, Ashe exuded precision, confidence, and a sense of belonging. "Paul Hornung had his harem, Ty Cobb his uncontrollable rage. Arthur Ashe has his cool," remarked one journalist. Even the mainstream press, long critical of the behavior of black athletes such as Jack Johnson and Muhammad Ali, concluded that Ashe represented a "gentleman's gentleman." He refused to scream, throw tantrums, protest a call, or showboat. Commenting on his calm demeanor, one writer suggested that someone check his pulse for signs of life.[2]

Yet Ashe was more alive and aware of his place in the world than ever before. He understood that his victory in front of thousands of cheering white fans meant a great deal to black America. Throughout the turbulent 1960s, America watched as African Americans held sit-ins at segregated lunch counters, rode in the front of buses, and marched on Washington and across the Edmund Pettus Bridge in Selma. Jim Brown dominated the gridiron, and Muhammad Ali shocked the world by defeating Sonny Liston and announcing his conversion to the Nation of Islam. Now, Ashe stood on the victory platform raising the U.S. Open trophy, crowned King Arthur of a sport controlled by white country-club elites. Ashe used his platform that day to do more than hold up a heavy trophy. He used it to talk about black America, to expound upon his belief in "nonviolent militancy." During and after his time as a student at the University of California, Los Angeles, Ashe had become aware of "a social revolution among people my age. I finally stopped trying to become part of white society and started to establish a black identity for myself."[3]

Ashe's "black identity" and the ways in which it shaped and was shaped by the black freedom movement stands at the heart of this book. Readers of African American sports history have grown familiar with the lives, times, achievements, and struggles of famous black athletes of the past, a long and celebrated list that includes Jack Johnson, Jesse Owens, Joe Louis, Jackie Robinson, Althea Gibson, Bill Russell, Jim Brown, and Muhammad Ali. Their stories and contributions to American society remain legendary: Louis's first-round knockout of German Max Schmeling in 1938, reaffirming American democracy on the cusp of the Second World War; Robinson's stoic ability to endure racial slurs, bean balls, and rabid discrimination in integrating Major League Baseball; and Ali's mastery in the ring, which was exceeded only by his outspokenness outside of it.[4]

For their part, historians and journalists have often categorized black athletes in one of two ways. On one side stand the accommodationists, athletes like Owens, Louis, and Gibson, who played hard, broke records, and achieved celebrity stardom but remained mostly silent on the issue of race. These prominent men and women contributed to the black cause by winning on the field and serving as positive examples for blacks and whites. They chose to pioneer through their athletic performances. "Someone once wrote," explained Gibson in her autobiography, "that the difference between me and Jackie Robinson is that he thrived on his role as a Negro battling for equality whereas I shy away from it. That man read me correctly."[5]

On the other side stand perceived radicals and militants such as Russell, Brown, and Ali—athletes who used their celebrity as a platform for social and political activism. No one personifies this category better than Ali, a superbly talented boxer who changed his name from Cassius Clay to Muhammad Ali just before winning the heavyweight championship in 1964. Ali inspired working-class African Americans by defying white America, joining the Nation of Islam, dabbling in Black Power politics and culture, and refusing to fight in the Vietnam War. This either-or approach to classifying black athletes, however, fails to consider how other African American sportsmen, such as Arthur Ashe, responded to racism, the civil rights movement, and Black Power in more moderate and nuanced ways.[6]

Ashe's center court was both physical and metaphoric. One of the top international players between 1966 and 1975, he routinely competed and won on center court, capturing the U.S. Open in 1968, the Australian Open in 1970, and Wimbledon in 1975. As a player and captain, he led the U.S. Davis Cup team to multiple titles. Sportswriters, players, and fans alike seemed in awe of his unmatched serve-and-volley game and the matter-of-fact way in which he overpowered and befuddled opponents. "Anyone who wouldn't watch Arthur Ashe play tennis wouldn't watch Picasso paint, Hemingway write, a diamond cut, Astaire dance, or Gielgud act. Nobody calls him 'Art,' but he is," declared Jim Murray of the *Los Angeles Times*.[7] And when his physical skills began to deteriorate in the mid-1970s, he proved he could outthink youngsters like Jimmy Connors, defying longtime African American stereotypes that characterized black athletes as physically gifted but intellectually inferior to whites.

Off the court and in the arena of international politics, Ashe positioned himself at the center of the black freedom movement, negotiating the poles of assimilation into white society and black nationalism. Fiercely independent and protective of his public image, he treaded the thin line between conservatives and liberals, reactionaries and radicals, civil rights and Black Power, the sports establishment and the black cause. Critics at both ends of the political spectrum, in the United States and abroad, accused him of doing either too much or not enough for the movement. In naming Ashe its "Sportsman of the Year" in 1992, *Sports Illustrated* recognized his "battered-from-both-sides balance" as a distinctive element of his black identity. His evolving approach to activism, located somewhere between moderate and militant integrationism, relied on patience, direct engagement with white leaders in the United States and South Africa, and open dialogue with his opponents and targeted direct action. Like most ordinary African Americans, Ashe adopted tenets of the civil rights and Black Power movements in arriving at his own form of activism. Wearing an Afro and embracing black empowerment, Ashe practiced a strategy of gradualism and nonviolence. He grew with the black freedom movement.[8]

Ashe's personal journey began in Richmond, where Jim Crow forced him to the back of the bus, denied his entry into local tennis tournaments, and relegated him to Brook Field Park, an undermaintained recreational facility located in the "black" section of town. Racism was the only game in town, and to survive Ashe had to learn the rules. Three African American men—his father, Arthur Ashe Sr.; a local tennis celebrity named Ronald Charity; and Dr. Robert Walter Johnson, a former coach and mentor of Althea Gibson—helped Ashe negotiate racism and segregation. Each believed in the philosophy of personal uplift espoused by Booker T. Washington. They instructed him to keep his mouth shut and his head down, absorb verbal abuse, and never challenge the racial status quo. To get out of Richmond he had to win, and to win he had to play by the rules.

In California, where Ashe attended UCLA from 1961 to 1966, he encountered yet another set of rules. While he broke racial barriers on the tennis court by winning a national championship, civil rights activists bravely joined the Freedom Rides, registered black voters in Mississippi, and marched in Albany and Birmingham. A newly popularized philosophy, Black Power, energized younger members of the black freedom movement and questioned the approach of movement veterans such as Martin Luther King Jr. And Ashe was caught in the middle. "There were times, in fact," Ashe wrote, "when I felt a burning sense of shame that I was not with other blacks—and whites—standing up to the fire hoses and the police dogs, the truncheons, bullets, and bombs. . . . As my fame increased, so did my anguish."[9] This anguish only grew as he engaged in conversations with black radicals, watched the Watts neighborhood of Los Angeles go up in flames, and followed the violence in the American South. He could no longer remain silent.

Ashe's racial awakening came in 1968, the same year that he emerged as America's top tennis player with victories at the U.S. Nationals and the U.S. Open. His expanding celebrity status and his position within the greater sports world led important civil rights figures such as King and Stokely Carmichael to lobby Ashe to embrace their philosophies and approaches to activism. King, Carmichael, and other activists understood that many Americans paid more attention to sports than to politics and civil rights. "Your eminence in the world of sports and athletics," King wrote to Ashe on February 7, 1968, "gives you an added measure of authority and responsibility."[10] By the spring of 1968 King had fallen victim to an assassin's bullet, but the movement would not die there. Ashe was ready to be a leader.

Between 1969 and his death in 1993, nowhere was his commitment to the black freedom struggle more evident than in South Africa, a nation that practiced an extreme form of racial discrimination known as apartheid. For four years beginning in 1969, ruling whites in the South African government refused to let Ashe compete in the South African Open, citing his public antiapartheid statements and his participation in the black freedom movement as the reasons for denying him a visa.

Ashe responded not as a militant but as a statesman. He engaged in formal and informal diplomacy, testifying before Congress and the United Nations and meeting privately with U.S. Secretary of State William Rogers and South African officials. His unwavering persistence and the eloquent way in which he challenged apartheid caught the attention of the South African government and radical antiapartheid activists. South African Prime Minister B. J. Vorster touted his rejection of Ashe's visa in campaign speeches across the country, hoping to convince racial hardliners that he deserved reelection. On the other side of the debate, critics such as South African exile Dennis Brutus and a number of black journalists demanded that Ashe boycott South Africa, call for the expulsion of South African athletes from the United States, and refuse to take the court against players from that nation. But Ashe was not one for giving in to demands. His independence and his reliance on reason, patience, and dialogue superseded his militancy. And when he finally entered South Africa in 1973, he did it on *his* terms.

This volume narrates the career of one of the most significant athletes of the twentieth century. It explains how Ashe overcame racial and class barriers to reach the top of world tennis in the 1960s and 1970s, a time when the sport exploded in popularity. It also follows Ashe's evolution as an activist who had to contend with a shift in the civil rights movement. As societal forces and historical events pulled him in many directions, Ashe made his own choices and crafted his own philosophy. He proved that black athletes could fight racism and injustice from the political center. Ashe was not merely an athlete who stood at the crossroads of sports and civil rights. He shaped the movement by forcing positive change in the United States and South Africa with an approach that borrowed from all elements of the black freedom movement.

# CHAPTER 1

# Richmond

Two public parks, one majestic, the other dilapidated, underscored the realities of "separate but equal" in the 1950s. For many residents of Richmond, Virginia, Byrd Park was the perfect place to escape the grind of city life. Located north of the James River in the city's West End, the park offered three man-made lakes for swimming and boating, a mile-long jogging green, and sixteen tennis courts, which attracted some of the region's best players. Those interested in a more relaxing experience could catch a play or a concert in the amphitheater or sit beside a loved one in the cool grass as the 240-foot Carillon Bell Tower played its fifty-three musical notes. Yet not all were welcome. In the eyes of one youth from North Side Richmond, Byrd Park represented something other than the ideal summer haven. A quick glance in the direction of Shields Lake revealed only white swimmers, and a visit to the tennis courts demonstrated a fact of life in the South: Byrd Park was not for blacks. In 1955, Richmond officials decided to close Shields Lake rather than allow African Americans to swim in it. When a local black tennis star attempted to register two black children in a city tournament, they were told to go home. Segregation ruled in Richmond.[1]

Less than five miles from Byrd Park and surrounded by small industrial businesses, Brook Field Park had neither a bell tower nor an amphitheater. Taking its name from Brookfield Gardens, a postwar federal housing project for low-income blacks, it contrasted sharply with Byrd Park, named in honor of William Byrd II, the founder of Richmond. The three-block, eighteen-acre park had benches, shade trees, horseshoe pits, three baseball diamonds, a basketball court, a football field, and a public swimming pool. Four asphalt tennis courts with one practice board served as a training ground for the tennis team at Virginia Union University, a historically black university. The park was, as one writer put it, "Richmond's largest recreational facility for black residents."

While Byrd Park catered to middle- and upper-class whites with outdoor Shakespeare performances and art festivals, Brook Field Park was for working-class recreation—football, not jogging; crap games, not plays. Nobody confused them.[2]

It was on the courts and fields of Brook Field Park that a skinny, six-year-old Arthur Ashe began a journey that would eventually lead to fame, fortune, and controversy. He would become a champion—of the U.S. Open and Wimbledon, of the antiapartheid struggle in South Africa, of civil and human rights movements around the world, and of the global battle against HIV/AIDS. He would also be maligned by many, from Afrikaner bureaucrats who denied him a visa in 1969 to black radicals who questioned his commitment to the black cause. Through it all he remained composed and stoic, refusing to give in to anger or bitterness. On the streets and courts of Virginia and in the homes of two men—his father, Arthur Ashe Sr., and his tennis coach, Dr. Robert Walter Johnson—Ashe learned to negotiate southern racism. By the time he left Richmond for St. Louis in 1960, his philosophy of moderate integrationism had been shaped by the racist environment he grew up in, his mentors' insistence on hard work and personal responsibility, and the racial and class dynamics of his sport.[3]

―∘·ᴑ∘―

"I grew up aware," Ashe wrote in 1981, "that I was a Negro, colored, black, a coon, a pickanniny, a nigger, an ace, a spade, and other less flattering terms." But on July 10, 1943, the same day that U.S. General George Patton's troops landed in Sicily during the Second World War, Arthur Robert Ashe Jr. was born at 12:55 p.m. at St. Phillip's Hospital, unaware of his place in the world. He was the first of two sons born to Arthur Robert Ashe Sr., a carpenter, chauffeur, and general handyman, and Mattie Cordell Cunningham Ashe, a housewife and department store clerk. As a child, he suffered from a variety of illnesses and ailments, including measles, mumps, whooping cough, chicken pox, and diphtheria. Inheriting a near-emaciated physique, his thin frame initially concerned his family. His maternal grandmother repeatedly instructed Ashe's father, "Don't let Arthur Junior stay out in the sun too long!" Amelia Johnson Ashe might have had an ulterior motive for keeping her grandson in the house. Raised on the stories of slavery, she understood that a lighter skin complexion would lead to greater economic and social opportunities and fewer instances of discrimination. During the slave era, plantation owners regarded lighter African Americans as more intelligent than darker slaves, and fairer-skinned slaves were more likely than darker slaves to work in the house, engaged in skilled labor.

These stereotypes persisted into the 1950s. A 1954 report in *Ebony* argued that many light-skinned blacks obtained more favorable employment than darker-skinned blacks. In addition to the dangers of sun poisoning, a tanner Ashe meant a greater chance of experiencing racism.[4]

Notwithstanding Arthur's poor health, growing up an African American in Richmond presented a series of racial challenges. Historians have argued that black communities in the South, such as Richmond's North Side, made up distinct communities connected to the wealthier white neighborhoods only by the city limits. Although scholars acknowledge greater residential fluidity in Richmond than in cities such as Atlanta or Memphis, they contend that the city's white leaders never reached out to middle-class blacks, leaving the North Side a "separate city," isolated by race and geography. To be sure, some Richmond blacks lived in more affluent neighborhoods. Most, however, crowded into one of three districts: Jackson Ward, Fulton, or the Seventeenth Street Bottom area. Robert Deane Pharr, a resident of Jackson Ward in the 1950s, remembered a poor yet vibrant neighborhood. During the postwar era, he recalled, "we had as much action on Second Street as you'll ever find in Harlem," referring to the restaurants and nightclubs that lined the borough's streets. Yet the city government, under the control of the white aristocracy, neglected African American neighborhoods, resulting in unpaved roads and decaying infrastructure. To maintain residential segregation, Richmond officials zoned each city block into black and white sections. Jim Crow mandated separate seating at theaters and athletic events and on buses and trolleys. Like nearly all American cities, North and South, Richmond was two worlds: one black, one white, separate and unequal.[5]

For a young Ashe, racial discrimination was a part of everyday life. "I never thought much about it," he explained. "Life was that way. There were certain theaters I couldn't go to, certain soda fountains and schools and playgrounds that weren't for me. There was no fuss about it—any more than you'd make a fuss if you couldn't get into a movie studio because you didn't know the right people, or couldn't enter a Moslem mosque because you weren't a Moslem. People in Richmond just took segregation for granted. I don't remember any racial unrest there." To him, racism and segregation were normal, and compliance with Jim Crow was the only option. Isaiah Jackson, a classmate of Ashe's, remembered Richmond in a similar way. "So much of the racial stuff you took for granted," he concluded. "We hadn't gotten bitter about it, or started to fight it, because it hadn't really interfered with us."[6]

Yet African Americans in Richmond had waged a campaign to integrate public transportation in the 1940s. In 1943, Sarah Pettaway and Lavinia Wilder boarded a Richmond trolley and sat down directly in front of a white woman, a clear violation of the city's segregation law. A police officer on the trolley who noticed the infraction confronted the women. "What are you trying to pull?" he asked. "You know better than this. Get up and move back." When both women refused, they were arrested and each fined $2.50 for disorderly conduct by police court judge Carleton Jewett. The defiant actions of Pettaway and Wilder, followed by the arrest of Lavalette Allen four years later for a similar offense, led Richmond women to organize a series of boycotts and protests between 1947 and 1953. By 1956, following the nationally recognized Montgomery Bus Boycott in Alabama, Richmond had voluntarily desegregated its buses and trolleys. Six years later, the city finally hired black drivers. Lost in the national publicity of Rosa Parks and Martin Luther King Jr., Richmond women paved the way for protests that followed.[7]

Ashe experienced firsthand the reality of segregated seating in Virginia. He and his mother sometimes boarded the bus on Chamberlayne Avenue, the unofficial divider between the black and white neighborhoods, and exited at the shopping district or transferred to the Number 6 to visit his grandmother. Getting on the bus was an instant reminder of his place in Richmond. "I can clearly recall the white line on the floor of the bus," he recalled. "It was just to the front of the rear door—and I understood that I was required to stay behind it. I don't ever remember discussing it; it was just understood." Despite his familiarity with the white line, he did challenge the racial hierarchy on at least one occasion. His Aunt Dot once recalled how the boy stood up for his mother on a city bus in the late 1940s. After boarding the bus and realizing there were no seats available in the front or the back, Ashe, in a characteristically polite fashion, asked a white man to give up his seat for his mother. He could have been verbally or physically abused for such a request, but instead the man looked at him and his mother and said, "If you have the nerve to ask me to get up and give your mother a seat, I'm gonna give her my seat." Ashe's bold act revealed a willingness to challenge the status quo in certain situations. It foreshadowed his strategy of caution—of sizing up his opponents before picking a fight.[8]

—◦ ◦—

The racial landscape of postwar Richmond shaped Ashe's early life, but his father was his greatest influence. On the surface they would become much different men: Ashe would be eloquent and educated, whereas his father lacked a formal education. As a writer for the *New Yorker* put it in 1969, "Arthur Junior's personality is contained, controlled, withheld. In Arthur Senior there is no studied cool. His smile is quick. He jokes a lot. He is easy to know." Despite differences of education and personality, Ashe and his father shared common traits. Critics accused both men of accommodating whites at the expense of fellow blacks, both reached out to whites as a means of problem solving, and both were polite, respectful gentlemen—one of Ashe's enduring legacies on the tennis court. More than anything else, Ashe Sr. taught his son to work hard, avoid selfishness, and not challenge the racial hierarchy.[9]

According to a genealogical study commissioned by the family, Ashe's white ancestors came from England and Ireland. The record of "Ashe families in America is that of an energetic, industrious, and resourceful race, strong of will and in many cases possessing the capacity for leadership," noted the report. Though it referred mostly to Ashe's white ancestors, the results of the study described him well. His family tree began in 1735, when an eighty-ton Liverpool rigger, the *Doddington*, docked on the banks of the York River in Virginia. The ship carried 167 West African slaves. On a trip to the Yorktown area, Robert Blackwell, a tobacco farmer from nearby Lunenburg County, was looking for a wedding present for his son. He found the perfect gift in the form of "a Negur girl," whom he acquired in a trade. The woman married a fellow slave, and together they had a daughter whom they named Lucy. Several generations later, Amelia Johnson Taylor, a descendant of Lucy's, married Edward Ashe, and together they had a son, Arthur Robert Ashe.[10]

Ashe's grandfather, nicknamed Pink because of his light skin complexion, was a proud tobacco farmer, carpenter, and bricklayer with a fierce temper. One day, while working a job on the roof of a home, Pink encountered a man who began barking orders at him from the ground. The seemingly calm Pink whistled a church hymn as he slowly descended from the roof. When he reached the ground, Pink took the piece of wood in his hand and without warning hit the man on the head. As he returned to the job, Pink finished his rendition of "Nearer My God to Thee," smiling as he worked.[11]

Pink, who wore a rather scruffy handlebar moustache, had many talents: whistling and singing, consuming large quantities of whiskey, and cozying up to women. "He loved drinks, hijinks, and girls," Ashe noted. He fathered a total of twenty-seven children with multiple women only to abandon them for an independent lifestyle in the 1920s. Eleven years after he left, Ashe's father entered a revival meeting in Durham, North Carolina, and found his father in the crowd

"singing louder than anyone else." Ashe Sr. resented his father, in part for fulfilling a number of African American stereotypes that many blacks worked hard
to avoid. Pink was a shiftless drunk who ran after women and left his family
without warning. To society, he was the black man who was a danger to all,
destroying the moral fiber of America.[12]

Pink's abandonment forced Arthur Sr. into the role of provider, a responsibility he did not shirk. He was determined to be what his father was not—
reliable, sober, and industrious. He would be a better role model for his sons
than his father had been for him. The second of nine children, Ashe's father was
born on April 27, 1920, and raised in South Hill, a town eighty miles south of
Richmond. Unlike his sons, who spent their afternoons playing in Brook Field
Park, Ashe Sr. worked throughout his adolescence. He was a jack-of-all-trades
who removed weeds from gardens, cleaned houses, and collected wood for
families in town. His employers, almost always white families, rewarded him
with fifty cents a week in addition to hand-me-down clothes that their children
had outgrown. His earnings always went to his mother. By the age of nine he was
making five dollars a week as a house servant for the president of a tobacco company. He attended public school in Mecklenburg County through the eighth
grade, often taking night classes with other day laborers. At sixteen he accepted
a job as a maintenance man for the Richmond railroad and eventually took the
same job for the city. Never one to remain idle, he supplemented his income by
mowing lawns, filling swimming pools, catering events, and chauffering prominent whites around town. One of those men was Al Smith, the 1928 Democratic
presidential nominee from New York, who lost to Herbert Hoover.[13]

In a city known for racial segregation, Ashe Sr. befriended a number of white
men and women in the 1930s and 1940s, many of whom would later help support
his son's tennis career. He was the driver for William Thalhimer, the Jewish
owner of Thalhimer's Department Store in downtown Richmond. On one occasion, he drove Thalhimer to the edge of the city to purchase a piece of land.
The Depression nearly bankrupted the seller, but despite his desperate need for
money, he was reluctant to sell his land to a Jew. "You should have heard [the
man]," Ashe Sr. told his sons years later. "He called Mr. Thalhimer all sorts of
things. Mr. Thalhimer never said a word. When the man finished all his ranting
and raving, they closed the deal." On the drive home, Ashe Sr. asked Thalhimer how he had tolerated the insults without changing his disposition. He
responded, "I came out here to buy that land and the end result is I got the land.
It's mine now. He can curse me out all he likes." Ashe Sr. learned an important
lesson from Thalhimer that he remembered for the rest of his life. No matter

what people say to you, he would tell Ashe, no matter how hard they try to make you feel inferior, you must always keep the end goal in mind. Later, on the tennis court, Thalhimer's strategy translated nicely for Ashe. Ignoring racial slurs from spectators and bad calls from white linesmen, he focused on one thing: winning the match.[14]

One evening, while taking a break from work, Ashe Sr. attended a function at the Westwood Baptist Church at which a tall young woman with a thin, gentle face caught his eye. Her name was Mattie Cordell Cunningham, but her friends called her Baby. A shy, unassuming young lady raised by strict parents, Mattie worked at Miller and Rhoads Department Store and was active in the church. She was kind and easy to get along with, yet she possessed a certain seriousness that instantly attracted Ashe Sr. Throughout their courtship they rarely argued, and in 1938 they were married by the Reverend William Hewlett in Richmond. Mattie was just sixteen and weighed a mere ninety-eight pounds.[15]

For a time, Mattie and Arthur Sr. lived with Mattie's widowed mother, Jimmie, who was affectionately nicknamed Big Mama. Her late husband, and Mattie's father, had been a "quiet hard-working railroad fireman" from Oglethorpe, Georgia, who moved to Richmond as part of the Great Migration. He and Big Mama had settled in Westwood, one of the city's predominately African American neighborhoods. With little money to buy their own home, Arthur and Mattie eventually left Big Mama's and moved into a small house on Brook Road owned by an uncle. There, on July 10, 1943, they welcomed their first child.[16]

As much as Ashe and his father had opposite personalities, the young boy and his mother were mirror images, and they built a strong bond around reading. Mattie read to Ashe at night and taught him how to read before the age of five. She barred him from reading *Superman* and any other comic books popular with young boys in the 1940s. Instead, she filled his bookshelves with novels and books on history and science, and he did not seem to mind. Years later, he still preferred the latest literature on Malcolm X or Benjamin Franklin over the comics. A writer for the *Richmond Times-Dispatch* in 1975 found his reading preferences quite odd. "There is a popular belief that pro athletes never 'read' beyond the centerfold of *Playboy*," he observed. "But Ashe may be seen in the dressing room reading a book. Usually a heavy book." On a tour of Ashe's apartment in 1968, writer John McPhee found books scattered everywhere. They included diverse titles such as *Ulysses*, *A Short History of Religions*, *Human Sexual Response*, and *The Rise and Fall of the Third Reich*. Neil Amdur of the *New York Times*, who would collaborate with Ashe on a 1981 memoir, learned that he often skipped lunch at the army officers' club to read at his desk. Amdur observed,

"He reads anything—magazines, newspapers and books like 'The Confessions of Nat Turner' by William Styron." He acquired a love for the printed page early in his youth. Yet another, more pressing love and fascination, as it turned out, was waiting for him just outside his own back door.[17]

In 1947 the city of Richmond hired Ashe Sr. as a special policeman in charge of patrolling Brook Field Park. As a requirement of the job, the family packed up their belongings and moved to a cozy, five-bedroom, one-level home at 1610 Sledd Street, right on the edge of the park. The job of park policeman required him to write citations for and even arrest fellow African Americans who violated any of the park's many rules. Washington, DC, native Willis Thomas, a friend of Ashe's, remembered that "because of [Ashe Sr.'s] job he locked up a lot of blacks, and so he was kind of known as an instrument of the white man down there." Petty crimes such as riding a bike in an unauthorized area, breaking soda bottles, or littering would earn the offender a ticket and a fine. Ashe Sr. did his job well—after all, he reasoned, the rules were clear. His by-the-book mentality did not, however, prevent cries of "Uncle Tom" from working-class African Americans. The custom was that blacks stuck up for blacks. By citing and arresting the sons of working-class African Americans in a white-run park, Ashe Sr., to some, could only be an Uncle Tom, a traitor to his race. Even Ashe was teased for his father's actions. His classmates sometimes stole his books or ripped his clothes to send a message to him and his father.[18]

Yet Ashe Sr.'s new job was a blessing for him and his son. Brook Field Park provided a world of endless entertainment for the young boy. In the summers he spent hours swimming and splashing in the pool, playing tag football with neighborhood kids, and hitting a tennis ball against the park's only practice board. "The field behind my house was like a huge back yard," said Ashe. "I thought it was mine. Brook Field was just an athletic paradise, a dream world for a kid who likes to play sports. . . . The pool was so full of kids in the summer you couldn't see the water. I had no problems at all. There was really no reason in the world for me to leave the place." His failure to share the facilities, however, sometimes presented a problem for other parkgoers. At age six, he often arrived at the park first thing in the morning to hit tennis balls against the practice board. As the morning turned to afternoon, and seemingly oblivious that other kids were waiting for the board, he continued to pound away using a racquet almost his size. It took a stern lecture from the park's policeman, his father, to pry him away from the fun.[19]

Brook Field Park was etched in Ashe's memory, however, for another, far more tragic reason. In March 1950 Mattie unexpectedly stayed home from her job at the department store. She had recently given birth to a second son, Johnnie, so it was reasonable to assume that she needed some rest. Her decision was a curious one for six-year-old Ashe. He knew that adults should never miss work, even if they were sick or tired. Yet he trusted his mother and began preparing for his daily foray into the park. As he left for the park, the image of his frail mother haunted him. She stood by the door of the family home in a blue corduroy bathrobe, waving goodbye for what would be the final time. Later that morning Mattie was taken to the hospital, where she was scheduled to have a minor operation to clear an infection resulting from her recent pregnancy. A procedure of little worry was a major concern for Ashe Sr., as Mattie suffered from high blood pressure and was susceptible to illness. Her family history included a number of aunts, uncles, and grandparents who had died young.[20]

Before Ashe Sr. took his ailing wife to the hospital that spring morning, he noticed a blue jay nestled in the family's oak tree "singing up a storm." "The bird sang for a week," he recalled. "I threw rocks at it. I shot at it with a .38, but not to kill it. The bird sang for a week and would not stop." Then, he remembered, "[a] call came at five-twenty one . . . from the hospital, and the bird stopped singing." The quiet blue jay proved ominous. Days earlier Mattie had suffered a massive stroke following surgery. The day the bird quit chirping was the day she died. Just twenty-seven years old, she was gone. The official cause of death was listed as toxemic pregnancy, certainly brought on by heart disease. When Ashe Sr. returned from the hospital after paying his respects to his dead wife, he called for Arthur and his young brother Johnnie. Ashe recalled, "He woke Johnnie and me, picked us out of the bunkbeds we shared, put my brother on his knee, squeezed me tightly, and told us that Mama had died." He repeated to them how important they were to him.[21]

Mattie's death profoundly changed Ashe's father. He joked less, abandoned his stylish clothes, and approached life more cautiously. Before she died, Mattie lectured her husband on familial responsibility. Aware that she was prone to illness, Mattie told her husband that if she died, the children were his to take care of. "I didn't born them for your mother and I didn't born them for mine," she instructed him. "I born the children for you."[22]

While his father suffered the loss of his young wife, Ashe remembered his mother's death much differently. He recalled the pink satin dress Mattie wore for the funeral, the sights and sounds of family members and friends paying a visit to Sledd Street, and the uneasy feeling in his stomach as he watched loved ones lose control when they viewed the casket. Emotional outbursts unnerved and scared Ashe, a major reason why he attended very few funerals in his life.

He described Mattie's death as traumatizing, an event that taught him to hide his emotions. "I don't remember grieving over my mother," he explained years later. "She died, and life moved on." His response, though seemingly detached and cold-hearted, was completely in line with Ashe's personality. When things did not go his way, he moved on. Whether it was a bad call by a linesman, a snub by the South African government, or his AIDS diagnosis years later, he was determined to make the best of life. That is why during his mother's viewing, as his father and others mourned Mattie, Ashe was equally transfixed on Brook Field's practice board. There, before his very eyes, was a young college student who played the game of tennis with grace and skill. As Ashe stared through the window of his home, Ronald Charity perfected his game. Soon, Ashe would join him.[23]

—cs cs—

Charity was, by all accounts, the perfect mentor for Ashe. A handsome nineteen-year-old African American part-time student at Virginia Union, he taught an afternoon tennis class for local boys in Brook Field Park. While shopping in a bookstore one day, Charity picked up a copy of Lloyd Budge's 1945 manual *Tennis Made Easy.* Charity became enthralled with the game at a time when there were approximately twenty African Americans, men and women, who played regularly in Richmond. Using the all-black YMCA, he taught himself how to hit backhands, forehands, and volleys. A quick learner with graceful strokes, he moved his workouts to Brook Field Park, where he developed a following. "His name," Ashe remembered, "was whispered around the gaggle of girlfriends, relatives, tennis buffs, and curious bystanders who drifted over from the football fields, baseball diamonds, and basketball courts. Ron Charity, they said, was one of the best black players in the country." He might have been the best in Richmond, but his status as a local celebrity did not guarantee his entry into tournaments. Every year he mailed a three-dollar check to play in the Richmond City Tournament, and every year his check was returned with the following explanation: "We regret to inform you your entry has been rejected." The tournament was to be played at the Country Club of Virginia, and blacks were *persona non grata.*[24]

In fact, a number of obstacles could have prevented Ashe, and did prevent others, from succeeding in competitive tennis, including issues of race, gender, and financial cost. To contemporary observers, a quick survey of Ashe's race and class made it clear that tennis was not for him. The sons of affluent families played tennis, not the sons of maintenance men. On the East Coast, it was played at wealthy country clubs on grass and clay courts, not in public parks on asphalt courts. On the amateur level in 1950, Budge Patty won the French Championships and Wimbledon, Art Larsen won the U.S. Championships, and Frank Sedgman won the Australian crown; all were white, upper-middle-class men. The sport's other heroes included Jack Kramer, an aging pro, and newcomers such as Tony Trabert. All of them had one thing in common: none were black. In a 1957 book titled *American Tennis*, Parke Cummings, perhaps sensing a transition, declared, "The days when tennis was the exclusive prerogative of [the wealthy] are long since past." In fact, Cummings's assessment was true. Pancho Gonzalez, a rising star, grew up in the barrios of Los Angeles and was raised in a working-class family. He had made it, so what prevented Ashe? Although the sons of working-class men and women had integrated junior tennis in California, they remained locked out on the East Coast. What Cummings had failed to mention in his romantic overview was that African Americans were not welcome in U.S. tennis circles. The facts were simple: a black man at a wealthy country club was almost certainly taking drink orders, not hitting a ball. Even Ralph Bunche, winner of the Nobel Peace Prize and a U.N. undersecretary, was refused a membership at the West Side Tennis Club in Queens, New York, because he was black. In the 1950s, white players wore white clothes, hit white balls, and played before white audiences. The game was as lily white as they come.[25]

Tennis also presented gender obstacles for Ashe. "As long as I have known it," Ashe wrote in a memoir, "tennis has always been considered, certainly in the crudest male circles, a 'sissy' sport, one mainly attractive to men of ambivalent sexuality." His contemporary Billie Jean King concurred, arguing, "You picture people sipping mint juleps under an umbrella, and it's not that way. People think of tennis as a sissy sport and this is what we have to get away from." A highly popular Broadway play that began its run in 1953 made the same connection. *Tea and Sympathy* was a story about Tom Robinson Lee, a prep schooler who preferred sewing to pranks, the theater to sports. A thoroughly feminine young man, Tom enjoyed tennis. The play reinforced the notion that tennis was a girly sport, played by boys who could not handle manly sports such as football, baseball, and basketball. Alfred Hitchcock's 1954 film *Dial M for Murder* also explores the theme of tennis as an effeminate sport. The protagonist is Tony Wendice, an aspiring tennis star who quit the sport at the request of his wife, Margot. Tennis, she concluded, would not provide for her lavish lifestyle. Wendice then took a job selling sports equipment, fulfilling the role of a traditional working husband. He began to resent his wife, eventually planning her murder. Margot's position in the film is clear: tennis did not allow her husband to be a man.[26]

Additionally, the high financial costs of the sport limited its appeal among poor and working-class youngsters. For many kids, black and white, sports like basketball and football were much more affordable. In a 1962 interview, Arnold E. Lynn, one of the few black tennis professionals of the time, called Ashe and Althea Gibson "special cases" because they were lucky enough to obtain sponsors. Those sponsors, black and white, helped Ashe cover his tournament costs, which included, in an average season, $750 for racquets and strings, $150 for shoes, and $60 for socks. Ashe's father, ever the penny pincher, initially regretted that his son had not chosen a more affordable sport. But before the sponsors sent in their checks, Ashe had to prove himself on the court, and Ron Charity would help him do just that.[27]

Ashe did not have the look of a future tennis champion when he first met Charity. Thin, bony, and frail, he seemed more likely to injure himself than to hit a powerful drive. "It was difficult to tell whether Arthur was dragging the racket or the racket was dragging Arthur," Charity recalled. Once, when he came home with a permission slip to join the football team, his father envisioned broken arms and legs and refused to sign it. Tall for his age, Ashe appeared lanky and slender, his bones and joints clearly visible. When held vertical in his left hand, Ashe's wood racquet stretched from his knee to just below his chin. Observers marveled at the power generated by such a thin physique.

But Ashe desperately wanted to fit in and play a sport other than tennis. Black children idolized Jackie Robinson, not Althea Gibson. "Baseball had special meaning for all colored boys because of Jackie Robinson," he remembered. "As soon as the Brooklyn Dodgers signed Jackie Robinson, every black man, woman, and child in America became a Dodger fan." For years he tried to follow in Robinson's footsteps, going so far as to join his high-school baseball team. Francis Foster, a retired dentist and one of Richmond's local African American historians, observed that Ashe "was a superior ballplayer. He had the speed of a gazelle and a sharp batting eye." Yet not everyone supported his baseball plans. One day, while Ashe was seated at his desk, his teacher at Maggie Walker High School received a note from J. Harry Williams, the school's principal. Ashe was to see him immediately. When he arrived in Williams's office, the principal sat the boy down and delivered a non-negotiable message: he was to quit the baseball team at once because he was too good at tennis to risk an injury on the diamond. Williams understood the importance of an African American breakthrough in tennis. By the early 1950s African Americans were represented on many Major League Baseball teams. In tennis, blacks remained locked out. For this reason, Williams brought Ashe's dreams of playing for the Dodgers to an abrupt end.[28]

It was clear, at least to others, that tennis was Ashe's future. His first official meeting with Charity came a day after he watched the Virginia Union protégé easily defeat players from another school. Following the matches, Charity was on the courts of Brook Field Park practicing his serve when he noticed a skinny young boy watching his every move. After several more serves Charity approached the boy and asked him his name. "Arthur Ashe, Junior," he replied. Charity instantly knew the name. "Your dad runs the playground," he said. Charity returned to practice, but Ashe did not leave. Finally he relented. "You play tennis?" Charity asked. Ashe shrugged. "You want to learn?" he inquired. Ashe politely nodded that he did.[29]

First Charity taught Ashe the Continental grip, in which a player places his palm on the upper right slant of the handle, shaking hands with the racquet. Then he stood six feet from the boy, on the same side of the net, tossing him balls. He taught him the backhand, the forehand, and later other strokes. Ashe's backhand, which Charity helped him perfect, would become one of his most intimidating shots. John McPhee observed in 1969, "Ashe's favorite shot is his backhand—a predilection that sets him apart from most tennis players on all levels. Nineteen years ago, when Ronald Charity began to teach him the game, Charity purposely led him to believe that the backhand was the easiest stroke." A good listener and an uncharacteristically astute seven-year-old, Ashe learned quickly, practiced hard, and began showing signs of brilliance. During the summers his schedule was consistent and compact: baseball from nine to noon, followed by a brief dip in the pool, lunch at home, then tennis practice with Charity until dinner.[30]

Yet despite his rigid schedule, Ashe was far from a perfect student. He showed enough promise that Charity allowed him to join the Richmond Racquet Club, a local, all-male African American tennis organization for adults. Ashe lit up at the chance to play with the men and proved himself worthy of the challenge. One day, however, he was playing a child his age when he looked around the park to see who might be watching. He knew he was good—really good—and liked the idea that a crowd might be observing him. Charity had been watching from a distance and objected to Ashe's behavior. "I bawled him out for [his actions]," Charity said. "I told him if he continued to do anything like that I wasn't going to be bothered with him anymore."[31]

Despite this momentary instance of arrogance, Charity believed that Ashe was ready for tournament play. At the end of each summer, Brook Field

Wearing his UCLA warm-up jacket, Ashe concentrates on his backhand stroke. His backhand was one of the best in the history of tennis. (UCLA Athletic Department)

Park hosted a tennis tournament for local African American youths, most of whom were eleven, twelve, or teenagers. Since they were barred from Richmond country clubs because of their race, the tournament was one of the only chances for the young blacks to display their talents and win a trophy. Ashe knew he would face older, more experienced opponents, but he believed he had a good chance of winning. The road to victory, as it turned out, would not be so easy. One summer day he left home and headed for the park on his bike. As with other segregated parks, the fields and courts of Brook Field served many purposes; the baseball diamond often substituted as a football field, and the tennis courts doubled as a bicycle track. On this particular trip, while racing on the asphalt, Ashe lost control of his bicycle and crashed to the ground. He knew he was injured, and a visit to the local black hospital confirmed that he had a broken collarbone. His dreams of competing in the tournament were suddenly in doubt, and Charity believed he would have to withdraw. Ashe spent the next two weeks in the hospital recovering from the injury, leaving him just ten days to train. A week and a half later he surprised everyone by not only competing but winning. In the final match, he defeated a young man three years his senior, leaving the mostly black spectators in awe of his talent. Having bested his African American competition, now he would try his hand against the top white players.[32]

Getting on the court with white players proved to be a formidable challenge. Like county clerks, park officials, and restaurant owners in the 1950s, tournament organizers often practiced racial discrimination in subtle ways. Just as clerks would suddenly close their office when a black man or woman attempted to register to vote, tennis officials would often receive a player's application "too late." In other instances, tournament officials accused black players and their coaches of filling out the wrong paperwork or never sending in an application. In 1959 John Southmayd, tennis chairman of the Congressional Country Club, in Bethesda, Maryland, claimed that he had not rejected Ashe for entry in the Middle Atlantic Junior Tournament. Rather, he accused Ashe of registering *after* the deadline had passed. He contended that Ashe's coach, Walter Johnson, "called the club the day after entries closed and he was told it was too late to enter. We never did receive a written entry from Ashe." He promised to present Johnson's grievance before the committee, though whether he actually did is unclear. Given his own experiences with Jim Crow and his careful attention to detail, it seems unlikely that Johnson forgot to file Ashe's paperwork. It is much more likely that Southmayd used the deadline as an excuse to bar Ashe from the tournament.[33]

Charity had his own trouble registering Ashe for a city tournament at Byrd Park. The explanation was different this time, but the underlying reason was the same. When Charity took Ashe and Sterling Clark, another African American youth, to register for the matches, the tournament director, Sam Woods, confronted them. "I'm sorry, we can't let you play," Woods said. Charity demanded that Woods tell him why, though he already knew the answer. "The time's not right yet," he responded. "I can't break the rules as they exist now." As late as 1968, *World Tennis* magazine offered a few sarcastic yet perhaps real reasons why a tournament director might bar an African American from a white event: "Perhaps he thought that black or brown would come off on white balls or that only white children should be allowed to play sports. Maybe he thought the white skins would turn black upon exposure to a person of another color. Or perhaps he thought that any little boy or girl with a skin that was not pure white would give a bad call or would carry a contagious disease."[34]

_◌ ◌_

Although Ashe's most direct experiences with racial discrimination in the 1950s came on the tennis court, de facto and de jure segregation affected all blacks in one way or another. In 1954 the U.S. Supreme Court ruled unanimously in *Brown v. Board of Education* that segregated schools were inherently unequal and therefore unconstitutional. The ruling struck down *Plessy v. Ferguson* (1896), which declared segregation legal as long as black and white facilities and services were equal. Of the four cases consolidated into the *Brown* challenge, one was litigated by Oliver Hill, a high-profile African American attorney and civil rights activist in Richmond. Along with two other lawyers, Samuel Tucker and Spottswood Robinson III, Hill was a member of the National Association for the Advancement of Colored People, or NAACP, an organization that documented instances of discrimination in schools, restaurants, transportation, public facilities, and housing. He contributed to the NAACP's legal strategy of challenging segregation in the court system. Hill had enemies, among them Senator Harry Byrd, who controlled Richmond's Democratic political machine from the 1920s to 1966, and James Jackson Kilpatrick, editor of the conservative *Richmond News Leader* and a fierce defender of school segregation. Kilpatrick's treatise, plainly titled *The Southern Case for School Segregation*, served as the basis for Richmond's Massive Resistance (MR) campaign against the *Brown* decision.[35]

On May 17, 1954, following the *Brown* decision, nine governors and forty-one southern leaders gathered at the John Marshall Hotel in Richmond to discuss the ruling and form an action plan. All of them opposed the decision, and many had campaigned on platforms defending segregated schools. What the delegates sought, then, was resistance, not compliance, a way to "follow" the law without following it. The leaders left without a consensus. Soon thereafter, however, southern opposition to *Brown* crystallized in a series of Massive Resistance campaigns. The MR strategy included the passage of local and state laws designed to block school integration, as well as a media campaign to rally the public in defiance of *Brown*. Virginia passed a law establishing a Pupil Placement Board to review African American applications for entry into white schools. More times than not, black applications were rejected. In the event that a district judge ordered compliance, a new state law allowed the governor to close a school rather than integrate it. Any school that admitted black students risked losing funding. Day after day, Kilpatrick heralded the virtues of "separate but equal" in the *Richmond News Leader*, forcing many white moderates into silence out of fear. In Virginia, only two blacks attended a white school in 1960, thirty-seven in 1961, demonstrating that implementation of *Brown* was difficult in Virginia, as it was in the rest of the United States.[36]

The Massive Resistance campaign only emboldened Richmond's black citizens. Oliver Hill and others were too determined to give in to segregationists. In fact, historians credit the *Brown* decision and MR for sparking the civil rights movement in Richmond. Black leaders formed the Richmond Crusade for Voters to fight segregation at the ballot box, aiming to elect moderate and progressive officials committed to civil rights. In 1960, just after black students from North Carolina A&T University demanded service at a Woolworth's lunch counter, Richmond students staged their own sit-in at a local segregated Woolworth's, occupying all thirty-four seats before the manager closed the store. Later, other students held sit-ins at G. C. Murphy's, People's Drug Store, W. T. Grant, Sears & Roebuck, and Thalhimer's. Far from preventing integration in Virginia, the MR campaign served as a catalyst for protest and eventual reform.[37]

Ashe's father was well aware of the *Brown* decision and the MR campaign that followed. Though he sympathized with Oliver Hill and supported the voter registration drive, any form of protest, nonviolent or otherwise, made him uneasy. "My father respected the skilled, courageous leaders in the black community in Richmond," Ashe explained, "including lawyers such as Oliver Hill and Spottswood Robinson III, who had strong connections to the legal side of the movement; but protesting was for other people." A native of Virginia, Ashe Sr. had witnessed the violent ways that whites reacted to direct-action campaigns. The widower was not prepared to place his family at risk.[38]

Ashe Sr. knew that the South was a dangerous place for black youths. In 1955 Emmett Till, a fourteen-year-old African American from Chicago visiting relatives in the Mississippi Delta, was kidnapped from his uncle's home by Roy Bryant and J. W. Milam, two local white men. Bryant accused Till of making a sexual comment to his wife, Carolyn, who worked behind the counter of the family's store. Some witnesses claimed that Till had grabbed Carolyn's hand, while others said he had yelled "Bye baby" as he left. Till's mother, Mamie Till Bradley, refused to believe the accounts and suggested that her son's stuttering problem might have been misinterpreted by Bryant. Till's body was found days later floating in the Tallahatchie River. He had been beaten and shot, and his body had been wrapped in a fan from a cotton gin. In Chicago, Till Bradley chose to display her son's body in an open casket, and *Jet* magazine published images of Till's mutilated corpse. Bryant and Milam stood trial in Mississippi but were quickly acquitted by an all-white jury, who argued that prosecutors had not proven the identity of the body. For Ashe Sr., Till's murder was a stark reminder of what could happen to his sons: "My father tried to keep us out of harm's way, and the possibility of harm was real. We all knew what had happened to Emmett Till, whose death in 1955 cast a shadow over my youth and that of virtually all black kids in Richmond and no doubt across America."[39]

In part to avoid what had happened to Till, Ashe Sr. kept a close eye on his sons. As a parent, he was stern and unequivocal, his methods of discipline bordering on overprotection. On Ashe's first day at segregated Baker Street Grammar School, for instance, Ashe Sr. walked with him from Brook Field Park to the school's entrance, a ten-minute trek. His father commanded that he return home exactly ten minutes after dismissal, and not a minute later. Ashe's father did all he could to keep his sons out of trouble. In high school, Ashe was elected to a committee in charge of purchasing a gift for the class-room. His peers recognized him as a responsible straight-A student, an ideal choice for such an important task. Ashe was excited, but he knew better than to take the bus downtown to shop with his classmates without his father's per-mission. He was sure his father would say yes, but instead Ashe Sr.'s response was, "No, you get right home." Ashe recalled what happened next: "I hated it but I went home. An hour later we heard that the group I would have been with had been picked up for shoplifting." The guilt or innocence of his friends was not the issue. What mattered was that an African American in a white-owned store was an easy target for overzealous and racist clerks and police officers, and Ashe Sr. knew that all too well. Like Ashe, a classmate of his, Isaiah Jackson, had a father who kept him away from potentially dangerous situations. "Our parents were smart," Jackson explained. "They just kept us away from what was socially poisonous, the things that would make life difficult or embar-rassing for us." Though Jackson and his friends begged to see a movie at the segregated Loew's Theatre, his parents insisted that he patronize the Booker T or the Walker Theatre instead.[40]

Ashe Sr. was an old-fashioned disciplinarian, a man who would not tolerate insubordination. His view of the world left little room for nuance or debate. On the few occasions when Ashe returned home late, forgot to do a household chore, or misbehaved, his father ordered him to retrieve his thick, "first quality cowhide" belt for a beating. "Only grade-A leather would do for my behind," Ashe reminisced. In an interview just before he died, Ashe revealed that well into his twenties and thirties he believed that "if I got out of line my father would kick my ass." He feared punishment at the hands of his father and worked hard not to disappoint him.[41]

One of Ashe Sr.'s commandments was to remain busy and productive at all times. "There's to be no hanging around," he instructed his sons. "If you don't have to be somewhere you should be home." Aside from the dangers of falling in with the "wrong crowd," more time at home meant less chance of becoming the victim of racial violence. And Ashe had plenty of chores to keep him busy at home, including making his bed, cleaning his room, feeding the dogs, and chopping wood for the fireplace. Once he finished the household chores, he would devote his time to his schoolwork. Later, he reflected on his upbringing: "Daddy instilled self-sufficiency in us. . . . Hard work and discipline helped shape my personality. I studied in school and read extensively because Daddy wanted me to be the 'best reader in school.'" Ashe Sr. understood the importance of a good education. In an interview with John McPhee, he summed up his philosophy. "I kept the children home pretty close," he explained. "My children never roamed the streets. A regular schedule was very important. A parent has got to hurt his own child, discipline him, hold him back from things you know aren't good for him." For the remainder of his life, Ashe adopted his father's philosophy of industriousness. Even after he became a celebrity, and to the chagrin of many sportswriters, he was often too busy for interviews.[42]

Ashe Sr.'s commitment to hard work is most evident in a home that he built himself. In 1955 he married a widow, Lorene Kimbrough, who had two children from her previous marriage. As a wedding gift, Kimbrough's father gave the couple five acres of land in Gum Spring, a town northwest of Richmond just off of Interstate 64. That same year, the state of Virginia began razing neighborhoods in the black section of Richmond to route Interstate 95 through the city. Ashe's Aunt Dot and many other local blacks were forced from their homes by the government-funded construction crews. A moment of crisis for many African Americans was an opportunity for Ashe Sr. Whenever he had the time, he began collecting cinder blocks and other scrap materials from the construction site to build his own house. On the weekends, Ashe and his father drove truckload after truckload of scrap materials to Gum Spring. Some blacks and whites criticized Ashe Sr. for "hustling" building materials. But rather than lamenting or protesting the destruction of historically black neighborhoods, he focused on recycling the wreckage.[43]

Along with giving them a steady diet of hard work, Ashe Sr. taught his boys how to keep their emotions in check and avoid conflict with potentially hostile whites. He urged his sons never to give in to bitterness or feel sorry for themselves; there were just as many "good" whites, he assured them, as there were bad ones. "I tried to impress on Arthur an old saying a woman who raised me in South Hill once told me," he told a Richmond reporter in 1968. "She said, 'A seeing eye and listening ear, a silent tongue and faithful heart, time and patience will accomplish everything.'" Ashe and his brother were to be observant, deferential, and respectful to others regardless of how they were treated. Their father was a positive example to them, rarely fighting or arguing with anyone.[44]

But living in Richmond in the 1950s was a constant reminder to Ashe of his position in the racial hierarchy. "To whites," he later observed, "being black is like being pregnant—you can't be a little bit of either." He could not ride in Yellow Cabs, play in Byrd Park, drink from "white" water fountains, or compete in the elite local tennis tournaments. He attended only segregated schools in Richmond, and early on he developed an antenna, as he called it, for detecting potential conflict. He explained, "Growing up black in the South, for survival and protection your antennae were always out. My grandmother often used the phrase 'good white people' to describe those who helped us. She also talked about 'bad white people'; the ultimate bad white people were the Klan—the Ku Klux Klan." Despite his father's belief in the inherent goodness of people, Ashe's experiences taught him that "collectively, white people didn't really like blacks."[45]

For this reason and others, Richmond, with its crumbling asphalt courts and segregated tournaments, was no place for an emerging African American tennis star. Ronald Charity knew it was time for Ashe to move on. One of Charity's best friends in 1953 was Bobby Johnson, a fellow black tennis player who lived in Lynchburg, Virginia. "I used to get up around seven on Saturday mornings," Bobby remembered, "and Charity would be sitting on the back porch waiting for me to come out. . . . Then we'd play tennis all day, and afterward, he'd drive back to Richmond." Bobby's father was Robert Walter Johnson, a local physician and a prominent member of the American Tennis Association (ATA), the country's premier organization for black players. Each summer, Johnson invited a handful of junior players to his home in Lynchburg for a tennis training camp.

His goal was to find one or more young men who played well enough and had the right demeanor to integrate the National Interscholastic Championships, held in Charlottesville, Virginia.[46]

One day while visiting Bobby, Charity mentioned Ashe to Johnson. He was young, Charity admitted, but he had enormous potential and just the right attitude to handle the physically grueling camp. The following Sunday, Charity loaded Ashe into his car and drove to Lynchburg. When he first laid eyes on Ashe, Johnson wasn't sure what to think: "The doctor's eyes narrowed when he saw him, and he wondered if the child had been a victim of rickets, he was so bony and frail. Arthur hit a few tennis balls, and Dr. Johnson, watching him run, was afraid he would pitch forward and fall." He was young and brittle, Johnson observed, but he had talent—and lots of it. And although Ashe Sr. liked to keep his son home and away from potential danger, he was aware of Johnson's credentials and agreed with his vision and his methods of discipline. With his father's permission, then, Ashe was off to camp.[47]

On the surface, Johnson was the opposite of Ashe's father. Ashe Sr. was reserved and careful; Johnson was not afraid to take chances and challenge the status quo. Ashe Sr. was an activist in spirit; Johnson was one in practice, joining sixty black students in protest outside of a Woolworth's in 1960. A member of the black middle class, he owned a big house in a white neighborhood and drove an Electra 225. Five foot nine, Johnson carried himself in a strong and proud manner. To Ashe he was "an immensely rich Negro, with his tennis court and his Buick, and his seemingly endless supply of money. At ten and eleven years old, I was rather awed by the guy." Differences aside, Johnson and Ashe Sr. agreed on how the young tennis player should conduct himself in public. For both men, discipline was key. Once when Ashe threw his racquet in anger in Brook Field Park, "he heard the screen door of his house slam before the racquet hit the ground." Ashe Sr. would not stand for poor sportsmanship or childish tantrums. Likewise, when Ashe initially refused to alter his grip on the tennis racquet, Johnson immediately phoned Ashe Sr. and asked him to pick up his son. Stubbornness would not be tolerated by either man.[48]

Like many southern blacks in the Jim Crow era, Johnson overcame many obstacles in his lifetime. Born in 1899 to Jerry Johnson, "an astute businessman" and logger, and Nancy, a housewife, he worked at the Plymouth Box and Panel Company, making sixty-five cents a day. His father was a diligent worker with a keen entrepreneurial sense, often taking difficult logging jobs for additional wages. Achieving middle-class status, Jerry eventually owned a furniture store, a grocery, and an auditorium where local teens gathered to view movies. As a young man, Jerry's son preferred leisure to work, girls to logging. When he was seventeen, a girl accused him of fathering her child. Though he denied that he was the father, his parents seemed to think otherwise and helped to financially support the child. Johnson later attended Shaw University, a historically black college in Raleigh, North Carolina, doing, as his biographer, Doug Smith, noted, "what he loved to do best: play sports and play around with pretty young women." A star in football, baseball, and basketball, Johnson began courting Annie Pate, a sixteen-year-old with light skin and straightened hair. Dismissed from Shaw his sophomore year for staying overnight in the girls' dormitory, he was subsequently expelled from Virginia Union, his next stop, for hosting illegal poker games. He soon married Annie at a Methodist church in Greensboro and then left her behind for the football program at Lincoln University.[49]

In the fall of 1922, Johnson enrolled at Lincoln, where he dazzled football fans with his speed and toughness. Refusing to wear a helmet, he streaked downfield, his long hair streaming behind him, held up by the wind. A teammate, Hildrus Poindexter, said he looked like a whirlwind. The name stuck. Though he was named to the Negro All-American team, football did not offer a young black man much of a future. The professional leagues were still in their infancy in the 1920s, many spectators preferred the college game, and few blacks had made it to the professional ranks. Johnson's future, as it turned out, was in medicine and not on the gridiron. Following brief coaching stints at Virginia Seminary College, Morris Brown College, and Atlanta University, he attended Meharry Medical College in Nashville, Tennessee, and worked to become a general practitioner. After his graduation in 1932, he accepted an internship at Prairie View Hospital in Prairie View, Texas. There he met a number of black professionals who played tennis in their spare time, and Johnson, ever the competitor, usually joined them. He "became addicted" to the sport and transplanted his hobby to Lynchburg, where he replaced the town's recently deceased black doctor. His practice thriving in 1936, Johnson moved into a large, two-story home at 1422 Pierce Street and built a clay tennis court in his backyard.[50]

Yet well before Johnson built his tennis court in Lynchburg, African Americans were involved in competitive tennis in the first half of the twentieth century. As early as 1898 an interstate tennis tournament held at the Chautauqua Tennis Club in Philadelphia featured the region's best black players. By 1916, black players from Washington, DC, New York, New Jersey, Massachusetts, and Pennsylvania, representing fifty-eight tennis clubs, competed at various times throughout the year. To the sport's backers, however, the occasional tournament was not enough. Blacks needed more tournaments, greater financial support, and increased player development programs. On Thanksgiving Day 1916 the American Tennis Association (ATA), the nation's first black tennis organization, was created. Representatives from the twenty tennis clubs that made up the ATA's membership laid out a series of goals that included founding new clubs, bringing local and regional tournaments under the auspices of a single organization, promoting the standards of the game, and hosting an annual championship tournament. The doctors, lawyers, and other professionals who made up the ATA's leadership hosted their first championship matches at Druid Hill Park in Baltimore in 1917. By 1940 the ATA claimed 145 clubs with a combined membership of one thousand, including Robert Walter Johnson.[51]

As a member of the ATA, Johnson's main contribution was working with black youths. His summer tennis camp, the Junior Development Program, developed by happenstance. One afternoon while driving from Lynchburg to Washington, DC, Johnson made an impromptu stop to watch the National Interscholastic Tennis Championships in Charlottesville. The competitors, many of whom hailed from wealthy suburbs, were good but not unbeatable, Johnson believed. He knew that with months of intense training and the proper financial backing African Americans could compete against white players. At the Interscholastic Championships he struck a deal with Edmund "Teddy" Penzold, the director of the event. Penzold promised that if Johnson succeeded in producing black players with outstanding talent, he would support the entry of one or two of them. With the deal in place, Johnson needed to find and train his athletes.

Returning to Lynchburg, Johnson made a few phone calls to ATA officials, laying the groundwork for his first summer training camp. The plan was simple. Each summer he would invite a handful of the region's most talented black players to his home based on recommendations from ATA members. Once he identified the players, Johnson mailed invitations to high-school tennis coaches with a list of rules and expectations. The students would live in his house, eat wholesome meals, train in his backyard, watch film of tennis matches in the evening, and learn proper etiquette. A participant in the civil rights movement, he was aware that his tennis pioneers had to have the right temperament and demeanor as well as athletic talent. How they conducted themselves in hotels, restaurants, and at tournaments was perhaps more important than how they behaved on the court.[52]

Initially, the results of Johnson's camp were disappointing. In 1951, Victor Miller and Roosevelt Megginson, both students at Dunbar High School, became the first African Americans to enter the Interscholastic tournament. Johnson promised officials that he would drive his players to Charlottesville and leave immediately following their matches, without staying overnight or lingering in town. Intimidated by hostile white crowds and their white opponents, Miller and Megginson suffered humiliating defeats, both losing 6-0, 6-0. The performances of the two young blacks highlighted a major problem for Johnson in the camp's early years: many blacks were reluctant to attend because of race, class, and gender stigmas. Just when Johnson might have given up, little Arthur Ashe appeared in his driveway. It would take six years, but the scrawny boy would help Johnson accomplish his most sought-after goal: victory at Charlottesville.[53]

Johnson maintained and enforced strict rules for the participants in the Junior Development Program, complete with a proper code of conduct. Failure to follow the rules would result in a swift dismissal, a fact Ashe quickly discovered during his first three days in Lynchburg. When Johnson's son Bobby, who assisted his father with the camp, tried to teach him the Eastern and Western racquet grips, Ashe refused to learn, believing that Charity had already taught him the appropriate grip. "I wasn't taking any shit," Bobby remembered, telling the young man, "Well, if you want Ron Charity to teach you . . . why don't you go home?" The elder Johnson learned of Ashe's stubborn behavior and phoned Ashe Sr., who immediately drove to Lynchburg. After talking with Johnson, Ashe Sr. approached his son and in a stern, forthright manner told him, "Dr. Johnson is teaching you now, Arthur Junior. You do what they say." "It was that simple," Ashe recalled. "I always obeyed my father. [Johnson and his son] had no more trouble with me." "But to tell you the truth," he wryly explained, "I didn't really change the grip on my backhand that much." Ashe was not a passive subject.[54]

Resembling an army boot camp, Johnson's program was rigorous and demanding. Players began the day by making their beds before tending to a variety of other chores, including clipping the rose bushes, trimming the boxwoods, weeding the yard and garden, and, worst of all, cleaning up after the dogs. "Somebody had to clean out the doghouse—with lye," Ashe remembered. "Man, you should smell the mess it left every day." As the youngest kid in camp, he often received the more "rotten" chores. Mealtime was equally regimented. Ashe explained that Johnson "had a giant freezer that he stocked with fish, birds, and game he killed. Usually there were mountains of rice, which I loved. I had to learn to slow down and stop snatching, because Dr. Johnson insisted on perfect manners." A typical breakfast included one or more meats, like steak, lamb chops, sausage, beef, and bacon, two to four eggs, milk, unsweetened fruit juices, whole wheat bread, and cereal. A quick sandwich sufficed for lunch, and dinner consisted of a lean protein such as chicken or turkey, potatoes, vegetables, salad, soup, and ice cream for dessert. Under no circumstances were the campers to have sodas, chocolate, pie, cake, or candy.[55]

Johnson used a variety of methods and techniques to teach the game of tennis. For weight training and conditioning, daily exercises included twenty-five push-ups, weights, fifty knee-to-chest jumps, one hundred side straddle hops, and forward and backward sprints. Before graduating to a tennis racquet, each player had to show proficiency with a broom handle, a drill intended to improve hand-eye coordination. With the racquet, the young men served fifty times a day from all spots on the court. "We had daily contests," Ashe remembered, "to see who could hit the most forehands without making an error, the most forehand returns of serve, deep forehand shots, forehand approach shots and forehand passing shots. Then we ran through the whole series on the backhand." After dinner the participants retired to the basement, where they watched film of tennis matches and read old manuals and magazines. By nightfall the boys, physically and mentally exhausted, were ready for bed.[56]

More than a tennis camp, Johnson's Junior Development Program was a life lesson, offering strategies for survival in a world of tennis alien to blacks and the working class. To succeed in the predominately white, upper-class world of competitive tennis, his pupils had to be disciplined and tough, knowing when to fight and, more importantly, when to walk away. Johnson knew that Jackie Robinson's ascension to Major League Baseball had as much to do with his temperament as with his athletic abilities. Beaned, spiked, and taunted by racially motivated bench jockeyers, Robinson remained calm and composed, allowing his bat and feet to do the talking. Johnson's players had to imitate Robinson, he believed, because tournament officials would look for any excuse to disqualify them. On the court, he ordered Ashe and the others to play any shot within two inches of the out-of-bounds lines to avoid the appearance of cheating. The players were never to gloat, argue, complain, or celebrate in a visible way. They were to ignore calls of "nigger" and "coon." "His assumption," Ashe wrote of Johnson in his diary, "was that if you wanted to get into a poker game, and there was only one game in town, you had better learn to play by the prevailing rules at that table." Johnson told a reporter for the *Washington Post*, "I can't use a boy unless he can control his emotions." Johnson's pioneers had to understand and accept the official and unofficial rules of tournament play before he would let them take the court.[57]

Notwithstanding his initial run-in with Johnson and his son, Ashe was a near-perfect student. He was the first player on the court after breakfast and the last to leave before dinner. Johnson was impressed by Ashe's mechanical strokes, his ability to control his emotions, and his knack for intimidating opponents with his cool, calm demeanor. In the age of the hot-tempered Pancho Gonzalez, Ashe's court behavior was a refreshing sign to many, harkening back to the days when "gentlemen" played the game.[58]

During Ashe's second summer in camp, Johnson unveiled his young protégé by entering him in a number of tournaments. Both his opponents and the spectators quickly learned what made him successful. Armed with an overpowering serve, an above-average backhand, and fundamentally sound ground strokes, he possessed all of the physical attributes that made for a great player. Most observers agreed, however, that his most important asset was his head. Slow to anger and always in control, the young man impressed and intimidated his competition with unbreakable composure. A writer for *Life* magazine called this characteristic an "icy elegance," or the ability to remain stone-faced on the court while conducting himself in a dignified and professional manner. In 1955 Ashe won every twelve-and-under tournament he entered, repeating the feat a year later in the under-thirteen division. Traveling for the first time to northern cities such as New York, Baltimore, Philadelphia, and Kalamazoo, he won eleven ATA national titles in eight years. In 1957, following his victory in the fifteen-and-under ATA national championships, tennis backers and the mainstream press began to take an interest in him. Ranked thirty-first nationally, Ashe learned how to rush the net and play a more aggressive style of tennis. In 1958 he entered the all-black Maggie Walker High School, joined the tennis team, and dominated the competition. David Lash, head tennis coach at Carver High School in Durham, North Carolina, marveled at Ashe's abilities and attitude: "He couldn't have weighed more than 80 pounds," Lash recalled. "But he loved to play. As soon as he finished his match he would find a good grassy spot and read a book. But the first question he asked when he came off the court was 'When do I play again?' Some boys didn't want to play many times a day, but Arthur did. He was always ready." Referring to Ashe as Johnson's "guinea pig," the *Chicago Defender* reported that he had "developed deadly accuracy and perfect court strategy."[59]

Ashe's remarkable success on the court, however, did not lead to acceptance in white tennis circles. He was rarely allowed to compete against whites, and some incorrectly assumed that he was not good enough to earn a higher national ranking. In a 1967 memoir, Ashe argued that he had deserved a higher ranking in 1957 than thirty-first nationally. In 1959 he was denied entry to play in the Middle Atlantic Junior Tennis Tournament because his application arrived "too late." Similar exclusions plagued him in other southern cities as well. Aside from an outright ban, racism in tennis manifested itself in other ways, including editors profiling only white players in magazines and newspapers, white parents yelling racial slurs from the stands, and coaches' selecting only white players for junior traveling teams. "We could hear words like 'nigger' come through," he recalled. "We just couldn't let it affect us." Christine Beck, a young phenom herself in the late 1950s, remembered being "horrified" that Ashe and his teammates were not allowed to use the dressing room at a tournament in Wilmington, Delaware. Ordered never to challenge the status quo, Ashe and his friends found ways to cope with racism. "Blacks could not eat in restaurants," he explained, "so we brought our fried chicken, potato salad, and rolls in bags and passed the Thermos around the car." Refused entry to a local movie theater, the team simply left, no questions asked. Their strategies, however, did not spare them from occasional violence. Ashe's friend Bob Davis recalled one incident in which the Junior Development Team was staying overnight at a local YMCA. In the middle of the night the team was awakened by the sound of a fire ax smashing their door, a clear message from racist townspeople that blacks were not welcome.[60]

Racism and discrimination continued to follow Ashe on the junior tournament circuit, yet his interactions with white players remained mostly positive, a trend that never changed. He rarely heard any racial slurs from white players on the court, though parents often hurled them at him. "We talked to white players," he explained, "but we didn't mix. We kept to ourselves." Just as Jackie Robinson at first avoided his white teammates on the Montreal Royals and the Brooklyn Dodgers, Ashe waited for whites to approach him. The problem, he concluded, was the parents and not the competitors. "Their folks," he remembered, "drove up in big shiny cars or station wagons, and practically pushed Sonny Boy onto the courts. Some parents arrived late with their sons, and lit into the umpire if he had forfeited their match. . . . I heard them tell officials, 'Don't put my boy on an outside court. The crowd wants to see him.'"[61]

Despite the haunting presence of Jim Crow and racism, Ashe performed well on the tennis court. In 1960, at the age of seventeen, he became the youngest player to win the Senior ATA National Championship. With the Middle Atlantic Championships moved to Wheeling, West Virginia, he successfully entered the tournament and brought home the trophy. As his trophies, plaques, and cups quickly accumulated, his goal of winning the Interscholastic Championships in Charlottesville remained. Ever since Johnson's first two youths had integrated the tournament, officials, with the support of the University of Virginia's president, had allowed more members of the Junior Development Team to compete. None, however, matched Ashe in talent, and most were eliminated in the early rounds. By 1960, though, Ashe was one of the favorites to win it all. Ironically, one gentlemanly act and a deep respect for the rules proved to be his downfall that year. During a tough match with Bill Lenoir of Atlanta, a ball from a neighboring court rolled onto Lenoir's side just as the white competitor was rushing the net. Ashe was certain that Lenoir did not see the ball, but his instincts told him to ask. "Did that ball interfere with you?" he inquired. Lenoir responded that he had been distracted, and the point, which Ashe had won, was replayed. Angered and rattled, Ashe lost his focus and eventually the match.[62]

Returning home from the tournament, Ashe was unaware that his life was about to change. For a while, unbeknownst to Ashe, Johnson had been formulating a plan. Richmond, and the South in general, offered few resources to help Ashe improve as a player. With a lack of indoor courts, segregated tournaments, and a scarcity of talented young juniors, Virginia had nothing else to offer him. He needed a change of scenery, and Johnson knew just the place. One day he phoned Ashe and bluntly reported: "I've made arrangements for you to live in St. Louis."[63]

Late in the summer of 1960, Ashe left Richmond to live with tennis coach Richard Hudlin, who was a former ATA standout, and his family. Unlike Ashe's hometown, St. Louis had indoor tennis facilities, which allowed him to practice year-round, and the city was home to a number of promising young players. In leaving Richmond, Ashe was leaving behind more than tennis courts in disrepair and poor competition. "I left," he explained, "all that Richmond stood for at the time—its segregation, its conservatism, its parochial thinking, its slow progress toward equality, its lack of opportunity for talented black people. I had no intention then of coming back." As an African American youth growing up in a segregated southern city, Ashe had developed strategies to manage racism. He had followed his mentors' rules, working hard, avoiding potentially dangerous situations, focusing on long-term goals, and remaining deferential to white adults. The moderate integrationism that had served him well in Virginia would not fit so neatly his life as a teenager in St. Louis and Los Angeles. Moderate and militant influences would soon collide.[64]

# CHAPTER 2

# UCLA

As Ashe prepared to complete Mrs. Cox's homework assignment, his comfort zone suddenly eluded him. The freshman English teacher at Maggie Walker High School had instructed her students to write a short essay that required each of the young men and women to take a position on an issue. The assignment offered Ashe the opportunity to think critically and form an opinion, something that his father and Dr. Johnson had subtly discouraged. Surviving as a black youth in Jim Crow America, they preached, demanded being deferent, cautious, and inconspicuous, not loud, opinionated, and defiant. Those like Emmett Till, who said too much, were lynched, not praised. Yet this assignment represented an invitation to speak up, one that Ashe could not dismiss. He decided to write on the failures of black leadership. He took issue with those followers who did not properly evaluate the advice of their leaders. "I wrote," he explained, "that I had learned not to accept everything at face value just because you heard it from a teacher, that we had to scrutinize, criticize constructively, and question everything because black people were too much like sheep." When an apparent savior appeared—be it a pastor, a politician, a teacher, or an organizer—African Americans, Ashe concluded, all too often clung to his every word and were led in the wrong direction. The analytical depth of his essay so impressed Mrs. Cox that she read it to the entire class.[1]

Ashe's argument reflected an approaching shift in the civil rights movement. In April 1960 students and movement veterans, representing organizations such as Students for a Democratic Society (SDS), the National Student Association (NSA), and the Congress of Racial Equality (CORE), gathered at Shaw University and collectively founded the Student Nonviolent Coordinating Committee (SNCC). Conceived as a grass-roots, student-led organization, SNCC had no intention of following the leader. "Students have a natural claim to

leadership in this project," concluded one document from the Shaw conference. Forty years later, SNCC member Julian Bond wrote that SNCC "demonstrated that ordinary women and men, young and old, could perform extraordinary tasks." The events at Shaw University resonated with activists in
California, forcing Ashe and others to reevaluate their racial identities.[2]

"It would have been difficult for me to avoid getting involved in politics,"
Ashe reasoned in 1981. "Growing up in the South in the 1950s, studying at UCLA
in the 1960s, even playing tennis planted seeds of confrontation." The early to
mid-1960s were a period of sustained civil rights activism throughout the
United States that included the nationwide sit-in movement beginning in
February 1960, the Freedom Rides in 1961, and the March on Washington on
August 28, 1963. In 1964, Harlem and six other U.S. cities erupted in race riots,
and in the summer of 1965 the Watts neighborhood of Los Angeles went up in
flames in protest of police brutality.[3]

In the midst of the civil rights movement, and on the courts, fields, and diamonds of American sports, black athletes developed a heightened racial consciousness. Ashe described his own racial awakening as follows: "I was moved
into the world of tennis that had little in common with the black experience.
The game had a history and tradition [that] I was expected to assimilate, but
much of that history and many of those traditions were hostile to me." He and
other black athletes in the 1960s experienced what one scholar has called "split
existences." Drawing from W. E. B. Du Bois's concept of double consciousness,
he has argued, "On the one hand, black athletes were proud of their race for its
forbearance and ability to survive and fought against the negative images of
black inferiority. On the other hand, black athletes' aspirations to success in
American sport necessitated that they adhere to values upheld in the dominant
society." This dilemma of whether to conform to the social mores of his sport
or stand with fellow blacks against injustice represented an emotional struggle
for Ashe throughout the 1960s. His mentors' philosophies of avoiding confrontation and moderate integrationism became impossible positions to hold.[4]

The maturation of the civil rights movement, the emergence of budding
Black Power ideologies in Los Angeles, and the presence of a small but significant group of politically active students at UCLA challenged Ashe to reconsider
some of his childhood beliefs. Free from the rules and expectations of his father
and Dr. Johnson, he became interested in politics, debating classmates on topics of race and civil rights, speaking out on international political matters, and
developing a philosophy of his own somewhere in between moderate and
militant integrationism. For Ashe, however, early exposure to Black Power

and black nationalist ideologies did not result in complete conversion. Leaders such as Ron Karenga made Ashe more aware of his place in the movement yet more independent than ever. Living in Los Angeles and attending UCLA helped transform him from a youth who accepted the status quo to an opinionated black man coming to grips with his race and his role in the black freedom movement.

_⌒ ⌒_

In the summer of 1960, Ashe packed his bags, gathered his tennis racquets, and headed west to St. Louis, leaving behind Jim Crow—or so he thought. He quickly learned, however, that his new home in the Midwest, like Richmond, was a city of contradictions. Missouri's Democratic governor, James T. Blair Jr., announced after his election in 1956, "Always and everywhere I will identify myself with any victim of oppression or discrimination, whoever or wherever he may be, and I will support him." In addition to the governor's progressive rhetoric, the city's Board of Aldermen passed an ordinance in 1961 that prohibited the exclusion of blacks from public facilities, including restaurants, theaters, and swimming pools. But for many of the city's working-class African Americans, civil rights legislation failed to alleviate economic inequities and harsh segregation. Middle-class whites exited St. Louis in droves in the early 1960s, moving their families and their wealth to the fast-growing suburbs of Webster Groves, Kirkwood, and Florissant. In 1960, blacks made up 15.3 percent of the population in St. Louis. Of the 114,539 blacks who lived in the city proper, many resided in one of four housing projects: Pruitt-Igoe, Cochran Gardens, Darst-Webbe, or Vaughan. Pruitt-Igoe, for example, was a three-thousand-unit complex with undersized sinks, kitchens, and stoves. In the winter, the loose windows rattled in the wind and the pipes froze. The lack of regular police patrols gave muggers and other petty criminals easy hideaways in dark, cramped hallways. Though free from the de jure discrimination of Richmond, St. Louis blacks, more often than not, lived in segregated neighborhoods with inadequate housing.[5]

Sumner High School, which Ashe attended, was an obvious paradox in a city where the harshness of everyday life often trumped the promise of opportunity. Located in a beautiful brick building in a neighborhood known as the Ville, Sumner had the distinction of being the first African American public school west of the Mississippi River. The school's well-educated black faculty drew students from all over greater St. Louis. "I was blessed to be a student at Sumner High School," reminisced Lynn Beckwith Jr., of the class of 1957. "We had very learned teachers who had been educated all over the United States." Faculty members held degrees from Harvard, Yale, and Princeton, and some had earned master's and doctorates. Ashe, who enrolled at Sumner in 1960, took advantage of the school's quality of education and graduated with the highest grades in his class. He did not add the title of valedictorian to his resume, though, because he attended the school for only one year. What was a blessing for Sumner's black students represented evidence of occupational immobility for the faculty. For many black Ivy League graduates, Sumner offered one of few options for employment. Colleges and universities, such as the University of Missouri, often refused to hire black intellectuals and scientists. Besides Sumner, black professors sometimes taught at Lincoln University, a historically black college, or at Stowe Teachers' College. Although Sumner's faculty paved the way for a future generation of black scholars and professionals, they remained locked out of Missouri's university system.[6]

Despite the academic benefits of Sumner and the presence of indoor courts, Ashe was miserable during his stay in St. Louis. He suffered from bouts of homesickness, and his relationship with Richard Hudlin, a former ATA champion, prominent black tennis coach, and high-school teacher, lacked intimacy and affection. Strict and uncompromising, Hudlin closely regulated Ashe's schedule. Hudlin enjoyed tennis more than any other activity and forced his love of the game on Ashe. His coaching style was relentless, and he rarely acknowledged that Ashe was mentally and physically exhausted. Although Ashe appreciated the free room and board, steak dinners, and tennis instruction, he resented Hudlin's control over his life. Ashe thought a high-school senior should make his own decisions about diet, exercise, and schedule.[7]

As a former tennis star at the University of Chicago, Hudlin had a stake in Ashe's personal and professional development. Like Ashe, he had struggled in the 1920s and 1930s to find tournaments that would allow an African American to participate. An ATA standout, the first black tennis captain in the Big Ten Conference, and a darling of the *Chicago Defender*, Hudlin never had the opportunity to compete in the U.S. Nationals, the French Championships, or Wimbledon. He did, however, help the ATA grow into a national organization that eventually included players from the Midwest and the West Coast. According to Edgar Brown, an ATA star in the 1920s, "Each year Hudlin got more and more [Midwest] players to go [to the ATA Nationals] until the Nationals became the tournament that all the tennis players look forward to each year." After his days as a player ended, Hudlin settled in as a teacher and tennis coach, waiting, it seemed, for a black player to come along who could integrate the major tournaments. During a meeting with Wilbur Jenkins, another former high-ranking

ATA player, the two men decided that Hudlin should reach out to Dr. Johnson about helping Ashe. Under his guidance, Hudlin believed, Ashe would become an elite junior. Ashe saw an overbearing drill sergeant in Hudlin. Hudlin saw in Ashe a racial trailblazer and champion.[8]

Ashe's daily routine in St. Louis consisted of exercise, school, and tennis instruction. He did push-ups every morning before breakfast and ran a mile every evening following tennis practice. Immediately after school, he met his instructor, Larry Miller, at Washington University's outdoor courts or at the 138th Infantry Armory indoor courts, depending on the weather. In St. Louis there were no segregated courts, the indoor facilities were state of the art, and white juniors such as Cliff Buchholz and Jim Parker would serve as formidable opponents. Buchholz and Parker matured into talented players who offered Ashe a level of competition unlike anything he had experienced in Richmond or Lynchburg. As a result, he improved rapidly. In late November 1960 he defeated top-seeded Frank Froehling in a four-hour match to win the National Junior Indoor Championship in St. Louis. The mainstream press covered his first major victory, with *Sports Illustrated* naming him one of its "Faces in the Crowd," the title of a brief section in the magazine highlighting the achievements of unknown, often amateur athletes. Les Matthews of the *Amsterdam News* discussed him alongside boxer Joe Louis and Jackie Robinson as examples of blacks who had experienced "a rugged, heart breaking uphill climb to attain their present status in the sports world." To Matthews, Ashe's win was a sign of progress, evidence that blacks could excel in a white, upper-class sport.[9]

Six months after his Indoor win, Ashe experienced his first national controversy when he returned to Charlottesville, Virginia, to compete in the National Interscholastic Championships. Following his loss to Bill Lenoir the previous summer, he had focused more than ever on accomplishing Dr. Johnson's most sought-after goal: victory in the segregated South. Yet Ashe nearly missed his chance to win in Charlottesville. Although the University of Virginia (UVA) had hosted the annual tournament since 1946, school officials asked to be excused from their responsibilities in 1961, claiming "that interest in the tournament was dropping off." UVA's athletic director, Gus Tebell, argued that the tournament drew little interest from the West Coast and the Midwest and noted that ticket sales were down. The Interscholastics had become a financial burden on UVA, prompting calls for its relocation.[10]

A number of sportswriters and ATA officials, however, speculated that race motivated UVA's request. "People in Charlottesville have been unhappy at the university's role as tournament host since Negroes began to appear regularly," read an editorial in *Sports Illustrated*. The magazine reported that Williams College in Williamstown, Massachusetts, might replace UVA, because "the sight of a Negro in white flannels does not upset white citizens [in Williamstown] as it apparently does in Charlottesville." It is also possible that Virginia officials might have suspected that an improved Ashe would top the draw in 1961. A likely win, they feared, would embolden the ATA, leading to calls for more black participants, better housing accommodations in Charlottesville, and additional antidiscrimination measures. Critics believed that the university, under pressure from angry white parents and alumni, had asked to be released from its contract with the United States Lawn Tennis Association (USLTA) for these reasons. UVA and the USLTA ultimately reached a compromise: the tournament would be held in Charlottesville in 1961, then moved to Williamstown in 1962.[11]

Ashe made the most of his final opportunity to compete in Charlottesville. Unlike in the previous year, he breezed through the tournament, defeating Buchholz in the semifinals and Parker in the final, both in straight sets. Though the mainstream press had covered his matches since 1959, his Interscholastic win led to a number of profile pieces discussing his athletic abilities, his mentors, his future plans, and perhaps most importantly, his role as a racial pioneer. Marion Jackson of the *Atlanta Daily World*, a black newspaper, remarked after his victory, "Few [in the mainstream media] questioned that it was time for his liberation from the blanket of silence wrapped around him by press, radio, and TV." In addition to *Sport* and *Sports Illustrated*, *Time* and *Newsweek* also covered his breakout in the sport. To Ashe's dismay, some of the coverage depersonalized him by reiterating that he was the "first Negro" to do this or that. "Of course," he explained, "there was a great deal of fuss about being the 'first black' . . . to win at Charlottesville, etc. Those comments always put me under pressure to justify my accomplishments on racial grounds, as if sports were the cutting edge of our nation's move toward improved race relations." In 1961 he did not yet believe that sports served as a vehicle for social change. As a naive teenager, he wasn't quite ready to confront the problem of race. He quickly came to understand, however, that he could not escape his role as a racial pioneer. Blacks and whites found larger meaning in his wins and losses that reverberated far beyond the tennis court. Whether he liked it or not, he was Arthur Ashe, the *Negro* tennis player.[12]

One incident during the Interscholastic tournament revealed Ashe's personal growth and his increased willingness to challenge racial discrimination. During the final weekend of the tournament, he and some of his white competitors left their rooms and walked to a local movie theater. Although the white players purchased tickets without a problem, the management refused to sell Ashe a ticket because of his race. Visibly angry, he snapped back in an uncharacteristically defiant way. "What do you want me to do," he asked the ticket clerk, "paint myself with whitewash?" His comments shocked his friend Cliff Buchholz. "That was the only time I heard Arthur say anything about something he didn't like that was going on," he said. "At the time, he didn't want to make waves and didn't want to deal with a lot of pressure." Buchholz, Charlie Pasarell, and Butch Newman were inspired by their friend and demanded refunds. The incident showed how Ashe had changed since leaving Richmond for St. Louis. His time away from his father and Dr. Johnson had taught him to be independent and sometimes bold. He began to decide things for himself, choosing when to rebel and when to acquiesce, and his companions' response that day also hinted at his ability to inspire others to action.[13]

While visiting his family in Richmond, Ashe made his most important decision to date. In the late 1950s J. D. Morgan arrived in Kalamazoo, Michigan, to scout juniors in a local tournament. Morgan was the head tennis coach at UCLA, home to one of the nation's premier tennis programs. Ashe recalled that in the 1960s "every promising high school tennis player in the country felt that his competitive playing days were over if he didn't win a scholarship to one of the big tennis schools like UCLA." At the tournament, Morgan spoke to Dr. Johnson about the possibility of Ashe's attending UCLA in the fall of 1961. Both men agreed that California would be an ideal place for him to grow as both a player and a person. Several years after their discussion, during Christmas break, Ashe received a phone call from Morgan offering him a tennis scholarship to play at UCLA. Rejecting offers from Harvard, Michigan, Michigan State, Arizona, and a number of historically black colleges, he accepted Morgan's offer before the coach could finish his sales pitch. "You could have knocked me over with a feather," he remembered. "I was thrilled beyond belief." For Ashe, receiving a tennis scholarship from UCLA compared to a quarterback's receiving a full ride to Notre Dame. His childhood hero Jackie Robinson had graduated from UCLA, and blacks seemed to thrive there. He had dreamed of playing for UCLA ever since he was thirteen, and that dream was about to become a reality.[14]

—◦ ◦—

To a casual observer in the early 1960s, UCLA seemed a model of racial tolerance and equality. Despite an enrollment of fewer than one thousand blacks out of a total student body of more than thirty thousand, the university had a record of offering scholarships to talented black athletes. Football players

Kenny Washington and Woody Strode, decathlete Rafer Johnson, basketball player Don Barksdale, and, most notably, multisport athlete Jackie Robinson were all UCLA alumni. As one scholar has noted, the presence on campus of successful black athletes "created the myth that UCLA was a 'racial paradise' where equality reigned and Jim Crow dare not rear his head." Even Ashe subscribed to the myth. "Negroes have been doing okay at UCLA for thirty years," he explained. "Rafer Johnson . . . was elected a student body president. Dr. Ralph Bunche of the United Nations had been a UCLA student." What appeared to be signs of racial progress to Ashe and others were seen as instances of tokenism by the university's critics. By recruiting and publicizing star black athletes, they argued, campus officials could more easily ignore housing discrimination in the predominately white neighborhood of Westwood. Loren Miller, a local NAACP attorney, suggested in UCLA's student newspaper, the *Daily Bruin*, that it was "difficult for a Negro to find even a cellar [to rent] around [Westwood]." The strategy of using prominent black athletes to mask racial inequality was not confined to UCLA and other public and private universities in the 1950s and 1960s. A number of scholars have shown how the U.S. State Department used international goodwill tours that included athletes such as Althea Gibson and the Harlem Globetrotters as evidence of improved race relations in America. In the midst of these tours, civil rights battles in the South discredited the government's claims. Though overall more progressive and liberal than St. Louis, UCLA was no beacon of equality.[15]

Ashe offered a candid assessment of his time at UCLA. "My college career was a roller coaster of highs and lows," he wrote. "The good moments were great, and the bad times were just as unforgettable." He arrived in Los Angeles in the fall of 1961 on a cloudless fall afternoon. After meeting his roommate in Sproul Hall, he walked to the athletic offices for an appointment with J. D. Morgan. In Morgan he encountered a man with an intimidating figure; he was a tall man, five foot eleven, with a round, wide girth. His personality, however, was far from imposing. "From the first day I met J. D. Morgan," Ashe remembered, "my antenna told me to trust him." During their initial meeting they discussed everything from tennis to career goals. When Ashe told Morgan that he intended to major in engineering or architecture, Morgan asked, "Are you prepared to study five hours a day?" Business administration, he counseled Ashe, would be a more fruitful and less demanding occupation for the young man. Before the 1970s, most tennis players held actual jobs while they competed in tournaments. Clark Graebner, one of Ashe's contemporaries, eventually worked for a paper company, and Chuck McKinley left the U.S. Davis Cup team in 1965 for a job on Wall Street. Unable to accept prize money because of their amateur status, Graebner and McKinley had to work to make ends meet. From Morgan's perspective, an easier major like business administration would allow his young protégé to spend less time in the library and more time on the tennis court.[16]

Although Ashe might not have realized it at the time, Morgan's "advice" was a script commonly delivered by college coaches and athletic directors in the 1960s. Often, when an athlete such as Ashe expressed a desire to major in biology, chemistry, or engineering, for example—each a "demanding" field of study—coaches would "recommend" an easier major such as general studies, leisure studies, or physical education. This would allow an athlete to focus more on sports and less on academics, a blueprint not so secretly championed by administrators and boosters. In his widely read social commentary *The Revolt of the Black Athlete*, sociology professor and activist Harry Edwards identified the practice of "encouraging" black athletes to adopt easier majors as one of the ways in which colleges and universities exploited African Americans for their athletic talents. Though Ashe always claimed that Morgan looked out for his players' best interests, it is just as likely that Morgan was looking out for UCLA's best interests. He needed players to remain academically eligible and focused on tennis, and "easier" majors made this more likely.[17]

Morgan had came to Los Angeles from Oklahoma, where he had excelled as a four-sport athlete, dazzling small-town fans with his fierce competitiveness. He suffered a serious back injury near the end of his high-school career, prompting his decision to focus on tennis alone. Lacking a natural athletic ability, he had to work harder than his peers and train longer. "He played tennis like it was terribly hard work," recalled his coach, William Ackerman. Morgan joined the army after college and, like President John F. Kennedy, served as a PT boat commander during World War II. He loved to tell war stories, often equating the role of an officer to that of a tennis player. After the war ended, he returned to UCLA and took a job in the accounting department of the Office of Associated Students. Later he became an assistant tennis coach and eventually the head coach. He proved to be an able recruiter, a skilled motivator, and a father figure. And he loved to win. He had "great enthusiasm and competitive spirit," a colleague explained. He was superbly organized and easily identified a player's weaknesses. More than a talented coach, Morgan was a good man. He treated his team like family, often choosing to caravan in cramped vans rather than travel by airplane. The rides, he believed, built camaraderie. He respected all of his players—black, white, or brown. "I'd just say I don't think J.D. was a racist at all, in any way or sense," noted John Wooden, UCLA's legendary basketball coach.[18]

Morgan became Ashe's most important mentor at UCLA. Aside from his role as head tennis coach, he took an active interest in Ashe's future. To attend UCLA, for instance, each male undergraduate had to complete two years in the Reserve Officer Training Corps (ROTC). At the end of that time, a student could either drop out of the program or continue with the training and become a commissioned officer in the U.S. Army upon graduation. Before meeting with Morgan, Ashe viewed his decision in terms of patriotic duty. His family had a military background, including one uncle who had served in the U.S. Marines and another who had served in the navy. Morgan, however, understood the choice in more pragmatic terms. He knew the realities of war and the difference between entering the army as an enlisted man and entering as a commissioned officer. Concerned about potential military engagements around the globe, Morgan suggested that Ashe undergo ROTC training. If Congress and the president ever initiated the military draft, as some feared, Ashe would surely be classified 1A, making him eligible for combat. For this reason, Morgan advised him to remain in the ROTC for a full four years, a decision he never regretted. "If J.D. Morgan had not been such a great administrator," Ashe quipped, "he would have made a marvelous disc jockey. When J.D. Morgan talked, people listened."[19]

Morgan kept a close eye on his star player, something that Ashe did not always appreciate. In one particular image the two men pose for the camera, Morgan in a full suit and tie and Ashe in his UCLA warm-up jacket holding a plaque in his left hand. Morgan grips Ashe's right arm tightly, just as a father might grab his own son to keep him away from danger. Morgan's expression is one of pride. Ashe wears a half-smile, appearing more serious and annoyed than happy. Despite living apart from his father and Dr. Johnson, Ashe remained far from independent.

Morgan's coaching style offered a stark contrast to the strategies and techniques of Dr. Johnson and Dick Hudlin. He devoted little practice time to micromanaging his players and allowed greater freedom on and off the court. Never a rigid disciplinarian, he expected his team to complete a physical conditioning routine each day but rarely checked up on them. This style was a welcome relief to Ashe. In Richmond, Lynchburg, and St. Louis, adults had regulated his every move, stifling his independence and controlling his personal life. Ashe remembered Morgan as a "forceful high-voltage type" whose main coaching talent centered on motivating his players. He established a "reward-punishment system"

Ashe poses for the camera with UCLA's head tennis coach, J. D. Morgan. As his coach and mentor, Morgan kept a tight rein on Ashe from 1961 to 1966. (UCLA Athletic Department)

in which a player's performance in the previous match determined his status in the next one. During UCLA's championship run in 1965, Ashe and his teammate Charlie Pasarell alternated between the number-one and number-two spots depending on who was playing better at the time. Yet Morgan could be unpredictable and difficult to read. A victory never ensured praise from the coach. He was just as likely to scold a player after a straight-set win as he was after a straight-set loss, but he took credit for both the wins and the losses and deflected criticism from his players.[20]

In Ashe, Morgan could see that he had a potential superstar on his team. As early as 1961, Bill Brower of the *Los Angeles Sentinel* wrote, "Someday soon young Arthur Ashe is going to join the ranks of tan immortals. . . . [Ashe] will do for tennis (male variety) what Jackie Robinson did for baseball, what Joe Louis did for boxing, what Jesse Owens did for track, and what Althea Gibson did for tennis (female variety)." He predicted that Ashe would become a "hero" of the U.S. Davis Cup team in the coming years. In 1962 the *Pittsburgh Courier*'s analysis read, "Ashe is a brilliant shotmaker without a serious weakness and should steadily progress in national ranking as he garners experience in top-flight men's competition." Nearly all sportswriters agreed that Ashe's advanced maturity, overpowering serve, and mechanically sound ground game ensured his success in amateur tennis, and Morgan frequently sung Ashe's praises to the national media. "I detected potential greatness in Ashe that very first day," said Morgan, referring to a junior tournament he watched when Ashe lived in Virginia. "And by the time he arrived at UCLA, I felt he would become a world class performer if he made normal progress and maintained his desire." To the *Pittsburgh Courier* Morgan predicted: "Ashe . . . is destined to become one of the United States top tennis players in the next few years."[21]

Ashe's game, however, was not without a number of flaws. Sportswriters frequently focused on his loss of concentration during long matches. Once he assumed a commanding lead in a match, his mind often wandered away from tennis to other topics, including women, food, and world affairs. On too many occasions his lack of focus allowed his opponent to even up a match. Clark Graebner, his eventual Davis Cup teammate, noted that Ashe was "carefree, lackadaisical, [and] forgetful. His mind wanders." Ashe explained to Wendell Smith of the *Courier*, "I guess I hit my backhand shots 70 different ways. The only trouble is that sometimes I have trouble making up my mind which way to hit."[22]

Aside from his problems concentrating, some sportswriters suggested that he lacked a "killer instinct." The *Amsterdam News* concluded that he was too much of a "nice guy." "This has been as consistent an observation about Ashe as his concentration has been inconsistent," read the paper. The *Chicago Defender* stated bluntly that he had "everything it takes to be great except one thing—a killer instinct." Comments like these seemed to bother him more than statements about his concentration. He thought that emotional displays on the tennis court drained a player's mental and physical energy and resulted in a loss of focus, a belief instilled in him by his father and Dr. Johnson.[23]

Criticism aside, Ashe's record at UCLA between 1961 and 1965 supported claims that a promising career in tennis awaited him. Before Ashe and Charlie Pasarell arrived in Los Angeles, the University of Southern California (USC) dominated the rivalry between the nation's top two tennis programs. Even with Ashe and Pasarell on UCLA's roster from 1962 to 1964, USC won three consecutive national championships, finishing with a combined record of 34-1. "USC was an obsession for every UCLA coach," Ashe explained. "Our archrival was only twenty-five minutes away and our entire year depended on how we did against 'SC.'" USC's team included veteran players Dennis Ralston and Rafael Osuna and had solid depth in Tom Edlefsen, Ramsey Earnhardt, and Bill Bond. In 1963 Frank Deford of *Sports Illustrated* wrote that USC was "not only . . . the best college tennis team in the world today but probably the best in history."[24]

Despite USC's remarkable run, Ashe emerged as a tough opponent for Ralston and Osuna. He played "magnificent tennis" to defeat Ralston in the semifinals of the 1963 Southern California Intercollegiate Championships. After dropping the first set 6-2, he rebounded to capture the next two sets 6-0 and 6-4. He then topped his UCLA teammate Dave Reed in the final. George Toley, USC's head tennis coach, made the case that Ashe "wins or loses every match. Nobody really beats him in that sense." Toley's analysis mirrored a common observation of Ashe's game in the mid-1960s. He lost matches because of unforced errors and lapses in his concentration and not as the result of being outplayed. Thanks in part to his rapid improvement, a writer for the *Daily Bruin* labeled UCLA's team a "powerhouse" in June 1963 and gave them a "fighting chance" to unseat USC in the NCAA tournament. In 1963 Frank Stewart of the *Los Angeles Sentinel* commented, "There's no doubt that the [USC] Trojans and [UCLA] Bruins boast the top collegiate teams in the country this season, teams which may be the best ever assembled in rah-rah net history." Although the Bruins lost that year, by 1965 UCLA was the clear frontrunner for the intercollegiate crown.[25]

Ashe's achievements in 1965 left little doubt that he was America's best collegiate tennis player. Named a team captain along with Pasarell in 1964, Ashe easily dispatched his season opponents en route to the 1965 NCAA individual title. He was aided by the fact that USC had lost Ralston and Osuna to graduation and Edelfsen, the team's current number-one player, to academic ineligibility. Before the NCAA tournament began, a headline in the *Daily Bruin* read, "It's Ashe's tourney," and most experts picked UCLA to win the team championship as well. "While Trojan coach George Toley is hurting from a lack of depth," a

The 1965 UCLA national championship team. Ashe (*seated far left*) and Charlie Pasarell (*seated third from right*) stood out in a sport dominated by white elites. (UCLA Athletic Department)

*Daily Bruin* columnist wrote, "his UCLA counterpart, J. D. Morgan, is suffering from an embarrassment of riches. He has so many highly qualified men, that he can't decide how to distribute [them]." And Ashe wasted no time in the singles tournament, never losing a set and defeating second-seeded Mike Belkin of Miami University in the final. After trailing 3-2 in the first set, he answered Belkin's soft game by utilizing the drop shot and driving balls into the corners of the court. Along with his singles crown, Ashe and teammate Ian Crookenden won the doubles title, and UCLA captured the team championship with a total of thirty-one points, eighteen more than second-place Miami, Ohio.[26]

Despite his success on the tennis court, Ashe encountered racial discrimination throughout his time at UCLA. One day during his freshman year, Morgan called him into his office to discuss an upcoming weekend tournament. The event was to be held at the Balboa Bay Club, a lavish hotel and resort located on California's Riviera, halfway between Los Angeles and San Diego. From the moment Ashe sat down, Morgan's "deep serious tone" foreshadowed a problem with the tournament. Each year, Morgan explained, the Balboa Club sent tournament invitations to college teams, and although UCLA had received an invitation, Ashe's name was conspicuously absent from the list of players. Like most country clubs in the early 1960s, Balboa catered to upper-class whites and prohibited blacks from becoming members. Its tournament committee apparently decided that Ashe's entry would anger the club's clientele, resulting in membership cancellations and other problems. As he listened to his coach, Ashe realized that California was not "the land of milk and honey, free spirits and

golden opportunity" that it was advertised to be. "There would be no more riding in the back of the Number 6 bus," he understood, "but the sense of space,
palm trees, and ethnic diversity in Los Angeles could not hide other realities,"
like racism. Morgan presented Ashe with a choice: either the team would travel
to Balboa without him or they would boycott the tournament and "make an issue" of the exclusion. Perhaps Morgan sought to avoid controversy, knowing
that Ashe had been raised to adjust to the status quo and would not fight Balboa's decision. In asking Ashe to decide, Morgan placed a heavy and unfair burden on his young freshman player. "J.D. had opened the door," recalled Ashe. "If
I wanted to protest being excluded from a tennis event because I was black, I
had my chance." After careful deliberation, he decided against a boycott, reasoning that such a move would place his teammates in a difficult position and
force them to withdraw from the matches. He ultimately relied on the advice of
his father and Dr. Johnson, who encouraged him to play the hand he was dealt.
Morgan accepted this choice but offered words of guidance that proved valuable as Ashe's career progressed:

> You can't make a little issue. If you want to fight something like [the Balboa exclu-
> sion], you have to fight it to win it. And you have to prepare for it, get your ducks in
> order so to speak. There will always be clubs like that and people like that. If you
> want to make a career out of fighting them, your tennis is going to suffer. When
> you're more established, you can be a good tennis player and be in the position of
> fighting them on your terms.

Playing championship tennis and participating in activism would always be a
difficult combination, sometimes an impossible one. In the future, Ashe would
have to choose what to make the focus of his battles.[27]

—◌ ◌—

Not all African Americans agreed with Ashe's tepid approach. In the summer of
1966, as Ashe transitioned from college student to army officer, Stokely Carmichael was elected president of the Student Nonviolent Coordinating Committee, replacing the more moderate John Lewis. Born in Trinidad in 1941,
Carmichael lived in Harlem and the East Bronx before attending Howard University in 1960. Turning down a graduate scholarship to study at Harvard, he
left the academy for activism, joining SNCC and participating in the Freedom
Rides. Arrested numerous times for his work on behalf of the movement, Carmichael in 1965 registered hundreds of black voters in Lowndes County, Alabama,
where African Americans were disenfranchised. One year later he became the

head of SNCC and traveled to Mississippi to continue James Meredith's "March Against Fear."[28]

On June 6, 1966, James Meredith, the first African American to integrate the University of Mississippi, began a 220-mile march from Memphis, Tennessee, to Jackson, Mississippi, billed as a protest against racism. On just the second day of the march Meredith was shot in the back, neck, and legs by an assassin's buckshot, seriously wounding him and leaving the fate of the march in question. Yet within a day the nation's leading civil rights figures, including Martin Luther King Jr. of the SCLC, Floyd McKissick of CORE, and Carmichael had picked up the march. A march that initially forged unity among the various civil rights groups soon exposed division within the movement. During a media interview with King and Carmichael, Peniel Joseph notes, "King dutifully professed his unwavering commitment to nonviolence, while Carmichael casually proclaimed his tactical rather than philosophical support." Additional conflict manifested itself in movement chants (SCLC workers chanted "Freedom" as SNCC workers chanted "Uhuru," which is Swahili for "freedom") and positioning in the march line. But the most dramatic moment of the march came when the party reached Greenwood, Mississippi.[29]

Carmichael planned to reveal SNCC's new slogan in Greenwood, a town he knew well from his work as project director. Before the marchers reached their designated campsite, Stone Street Elementary School, the governor of Mississippi, Paul B. Johnson Jr., withdrew most of the police officers assigned to the march. Now facing armed hecklers, the group learned that Greenwood officials had barred the marchers from using the school as a campsite. Carmichael had had enough. In the midst of an argument with Greenwood's public safety commissioner, Carmichael took the advice of his aide, Willie Ricks, and let the police arrest him for trespassing. "We'll get you out of jail," said Ricks, "and you come out and make the speech tonight." Released after just a few hours, Carmichael arrived at Broad Street Park, where Ricks and the marchers were waiting. Standing on a makeshift stage, Carmichael began his impassioned address. "This is the twenty-seventh time that I've been arrested," he told the captive audience. "I ain't going to jail no more. The only way we gonna stop them white men from whuppin' us is to take over. What we gonna start sayin' now is Black Power!" After each passage of Carmichael's emotional speech, Ricks asked the crowd, "What do we want?" And with equal emotion in their voices they replied, "Black Power!"[30]

Until recently, most historians have identified Carmichael's Greenwood address as the birth of the Black Power movement. These scholars have either ignored or minimized the movement's origins, such as Marcus Garvey and his Universal Negro Improvement Association in the 1920s, militant influences in the labor movement in the 1930s and 1940s, and Robert F. Williams's call for armed self-defense in the late 1950s and early 1960s. Beginning in the 1990s, historians such as William Van Deburg, Jeffrey Ogbar, and most notably Peniel Joseph have concluded that Black Power was not born in 1966 nor did the civil rights movement die in 1968 following King's assassination. Joseph, for instance, states plainly that the Black Power movement "paralleled, and at times overlapped, the heroic civil rights era." He notes, "Early Black Power activists were simultaneously inspired and repulsed by the civil rights struggles that served as a violent flashpoint for racial transformation." Any black man or woman in the mid- to late 1960s certainly identified with elements of both of these major movements.[31]

Outside the Student Union, in the Kappa Alpha Psi fraternity house, and in the classrooms of UCLA, activists and students demanded that Ashe stand up for fellow blacks in the South and in urban America. Grass-roots organizers active in King's Southern Christian Leadership Conference urged Ashe to speak out in support of the UCLA students who traveled to Mississippi to register voters in 1964. Black militants like Ron Karenga called on Ashe to visit the black ghettos of Watts and criticize America's corrupt white leadership. "Those were the frenetic, psychedelic, schizophrenic '60s," Ashe told a reporter, "when the moderate progressive's hero could be the reactionary's nigger and the revolutionary's Uncle Tom." Both moderates and radicals agreed, however, that he *had* to do something. "As my fame increased," he explained, "so did my anguish. I knew that many blacks were proud of my accomplishments on the tennis court. But I also knew that some others, especially many of my own age or younger, did not bother to hide their indifference to me and my trophies, or even their disdain and contempt for me." The politically charged atmosphere of the 1960s helped Ashe transition away from the conservative and moderate approaches of his father and Dr. Johnson. Being an African American in college, a black athlete, and a racial symbol to blacks and whites alike moved him in the direction of militancy. Far from becoming a black nationalist, he incorporated elements of Black Power into his life while remaining committed to a belief in open dialogue with whites and nonviolence.[32]

Black Power ideology appeared on college campuses years before Carmichael popularized the phrase. In the mid- to late 1960s, black students started to demand the creation of black studies departments and black student unions, open admissions policies for minority students, and more soul food in school cafeterias. Some African Americans even called for segregated classes, arguing that whites stifled the creativity of black students. To the movement's converts, Black Power rested on the notion that black moderates like King were under the control of white elites. At UCLA, some activists accused Ashe of accommodating whites by remaining silent on the major issues of the day. He engaged in many debates over the years with black classmates, activists, and reporters who challenged his seemingly conservative to moderate world-view. One black journalist criticized him for his failure to empower African American youths, charging that he spent little time in the inner city teaching kids how to play tennis. As the movement became more militant, reporters increasingly injected politics into their interview questions. When confronted with the accusation that he had neglected black youths, a defensive Ashe reframed the question and asked the reporter, "Well, how many black kids in the mid-sixties have you taught how to handle a microphone?"[33]

Ashe agonized about his role in the civil rights movement. "There were times," he wrote, "when I felt a burning sense of shame that I was not with other blacks—and whites—standing up to the fire hoses and the police dogs, the truncheons, bullets, and bombs that cut down such martyrs as [James] Chaney, [Michael] Schwerner, and [Andrew] Goodman, Viola Liuzzo, Martin Luther King, Jr., Medgar Evers, and the little girls in that bombed church in Birmingham, Alabama." Even if he wanted to, he could not escape the call of fellow blacks. Each day, network newscasts aired stories of black workers being beaten and harassed for registering voters or participating in marches. The *Los Angeles Times*, the *Los Angeles Sentinel*, and UCLA's *Daily Bruin* featured front-page coverage of California activists who had traveled to Mississippi and Alabama in support of black southerners. "While blood was running freely in the streets of Birmingham, Memphis, and Biloxi," he admitted, "I had been playing tennis. Dressed in immaculate white, I was elegantly stroking tennis balls on perfectly paved courts in California and New York and Europe." To a reporter for *Class* magazine, he added, "Everybody—black or white—was angry about something," he explained. "If you were white, you were probably into the free speech movement, as they were up at Berkeley, our sister school. And if you were black, and in the South, you were probably sitting at some lunch counter or marching and demonstrating with someone. And I missed all that."[34]

Years later, he offered a geographic explanation for his lack of activism: "I was geographically isolated at UCLA, bounded on the north by Bel Air, on the east by Beverly Hills, on the west by Santa Monica, and on the south by Westwood. There weren't too many blacks that live in that section of Los Angeles."

Ashe conceded, however, that his physical isolation did not make him unaware of developments in the movement. In fact, on a near-daily basis the *Daily Bruin*, the *Los Angeles Times*, and *Los Angeles Sentinel* ran stories of the sit-ins, the Freedom Rides, the voter registration campaigns, marches, and demonstrations. Local activists in California distributed flyers and staged rallies in support of the movement, and Black Power advocates such as Ron Karenga gave speeches outside the Student Union. One *Daily Bruin* piece reported on Earl Lemont Avery, a former *Daily Bruin* sportswriter whose previous accomplishment had been to lead UCLA's flag football team to victory over their rival USC. Traveling South, Avery said, "is just something I have to do." In March 1965 a group of UCLA students held a rally protesting the violence in Selma. "Since Birmingham," student leader Jim Berland said, "we have stood by while the Negroes of the South have been denied again and again their constitutional rights to vote and the freedom to assemble. . . . The beatings in Selma should shake us out of our apathy." Ashe could have actively joined the cause, but he chose not to do so. Many factors contributed to this decision. The moderate integrationist teachings of his mentors, the class and social obligations of being an amateur tennis player, and Ashe's restrictive status as an ROTC cadet all contributed to his supporting the movement in spirit but not in practice.[35]

Ashe had many opportunities to get involved in civil rights activism. During his junior and senior years he was a member of Kappa Alpha Psi, an African American fraternity situated off campus on Crenshaw Boulevard, which accepted black members from both UCLA and California State University at Los Angeles. As a physical and community refuge from institutionalized racism, fraternities like Kappa Alpha Psi served as support groups for blacks facing economic, political, and social discrimination. Kappa Alpha Psi participated in community outreach, focusing on issues like housing discrimination in Westwood. Considered a "white area" near campus, Westwood's realty boards used deeds and titles to keep African Americans from owning homes in the neighborhood. With regard to student housing, Byron H. Atkinson, UCLA's associate dean of students, observed, "I don't see any changes in the student housing situation since this campus was founded. It was impossible for a Negro to room here in 1930. It is almost impossible now." Despite Kappa Alpha Psi's involvement in important issues, Ashe showed little interest in fraternity programs. He explained that his friend basketball star Walt Hazzard and others "sort of pressured me into joining" the fraternity. When he had some free time away from tennis, he paid attention to his studies, women, friends, and leisure activities. Working on behalf of Kappa Alpha Psi was not a top priority for him.[36]

Ashe also engaged in arguments with African and African American students at UCLA, many of whom questioned his commitment to the black cause. "How can you Negroes call yourselves Afro-Americans?" inquired one African student. "You've never seen Mother Africa. You don't speak any African languages. You don't know our customs. None of you ever visit the Afro-Asian Cultural Center here. All I see you do is play cards and play pool when you're not in class." Conversations like this one forced Ashe to think of himself in racial rather than athletic terms. Was he destined to become a great tennis player and nothing more, or was there a need for him and his opinions in the black freedom movement? Never one to remain quiet during a discussion, he pushed his counterparts to clarify their positions with pointed, direct questions. None of his intellectual opponents at UCLA, however, were as combative or insistent as Ron Karenga.[37]

Short, stocky, and bald, Karenga wore oversized black-tinted glasses, colorful dashikis, a "Fu Manchu" mustache, and, according to Ashe, "was known as the heaviest, baddest black dude on campus." Born Ronald Everett in 1941 to a poultry farmer and Baptist minister, Karenga moved to Los Angeles after high school and attended Los Angeles City College, becoming the school's first African American student body president. Following graduation, he earned a master's degree in political science and African studies from UCLA, where he also became fluent in Arabic and Kiswahili. He organized a Los Angeles chapter of the Afro-American Association, an association that encouraged the study of African history and culture and promoted self-help and black entrepreneurship. Breaking away from the AAA, Karenga later founded Organization US (as opposed to "Them"), which sought "a reclaimable African past through the adoption of creatively interpreted cultural, social, and political practices in an easily digestible and expertly marketed package." As "cultural nationalists," he argued, "we believe that you must rescue and reconstruct African history and culture to revitalize African culture today in America." US members adopted a philosophy called Kawaida (meaning "total way of life"), assumed Swahili names, dressed in West African clothing, and participated in rituals. Karenga took on the name Maulana, meaning "master teacher." At the height of his influence in the late 1960s, Karenga helped build black studies departments, black student unions, and black schools. He founded the Black Congress to revitalize Watts after the 1965 riots. When Ashe unexpectedly encountered Karenga at UCLA, before either had reached the peak of his fame, the US founder gave the tennis star an earful.[38]

One day while walking home from class, Ashe stopped at the Student Union after noticing Karenga surrounded by a gathering of supporters. Joining the crowd, Ashe listened carefully as Karenga talked about racism, discrimination, and injustice. Karenga encouraged African Americans to establish an identity apart from whites by partaking in cultural nationalism. After Karenga concluded his remarks and his audience walked away, Ashe approached him and the two engaged in a deep conversation about Ashe's role in the black freedom movement. In an assertive manner that Ashe described as "argumentative," Karenga explained the need for African Americans to learn African history and adopt African cultural practices. Ashe listened patiently but gave no indication that he agreed with Karenga. The conversation intensified. "It's attitudes like yours I'm trying to change," said Karenga. "Look, you're the cream of the black crop, you're in college, you're going to do fairly well in life. If I can't convince you, then what do you think about the black masses?" Ashe found Karenga persuasive, yet he equated black nationalism to separatism, echoing the arguments of the mainstream media and conservative blacks. Ashe's belief in integration and his faith in America's future, however slow or uneven the progress, clouded his views of black nationalism. Agreeing to disagree, the two parted and never crossed paths again. Growing up in Virginia, Ashe had contended with racism and segregation on a daily basis. Now in Los Angeles, he believed that Karenga was arguing for self-imposed segregation, a clear misinterpretation of Karenga's views. Considering Jim Crow segregation and black nationalism extreme positions, Ashe rejected both.[39]

The Watts riot of 1965 offers another example of Ashe's reluctance to participate in activism. In August of that year, Los Angeles police pulled over a young black man on suspicion of drunk driving. During the arrest, officers feuded with local black residents who had gathered around the patrol car. For years, residents of the Watts neighborhood had claimed that local police practiced racial profiling, resulting in unfair arrests and the beating of innocent citizens. To struggling blacks in Watts, who lived well below the poverty line, the August arrest was infuriating. When the police left the scene, residents began attacking white motorists, throwing stones at passing vehicles, and tipping over cars and setting them on fire. Investigators estimated that 35,000 adults participated in the riots and another 72,000 were "close spectators." Don Harrison, a *Daily Bruin* reporter covering the riots, observed, "Watts was no place for 'Whitey' that bloody weekend. A Caucasian, any Caucasian, represented to rioting Negroes 'the power structure,' which they thought responsible for their sub-standard living." Harrison described a scene in which fires burned all night, grandmothers and young children looted from local stores, and reports of "men with guns" filled the airwaves. When the rioting concluded, 4,000 men and women had been arrested, 1,000 had been injured, and Watts's business owners had suffered $200 million in property damage.[40]

"People have said to me," Ashe remembered, " 'Well, you were in Los Angeles [in 1965], couldn't you see Watts coming?' But I didn't know Los Angeles, even after several years." When he was not on campus or traveling for tennis, he only visited his fraternity house, which was located outside of Watts. He did not have any friends inside the riot zone, nor did he see any "social significance" in Watts prior to the riots. From his dorm room at UCLA, Ashe tracked the events in the South but took no action. As a member of the tennis team and an ROTC cadet, he stood to lose his athletic scholarship and his military status if he joined other activists in the South and urban America or said the wrong thing to the press. Further, his father had advised him not to protest. He could not, however, shake the persistent feeling that he should join the cause.[41]

_ゃ ᠙_

When Ashe wasn't on the tennis court or traveling to play tennis, he spent the little free time that he had studying, hanging out with his friends, fulfilling the obligations of his scholarship, and trying his hand at other sports. At Sumner High School in St. Louis, Ashe had graduated at the top of his class, earning A's on nearly all of his assignments. His academic career at UCLA was a different story. In part because tennis demanded so much of his time and energies, he did not prioritize education, and as a result he received mostly B's and C's. During a number of stretches at the height of tennis season, Ashe worked almost exclusively with tutors, who, he claimed, taught more in a couple of hours than professors taught in two or three classes. UCLA, like other major universities, provided alumni-funded tutors to athletes to ensure that they remained eligible to compete. In memoirs and interviews, Ashe rarely identified particular professors or courses that influenced him. One exception was a course titled "Outdoor Recreational Camping," which he described as a "cinch" course sure to improve one's GPA. Because Ashe and teammate Charlie Pasarell had missed a required camping trip, the instructor agreed to take the two men, along with some football players, on a make-up trip. On the drive to the campground Ashe, perhaps recognizing the absurdity of such a course, bluntly asked the professor, "Is it true they are going to stop your course because it's too easy?" The professor mostly ignored the question, choosing instead to speak with his actions: he gave Ashe a C in his "cinch" course.[42]

Away from the classroom and his tutors, Ashe enjoyed staying in as much as he did going out. His father's "commandment" that Ashe remain at home if he did not have a reason to be out stuck with him at UCLA, even though his father resided hundreds of miles away. He did not date for the sake of dating or party for the sake of partying. His teammate Jean Baker remembered Ashe attending few parties other than select dorm dances. He likewise associated with few African American women at UCLA, believing them to be secretly searching for husbands. But when Ashe did venture beyond his own dorm, he could be the life of the party. His friend and teammate Allen Fox recalled, "He dresses very well, very neat. . . . And I get a kick out of watching him dance. He's real loose." Sometimes Ashe's social life conflicted with tennis. On the eve of an important practice match with teammate John Lesch, Ashe attended a "pretty wild" house party hosted by his African American fraternity. Like many typical college students, he was slow to wake up the following morning. So slow, in fact, that Lesch had to physically pull him from under the covers. His lethargy carried over to the tennis court. Ashe vowed never to repeat that mistake.[43]

Ashe made some lasting friendships at UCLA, few stronger than his bond with basketball star Walt Hazzard. As black men enrolled at a predominately white university, he and Hazzard shared the experience of being outsiders. Hazzard had grown up in Philadelphia, where he quickly distinguished himself as one of the city's best basketball players. He led Overbrook High School to a record of 89-3 over four years, earning player-of-the-year honors and a scholarship to UCLA. During UCLA's undefeated national championship season in 1963–64, Hazzard was named the NCAA tournament's most valuable player. He and Ashe were both accomplished athletes, and both were conscious of their race. In fact, Hazzard introduced Ashe to the fraternity. And in 1971, just as Ashe fought against apartheid, Hazzard converted to Islam and changed his name to Mahdi Abdul-Rahman. While Hazzard was from the North and Ashe from the South, both men were raised by working-class parents in segregated neighborhoods, and athletics represented their escape. Yet neither Ashe nor Hazzard felt completely at home in Los Angeles. There was always the danger of fitting in too well with the white world. "If you're going to maintain your identity and your equilibrium," explained African American baseball player Tebbie Fowler, a native of Compton, "you can't associate too much, you can't assimilate. You can commingle, but not assimilate." More often than not, Ashe and Hazzard found fellowship with each other, attending the other's games and matches as well as playing pick-up sports.[44]

Other than Hazzard, Ashe hung out with African American basketball player Fred Slaughter, the team's center, white player Gail Goodrich, a guard, and his mostly white tennis teammates. Baker, Charlie Pasarell, and Ashe were always looking for new sports to try. These "sport kicks" included horseback riding, billiards, table tennis, and baseball. The three men continued to play a variety of sports even though J. D. Morgan had ordered them to stick to tennis. Once, when Ashe sprained his ankle on the gridiron, Morgan commanded, "No more football!" Ashe ignored his coach. Even he had to live a little.[45]

Although Ashe attended UCLA for four years, he remembered few professors and classes that advanced his intellect. More than his teachers, Ashe's classmates challenged his opinions and engaged him in long conversations about race relations, Africa, and world affairs. Ashe's impressive memory allowed him to remember much of what he read—and he loved to read. Early on, both his father and his mother had emphasized education, even at the expense of tennis. When he arrived at UCLA, then, his intellectual curiosity surpassed that of his peers. He also had the good fortune of traveling all across the United States and Europe for tennis. He had personally witnessed the lives and living conditions of African Americans residing in urban and rural, northern and southern communities. All of these personal experiences carried greater weight than any history, political science, or English course. Because Ashe attended UCLA during the pivotal years of the civil rights movement, years that included events such as the March on Washington, Freedom Summer, and the voting rights campaign in Selma, he faced more pressure to know about and have an opinion on the major issues of the day. For all of these reasons, Ashe left UCLA a very educated man.[46]

As an African American in tennis, Ashe reaped the financial and social benefits of being an "other," a novelty in a game filled with white faces. Yet although many whites cheered his accomplishments and flocked to local matches to see him play, others saw him as a danger to the sport of tennis, a man who might steal their white women and jeopardize the position of wealthy whites in a game dominated by the upper crust. "Arthur went through two extremes," observed his black teammate Luis Glass. "In the beginning he just wasn't wanted. Now everyone wants him. A more emotional person might have cracked in the beginning, or gotten a swelled head afterward. He must have a lot of internal strength." Glass's perceptive commentary reveals that Ashe's internal struggles at UCLA went beyond racism, civil rights, and Black Power. Because of his race and his athletic abilities, he had become one of the sport's main drawing cards. And while the press focused on his role as a racial trailblazer, he insisted that reporters evaluate him based on his tennis and not his race. On campus, he faced a number of dilemmas, including the prospect of interracial dating. In the mid-1960s, he struggled to be a normal college student, always aware that someone was watching.[47]

Despite his emerging celebrity status, Ashe continued to face racial discrimination. At UCLA he frequently roomed with Dave Reed, a white player, when the team was on the road. Once during a tournament at the Merion Cricket Club in Haverford, Pennsylvania, Reed approached the hotel's registration desk to get his room for the night. Ashe and most of his teammates had checked in earlier in the day, leaving Reed as the lone straggler. When he requested his key and room number, the white woman behind the desk asked, "Do you have any objections to rooming with Arthur Ashe?" Laughing at what he considered an absurd suggestion, Reed sarcastically responded that, yes, he did have a problem staying with Ashe. "Well," the woman said, "we can arrange so you won't have to."[48]

While some, like the hotel clerk in Haverford, were more than eager to isolate Ashe, most tennis fans—black and white—embraced him as one of the sport's top young talents. Eager spectators turned out in droves to see the young star with an overpowering serve and impeccable demeanor. The *New York Times* reported in 1965 that all gate and attendance records were broken at the U.S. Championships in part because of Ashe's "electrifying tennis." "I know people are staring at me when I play," he told a sportswriter. "I draw bigger crowds than I would if I were white." Black athletes such as Ashe have always been drawing cards. The Brooklyn Dodgers repeatedly sold out their games following Jackie Robinson's entry into Major League Baseball in 1947. In that year, the Dodgers drew a record 1.8 million fans, and four other teams set attendance records. Love him or hate him, fans assembled to see Robinson perform. When asked about being a black tennis player, Ashe conceded that "it's almost like money in the bank for me," referring to the gate receipts. He realized the benefits of being a "novelty," yet he remained uneasy about the role race played in his success. "I wouldn't like to feel that I am considered a representative of the Negro race, but I know I am," he told a reporter. "I just want to be taken as another tennis player. If I make it, fine. If I don't—well, lots don't."[49]

As just "another tennis player," he found himself attracted to women of all colors, a fact that did not sit well with some black and white critics. "I have absolutely no prejudice," he told the *New York Times*. "I take out colored girls and white girls. I just like girls." Initially, he found black women "stuck up" and constantly on the hunt for a husband. Perhaps out of curiosity, then, he favored white and Asian women during his first two years at UCLA. He knew, however, that interracial dating was controversial at best and dangerous at worst. In the Jim Crow era, some state laws criminalized intermarriage, and a number of whites even suggested that the civil rights movement was a ploy by black men to have relationships with white women. Many Black Power advocates op-posed intermarriage on the grounds that it diluted the African race.[50]

In a provocative, multipart series on black athletes in 1968, journalist Jack Olsen of *Sports Illustrated* examined the hidden world of interracial dating. "The first message that is passed on by the coach to the uneasy Negro is often: Stay away from white women," he wrote. The future NBA star Elgin Baylor once escorted a white woman to a campus dance at Seattle University only to be stopped at the door by a coaching assistant who ordered him to "cease and de-sist." In addition to the direct approach, coaches exercised more subtle means of discouragement. Harold Busby, a sprinter and football player at UCLA, told Olsen, "Sometimes if you're walking with a white girl the coaches will look at you kind of funny. . . . Nothing is said about it, but you can get the message." In extreme cases, coaches withheld an athlete's playing time. Junior Coffey, a football starter for the University of Washington, was benched and never started another game after refusing to end a relationship with a white woman. Walt Hazzard, who often was seen on campus with white women, described a persistent "feeling of apprehension, even when you were just going from one class to another."[51]

Ashe understood the stigmas and dangers that came with interracial dating. Though UCLA had a progressive reputation and a history of treating black play-ers well, he acknowledged the presence of racial prejudice in academics and athletics. Several of his friends on the football team had told him that coaches instructed the players, "Don't bring a white girl to the football banquet." Despite the experiences of other black athletes at UCLA, there is no evidence that J. D. Morgan advised him against dating white women, nor does Ashe men-tion that he encountered any problems as the result of his dating preferences. A tennis player, black or white, was considered less threatening to white women than a muscled football player. Teammate Luis Glass made the common obser-vation that Ashe had "white" features, including a light skin complexion. Years later, a South African newspaper commenting on Ashe's antiapartheid views noted, "The biggest surprise is that he is not black at all. The pigmentation of the player who represents blacks in world tennis is more brown or Oriental yel-low." Ashe rarely attended parties where there would be white women present that went late into the night, which would make him an easy target for those who did not share his views.[52]

His strategies for avoiding controversy did not spare him from racism. At a dorm dance his sophomore year, he became fixated on a white woman with dark hair who wore a matching green skirt and turtleneck. He got up the courage to approach the young woman, and the two ended up talking for three hours. "Talk about old southern taboos coming back to haunt you," he remembered. "I was scared, thrilled, excited, sweating and numb—all at the same time." The relationship ended, however, when the woman's mother learned from TV sports coverage that he was black. "You didn't tell me he was a Negro!" she exclaimed. "I don't ever want him in my house."[53]

Even aside from his race, Ashe proved to be an enigmatic dating partner. His friend Jean Baker observed how he would be enamored with a woman for one or two weeks only to break up with her soon thereafter. "He'd get interested in some girl, then get bored—or scared, maybe—and wouldn't want to see her," Baker recalled. "But he always kept friends with her." His biggest relationship mistake occurred when he proposed to Dianne Seymour, an African American telephone operator who lived in New York City. Ashe met Seymour during a tennis tour, and the two began exchanging letters. "They had a good time and Arthur asked her to marry him," Baker remembered. "Right like that! Took ten minutes to make the decision." Ashe's impromptu proposal was out of character for him given his usual caution and contemplation. On March 19, 1966, the New York Times ran an advertisement announcing the engagement, with the wedding scheduled for June 5 in Richmond. When he returned to Los Angeles following the announcement, he began having second thoughts. Seymour telephoned him repeatedly and demanded more of his time than he was willing to give. Ashe grew bored with the relationship and missed his independence, which he valued above most other things. Over Easter vacation he met Seymour in Puerto Rico, where he broke off their engagement. Baker, perhaps sarcastically, noted, "She took it nicely." The engagement would be one of the few impulsive decisions that Ashe ever made.[54]

—◌ ◌—

At UCLA, Ashe shied away from activism, choosing to focus instead on his tennis and his studies. In June 1964, however, a controversy in Europe would place him at the center of a civil and human rights battle involving the United States and the Soviet Union. Since the end of World War II, both nations had engaged in propaganda campaigns, each arguing that the other committed human rights abuses. The Americans accused the Soviets of quashing internal dissent in Eastern Europe, executing political prisoners, and secretly financing the North Vietnamese. The Soviets pointed to segregation in the American South as evidence that the United States violated the civil rights of its citizens.[55]

Over time, both nations increasingly focused on South Africa and the role it played in the Cold War. An ally of the United States, South Africa exported diamonds and other raw materials to the United States and was seen as a staunch defender of capitalism in Africa. To maintain control over native blacks, ruling whites, known as Afrikaners, governed under a series of draconian laws known collectively as apartheid. Apartheid included laws that required blacks to carry a pass with them at all times, forbade labor organizing, and mandated segregation in housing, hospitals, schools, public facilities, and public transportation. Beginning at midcentury, Afrikaners relocated thousands of blacks away from their homes and into homelands, makeshift communities that resembled refugee camps more than cities. Afrikaners ruled South Africa with a heavy hand, arresting and jailing those dissidents who dared to oppose them, like Nelson Mandela. Critics of U.S. foreign policy argued that America was hypocritical for supporting a decidedly undemocratic regime. Soviet propagandists were also quick to point out the gap between America's progressive rhetoric and more strategic foreign policy decisions.[56]

On many occasions, Cold War battles between the United States and its allies and the Soviet Union and its allies were fought in the arena of international sports. In the middle of the 1964 Wimbledon championships in England, Alex Metreveli of the Soviet Union forfeited his match rather than take the court against Cliff Drysdale, a white South African. Soon thereafter, Hungary's Istvan Gulyas withdrew from his match with South Africa's Abe Segal. Metreveli and Gulyas almost certainly had received orders from Moscow to forfeit their matches in an attempt to draw attention away from Wimbledon and toward South African apartheid. Suddenly, all of England and the tennis world were in an uproar. Wimbledon—the crown jewel of tennis—was supposed to be a sacred place, a sanctuary undisturbed by the Cold War and geopolitics. When asked by an Associated Press reporter about Metreveli and Gulyas, Ashe criticized the two men for their decision and suggested that sporting events were not the proper arena for political protests. "This no doubt is some sort of political strategy on the part of the Russians," he reasoned. "I don't think you want political protests of this kind in sports—especially here at Wimbledon." Tennis players, he believed, had to be viewed as individuals and not punished because of their countries' actions. Furthermore, he argued, if tennis players, fans, and officials accepted the withdrawals, what would stop an American from forfeiting a match with a player from the Soviet Union, or an Egyptian player from refusing to take the court against a player from Israel? "I am a Negro and apartheid objectively concerns me," he said. "But I would play Segal any time." Thus, although he was moving incrementally away from moderate integrationism, Ashe remained steadfastly opposed to athletic protests, especially the kind that resulted in forfeitures. The sport of tennis mattered more than what he viewed as an empty protest that harmed other competitors.[57]

Ashe's statement against the boycott and his tepid condemnation of apartheid touched off rounds of criticism from Sam Lacy of the *Baltimore Afro-American* and other black sportswriters. In a scathing piece titled "A Communist without a Card," Lacy questioned Ashe's knowledge of world affairs and suggested that he play tennis and keep his mouth shut. Lacy wrote, "It is most unfortunate that Ashe couldn't have just gone on and played the role of juvenile as a 19-year-old tennis player. . . . That he presumes to [be an] expert on international 'politics' . . . clearly demonstrates that he is either educationally puerile or politically naïve." The time would surely come, Lacy knew, when Ashe would have to face a South African in a major tournament. Would he have the guts to withdraw, or would he be a coward and hide behind tennis etiquette? Withdrawal, Lacy acknowledged, would certainly jeopardize Ashe's standing in tennis and cost him a tournament win, yet his sacrifice would pale in comparison to the actions of men like Medgar Evers, who gave their lives in the pursuit of justice. Lacy implored Ashe to consider the thousands of struggling South Africans and blacks in the U.S. South before he made another naive statement to the press.[58]

Lacy was not the only African American sportswriter to question the tennis star. Clayton Moore of the *Los Angeles Sentinel* offered a balanced yet critical take on Ashe's comments. Yes, Moore agreed that Drysdale and Segal were individuals who should be treated as such. "But if one is too refined," he argued, "to speak out against injustice and intolerance we find little comfort in knowing that he represents this nation and certainly not the Negro people." Moore had always admired Ashe but wished he understood the "facts of life" as they related to blacks in the United States and South Africa. Both Lacy and Moore had covered the most politicized African American athletes of the twentieth century, including Jackie Robinson, Bill Russell, Jim Brown, and Muhammad Ali. Lacy, for one, had reported on Robinson's encounters with racial discrimination during spring training in Florida, where Lacy was also involved in an incident in which he and Robinson were refused accommodations at a local hotel. Lacy was no ordinary sportswriter. He was a force for change who helped to integrate Major League Baseball and placed a spotlight on injustice once he identified it. Sam Lacy had battled racists in the past and often won.[59]

Ashe waited three years to answer Lacy and other critics in *Advantage Ashe*, his first of many memoirs. Striking a defiant tone, Ashe insisted that his mistake had been not to anticipate a backlash from black sportswriters, even though he summarily dismissed their views. He defended his own statement and his right to offer his opinion. "I don't care how Lacy feels," Ashe noted. "He has the right to his opinion. But in this case I think he's sorry he popped off." He concluded that since South African tennis players could not end apartheid or sway the government, their views were virtually irrelevant to him. And if South Africa offered him a large sum of prize money to compete in the land of apartheid, he wouldn't turn them down. He agreed that apartheid was a clear human and civil rights violation that affected thousands of lives, but someone else would have to play the role of militant.[60]

― co co―

As Ashe prepared to graduate from UCLA and become an officer in the U.S. Army, he was no longer the shy and unassuming youth who had left Richmond in 1960. The events of the past five and a half years—both locally and nationally—had led Ashe to develop a racial consciousness that oftentimes stood in opposition to his role as a tennis player. He had learned to negotiate the myriad voices telling him to speak up or be quiet, demand freedom or remain patient, and contribute to the cause as an activist or as a tennis player. With the late 1960s fast approaching, the microphones and tape recorders would follow Ashe from New York to London and elsewhere around the world. His emerging celebrity status and role as an African American icon sealed his fate. When Arthur Ashe talked, people listened. And Arthur Ashe, as it turned out, had much to say.

# CHAPTER 3

# An Emerging Activist

"It was a time of horror, embitterment, despair, and agony," wrote one historian about 1968. Another scholar, offering a more balanced perspective, remarked that "1968 combined both revolutionary bombast and spiritual fulfillment, ecstasy and self-destruction, success and failure." In 1968 America launched Apollo 7 and 8 into space and elected Richard Nixon as the thirty-seventh president of the United States. Americans witnessed the assassinations of Martin Luther King Jr. and Robert F. Kennedy, student-led riots protesting the Democratic National Convention in Chicago, and the Tet Offensive in Vietnam. The latter event led Americans to question whether the United States was really winning the war in Southeast Asia. Nineteen sixty-eight also represented a decisive year for African Americans frustrated with uneven enforcement of the Civil Rights Act of 1964 and the Voting Rights Act of 1965. Increasingly, blacks demanded an end to police brutality, voting disfranchisement, and housing and workplace discrimination and called for equal protection under the law.[1]

For black athletes, both amateur and professional, 1968 was a year in which African American sports figures participated in civil rights activism at an unprecedented level. Harry Edwards, a former multisport athlete and current instructor of sociology at San Jose State College, led a movement calling on black athletes to boycott the 1968 Olympic Games in protest of worldwide racial discrimination. At the Games in Mexico City, Tommie Smith and John Carlos raised their black-gloved fists in defiance from the victory podium after the 200-meter race, a Black Power salute that got both men banned from the Olympic Village. At colleges and universities across the United States, black athletes challenged racial discrimination and threatened to boycott competitions until coaches and administrators met their demands for racial equality. Muhammad Ali fought a Vietnam draft order in the courts, NFL all-pro Jim Brown founded an organization to aid inner-city blacks, and the St. Louis Cardinals football team planned a walkout unless the league disciplined racist players and coaches.[2]

Black athletes' participation in the black freedom movement increased the visibility of black activists as a whole, drawing attention to African Americans who suffered racial discrimination in sports and society. By assuming the role of social and political activists, black athletes actively contributed to the black freedom movement, requiring leaders like Martin Luther King Jr., Whitney Young, and Stokely Carmichael to seek their counsel and enlist them in the cause. This activism, however, frequently overshadowed the athletic achievements of black athletes in the late 1960s. O. J. Simpson's Heisman Trophy, Bob Gibson's MVP and Cy Young awards, and Bill Russell's selection as *Sports Illustrated*'s "Sportsman of the Year" drew far less attention than the actions of Smith, Carlos, Ali, and Brown.[3]

Like many black athletes, Arthur Ashe juggled his role in sports and politics in 1968. In September 1968 he became the first African American man and amateur player to win the U.S. Open in Forest Hills, New York. Three months later he led the U.S. Davis Cup team to a 4-1 victory over defending champion Australia to capture the Davis Cup crown for the first time since 1963. He finished the year ranked number two in the world behind Rod Laver of Australia and ranked number one in the United States. As he found his game, he also found his voice. In the late 1960s, sportswriters and reporters began asking him about race, Black Power, and apartheid, and he often responded with unambiguous statements. He also spoke directly to the public. On March 10, 1968, he gave his first civil rights address by invitation at the Church of the Redeemer in Washington, DC, where he outlined his political and economic philosophies. Although he offered a tempered solution to the problems of racial discrimination, the army reprimanded him for violating a rule that prohibited officers from making political speeches. From 1968 on, tennis and activism would go hand in racquet for the American star.[4]

From 1966 to 1968 Ashe lived a life of contradiction. He was a commissioned officer in the army and a proud member of the U.S. Davis Cup team, yet he privately questioned the Vietnam War and acknowledged the persistence of American racism. When he spoke out on race, class, or politics, radical blacks accused him of selling out to whites, while conservatives, black and white, assailed him for adopting a militant posture. Perhaps most important, winning the U.S. Open and the Davis Cup gave him an international platform that he used to rally others to the causes of civil rights, poverty, and apartheid.

_C. C_

The time had come for Ashe to make a decision. For years he had tried to accommodate everyone, sacrificing his own personal interests for the sake of others. Now, he had to disappoint one of his mentors. The Davis Cup team needed him to steal the crown from the Australians, a commitment that promised to take him around the world. Australian tennis officials and boosters expected America's "Negro star" to compete in their summer circuit, dazzling fans and keeping the turnstiles moving. Both opportunities, however glamorous, would require him to miss the fall semester of his senior year at UCLA, a prospect that made him uneasy. As a child, he had received repeated lectures from his grandmother on the importance of a formal education, and he was the first member of his family to attend college. But the Davis Cup and the Australian circuit represented tickets to stardom. The competition would be intense and the schedule grueling, but the reward included international recognition and the possibility of landing endorsement deals. His father, J. D. Morgan, and Dr. Johnson offered advice, but the decision remained his. After careful deliberation, he chose tennis over college. His cap and gown would stay in the closet for another year.[5]

Ashe's selection to the Davis Cup team marked an impressive achievement for a black man who had grown up in the segregated South. In August 1963 he became the first African American named to the U.S. Davis Cup team, joining stars such as Dennis Ralston and Chuck McKinley. His long-anticipated selection was met with cheers in the African American community. A reporter for the New York Times traveled to Harlem and observed tennis courts filled with young blacks, each hoping to become the next Arthur Ashe. After interviewing Clifford Blackman, the president of the New York Tennis Association, and speaking with some of the city's estimated six thousand black players, the reporter discovered that Ashe was the idol of many black boys and girls who lined Harlem's makeshift courts. The reporter also noted a socioeconomic disparity between Ashe and the young blacks who idolized him. The children of Harlem played on asphalt courts in such disrepair that it was often dangerous to use them. Blackman's organization unsuccessfully lobbied the New York City Council to build clay courts in Harlem. Ashe was a rising star, a black man in a white man's game, yet the promise of new tennis courts in Harlem remained unfulfilled. Any young Harlemite hoping to become the next Arthur Ashe would have to contend with broken pavement, curbs, and passing cars.[6]

Selection to the U.S. Davis Cup team represented a major honor for any American player, black or white. Conceived by Dwight Filley Davis in 1900, the Davis Cup competition began as a friendly tournament that promoted good-will among participating nations. From 1900 to 1903 only the United States and Great Britain competed, but by 1905, France, Belgium, and Australia had entered as well. With a total of seventeen nations involved in 1923, Davis Cup officials divided the tournament into two zones, the American and European zones. An Eastern Zone followed in 1955, and by 1967 the American and European zones had each divided into two.[7]

Each match between two nations, or "tie," is divided into five separate matches. On the first day of a tie, the number-one player from country A plays the number-two player from country B, and vice versa. On day two there is a doubles match between the two countries. On the final day, the number-one player from country A plays the number-one player from country B, and the number two from A plays the number two from B. The country that wins three out of five matches wins the tie and moves on to the next round. The higher-ranked country hosts the tie and chooses the court surface and location of the matches. Before Ashe's selection in 1963, Australia dominated the competition, winning four consecutive cups in 1959–62.[8]

Ashe considered himself a patriot, a man who represented his country with intense pride. He told more than one reporter that he would rather win the Davis Cup as a team than win Wimbledon as an individual. He preferred to hear "Point USA" from a referee than "Point Ashe." Wearing the U.S. colors in international competition meant a great deal to him. His uncles had fought during World War II, a time when many blacks sought full citizenship by enlisting in the war effort. As historian Lizabeth Cohen has noted, "Black organizations envisioned the patriotic route as a means to participate in the public life of the nation and broaden the meaning of democratic citizenship." Blacks joined the army to show that they too would sacrifice their lives for the nation. On the homefront, black men and women embraced price, rent, and rationing controls just as everyone else did. All too often, however, the promises of equality went unfulfilled. Black soldiers served in segregated units and returned to the United States to face the same discrimination as before. Service did not result in full citizenship. Although Ashe understood this reality, he remained a patriot.[9]

Despite his selection for the Davis Cup team in 1963, he spent almost two years training, learning, and watching Ralston, McKinley, and others play the important matches. Sitting on the bench proved difficult for him, especially

Clean-cut and wearing his signature glasses, Ashe prepares for a Davis Cup match. In 1963 he became the first African American selected for the U.S. team. (Edward Fernberger / International Tennis Hall of Fame & Museum Archives)

because he had to comply with his coach's strict training regimen and rules. A thin and demonstrative Mexican American with two U.S. championship trophies, Richard "Pancho" Gonzalez was no ordinary Davis Cup coach. Like Ashe, he had overcame racial and class discrimination to become one of America's best tennis players. Known for his persistent temper, which rattled referees and opponents, Gonzalez won an unprecedented eight professional titles between 1954 and 1962. Years after his death in 1995, *Sports Illustrated* eulogized Gonzalez: "Before the groundbreaking wins by Althea Gibson and Arthur Ashe in the '50s and '60s, before the brattiness of Jimmy Connors and John McEnroe in the '70s and '80s, before the complaints about Pete Sampras's untouchable serve in the '90s, Gonzalez smashed through the game's class and ethnic barriers, abused officials verbally and paralyzed opponents with a serve so powerful that it inspired cries to remake the sport."[10]

Personality and demeanor aside, Gonzalez saw much of himself in Ashe. Both men had grown up in segregated neighborhoods, both had joined the armed forces at a young age, and both possessed a devastating serve that intimidated opponents. Because he felt a connection to Ashe, Gonzalez pushed his young protégé to work harder, play smarter, and avoid distractions. Gonzalez frequently criticized his pupil in the press. He once told the *New York Times*, "Arthur Ashe doesn't train or practice hard enough; there are ten players better than he is." To *Sport* magazine he lamented Ashe's shot selection. "Ashe has about 16 different backhands," he quipped. "I wish he'd settle on a couple. He doesn't need that many." Although he certainly exaggerated in both statements, Gonzalez criticized the young Davis Cupper to ensure that his dedication would match his talent.[11]

Working with Gonzalez was like a dream come true for Ashe. "The only idol I ever had was Pancho Gonzalez," he told a reporter in a 1966 interview. "Skinwise, he was the nearest thing to me [in tennis], and he was also the greatest player in the world." He related to Gonzalez as one of the few "others" in a white man's game. As a child in Richmond, he saw Gonzalez play in person when he came to town with a professional tour group. Years later, Morgan brought Gonzalez to UCLA to work with the team. Observing the former champion, Ashe modeled his own game after Gonzalez's. "When Pancho Gonzalez plays it's all reflex," he told a sportswriter. "He doesn't have to think. That's what I'm trying to achieve." Gonzalez spent countless hours with Ashe, at times working him harder than Dr. Johnson or Dick Hudlin ever had. Ashe once joked, "It is a good thing I wasn't paying him" for all of the time Gonzalez devoted to the young player. Sportswriters often compared the two men. Arthur Daley observed in his column that "Ashe is a quite remarkable young man who has moved gracefully and naturally into championship stature, another in the long line of big hitters," a line that included Gonzalez. In Ashe, sportswriters and tennis fans saw a calmer, more mature version of Gonzalez, one who could intimidate his opponents with an "icy elegance" rather than an explosive temper.[12]

As a coach, Gonzalez resembled Walter Johnson more than he did J. D. Morgan. He demanded that his team wake up promptly at eight in the morning and eat a high-protein breakfast of bacon and eggs. Because of his high metabolism and lean frame, Ashe was allowed and even encouraged to drink whole milk instead of skim. His bulkier teammates were not afforded such a luxury. After breakfast the team jumped rope for fifteen minutes, ran 300-yard sets, and practiced specific shots for an hour and a half. "I don't go for all that getting up at five a.m., lifting weights, running through parks and jumping up and down," Ashe complained to a reporter. Yet he dared not defy Gonzalez. For lunch the team ate small quantities of meat and fruit. This was followed by a rest period. While the other players napped or watched television, Ashe often read a book, magazine, or newspaper or listened to music on the radio. "Ashe does not seem to be quite together unless a radio or a tape recorder is playing," noted John McPhee. "He irritates friends by turning up the music and flipping through books or magazines in the middle of conversations." He relied on the radio and music to put his mind at ease, to help him cope with the pressures of tennis. After the rest period, the team members played three- or four-set matches against one another.[13]

Gonzalez was a tough coach, but he joked with his players and kept the mood light on the court. He did, however, have a dark side. During a practice match with Ralston in Australia, Gonzalez quickly lost his temper after going down four sets to none. Without provocation, he screamed at Ralston, "Listen, you son of a bitch, you crybaby, all you do is cry." He then walked away from the match. Although Gonzalez later apologized, the coach's erratic behavior upset Ralston. "I was heartbroken," Ralston remembered. "This was my idol." Fortunately for Ashe, he managed to avoid a similar episode with Gonzalez.[14]

Ashe's one and only Davis Cup match before 1965 occurred on September 15, 1963, when he easily defeated Venezuela's Orlando Bracamonte. Known as a "dead rubber," the match was essentially meaningless. The United States had won the first four matches against Venezuela, clinching the American Zone final for the Americans before Ashe took the court. Just as football and basketball coaches play their backups at the end of a blowout game, Davis Cup captains often replace seasoned players with inexperienced ones in a dead rubber match. Looking more like a veteran than a Davis Cup rookie, Ashe overpowered Bracamonte, forcing the action with "blazing serves and stinging return shots." He won twelve games in a row in besting the Venezuelan 6-1, 6-1, 6-0. Both the press and Gonzalez took notice of Ashe's dominating performance. He had defeated Bracamonte by a wider margin than his teammate Dennis Ralston had managed several days earlier. Ralston had lost five games in three sets. Still, Ashe struggled on slow clay court surfaces. He and Gonzalez knew that learning to win on clay held the key to becoming a Davis Cup regular. Every time he played on clay, his feet began to slide, reminding him more of a roller rink than of a tennis court.[15]

Two years later in Dallas, the new Davis Cup captain, George MacCall, unexpectedly inserted Ashe into the lineup against Rafael Osuna, Mexico's top-ranked player. Mexico's captain, Pancho Contreras, assumed that Osuna would dominate Ashe in an easy opening-match win. No one, however, told Ashe that he was supposed to lose. Frank Deford, in Dallas to cover the tie, observed, "In the very first match the show went haywire: a supporting player, not really a principal, decided to become a star." *Time* magazine exclaimed, "Unleashing the strongest serve in U.S. amateur tennis, Ashe aced the abashed Osuna 15 times, volleyed with unerring accuracy, and walloped his opponent."[16]

In most matches, Ashe played "gangbusters style," relying on power and quickness to take down his opponents. Against Osuna, however, he embraced Gonzalez's counsel and focused on accuracy and control. The victory proved to an international audience that he was not only a skilled player but a smart one as well. In the mid-1960s, academic and popular literature described black athletes as fast, muscled brutes who fell victim to the intelligence, wit, and strategy of white players. Ashe's smart performance undermined such a racist and uninformed theory. After the match, MacCall heaped praise on the rising star. "Today Arthur became a man," he told a reporter. "He was under terrific pressure, and he came through." Two days later Ashe topped Antonio Palafox to clinch the American Zone final for the United States. Following the matches, he and his teammates visited the Levee Club in Downtown Dallas for a victory celebration. When he entered the club, the band immediately stopped playing. He worried that the club's employees would ask him to leave because of the color of his skin. Then the master of ceremonies announced over the loudspeaker: "Arthur Ashe, the hero of the Davis Cup triumph over Mexico." A private club that traditionally banned people of color not only welcomed Ashe but celebrated his achievement.[17]

Although he was the hero of Dallas, Ashe struggled with his role as the only black player in top-flight tennis. With each new achievement, newspapers continued to label him a racial pioneer, "the first Negro" to win a particular tournament or as "the first Negro" named to the Davis Cup team, references that perpetually annoyed him. He viewed himself as a member of the American team, and not as an individual African American, though he knew that he remained a novelty. At times he seemed uninterested in carrying the burden of race representation. His "burdens" were his alone, and no one else should have to assume them. When sportswriters focused on his race, declaring him America's Negro star, they neglected his individuality, wrote Frank Deford of *Sports Illustrated*. To *Sport* magazine a frustrated Ashe announced, "I'm a tennis player who happens to be Negro. . . . I want to be No. 1 without an asterisk next to my name." His goal was to be the top player in the world, not the top Negro player.[18]

Racial conflict manifested itself at other times during Ashe's Davis Cup days. At country clubs, white members, mistaking him for the help, sometimes asked, "Hey, boy, where's the bar?" A number of country clubs told USLTA officials in no uncertain terms that they would not host matches if Ashe traveled with the team. Internationally, the issue of apartheid continued to haunt him. What if the United States played South Africa in a Davis Cup round? Would he withdraw from the matches in protest or risk condemnation by playing? Everyone had an opinion on the matter. To Ashe's chagrin, he had become a lightning rod, a player whose actions were infused with meaning by critics and defenders alike.[19]

The issue of race followed Ashe wherever he went, and nowhere was this burden more evident than in his hometown of Richmond. In 1966 the city honored him with an "Arthur Ashe Day" that included formal dinners, speeches, and tennis exhibitions benefiting the ATA's Junior Development Program. He returned to Richmond with mixed feelings, thankful for the honor but mindful of how the city had once treated him. The dinner took place at the John Marshall Hotel, the same place where twelve years earlier southern leaders had planned the Massive Resistance campaign against *Brown v. Board of Education*. As afternoon faded to evening, middle- and upper-class whites slowly trickled into the banquet hall wearing their finest attire. More than half of the attendees were white. Although he enjoyed the congratulatory applause, he believed that most white Richmonders took an interest in him simply because he was famous. This phenomenon was not unique to Ashe. Many black celebrities, including Sidney Poitier, Sammy Davis Jr., and Joe Louis, found themselves the toast of white America—once they became famous, of course. Where had these white benefactors been five years earlier?, he wondered. When Ashe took the podium, he spoke about his father, Dr. Johnson, and the honor of being back home. With so many negatives to dwell on, he instead focused on the city's attempts at racial reconciliation. Times had changed. Blacks and whites attended the same schools, played on the same tennis courts, and used the same public facilities. The future Arthur Ashes would not be relegated to Brook Field Park. The day after his speech, the *Richmond News Leader* published a scathing editorial criticizing the city for its resolution passed in honor of Arthur Ashe Day. "The resolution," it began, "probably would have meant more if it had contained at least an implied regret that while he was growing up the inherited mores of the rest of us prohibited him from playing at Byrd Park." The editorial urged the city to take stock of itself, to admit to past mistakes in the hope of redefining the racial landscape of Richmond. Like Ashe, Richmonders themselves understood the irony of Arthur Ashe Day.[20]

Although Ashe struggled with his role as a racial pioneer off the court, on the court he was not struggling much at all. If his widely praised Davis Cup play elevated his profile in the world of tennis, then his dominance of the world's best players in Australia in the winter of 1965–66 made him a household name among international fans. In the mid-1960s Australia produced the best international players. The winners of four straight Davis Cups as a team, Australians dominated the major tournaments. Rod Laver also topped the professional ranks. In both 1964 and 1965 Roy Emerson defeated his teammate Fred Stolle to win at Wimbledon. Australians won a remarkable seven of eight Wimbledon crowns between 1964 and 1971. Ashe knew that if he was to become an elite international player, he had to defeat the Australians.[21]

If attending Dr. Johnson's camp and moving to St. Louis represented watershed moments in Ashe's life, his performance in Australia's summer circuit proved to be equally important. His dominance placed him among the world's best young players, a star who could stand toe to toe with the world's best. He went 18-6 against foreign players and defeated nine top Americans during his play on the circuit. A year earlier he had defeated Roy Emerson, the world's top amateur, in the quarterfinals of the U.S. Nationals at Forest Hills. The pundits quickly declared the victory a fluke. They said that Emerson was rusty, too tired, and off his game and that a rematch would certainly prove his superiority. Ashe's own statements to the press did not help his cause. The humble star told *Sport* magazine that Emerson was a better player, suggesting that the Australian would certainly win a best-of-five or best-of-seven series. Ashe did not give himself enough credit. In Australia, Ashe bested Emerson again, *after* he "demolished" three more top-ranked Australians "with wonderful ease." He dispatched Stolle in an hour and a quarter and John Newcombe in just over an hour. "He aced me 21 times," an exasperated Stolle told a reporter. "That's never happened to me before." Australia's legendary tennis coach Harry Hopman named Ashe Australia's biggest threat to Davis Cup victory. No American player in recent memory had performed so well in Australia.[22]

As a visitor in Australia, Ashe observed how the government, employers, and local officials mistreated native blacks. Beginning in the early twentieth century, Australian officials had forced aborigines to attend segregated missionary schools. Woefully understaffed and underfunded, these schools aimed to strip the aborigines of their native culture with instruction that focused on manual labor. Like African Americans in the Jim Crow era and black South Africans under apartheid, aborigines were relegated to the most dangerous and lowest-paying jobs. Ashe empathized with the aborigines, who reminded him of the poor blacks he had known growing up in Richmond. He noticed a striking similarity between American and Australian white racism. Tennis players from Australia often remarked to him that aborigines were unmotivated, lacked focus, and showed up late for work. Whites in Richmond had used these same stereotypes to describe the city's black workers in the 1950s, arguing that blacks were too lazy and too stupid to qualify for management or other positions of authority. These perceptions were untrue in Richmond and in Australia. As he walked the streets of Australia, native whites stared at him, and not always with admiration. John McPhee described the attention as "not malicious," though Australia's history of racial violence might have suggested otherwise. Years later, Ashe wrote that overall Australia had treated him well. Many fans and local officials had gone out of their way to make him feel comfortable. In spite of this hospitality, he would never consider living there. He had heard enough rumors, noticed that nearly all of the black Australians were segregated outside of the city proper, and observed enough subtle racism to know that Australia was not for him. Racism in tennis was not only an American phenomenon. In Australia, South Africa, and parts of colonial Africa racism and tennis seemed to go together.[23]

Even in the segregated seats of Australia's many tennis venues, local white tennis fans cheered Ashe as if he were one of their own. White spectators flocked to see America's Negro star, a curiosity not to be missed. As white Australians packed into local venues and stadiums, Ashe became a drawing card yet again, a novelty because of his race and his remarkable talents. "Ashe has been completely accepted by the vast bulk of his fellow players, and by spectators almost everywhere he has played," commented Harry Gordon of the *New York Times*. "The galleries in Australia, which has a whites-only immigration policy, have made him a particular favorite." Sportswriters in the United States wondered aloud why the Australian public took such a liking to Ashe. One Chicago reporter contended that his "court manners" endeared him to fans. Another writer insisted that fans admired and respected him because he "stood tall in defeat." A woman in Western Australia wrote to Ashe praising his demeanor on the court and suggesting that he was a credit to his race. She commented that he had "done a great job for your folk and yourself." By the time he returned to UCLA for the spring semester of 1966, Ashe was an international star with major victories to his name.[24]

—◌ ◌—

Ashe returned from Australia, but his commitments were not over. In fact, he had more to do than ever before. There were television interviews to give, products to endorse, and a college degree to finish. At times it was all too much. There was not enough Arthur Ashe to go around. In June 1966, though, he had only one place to go, whether he liked it or not. For months he had delayed army basic training so that he could continue to play tennis. Finally, Uncle Sam called, and Ashe traded his racquet for a gun.[25]

Ashe's position as a first lieutenant in the U.S. Army limited his ability to actively fight against racial discrimination. Participation in the ROTC program required him to serve as a commissioned officer in the army upon graduation from college, and many sportswriters and columnists initially predicted that he would serve in Vietnam. In 1966 the military draft affected a number of prominent athletes, threatening to remove them from the playing fields, boxing rings, and arenas and place them on the battlefields of Southeast Asia. The draft status of Muhammad Ali drew the attention of almost all Americans. After a local board initially declared him ineligible for the draft, it subsequently reversed its decision, listing him mentally and physically fit for service. Immediately following the ruling, Ali labeled himself a conscientious objector to the war and reinforced his earlier comment, "I ain't got no quarrel with them Viet Cong." He argued that the army should exclude him from combat because of his religious beliefs. In his opinion, the government had targeted him: "I can't understand out of all the baseball players, all of the football players, all of the basketball players—why seek out me, the world's only heavyweight champion?"[26]

If Ali was in one corner of the Vietnam debate, Ashe was in the other. Whereas Ali made anti-American statements and fought the draft, Ashe, at least in public, praised the American war effort and joined the army voluntarily. "Those bullets don't have much appeal for me, I'll admit," he said about Vietnam. "But if there's a job to do over there, the sooner it's over the better. I'll be proud to serve." Privately, he expressed doubt about the war's purpose. Years later, on a trip to Vietnam, he told General Creighton Abrams that he did not believe in the war. But for now he chose to remain silent, serving as the "good Negro" soldier opposite Ali.[27]

Ashe's army career began in June 1966, when he flew to Fort Lewis, Washington, to undergo six weeks of basic training. The camp was a training school for future officers where drill sergeants pushed cadets to their mental and physical limits. Ashe would face overbearing superiors who called him names, forgetting entirely that he was a star tennis player. The army had little interest in making its cadets feel welcome; it wanted to create disciplined soldiers who excelled at the simplest tasks. As a young man who began to see the world in nuanced terms, Ashe was put off by the black-and-white world of the military. He did, however, embrace the army's focus on personal and collective responsibility. The army was like a team. If one cadet messed up, the entire group faced punishment.[28]

On his first day at Fort Lewis, Ashe learned how little his celebrity status mattered. Fort Lewis placed cadets in leadership positions from day one. Each trainee was assigned to the role of deputy brigade commander at least once, and as luck had it, Ashe was first in line for the position. After fifteen yards of marching, the brigade commander stepped on a broken piece of pavement and sprained his ankle. Left completely in charge of nearly eight hundred cadets, Ashe led the march, eventually returning to the barracks for the unit's dismissal. He was quite proud of himself until he discovered that something was not right: he had lined the unit up backwards. "You've really got it fucked up, mister," shouted his training officer. The officer ordered him to repeat the march, an embarrassing moment for the young soldier.[29]

Ashe survived the six weeks of basic training. He learned to fire weapons, toss grenades, and read military maps. Officers trained him in tactics and strategy, and he excelled in the classroom. To his surprise, the army allowed him to play in several tennis tournaments while his fellow cadets in Fort Lewis continued drills. It soon became clear that Ashe would not be fighting in Vietnam. The army's insistence that he compete in tournaments during basic training proved that the military viewed him, as it had famous athletes in the past, more as a goodwill ambassador than as a combat officer. As an enlisted army officer and an international tennis star, he would showcase American freedom for the world rather than fight in the jungles of Southeast Asia. Ashe, it seems, allowed the military to use him for its own political and propaganda purposes. He could have resisted or demanded that the army send him to Vietnam alongside most of his fellow young officers. Instead, as a goodwill ambassador who would play exhibitions and meet with the troops, he escaped the front lines, an arrangement that benefited him and the army. He stayed safe and continued to improve as a tennis player, and both the army and the State Department used him as evidence of racial progress in the United States. Ashe later objected to his role in the propaganda campaigns, but in 1966 he lodged no complaints. Lieutenant Ashe obeyed orders.[30]

The army had a history of using black athletes as morale boosters, propaganda, and goodwill ambassadors around the globe. Boxers Joe Louis and Sugar Ray Robinson fought more than one hundred exhibition matches for U.S. troops during World War II. Louis donated his winnings from his fight with Buddy Baer to the Navy Relief Fund and appeared in Frank Capra's propaganda film *The Negro Soldier*. In a 1942 speech orchestrated by the army, Louis argued that America was "on God's side" and encouraged ordinary citizens to aid the war effort. He became a symbol of American patriotism, appearing on propaganda posters in full uniform holding a rifle.[31]

In 1968 the *Daily Bruin* included Ashe in an army advertising campaign asking UCLA students, "How Will You Fulfill Your Military Obligation?" Ashe and J. D. Morgan, both military men, appeared smiling in the ad. Now a first lieutenant, Ashe was a success story, a testament to the ROTC program. The army also encouraged him to play in specific tennis tournaments, such as the Pan-American Games and Wimbledon, and not in those in which his patriotic image would matter less. At the Pan-American Games, for instance, the press often referred to him as "Lieutenant Ashe," a clear military reference. Sportswriter Sam Lacy of the *Baltimore Afro-American* objected to the army's plan, arguing that Ashe had no voice in the army's strategy and that his was a voice that could be powerful if someone allowed him to speak. Lacy believed that Ashe was a natural politician, a smart man whose words would accomplish more than his picture.[32]

While Lacy and others waited for the army to offer Ashe a more meaningful position, the young star was happy to stay out of Vietnam. Instead of fighting the Vietcong, he accepted a position as a data processor and tennis coach at West Point Military Academy, located fifty miles north of New York City. Sportswriter Neil Amdur described the data-processing center as a building that "is Modern Army, a combination of the wooden interiors of World War II quonset huts and today's newer administrative offices." Ashe's personal "cubbyhole" included books, a picture of him at the White House with President Johnson, and a small array of products he had agreed to endorse: gum, razors, and breath fresheners. He read *Life* and *Sports Illustrated* for fun, *Business Week* and *Forbes* to improve his business acumen, and the *New York Times* and the *Afro-American* to keep abreast of local and global politics. At times he struggled with army regulations, specifically those that prevented him from making political statements to the press. He knew that the army used him "as sort of [a] showpiece," which did not make him popular among more radical blacks. He often wondered how radical and moderate blacks viewed him as an army officer. Were they proud of him for his service to the nation, or did they consider him a sellout for seeming to condone the war effort? He feared that the latter was more likely. He also felt guilty about avoiding the war. On more than one occasion he received phone calls at his desk from angry parents wondering why he was safely holed up in New York while their sons fought in Vietnam. By joining the army and accepting their position for him, he had chosen to stay out of combat. He could blame no one but himself.[33]

In 1966 Ashe sat down with *New York Times* sportswriter Harry Gordon and gave his most revealing interview. Although some of the questions focused on recreation, dating, his work ethic, and tennis, Gordon was interested in Ashe's encounters with racial discrimination and his role as a racial symbol and pioneer. "As a Negro in a game that is one of the last sporting strongholds of the white man," Gordon began, "Ashe is acutely aware that he is an athletic oddity, a kind of pioneer in short white pants." "Let's face it," Ashe admitted, "being known as the only Negro in a game probably puts me a hundred dollars a week ahead of the others in market value. You have to be realistic. . . . People will usually pay a little more for a product that's *different*—and that's what I am." He knew that he attracted white fans to the sport, yet he hoped that with every magazine cover, television interview, endorsement deal, and tournament victory, he would draw blacks to the sport as well. Jackie Robinson, Willie Mays, and Wilt Chamberlain had all led by example, allowing their athletic abilities to inspire young blacks to take control of their lives. Ashe believed he would do the same. "I want to do something for my race," he confided to Gordon, "but I figure I can do it best by example, by showing Negro boys the way." He was determined not to let racism get the best of him. "I don't want to spend my life fuming. What good would that do? It's like beating your head against a brick wall. If you go looking for discrimination, you can find it in a lot of places." He was familiar with the cold shoulders, the disapproving stares, and the occasional hate mail. Gordon concluded that Ashe's "detachment," or the ability to tune out distractions, was his most striking feature, a survival mechanism that few others possessed.[34]

When he was not working at West Point, Ashe kept busy with Davis Cup matches and tournaments, inner-city tennis clinics, and endorsement obligations. He finished 1966 ranked seventh in the world, behind Ralston, and ended 1967 ranked ninth, behind his Davis Cup teammate Clark Graebner. Despite his individual success, the U.S. Davis Cup team suffered a humiliating defeat at the hands of Ecuador in June 1967. Ashe played poorly against his "lightly-regarded" South American opponent, falling to Francisco Guzman in five sets. He was "unavailable for comment" after the match, but team captain George MacCall, stung from the loss, told a reporter, "When you lose, you keep your mouth shut." The 3-2 loss was a devastating defeat for the United States, which had hoped to dethrone Australia in 1967. Many fans and sportswriters blamed Ashe and the army for the Ecuador fiasco, arguing that the army should have allowed him to compete in more tournaments so that he would be fresh for the Ecuador tie. Australia's Harry Hopman agreed, commenting, "It seems to me that Arthur

Ashe has not had enough tennis to bring him to his peak. Obviously his army duties have restricted his match practice and general condition." *Sports Illustrated*'s Bud Collins, a veteran tennis reporter, disagreed. Acknowledging that Ashe was "rusty," Collins argued that the problem was the star's motivation and concentration. "He obviously has talent," Collins wrote, "but his performance has lagged behind his publicity." He believed that Ashe focused too much on his endorsement deals and too little on his tennis. He was stretched too thin, and balancing tennis, the army, and his celebrity status was simply too much to handle.[35]

Collins might have been right. Ashe juggled a number of commitments in 1967. He was an army officer and a goodwill ambassador, a top-ranked tennis player and a Davis Cup stalwart, an inner-city tennis instructor and an entrepreneur, a best-dressed celebrity and an eligible bachelor. *World Tennis*, the *New York Times*, the *Chicago Defender*, and late-night TV shows clamored for interviews, and civil rights organizations sought his time and help. A year earlier, Philip Morris hired him to appear in advertising promotions, including campaigns for chewing gum, razors, and men's toiletries. As a spokesman for Philip Morris, he worked closely with the company's overseas branches and attended business functions while in Europe. He was also under contract to Coca-Cola, his main task being to "drink plenty of the stuff, preferably in public." "The idea," Ashe explained, "is to have a Coke in one hand, and a Wilson racquet in the other while donning a Fred Perry shirt when they take my picture." Then came 1968, with its assassinations, riots, and protests. A "Revolt of the Black Athlete" threatened to overwhelm American sports, pressuring Ashe to take a stand.[36]

_—◌ ◌—_

On October 16, 1968, African American sprinters Tommie Smith and John Carlos prepared to run the 200-meter race at the Olympic Games in Mexico City. Both had actively supported Harry Edwards's campaign for black athletes to boycott the Games in protest of racial discrimination. Although the boycott failed, International Olympic Committee president Avery Brundage and other Olympic officials worried that black athletes might engage in political protest at the Games. Like other black athletes, Smith had grown tired of being treated as a second-class citizen but was sorry that he had not taken action sooner. If he won a medal, he promised himself, the victory podium would become his political platform, a vehicle for expressing black pride and defiance. After winning the gold medal, Smith walked over to his gym bag, removed a black scarf, and tied it around his neck. He then took off his track shoes and rolled up his pants, exposing his black socks to the world. Finally, he pulled out a pair of black gloves and handed the left glove to his teammate Carlos, who had captured the bronze medal. Then, as the American national anthem played over the loudspeakers, Smith and Carlos gave the Black Power salute, each with a fist held high and his head down. "We want people to understand," Carlos told a reporter, "that we are not animals or rats. We want you to tell Americans and all the world that if they do not care what black people do, they should not go to see black people perform." Though praised by many blacks and some whites, Smith and Carlos paid a heavy price for their activism: Brundage banished them from the Olympic Village.[37]

The Mexico City protest was the most visible and direct example of what Harry Edwards labeled the "Revolt of the Black Athlete." In the late 1960s many African Americans had given up on the belief that government would enact real social change. Enforcement of the 1964 Civil Rights Act was slow, schools remained segregated, and inner-city neighborhoods continued to deteriorate. There were riots in Harlem in 1964, in Watts in 1965, and in Detroit and Newark in 1967. And new organizations such as the Black Panthers added their voice to the movement.[38]

The Black Panther Party, argues Black Power scholar Peniel Joseph, "represented the most visible face of radicalism in the 1960s. Armed with guns, law books, and menacing bravado, the Black Panthers projected a militant swagger that made their threats of starting a violent revolution for black liberation seem plausible despite considerable evidence to the contrary." Founded in Oakland, California, in October 1966 by Huey Newton and Bobby Seale, the Black Panther Party for Self-Defense, as it was initially called, counted as its members "maverick black nationalists and unconventional Marxists." Newton, for one, believed that black nationalism and class conflict were inextricably linked. The Panthers' Ten-Point Program sought, among other things, social justice, economic equality, peace, and an end to police brutality. Although the mainstream media fixated on their guns, their uniforms, and their sometimes violent rhetoric, the Panthers were known locally in black communities for a number of service programs, including free breakfasts, health clinics, and liberation schools. "Enormously popular," writes Joseph, "the Panthers' community service programs represented a softer, more practical side of revolutionary politics, one that contradicted FBI fears and local antagonisms that mistook the Black Panthers for armed terrorists." The historian Jane Rhodes found that the media consciously ignored or downplayed these community-based initiatives and multiracial outreach in favor of violent imagery, a development relished by many national leaders of the BPP. Whenever Ashe turned on his television or paged through the newspaper, he was likely to see the Panthers portrayed as a threat to society and a dangerous rival of the nonviolent civil rights struggle.[39]

But Carmichael, Edwards, and the Black Panthers represented just a few of the immediate influences that shaped Ashe's approach to activism. Martin Luther King Jr. and his understanding of Black Power served as another. In *Where Do We Go from Here: Chaos or Community?*, published in 1967, King argued that Black Power was an "emotional concept" that took on different meanings depending on the person or the circumstances of a particular situation. He defined Black Power as "a cry of disappointment," a term that symbolized the frustration of African Americans with the lack of federal law enforcement, the deteriorating conditions in northern ghettos, and the hypocrisy of white politicians. He contended that "Black Power, in its broad and positive meaning, is a call to black people to amass the political and economic strength to achieve their legitimate goals." King also argued that Black Power, properly understood, was "a psychological call to manhood," a reassertion of one's self. He recognized, however, that other African American leaders, such as SNCC head Stokely Carmichael, had a different understanding of Black Power. King predicted that the "negative values" of Black Power would keep it from becoming a substantial enough strategy to drive the civil rights movement. He disagreed with Carmichael's questioning of the movement's nonviolent approach, his insistence on black nationalism, and his abandonment of hope. "Black Power alone," King concluded, "is no more insurance against social injustice than white power."[40]

Despite King's understanding of Black Power as a positive ideology, historians and journalists of the late 1960s and 1970s focused instead on the widely held notion that Black Power undercut the aims of the civil rights movement. Peniel Joseph has argued that for these scholars and writers, "black power stands at the center of declension narratives of the 1960s: the movement's destructiveness poisoning the innocence of the New Left, corrupting a generation of black activists, and steering the drive for civil rights off course in a way that reinforced racial segregation by giving politicians a clear, frightening scapegoat." In this context, Black Power became the "evil twin" of the civil rights movement. More recent studies by a number of other historians, however, have examined the fluidity of Black Power as a political and cultural ideology and concluded that the movement was more diverse, widespread, and complex than earlier historians had concluded. This view is much closer to King's initial conception of Black Power than to popular representations "of violent rhetoric, misogyny, and bravado by black power advocates."[41]

In the late 1960s Ashe had very distinct opinions of King, Whitney Young, Carmichael, and Black Power. He identified most with King and Young, two well-respected leaders whose philosophies of nonviolence, integration, and open dialogue with whites echoed what his father and Dr. Johnson had taught him. Ashe argued, "I am with Thoreau, Gandhi, and Martin Luther King, Jr., in their belief that violence achieves nothing but the destruction of the individual soul and the corruption of the state." Ashe labeled King one of his heroes and even compared himself to the iconic leader. "Like Martin Luther King's role gave him pleasure," he told a *New York Times* reporter, "so does my struggle for equality," referring to his own current and future activism.[42]

Although Ashe agreed with Carmichael in principle, he was skeptical of the new SNCC leader. To the *Los Angeles Times* Ashe contended, "We need aggressive militants, the Stokely Carmichael and Rap Brown and Leroi Jones figures. You need men with charisma who can appeal to emotions." But, he added, "without guys like me they are dead." He believed that militants could not function without moderates, and vice versa. Ashe admired Carmichael's passion and agreed with his demand for freedom now, but he opposed Carmichael's seemingly violent rhetoric, his unwillingness to work with white leaders, and his lack of faith in America's political system. "Stokely shouts that black is beautiful and so it is, but that doesn't mean that white isn't beautiful," Ashe explained to a *World Tennis* writer. To the press, Ashe made it clear that King and Young, not Carmichael, best represented his position. In an interview printed in the *Chicago Tribune*, Ashe echoed Young's approach when he argued that "the only way to advance materially this whole human rights struggle is to have us hold out a hand to the slums, saying, 'Look, I'm going to help you!' And keeping the hand out until we've proved it. Meanwhile the other hand is out, raised up toward the white establishment steadily insisting, but also slowly building up its confidence." Ashe viewed himself as a bridge between black and white America, and in this respect he was akin to Young, whose biographer Dennis Dickerson described him as a "militant mediator."[43]

On his conception of Black Power, Ashe was quite clear, stating in an interview, "I'm in favor of black power as far as it pertains to the exercise of power by black people in a bloc, if they so desire. This power is not only good, it's just and it's American. It's democracy in action. . . . We want certain things and we've got to lobby for these things, to ask Congress for them. That's the only place we're going to get it. In that respect, I'm all for black power." Like King, Ashe was a militant integrationist who argued that the federal government should immediately enforce the Civil Rights Act and the Voting Rights Act. But he did not support all understandings of Black Power. "There's nothing constructive about people living in a self-styled state of quarantined isolation," he concluded. The most important element of his future activism, Ashe believed, would be "to balance the practical and the emotional."[44]

Since the beginning of the twentieth century African American athletes had fought publicly against racism. In July 1949 Jackie Robinson, in testimony before the House Un-American Activities Committee, criticized government officials who condoned racism. "White people must realize," he said, "that the more a Negro hates Communism because it opposes democracy, the more he is going to hate the other influences that kill off democracy in this country—and that goes for racial discrimination in the Army, segregation on trains and buses, and job discrimination." In 1952 Robinson assailed the New York Yankees organization for its treatment of black ballplayers, and four years later he criticized Major League Baseball for not pressuring the South to change its racist practices. Hotel managers and restaurant owners frequently forced blacks to leave their establishments because of their race. Although some black radicals attacked Robinson for some of his conservative opinions, he stood as a voice against oppression.[45]

The Boston Celtics All-Star center Bill Russell similarly challenged the racial status quo. A frequent victim of racism on road trips and in Boston, Russell was an outspoken advocate for civil and human rights in the late 1950s and throughout the 1960s. He attended the March on Washington in 1963 and became an ardent defender of Muhammad Ali when the boxer refused a draft call. "I'm not worried about Muhammad Ali," he told a *Sports Illustrated* reporter. "What I'm worried about is the rest of us," referring to himself and other blacks. Russell urged black athletes to support human rights causes, and he used his autobiography *Go Up for Glory* to expose racism in American sports and society.[46]

Ashe became a player in the black athletic revolution as early as 1968. While in Atlanta for a tournament, he attended an informal gathering at the home of civil rights activist Andrew Young, an officer in Dr. King's Southern Christian Leadership Conference. Also present were Donald Dell, Ashe's Davis Cup captain, Jesse Jackson, the head of the SCLC's Operation Breadbasket, and several other black activists. The men discussed world affairs, civil rights, and the best ways to confront racism. At one point in the conversation, Jackson challenged Ashe to be a more vocal agent for the black cause. "Jesse," he responded, "I'm just not arrogant, and I ain't never going to be arrogant. I'm just going to do it my way." In 1968 his "way" finally included public statements on Black Power, racism, African American youths, and apartheid. Any black athlete who remained silent while others struggled risked criticism from black radicals and moderates. Was it even possible for Ashe and others to excel athletically and remain committed to civil and human rights? As racial strife intensified, he and others struggled to choose a position. One thing was clear: the status quo was not an acceptable choice.[47]

A single invitation soon changed Ashe's life. Reverend Jefferson Rogers of the Church of the Redeemer in Washington, DC, believed that African American athletes were important agents for change. Reverend Rogers began hosting a political forum in which activists, politicians, artists, and athletes addressed his congregation on the topic of civil rights. Early in 1968 he invited Ashe to speak at his church. As the sole African American star in a predominately white sport, Ashe had a different perspective than Bill Russell, Brown, or Ali. His previous statements to the press showed intelligence and revealed a man who was struggling to reconcile the philosophies of his early mentors, King, Carmichael, and others. Initially, Ashe politely refused Rogers's invitation, citing army rules that prevented officers from giving political speeches. Rogers called Ashe's bluff. He accused the tennis star of "copping out" of the address because he refused to take a stand, not because of the army. Rogers's response triggered something in Ashe. In effect, Rogers was calling him a liar, and that was not something he could live with. He agreed to give the speech, with or without the army's permission. The army was not his only concern, however. He also worried about his reception among church members and in the African American community. He questioned whether his athletic accomplishments qualified him to offer advice. Why, he wondered, did African American athletes and entertainers feel compelled to speak out on political matters? How was Sammy Davis Jr., among other athletes and entertainers, an "expert" on racial prejudice? He determined that if he was going to deliver a speech, he would work hard on his remarks. The address would be personal, heartfelt, and genuine, not simply a repetition of the ideas of King, Carmichael, Ali, or anyone else.[48]

His speech was scheduled for March 10, 1968, at 6:00 p.m. In a phone interview with Mark Asher of the *Washington Post*, he offered a preview of the address. Asher reported: "Ashe will speak on the role of the Negro athlete in general, 'nothing specific' he said because 'everything is sorta based on what I can say and do as an Army officer under Army regulations.'" He described Ashe as a black activist but no militant, a fiercely independent thinker who planned to challenge the established black leadership. His opinions on black athletic activism had not changed, but his role had. "A long time ago," he explained, "I was standoffish about everything. I wasn't aware that what I said carried any weight.

It obviously carries weight now; it would be almost sinful not to throw it around in the right direction." He reiterated, however, that he made and would continue to make his own decisions. No activist, however persuasive, would force him to participate in the movement. Ashe's confident words masked feelings of uncertainty and inadequacy. In fact, he was not entirely sure that his words would matter or that the congregation would take him seriously.[49]

To his friend Neil Amdur of the *New York Times*, Ashe revealed some of his insecurities. He regretted his absence from the civil rights movement and admitted that he had been both "flattered and embarrassed" when Rogers contacted him to speak. He had been silent in part because he distrusted reporters and was concerned that they would take his statements out of context. Amdur described how Ashe constructed his speech: Whenever an idea or a thought came to mind, he scribbled it onto a yellow pad in his army cubicle. His outline included statements like "Poverty is one-half laziness," "Everything yields to diligence," and "NO VIOLENCE." The speech would include references from Voltaire, the Bible, and *Forbes* magazine and would focus on Ashe's "personal philosophies." "I guess I'm becoming more and more militant," Ashe stated at the end of the interview, smiling as he reflected on the word *militant*.[50]

Late on a Sunday afternoon in March, Ashe stepped up to the podium before a standing-room-only audience and gave a passionate though politically tempered address. As he stared at the mostly African American men and women who attended the Church of the Redeemer, something came over him. He felt empowered and emboldened, and he realized that his words meant something to the audience. Drawing from the integrationist philosophies of his father and Dr. Johnson, he focused on personal uplift and encouraged the congregation to concentrate on the elements of their lives that they could control. He labeled this "a do-it-yourself blood-and-guts, Me Power kind of philosophy." "There is a lot we can do and we don't do because we're lazy," he told the crowd. "This may be brutal, but poverty is half laziness." This mode of thinking was nothing new to members of the congregation. As far back as the 1880s Booker T. Washington had called for personal uplift and economic empowerment within African American communities. Inherent in the civil rights movement was the notion that African Americans had to take responsibility for themselves and their families. Like his father and Dr. Johnson, Ashe urged African Americans not to blame white leaders for their current predicament. He pointed to football All-Pro Jim Brown as someone who was making a difference in the African American community. Brown had founded the Negro Industrial Economic Union (NIEU) to help create "producers instead of consumers, achievers instead of orators." Brown, he believed, was correct to focus on personal income and community investment. At the end of his speech, Ashe promised to be more active in the black freedom movement. He asked the audience where they should start to improve their lives, and the congregants responded in unison, "At home!" He received a standing ovation from the Washington audience, vowing to himself to give more speeches and actively contribute to the black freedom movement.[51]

The Church of the Redeemer speech marked a turning point for Ashe, the moment in his life when he transitioned from being just an athlete to being an athlete *and* an activist. In this short address he answered critics who assailed him for being silent, and he promised to be more active in the movement. The speech briefly alleviated years of guilt, as he had finally said something, participated in the movement, and joined the African American cause. His defiance of the army, however, came at a cost. When he returned to West Point following the speech, his army superiors had already read a *Washington Post* article summarizing his address. As an officer of the U.S. Army, they told him, he was not to give political speeches. Ashe left the meeting feeling angry at both himself and Reverend Rogers and wondering if Rogers had used him to score political points. Quickly, though, his anger faded into satisfaction and relief. "I knew there would be trouble [with the army] if I made the speech," he admitted, "but I accepted rebuke as my way of paying dues to the [African American] cause." In the early 1960s he had played tennis, received a free education, and basked in the sun of Southern California. The late 1960s, he vowed, would be different.[52]

The speech and his statements and actions immediately thereafter transformed Ashe from a peripheral actor in the black freedom movement to a prominent activist within the sports world. Leading African American figures recognized his growing influence in the African American community and reached out to the young athlete. Harry Edwards encouraged him to join the Olympic Project for Human Rights (OPHR), a coalition made up of African American athletes, actors, entertainers, and activists that focused on the discrimination and exploitation of African Americans in sports and society. The OPHR resolved to boycott the 1968 Olympic Games. When Edwards discussed the boycott with Ashe, however, the tennis star resisted the plan. Although he agreed with the goals of the OPHR, Ashe argued that an African American athletic boycott would damage the reputations of the Olympians. His comments were a direct affront to Edwards but also a sign of Ashe's expanding independence. "Well I'll be damned," Edwards said to himself, "Arthur Ashe is an Uncle Tom."[53]

Although Ashe disagreed with Edwards's position, he signed a letter supporting a boycott of the Games by African athletes. In 1964 the International

Olympic Committee had barred South Africa from the Games for refusing to field an integrated team. Four years later, South Africa gave in to international pressure and agreed to send an integrated team, with several important caveats. The nation's black and white athletes still had to compete in segregated trials, and blacks had to earn their way onto the team. Under this scenario, white athletes, who trained on state-of-the-art fields and tracks, had a decided advantage over blacks, who practiced in decaying townships. The Supreme Council for Sport in Africa, a union made up of representatives from African nations, argued that South Africa's 1968 concessions were superficial and failed to dismantle racism in sports. On February 15 of that year, disappointed SCSA members learned that the IOC had officially readmitted South Africa, paving the way for South Africa's participation in Mexico City. At a meeting in Brazzaville, Congo, on February 26, SCSA members voted overwhelmingly for African athletes to boycott the Games if South Africa did not eliminate racism in sports.[54]

A few weeks before the vote, Ashe joined thirty other amateur and professional athletes in supporting the SCSA. Other famous athletes who signed the petition included Wilt Chamberlain, Jim Bouton, and Oscar Robertson. Shortly thereafter, the IOC reversed its decision and barred South Africa from the 1968 Games after a number of other nations threatened a boycott if South Africa was allowed to compete. Unlike in the United States, South African rules prohibited racial and ethnic minorities from competing at the Olympic level. Although race relations were far from perfect in America, African American athletes such as boxer George Foreman still represented the United States at the Games. Simply put, Ashe supported the SCSA because South Africa denied its black athletes real opportunities to compete.[55]

In addition to his role in the African Olympic boycott, Ashe became a popular public speaker. From 1968 on, he gave numerous speeches to women's groups, businessmen, community organizers, and activists on a variety of non-sports topics. In December 1968 the FBI discovered that the Black Unity Congress had targeted Ashe as a potential speaker for its 1969 Black Convention. The BUC's other potential speakers included Ali, Carmichael, Adam Clayton Powell, and Le Roi Jones. The fact that Ashe's name appeared alongside the names of established activists attests to his increasing militancy and his growing influence in the black freedom movement. The FBI considered the BUC a radical Black Power organization, which is one of the reasons why the bureau monitored plans for the group's upcoming convention. If Ashe agreed to address the organization on the topic of youth education, he would certainly face a much more radical audience than the Church of the Redeemer congregation. The BUC's invitation to Ashe, then, shows that his approach to activism was militant enough for the Black Power group.[56]

Even Martin Luther King Jr. recognized Ashe as an emerging leader whose moderation and intelligence made him quite effective as an activist. "Your eminence in the world of sports and athletics," King wrote to Ashe, "gives you an added measure of authority and responsibility. It is heartening indeed when you bring these attributes to the movement." Although King had never met Ashe, his associate Jefferson Rogers assured the civil rights icon that Ashe could play an active and prominent role in the black freedom movement. Ashe had always admired King's pragmatism and his ability to inspire others to action. Ashe explained, "What was so great about him was that he could use emotional power to stir black people at rallies and so on and then use sophisticated political techniques to achieve practical ends." Now America's most prominent civil rights leader was reaching out to America's most prominent tennis star, affirming his importance to King and to the movement. King believed that Ashe had an obligation to join with other African Americans who were fighting discrimination and racism, and the tennis star agreed.[57]

Just weeks after his Church of the Redeemer speech, Ashe was driving across the George Washington Bridge into New York City when news of King's assassination hit the airwaves. The initial radio reports indicated that an unnamed assassin had shot King as he stood on a hotel balcony in Memphis, Tennessee. King had come to Memphis to support striking African American sanitation workers. The news of King's untimely death shook Ashe to the core. As soon as he arrived in New York, he stopped his car on Amsterdam Avenue and listened to the reports along with several other African American motorists. "Their reactions ranged from sorrow to anger," he later wrote. "We all assumed some white man did it." King's death both saddened and worried Ashe, who shared King's belief in nonviolence, his rejection of separatism, and his views on Black Power.[58]

After King's death, Ashe feared that men such as Carmichael might take control of the movement. He admired Carmichael, H. Rap Brown, and others for their courage, outspokenness, and dedication to the cause, but he did not always agree with their methods. Both men, he believed, genuinely desired to help African Americans and had the guts to say what he and other African Americans felt. "I wouldn't move that far left myself," he told the *Amsterdam News*, "but I agree with some of the things they say, and you need a few extremists when you want to change something." To a *World Tennis* reporter he asserted, "Men like Stokely are absolutely right to demand and insist that it must happen now. What Stokely is doing is wonderful. I've met him and talked with him quite a lot and I'm full of admiration for the guy." But Ashe's public statements directly contradicted his private feelings and concerns about Carmichael's vision of Black Power. For example, he avoided appearing publicly with the young radical. When Carmichael's representatives invited Ashe to participate in a freedom march, he politely declined and instead spent the day on a Milwaukee playground, leading a tennis clinic for African American and white kids. A reporter for the *Amsterdam News* explained in 1968 that Ashe "was not a moderate on racial matters, but that he was also not a militant along the lines of a Stokeley [*sic*] Carmichael or a Rap Brown."[59]

—◌ ◌—

In the first eight months of 1968, Ashe had given a civil rights address in a prominent black church, publicly commented on the Olympic boycott movement, and offered his opinions of Black Power and Stokely Carmichael in the press. Nineteen sixty-eight also happened to be the year in which he played the best tennis of his young life. By the late 1960s Ashe's body had filled out. Sportswriters no longer described him as lanky and frail, a man desperately in need of a good meal. The new and improved Ashe remained lean, but well-defined muscles now covered his body. His stronger physique made his serve even more powerful and his reflexes quicker. Another physical feature also improved his game. During a basketball game at UCLA Ashe had difficulty reading the scoreboard from his seat in the arena. A trip to the eye doctor revealed what many of Ashe's friends already knew: he suffered from nearsightedness and needed glasses. His new glasses, supported by thick frames, sharpened his vision and helped him see the ball more clearly. They also became one of his most defining physical characteristics. Many remarked that the glasses made him appear even more intellectual.[60]

Beginning on July 22, he won twenty-six consecutive matches, including a victory over Bob Lutz to win the U.S. Amateur Championship. In the two-hour, forty-five-minute match at the Longwood Cricket Club in Brookline, Massachusetts, he aced his opponent twenty times to recover from an early deficit. Despite gusty winds, his explosive serve proved too much for Lutz. With the win, Ashe became the first African American man to capture the U.S. title and the first American to take home the trophy since Tony Trabert in 1955. He returned to West Point ranked as the top amateur in the United States. He had little time to prepare for his most important athletic challenge to date, the first-ever

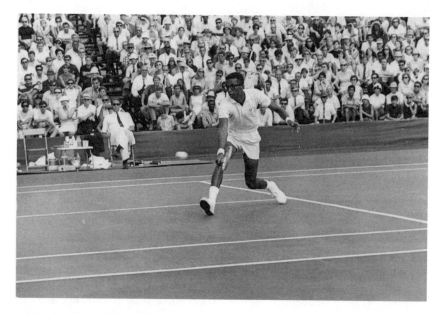

Ashe rushes the net as hundreds of mostly white spectators look on. By the late 1960s he had improved his physique with a weight-training regimen. (Edward Fernberger / International Tennis Hall of Fame & Museum Archives)

U.S. Open Championship in Forest Hills, New York. There the professionals would be waiting.[61]

Prior to 1968, the major championships—the Australian, French, Wimbledon, and U.S.—were amateur tournaments, won by players who refused to sign a professional contract or accept prize money. For years the game's greatest players, including Jack Kramer and Pancho Gonzalez, were barred from the majors after they began competing on the professional circuit. The amateur/professional divide limited tennis's popularity. Gate receipts were down, the major television networks declined to broadcast matches, and fans lost interest. Because amateurs could not compete against professionals, the best player in the world could not be identified. Was it Roy Emerson, the rising Australian amateur? Or was it Gonzalez, the seasoned pro? "The game of Tennis died early one morning sometime in the late or middle '50s," wrote columnist Jim Murray. "The game's long, misleading coma had been brought on by acute schizophrenia. Torn between being amateur and professional, it became catatonic." After years of discussion and fed up with poor attendance and low television ratings, the British Board of Governors finally voted to make Wimbledon an "open" tournament in 1968. Purists attacked the decision, claiming that it polluted a gentleman's game with prize money. Supporters responded that "amateurs" had been paid under the table for years. One British writer stated bluntly, "After years of hypocrisy and increasingly flagrant breaches of the unworkable amateur rules the game at last became honest." Shortly after the Wimbledon announcement, U.S. officials followed suit. Forest Hills would be an open tournament.[62]

Several storylines dominated the U.S. Open coverage. Earlier in the summer, a number of amateurs had upset established professionals at the French Open and Wimbledon. One of the biggest surprises had come when Ray Moore, a relatively unknown South African amateur, knocked off third-seeded Andres Gimeno of Spain at Wimbledon. At the French Open, Gonzalez had become the first professional to lose to an amateur, falling to Great Britain's Mark Cox in five sets. "Many of the pros were jittery," explained Bud Collins. "They knew their reputations were on the line, and the most discerning realized they were ill prepared, given long absence from best-of-five-set matches." Before the U.S. Open, sportswriters wondered if amateurs like Ashe and Clark Graebner would continue to give the pros fits.[63]

Another storyline centered on Ashe and Rod Laver. Despite his remarkable run in the summer of 1968, Ashe had yet to defeat the Australian phenom. "Playing tennis against Rod makes you feel like Don Quixote tilting a windmill," he told a reporter. "He can so overwhelm you that you can't get started." In 1959 a teenage Ashe drew Laver in the first round of the U.S. Nationals. He was so nervous prior to the match that he vomited. Incidentally, his winning streak in 1968 began *after* a loss to Laver. If all went according to plan, the two men were set to face off in the quarterfinal round of the Open. A final storyline concerned a potential matchup between Ashe and one of the South African players, such as Cliff Drysdale. If Ashe were to meet one of these men, black radicals would surely call for him to withdraw from the match, forfeiting his chance to win the tournament.[64]

The first-ever U.S. Open proved to be an exciting tournament, filled with surprises and twists. A polished and determined Ashe ripped through his first four opponents en route to a quarterfinal match, likely with Laver. The Australian pro, however, would never reach the quarterfinals, falling victim to Cliff Drysdale in the fourth round. Labeling the match the "tennis upset of the year," Jeff Prugh of the *Los Angeles Times* observed the "agony [that] was plainly etched into the pallid face of Rod Laver" following his defeat. He had lost to a sixteenth-seeded player, a man who had failed to reach the quarterfinal round at Wimbledon earlier in the summer. In another fourth-round upset, Gonzalez defeated second-seeded Tony Roche of Australia, a victory that thrilled a sellout crowd at Forest Hills. The forty-year-old Gonzalez, a "darling" of the grandstands, fed off the crowd and used his soft game to keep Roche off balance. With unexpected losses by Laver and Roche, the tournament was suddenly quite winnable for Ashe. Of the remaining players, he was arguably the best.[65]

A discussion of politics, not tennis, dominated the media's coverage of Ashe's quarterfinal match with Cliff Drysdale. Though an opponent of apartheid, Drysdale represented a nation that barred interracial athletic competition, jailed political dissenters, and forced its black citizens into shantytowns called "homelands." Drysdale, though, was not responsible for apartheid, and Ashe understood this well. In the locker room, Ashe and other South African players enjoyed a friendly relationship, rarely letting politics get in the way. Because he knew Drysdale to be progressive and a liberal, he ignored those who called for him to withdraw from the match in protest of apartheid. Still, the politics weighed on him. In April he had told a *Los Angeles Sentinel* columnist that he would consider boycotting a match against a South African player. Now he opted to compete. A withdrawal would solve nothing, and it would punish his friend Drysdale for policies he did not condone or control. Although black radicals and some in the black press would praise Ashe if he decided to withdraw, most would criticize the move. In the end, he believed that beating Drysdale on the court would do more for the black cause than withdrawing in protest. He defeated Drysdale in four sets, moving on to face his teammate Clark Graebner in the semifinals.[66]

*New York Times* sportswriter Arthur Daley praised Ashe for accepting "direct confrontation" over withdrawal. "He proved his own superiority," Daley wrote. "If he had withdrawn in protest at South Africa's racial posture, he would have proved nothing. The impact would have been smothered in the continuing drama of the tournament as Drysdale perhaps might have gone on to gain recognition as the world's premier tennis player." Contrasting Ashe to Harry Edwards, Daley argued that withdrawals and boycotts were misguided actions that denied medals and trophies to deserving black athletes. Ashe was right to set aside "sociological overtones" and fight apartheid on the court by defeating a white South African.[67]

After defeating Graebner in the semifinals, Ashe met professional Tom Okker on September 9 to compete for the U.S. Open title. Officials moved the match from Sunday to Monday because of a rainstorm that left the grass courts drenched and slick. "The meeting," reported amateur player Gene Scott, "is as contrasting a confrontation as Dr. Jekyll lunching with Mr. Hyde." Okker worked like a surgeon, relying on precise ground strokes and a solid forehand. Scott predicted that Okker's topspin drive would give Ashe fits. Unlike Ashe, Okker had a weak backhand. "Ashe," reported Scott, "has no visible foible on which to concentrate. Service, volley, forehand, and assortment of backhands, an imaginative combination of each are all present to be called upon in crisis." If he remained focused, Ashe was without weakness. Okker was an able opponent, forcing twenty-six games in the first set before Ashe prevailed, 14-12. Okker won two of the following three sets, resulting in a definitive fifth set. At West Point, Ashe had begun a weight-training program designed to increase his strength and endurance during long matches. The regimen proved effective, as Ashe overpowered Okker in the final set, 6-3. The young man from Richmond had won the first U.S. Open.[68]

Ashe Sr. was at Forest Hills to witness his son's victory. Throughout the match, he sat quietly in a personal box, leaning one way or the other as the match intensified. Robert Kelleher, Ashe's former Davis Cup captain, observed that Ashe Sr. was entirely focused on his son's performance, refusing to make small talk with other spectators. At the conclusion of the match, Kelleher embraced the old man and invited him to join his son on the court. Ashe Sr. politely refused, believing that his son alone should bask in the glory. When Kelleher reached center court, he looked up at his personal box and waved for Ashe Sr. to come down, and finally the proud father succumbed. Hugging his son by the shoulders, Ashe Sr. stared up at the nearly seven thousand fans applauding his son's win. Ashe had found a home in a white man's game.[69]

Dr. Johnson also attended the match. He had trained the skinny boy from Richmond from a young age, teaching him how to swing, strategize, and survive in a world alien to blacks. After Ashe left Richmond for good in 1961, he remained in close contact with Dr. Johnson. Johnson relished their conversations and thought of Ashe as one of his own sons. "I don't think Ashe realized the degree to which my father loved him," Johnson's daughter Waltee told biographer Doug Smith. "I thought he cared for Ashe more than he did for me. I thought he was prouder of Ashe than he was of me." During the trophy presentation at the U.S. Open, Johnson was not invited to join Ashe and his father on center court. As he watched the two men embrace another with such joy, he worked through mixed feelings. He was proud of Ashe for his remarkable achievement, but he too should have been with his protégé. Although he never admitted it, the slight was one that he always carried with him.[70]

The public reaction to Ashe's win was overwhelming. He received scores of telegrams from fans, politicians, and celebrities. Jackie Robinson wrote, "Proud of your greatness as a tennis player[,] prouder of your greatness as a man. Your

Ashe embraces his father, Arthur Ashe Sr., after becoming the first African American man to win the U.S. Open in 1968. (AP Photo/Marty Lederhandler)

stand should bridge the gap between races and inspire black people the world over and also affect the decency of all Americans." Robinson understood that Ashe's victory represented more than a trophy or a title. It was a sign that blacks could excel at all things, even in areas of American life dominated by racial prejudice. Overwhelmingly, the telegrams from white fans focused on his athletic achievement, while the telegrams from black fans labeled him a credit to his race. In addition to telegrams, he received nearly three hundred letters in the weeks following his win, including two marriage proposals. He also received an unusual gift: one hundred shares of General Motors stock, valued at $8,912.75. Because he was classified as an amateur, he was unable to accept the U.S. Open prize money, which was $14,000. An anonymous donor, angry that Ashe walked away with nothing, offered the stock as compensation. Since it was "an unsolicited, independent gesture," Ashe was allowed to keep the gift. "It's like 'The Millionaire' TV show," he joked. "Only it's about $990,000 short."[71]

Press reaction to Ashe's win varied from outright praise to reflections on the current state of race relations in America. Robert Markus of the *Chicago Tribune* argued that Ashe would help usher in the "boom years" of tennis. An eloquent gentleman with unmatched talent, he was perfectly suited to lead the United States past Australia in international competition. He had also proven, once and for all, that amateurs were just as exciting and talented as the professionals. To Markus, Ashe was the poster child of American tennis, "the hottest amateur property since Rod Laver." Instead of writing about his image and his international appeal, Jeff Prugh of the *Los Angeles Times* explained how far Ashe had come since his Richmond days. He had overcome race and class to become one of the best players in the world. Yet there was more work to be done. Focusing on Ashe's role as an activist, Prugh told his readers that the new champion planned to work with Whitney Young and the Urban League to help underprivileged kids escape the ghettos. "Well, I'm definitely not conservative, and definitely not moderate in these [racial] matters," Ashe explained to Prugh. "I guess I'm a militant, but there are varying degrees of militancy. . . . I guess I'm somewhere in between." Prugh's candid interview with Ashe revealed that the sportswriter viewed him as both an activist and an athlete. In the excitement of a U.S. Open title, Prugh believed it was important to ask him about race, Carmichael, and the future of the black freedom movement.

Dick Edwards of the *New York Amsterdam News* also used Ashe's victory to discuss race relations in America. He reminded Americans that despite his win, country clubs barred Ashe and other blacks from becoming members. Edwards stated bluntly, "He can't join 99.9% of the tennis clubs in the United States."

Edwards also complained about the Open coverage. "The news media," he argued, "even let the hope that Dutchman Tom Okker would win this first United States Open over Ashe seep through their writing. The huzzahs and hudos were pointing up the feats of the Hollander despite the fact that home-bred Ashe had a 5-1 overall edge over him." This claim was greatly exaggerated. Most mainstream American newspapers had hinted at an Ashe victory, and some had openly cheered for him to win. Edwards's point, however, was that Ashe continued to face racial prejudice despite his athletic success. "Americans," he exclaimed, "still place Arthur Ashe in the back of the bus."[72]

Columnist Jim Murray compared Ashe's achievement and talent to those of other great athletes, actors, and artists. As one who always had had a way with words, Murray captured Ashe's importance like no other sportswriter. "Arthur Ashe Jr. came along at just the right time. Like The Babe or [boxer Jack] Dempsey, he found a sport chained in the dungeon and subsisting on bread and water. Everybody was playing tennis but nobody was watching it." Ashe was a phenomenon comparable to Hemingway or Picasso. Executing his shots and his movements with "nonchalant perfection," Ashe was the epitome of calm, making a librarian look like a fighter pilot by comparison. "Ashe," he wrote, "is as impassive as a Madonna, has a pulse rate so slow he has to fight off the heart transplanters. He is as unflappable as an English butler." The USLTA would be wise to bet everything on Ashe, to make him the centerpiece of its marketing campaign. Murray concluded, "When he was a boy breaking out of the Richmond ghetto, he needed tennis. Now, tennis needs him to get out of its ghetto."[73]

# CHAPTER 4

# Bright Lights and Civil Rights

September 15, 1968, began like any other Sunday in America. While some families readied for church or prepared to run errands, others turned on their television sets to watch the weekly news programs over breakfast and coffee. Since its debut on November 7, 1954, CBS's *Face the Nation* had been a must-see for political junkies, businessmen, and socially conscious men and women. It featured presidents, pundits, activists, and economists who debated one another before a national television audience. The show engaged politicians, not athletes; world affairs, not sports. But when Americans tuned in on the morning of September 15, they did not see President Johnson or Stokely Carmichael answering questions from moderator Martin Agronsky. Instead, they watched the black U.S. Open champ from Richmond, Virginia, present and discuss his ideas. On that Sunday Arthur Ashe was in the hot seat.[1]

CBS did not invite Ashe on the program to discuss his historic U.S. Open win or his general athletic achievements, even though these accomplishments made him well known to the viewing public. Instead, he appeared on the show as an African American activist, weighing in on the Civil Rights Act and the Voting Rights Act, Black Power, and the role of the African American athlete in society. He argued that African Americans remained frustrated because the U.S. government failed to enforce federal civil rights legislation. Offering a thoughtful assessment of race relations in the United States, Ashe outlined a nuanced path, embracing African American empowerment while opposing elements of black nationalism and violence. Mainstream and African American newspapers applauded his segment on the show. One mainstream paper explained that Ashe had impressed viewers with his "intelligence, candor, grace, and good will." An article in *Muhammad Speaks*, the newspaper of the Nation of Islam, also approved of his appearance. One writer declared that Ashe had accepted militancy and vowed to fight for his race. All sides seemed to agree that Ashe had delivered a winning performance.[2]

Ashe's U.S. Open and Davis Cup victories in 1968 gave him the platform he needed to engage in international activism in 1969. He now stood as a famous sports figure, a celebrity willing and able to deliver a strong civil rights message in the media. The South African government took notice of his increasing activism. In March 1969 Prime Minister B. J. Vorster personally rejected Ashe's request for a visa to compete in the South African Open, an ILTF-sanctioned event. South Africa claimed it had denied Ashe's visa because of his antiapartheid statements in the press, his general support for African liberation movements, and his overall opposition to apartheid. Opponents of Vorster contended that South Africa had rejected Ashe as a result of his race, not his controversial opinions.

In 1969 Ashe joined a growing list of black athletes barred by the South African government. Instead of remaining silent, he used his celebrity status to argue for sanctions against South Africa in the U.S. Congress, the United Nations, the Davis Cup Committee, and the ILTF—activism that resulted in tangible action. Near the end of 1969 a collection of international sports bodies, including the International Olympic Committee, removed South Africa from almost all world sporting events. In the United States, Secretary of State William Rogers personally oversaw Ashe's visa negotiation with Vorster, proving that Ashe's application represented much more than a sports matter. His bold action was a direct affront to apartheid, one that required the attention of top officials in the United States and South Africa. Ashe, and sports by extension, was helping to break down apartheid in ways that elected officials could not.

In the United States, some radical activists assailed Ashe for focusing on apartheid in South Africa rather than racial discrimination in his own backyard. Ashe, however, had chosen antiapartheid activism because of a political decision that directly affected his athletic career. His visa denial represented a racist action focused solely on him, not generalized racism and institutionalized discrimination characteristic of Jim Crow. For him it was personal. In his memoirs, Ashe revealed that his antiapartheid activism became a way for him to compensate for his relative inaction during the 1960s. Antiapartheid protests would become *his* contribution to the black cause.

Throughout 1969 Ashe struggled to balance activism and tennis. At Wimbledon and the U.S. Open he met with protesters and antiapartheid activists, all of whom demanded his attention. His hectic schedule arguably took a toll on his tennis, as he failed to win a major tournament in 1969, finishing the year ranked six spots below his 1968 ranking. No longer considered one of the world's top three players, he began to fear that a drop in his athletic standing would threaten his status as an activist.

_⚬ ⚬_

On the heels of his U.S. Open victory and his appearance on *Face the Nation*, Ashe turned his attention to the upcoming Davis Cup championship in Australia. Beginning with his selection to the team in 1963, black and white sportswriters had depicted him as America's tennis savior, an unstoppable force who would lead the United States to Davis Cup glory. If he focused on tennis and avoided distractions, the Americans could not lose, argued sportswriters. For Ashe, however, tennis sometimes took a back seat to other obligations. Robert Bradford of the *Chicago Tribune Magazine* reported that Ashe fielded phone calls every day requesting meetings, TV and other media interviews, and attendance at exhibition matches. His roommate, Hank Friedman, told Bradford that Ashe managed his affairs well, recording all of his commitments in a leather appointment book. An organized and mature twenty-five-year-old, Ashe nonetheless struggled to please everyone. His schedule included working on behalf of the Urban League, fulfilling endorsement contracts, appearing on late-night television programs such as *The Tonight Show*, and practicing his tennis.[3]

As Ashe worked to honor his commitments, help arrived in the form of Donald Dell, a lawyer, manager, political insider, and former tennis star who became the U.S. Davis Cup captain in 1968. An alumnus of Yale and the University of Virginia Law School, Dell enjoyed a promising career working for Sargent Shriver, the head of the U.S. Office of Economic Opportunity and the Peace Corps. He had served as a campaign manager for Robert F. Kennedy prior to his assassination in 1968. A former Davis Cup competitor himself, Dell was chosen to captain the team in 1968 at the age of twenty-nine. He first met Ashe in 1964, when the two men faced off in a tournament in Fort Worth, Texas. "He had a big serve," Dell remembered of Ashe, "a very whiplash-like serve. I couldn't break his serve on those lightning-fast cement courts." After Dell assumed the captainship early in 1968, he and Ashe became very close. Ashe admired Dell's ability to work with and befriend people from all backgrounds. "Donald has always been something of a contradiction: a flaming liberal with southern friends," he wrote in his diary. Dell was no George MacCall. He wore double-breasted blazers over turtlenecks and allowed his team members to grow their hair, a development that disappointed tennis purists. Labeling themselves "The Mod Squad," the Davis Cup team had a new attitude, more in line with the radical sixties

Ashe, his father, and other family members take a break from tennis. Dressed in a turtleneck, sweater, long necklace, and dark sunglasses, Ashe presents a contrast to his father's formal attire. (Edward Fernberger / International Tennis Hall of Fame & Museum Archives)

than with the conformity of the fifties. Dell became Ashe's personal manager and lawyer, helping him deal with contracts and other distractions.[4]

Some blacks criticized Ashe for hiring a white manager. Walter Johnson, for one, worried about Ashe's close relationship with Dell. For years he had seen how white managers and agents embezzled money from their black clients, leaving former stars penniless in their old age. There was also the issue of race. How could Ashe preach the doctrine of black empowerment and pride *and* hire a white manager? Johnson's son Bobby questioned Ashe's racial authenticity in a *Black Sports* editorial, suggesting that he was trying to "mask his origin" by working so closely with Dell. Ashe defended his decision to hire Dell, citing his impeccable credentials, his superior management skills, and his commitment to civil rights. He had no history of ripping anyone off. Ashe had found the best man that he knew for the job, and that man just happened to be white. At the National Press Club, he gave Dell a full vote of confidence, telling his audience that he trusted only two men with his life: his father and Dell. Both of them, as it turned out, would play key roles in the upcoming Davis Cup matches.[5]

Although they were the challengers, Team USA was the squad to beat in Adelaide. The *Washington Post* declared the U.S. team 10-to-1 favorites to defeat the Australians. The Australians had lost a number of top players to the professional ranks, and the United States fielded an impressive team of amateurs, including Graebner, Stan Smith, and Bob Lutz. Before the matches began, though, Ashe and Graebner both suffered injuries that threatened to sideline them during the tournament. Ashe had tendonitis in his elbow, resulting in acute pain when he served, and a muscle pull plagued Graebner. Both stars planned to travel with the team, and Dell planned to make a decision by December 16. Fortunately, Ashe and Graebner responded well to treatment by the deadline, and Dell inserted them into the lineup. In London, the *Guardian* predicted that the Americans would roll over the Australians, marking the end of Australia's dominance and ushering in a new era. The Americans were overwhelming favorites because of Ashe, the first African American to reach the Davis Cup final. The team would go as far as he would take them.[6]

A surprise awaited Ashe just days before Team USA took the court. While he ripped through the competition at the Queensland tennis championship, an array of tennis benefactors and wealthy friends donated the money needed to send Arthur Ashe Sr. to Australia for the Davis Cup matches. Beginning with his son's first lessons in the late 1940s, Ashe Sr. had stood on the sidelines, admiring the young star from a distance but rarely traveling with his son. He had a family to care for, property to attend to, and work obligations to fulfill. Once, when Ashe returned to Richmond for a match, his father readied the court and emptied the trash cans. Ashe learned from his father's example, understanding the value of hard work and dedication. Richmond's tennis backers aimed to reunite the two men halfway across the world. One afternoon Ashe heard a knock on the door of his Adelaide hotel room. It was his teammate Clark Graebner, who insisted that Ashe join him in the lobby. Graebner seemed relaxed, so Ashe thought nothing of the request. When they reached the first floor, Ashe caught a glimpse of his father, and his emotions got the best of him. The two men teared up, embracing with a manly hug. Even the press covered the event. The *New York Times*, the *Chicago Tribune*, and Richmond, Virginia, papers reported that a group of anonymous donors had sent Ashe Sr. to Adelaide.[7]

*Sports Illustrated* anticipated a solid performance by the United States. Dell would not allow anything else. "Sitting beside a tennis court during a Davis Cup match, Donald Dell invokes about as much humor as a death-watch," the writer observed. "As captain of the U.S. team, he is equal parts coach, cheerleader, psychologist, and baby-sitter." He made tough decisions for the good of the team. Before the Interzone final in Puerto Rico, he informed Charlie Pasarell, a Puerto Rican native, that he would not play in the tie, opting instead for Ashe and Graebner. The local media criticized Dell, but his decision turned out to be the right one, as the U.S. team cruised to victory. Always in a "high state of agitation" during a match, he carefully inspected his players, looking for mechanical flaws. By Christmas, Dell had penciled in his lineup: a healthy Ashe and Graebner would play the singles matches, and Smith and Lutz would represent the United States in doubles. The *Chicago Defender* reported that the Australians would counter with a "psycho attack," relying on stalling techniques and mind games designed to rattle Ashe and Graebner. "A crying baby or a disputed line call can wreck Graebner's concentration under the tension of a challenge round final—and the Australians know this," explained the *Defender*. Unnerving Ashe would be much more difficult. Their best bet would be to break his concentration with delays.[8]

The heavily favored Americans took a commanding lead after the first day. In a three-hour, ten-minute match before fifty-five hundred fans, Clark Graebner outlasted Bill Bowrey, giving the U.S. a 1-0 lead. "The American's smoking service was bringing up chalk from the lines and he moved around the court like a tiger putting away overheads and volleys," reported the *Chicago Tribune*. In his match with the streaking Ray Ruffels, Ashe quickly went down one set to none before receiving advice from Dennis Ralston and Dell. Because Ruffels was left-handed, Ralston urged Ashe to move several strides to his left to combat the Australian's wide serve. Dell ordered Ashe to be more aggressive and take advantage of volley opportunities. The strategy worked, and he defeated Ruffels in four sets, needing just twenty minutes to win the final frame. The next day, as Smith and Lutz took on Ruffels and John Alexander, Ashe was nowhere to be found. He and Graebner were too nervous to watch their teammates, choosing instead to drive around Adelaide listening to the match on the radio. Rarely nervous when he played, Ashe could not stand to watch his teammates compete. "The reality of winning was beginning to sink in," he recalled. "I thought of sitting in the dollar seats as a twelve-year-old in Richmond, watching the Aussies play. I was so close to getting my name on that old bowl." After three quick sets the match and the tie were over; Ashe and his teammates were Davis Cup champions. The final score was 4-1. Graebner defeated Ruffels in a dead rubber match, and Ashe fell victim to Bowrey for the team's only loss. Despite its unimportance, Ashe's loss to Bowrey was disappointing for America's top player. The sight of the Davis Cup, however, lifted his spirits. Dell and his team wept openly as Sir James Harrison, the governor of South Australia, presented the U.S. team with the silver bowl. "Believe me," Dell told the crowd over the microphone, "we are not going to surrender the cup easily."[9]

_⌒ ⌒_

As the newly crowned Davis Cup champions, Ashe and his teammates returned home to a barrage of interview requests, dinner invitations, and fan mail. The team made the rounds, being photographed with politicians and celebrities, discussing their personal lives on late-night television, and agreeing to product endorsements. In mid-January 1969 the team embarked on a goodwill tour of war-torn Southeast Asia. Sponsored by the U.S. State Department, the goodwill tour included stops in South Vietnam, Laos, Burma (now Myanmar), Thailand, and Indonesia. The team represented the United States, visiting the wounded, playing exhibitions with soldiers and native Asians, touring the battlefields, and promoting American foreign policy. It was a timely visit, taking place just one year after the Tet Offensive, a battle in which the North Vietnamese and the Vietcong targeted American military installations in South Vietnam. A military and tactical failure for the Vietcong, Tet had become a public-relations nightmare in the United States. Americans turned on their televisions and witnessed bombs exploding, buildings on fire, and the U.S. military scrambling to regain control in Saigon. "The cities are no longer secure," reported Frank McGhee of NBC News. "From all this," he continued, "we must conclude that the grand objective—the building of a free nation—is not nearer, but further from realization." Walter Cronkite, a legend of American journalism, declared Vietnam a stalemate. The Davis Cup team traveled to Vietnam at a time when American morale remained low, opposition to the war was high, and some policymakers were discussing withdrawal rather than victory.[10]

After arriving at the airport, the team met Willis Johnson, a no-nonsense major in the U.S. Army. He took one look at Ashe and his teammate Charlie Pasarell and issued a non-negotiable order: "Okay, fellows," he told the two men, "the first thing you're going to do is get a haircut and wear your [military] uniform." Ashe and Pasarell, still reveling in their Mod Squad fame, had arrived in street clothes, Ashe wearing an Afro and Pasarell resembling a Haight Street hippie. With the Black Power and antiwar movements gaining momentum in the United States, the army refused to accept a pair of hipsters as goodwill ambassadors. Following the verbal undressing, the team piled into an army vehicle and headed for downtown Saigon. Then Pasarell made an almost deadly mistake: he rolled down his window to take in some cool air. Barking at Pasarell, the major commanded him to roll it up. The Vietcong, he explained, sometimes tossed grenades at military escorts from passing bicycles. The naive men quickly learned the reality of life in Vietnam: there was no battlefront; the war was everywhere.[11]

In Saigon the team played a series of exhibition matches for the troops. Unaccustomed to the sounds of artillery in the background, the team suffered an embarrassing moment. In the middle of a match, Ashe and his teammates fell to the ground after hearing what sounded like incoming artillery. Assuming they were under attack from the Vietcong, they covered their heads and clung to the court. What they heard next was a chorus of laughter coming from the U.S. troops, laughter so loud that it almost drowned out the noise of live rounds. Someone in the crowd pointed out that the artillery was outgoing, not incoming. The tennis stars would have to learn the difference. The team remained uneasy throughout their stay in Vietnam. On a tour of the Vietnamese countryside, they witnessed impact craters, destroyed farmland, and immense poverty. They met U.S. Ambassador Ellsworth Bunker for lunch at a restaurant that was located next door to a brothel, where local Vietnamese women catered to America's fighting men. Sportswriter Bud Collins, who traveled to Vietnam with the team, observed, "Ashe sits by the window eyeing everybody on a Honda suspiciously," worried that he might become the victim of an attack. Before arriving in Vietnam, Ashe suffered from a terrible headache. It would get no better during his stay.[12]

Ashe voiced his concerns to General Creighton Abrams, who briefed the team on the war. Abrams told the team that if South Vietnam fell to the communists, then Japan, South Korea, and other Southeast Asian nations would be in jeopardy as well. This domino theory, first articulated by President Eisenhower in the 1950s, compared communism to a disease: the United States had to contain the threat or capitalism would crumble in Southeast Asia. Ashe found the domino theory "ridiculous"; he believed that it was simply a pretense to justify the U.S. occupation of Vietnam. As a data processor at West Point, he walked past two or three funerals a day for fallen servicemen. Death in Vietnam, he believed, was "senseless." When Abrams concluded his briefing, Ashe pressed the general on the topic of black soldiers and drugs. The two men discussed drug abuse in Vietnam, including the widespread availability of heroin, cocaine, and marijuana. Blacks and whites returned home from the war addicted to a variety of drugs, and the U.S. government failed to provide adequate rehabilitation programs for these soldiers, resulting in high rates of homelessness, suicide, and crime. Race also mattered. Poor men fought and died for the United States, and more often than not those men were black. A number of prominent black leaders, including Martin Luther King Jr., had opposed the war on these grounds. Ashe became only the latest to question America's commitment to black soldiers.[13]

Despite his private criticisms of the war, Ashe made a positive impression on the soldiers. Armed with a blazing serve and a warm personality, he played in fifteen exhibitions in ten days, signing autographs and talking with the troops after each match. Many of the soldiers, raised on the stories of Lou Gehrig, Red Grange, and Joe Louis, were unfamiliar with amateur and professional tennis; however, something about Ashe and his teammates thrilled them. In Laos, local villagers also flocked to see the American stars perform. "Fewer than 300 people play tennis in struggling, uneasy Laos," reported Bud Collins, "but there are nearly 50 kids at the morning clinic—in Vientiane, and they all know Arthur Ashe and want to hit with him." In a country where tennis balls were hard to come by, Ashe and Stan Smith drew eleven hundred locals for an exhibition. Collins declared the trip an overwhelming success. "Few are aware of how much good the team did for America (and for tennis)," he told *World Tennis* readers. Although Burma frequently rejected American visitors, it "warmly received" the Davis Cup champions. Collins explained that the trip was a good way for Asians to see another side of America. An embassy official told him that the Davis Cup team did more for relations between the United States and Burma than U.S. diplomats. It is doubtful that the Davis Cup tour changed the minds of any Burmese officials—the United States, to them, represented an imperial power that threatened the Third World. Yet on a personal level the trip did matter. American soldiers, South Vietnamese fighters, and Laotian laborers all took a break from the realities of war to watch a tennis match or two. If nothing else, the tour was a mental break for those directly involved in the fighting.[14]

Ashe left Vietnam more opposed to the war than ever. The images of soldiers with limbs missing, villages destroyed by machine gun fire and grenade attacks, and black servicemen addicted to heroin and other drugs convinced him that the war was wrong. "I never thought this war made sense," he confessed. "Seeing the dead and knowing that a disproportionate number of young blacks were paying the ultimate price for faulty American foreign policy, moved me toward firm opposition to our involvement in Southeast Asia, even with my military status." On the one hand, the Civil Rights and Voting Rights acts promised universal equality under the law. On the other, working-class blacks were disproportionately drafted into the army to fight for a nation in which they remained second-class citizens. Something did not make sense. Ashe was no Ali, however. He would lodge his objections to the war in private, away from the television cameras and sportswriters. He remained astutely aware that expressing opposition to the Vietnam War in public would cost him dearly. The U.S. Davis Cup team might drop him from the squad; his corporate employers, including Coca-Cola, Philip Morris, and Head, might cancel his contracts; and future employers would think twice about hiring him. He envisioned headlines detailing the story of an American hero gone bad. Ashe could not risk his reputation and his standing in world tennis, at least not yet.[15]

Leaving his teammates in Southeast Asia before the end of the tour, Ashe flew to Syracuse, New York, to accept an award from the National Jaycees, which the army insisted he receive in person. He was named one of the Ten Most Outstanding Young Men of 1968 for his U.S. Nationals and U.S. Open victories, his Davis Cup triumph, his community service, and his dedication to human and civil rights. Eight years earlier the Jaycees had barred him from a tournament because of his race, and now the exclusive club honored him. Two months later the army discharged Ashe after three years of service. "I'm excited as hell," he told Neil Amdur regarding his upcoming independence. "Some of the strains have been cut. I'm a tennis player with one hat on, and I can be a businessman with another hat on. I've got the whole world at my feet and I can pick and choose."[16]

Ashe valued his independence over the prospect of a lucrative salary. In late February he turned down a five-year, $400,000 contract offer from promoter George MacCall to join his professional tennis tour. "I just got out of the Army and I relish my freedom," Ashe told Arthur Daley. Signing a professional contract would require that he play according to MacCall's rules; his schedule would be hectic, his tournaments would be selected for him, and he would be disqualified from future Davis Cup play, which remained an amateur competition. After having the army tell him what to do for three years, he was not about to transfer that authority to MacCall. "For the first time in two years," he told Daley, "I can go where I want and do what I want." His independence would also allow him to devote more time to Whitney Young and the Urban League. Ashe wanted to be his "own boss," and that included expanding his endorsement deals with Philip Morris and Hobson-Miller (a paper company) and purchasing a coin laundry. Nowhere would he showcase his newfound independence more than in South Africa.[17]

—◌ ◌—

"What are the chances of me playing in South Africa?," Ashe asked his friend Cliff Drysdale in 1968. "I think you have no chance of getting in now," replied Drysdale, a South African citizen. "You have to keep in mind that the reason you can't get in is not because of the South African Lawn Tennis Union but because of the government." "The government," he informed Ashe, "won't give you a visa." In fact, Ashe had not been kind to South Africa. "Because of apartheid," he once told a reporter, "I would like to drop a hydrogen bomb on Johannesburg." On a *Tennis South Africa* questionnaire inquiring about open tennis, he wrote: "Abolish apartheid first. . . . Print that if you like—nothing against you personally, just your god-damn, stinking country." In subsequent interviews, Ashe claimed that he regretted both statements, though the damage had already been done. These inflammatory comments gave Prime Minister Vorster the perfect reason to deny Ashe a visa. He was, as the South African government asserted, a rabble-rousing militant who lived under the guise of an apolitical tennis player. He wanted to destabilize the government of South Africa and further embarrass a nation that had come under increased scrutiny for its racial policies. Vorster would have none of it, and he personally denied Ashe a visa. Sports and politics had collided once again.[18]

In 1960 the Sharpeville massacre drew the world's attention to apartheid. A black protest group known as the Pan Africanist Congress, or PAC, had organized a demonstration to protest the pass laws. Under apartheid, black South Africans had to carry a passbook with them whenever they left their homelands. The passbooks restricted the movement of persons of color, confining them to select locations. At Sharpeville, anywhere from 3,000 to 20,000 protesters descended on a local police station, all without their passbooks. The police opened fire on the nonviolent crowd, killing 69 and wounding an additional 186. Most of the victims were shot in the back as they attempted to run from the scene. The government responded by banning the PAC and the African National Congress. The Sharpeville massacre and dissolution of the ANC would force international sports bodies to take a hard look at South Africa and its athletic policies.[19]

The draconian actions of the South African government and police led to near-unanimous condemnation from the international mainstream media. The press portrayed South Africa as a racist nation that quashed human rights and thumbed its nose at the international community. One year before Sharpeville, South Africa's government had rejected a visa request by Pancho Bathacaji, an Indian boxer who planned to fight in South Africa. Egypt's entire table tennis team was also turned away. The most notable exclusion prior to Ashe involved Papwa Sewgolum, a South African golfer of Indian origin. Sewgolum was a world-class golfer who had recently won the Dutch Open. In 1961 he applied to play in the Natal Open. The South African Golf Union, under orders from the government, never ruled on Sewgolum's application, and as a result he missed the tournament. Later, Sewgolum applied to compete in the South African Open. The government informed him that under the Group Areas Act he needed an additional permit to play. He eventually secured the permit but was told not to practice on the course or to enter the clubhouse. The following year, the government again barred him from the Natal Open, explaining that "the policy of the Government is against mixed participation in sport." Facing heavy international pressure, the government begrudgingly accepted his entry the following year. Sewgolum played the best golf of his life, defeating 113 whites to win the championship. An elated Sewgolum received his trophy in the pouring rain, as mixed-race South Africans were not allowed in the clubhouse. The South African Broadcasting Corporation refused to announce the results of the tournament, depriving Sewgolum of nationwide accolades. "Papwa Sewgolum," noted scholar Richard Lapchick, "became the first real martyr for those opposing South Africa's sports policy."[20]

In South Africa, sports were a civic religion, observed by all segments of the population. White fans turned out in droves to see the nation's cricket and rugby stars battle one another on the fields of Johannesburg, Cape Town, and Durban. More often than not, sports news made the front pages of the *Rand Daily Mail*, the *Johannesburg Star*, the *Daily Express*, and other Afrikaner newspapers. Antiapartheid activists quickly learned that sports served as an ideal vehicle for applying international political pressure.

Tennis was not the only sport to tangle with apartheid. Between 1948 and 1960 the South African government slowly took control of the nation's independent sports bodies. For twelve years, beginning in 1946, white sports bodies enacted color bans in their constitutions. In 1956 Minister of the Interior Dr. T. E. Donges first articulated South Africa's official sports policy, which prohibited mixing among black and white athletes, coaches, and administrators. The government barred nonwhites from the grandstands, bleachers, stadiums, and fields. In response, a number of black protest organizations, including the South Africa Sports Association (SASA), led direct-action campaigns targeting white sports bodies. Dennis Brutus, the leader of SASA, asked international sports bodies such as the Amateur Athletic Union to bar South Africa from international sports competitions because of apartheid. In 1963 the International Olympic Committee placed South Africa on notice, ordering the country to integrate its sports teams or risk sanctions. South Africa chose the latter.[21]

The hardening of apartheid in sports and society led to increased attention from the international community. In New Zealand, Australia, and England, union leaders threatened to discontinue their services if a South African team visited their country. South African athletes such as Cliff Drysdale and Gary Player met with organized protests as they competed abroad. In 1964 the Soviet Union ordered a tennis player to forfeit his match at Wimbledon rather than play a South African. Clergy from a variety of denominations stood united against apartheid. In the United States, Great Britain, New Zealand, and Australia, newly formed pressure groups joined with SANROC, the South African Non-Racial Olympic Committee (formerly SASA), to lobby national governments to take action.[22]

Not all athletes and administrators agreed with the concept of direct action. Some concluded that active engagement, including competitions between multiracial and South African teams, were the only way for South Africa to see the benefits of race mixing. Others, like Avery Brundage, wished that the problem would simply go away. Margaret Court, the great Australian tennis player, had no problem at all with South Africa's racial exclusions. "I love South Africa," she told the *New Zealand Herald*. "I have many friends there. Of course, I will keep going to play. It is a tragedy that politics has come into sport—but if you ask me, South Africa has the racial situation rather better organized than anyone else, certainly much better than the United States."[23]

By 1964 the IOC could no longer ignore South Africa. On June 26 it issued an ultimatum: South Africa had to publicly renounce racial discrimination in sports and integrate its Olympic trials or face expulsion from the 1964 Games in Tokyo. The South Africans had until August 16 to make a decision. An announcement condemning apartheid never came. Therefore, on August 18, in Lausanne, Switzerland, the IOC announced that it had removed South Africa from the Games. Dennis Brutus, in prison for opposing apartheid, gained a small sense of satisfaction from the IOC's ruling. "The cheering in the quadrangle at Robben Island, where we were breaking stones, must have deafened the guards," he later wrote. The *Amsterdam News* wondered if Tokyo marked only the beginning, suggesting that other nations would follow the IOC's lead and bar South Africa from international competition.[24]

From 1964 to 1968 South Africa and the international community each held to their positions. South Africa continued to bar race mixing in sports, refused to integrate seating at sporting events, and publicly defended its sports policies. As a result, protests intensified. In May 1964 antiapartheid demonstrators disrupted a Davis Cup match between South Africa and Norway in Oslo. Angry protesters rushed onto the court, resulting in fifty arrests. In 1968 South Africa's government informed Basil D'Oliveira, a black South African cricket star playing professionally in Great Britain, that he could not travel with his team to South Africa. Rather than issue a formal ban, Vorster attempted to bribe D'Oliveira, hoping to keep him out of South Africa. D'Oliveira did not take the bait, and the media praised him for his actions. D'Oliveira, however, claimed that he wanted to play cricket, not criticize his homeland. Before the 1968 Olympic Games in Mexico City, South Africa made one final plea to the IOC. In a statement issued before the IOC's Tehran meeting in May 1967, South Africa promised that it would send a mixed-race team to the Games. All of its competitors would wear the same uniforms and march together during the opening and closing ceremonies. A committee of whites and nonwhites would assemble the team. It was all a pretense, however. The South Africans had no intention of fielding an interracial team, nor did they intend to condemn apartheid. When a united group of African nations threatened to withdraw from the Games in protest, the IOC had to act. South Africa was once again expelled from the Games.[25]

Less than a year later, with the Mexico City Olympics over, antiapartheid activists in the United States focused their attention on South African Airways. On February 23, 1969, South African Airways, a government-controlled company, began advertising a flight from New York to Johannesburg for $784. "South African Airways Invites 139 Distinguished Americans to be first to fly the last ocean," read the ad. African Americans reading the ad in the *New York Times* understood that the offer was not for them. The "139 Distinguished Americans" meant white Americans. A number of prominent black leaders, including Ashe, responded with an ad of their own. "We are black Americans," the ad announced, "non-whites like 80 per cent of the population of South Africa. And we know that the first thing to 'welcome' us on arrival in Johannesburg would be racially designated areas—signs which say 'European' and 'Non-European' (which means white and black)." The airline represented an arm of apartheid, a way for the government to maintain its racial policies in international commerce. The responding ad's signatories included actor Harry Belafonte, congressman Charles Diggs, union and civil rights leader A. Philip Randolph, and Urban League president Whitney Young. They would not allow South Africa's government to take in an estimated $5 million a year without a fight. "Black Americans," the ad continued, "aren't welcome at the splendid bathing beaches you take pride in advertising. Black Americans wouldn't be served at your sophisticated night clubs, your luxurious restaurants. Black Americans couldn't get inside your modern, comfortable hotels." After citing the realities of life under apartheid, the ad asked Americans to support U.N. sanctions against South Africa. It encouraged black and white Americans to write the president of the U.S. Civil

Aeronautics Board, their congressmen in Washington, or President Nixon to express their dissatisfaction.[26]

Two months before he signed the anti-airline ad, Ashe had quietly inquired about obtaining a visa to compete in the South African Open. He did not notify the press, nor did he apply for the visa in person. Although the South African Lawn Tennis Union (SALTU) had accepted him as a competitor, Vorster's government promptly rejected his visa request. Ashe had become accustomed to rejection. For the first twenty-six years of his life he had been barred from country clubs, tournaments, and some public places, all in the name of Jim Crow. South Africa's rejection, however, differed from the usual racial slights. The Ashe of 1969 represented no ordinary black man. In addition to holding the title of U.S. Open champion, he publicly advocated for civil and human rights and lived as a world-class celebrity. How could South Africa, or any nation for that matter, prevent the number-one American player from competing in a tournament? The Sharpeville massacre and the 1964 and 1968 Olympic bans had shown that many, if not most, in the world community refused to tolerate South Africa's racial policies. The world was prepared to stand with Ashe, or at least he thought. Perhaps most importantly, South Africa targeted Ashe as an individual. This was not some case of general racial discrimination or exploitation, nor was it an example of racism perpetrated upon someone else. South Africa planned to make an example of him. In light of these facts, Ashe declared, rather boldly for him, that the International Tennis Federation must remove the South African Open from its circuit or South Africa must let him play. For once, Ashe refused to compromise.[27]

While at Wimbledon, Ashe chose the *London Times* as the vehicle for his first public statements on his visa denial. A widely circulated international paper, the *Times* was available throughout the world. An interview with the *Times* would ensure the largest possible readership. To John Hennessy, Ashe declared that South Africa should be excluded from the Davis Cup if it did not reevaluate his visa status. He appeared before the International Tennis Players Association, a de facto union, and urged the body to issue a statement on his behalf. The government's poor treatment of himself and D'Oliveira, Ashe argued, proved a pattern of racial discrimination by South Africa. Although the players' union expressed "sympathy for Ashe's views," it voted 19-17 not to issue a formal statement. South Africans Cliff Drysdale and Bob Hewitt voted with the majority. The ITPA's vote saddened but did not shock Ashe. Tennis players had always been apolitical, and many believed that international politics had no place in sports. A number of players privately supported Ashe but were unwilling to stand with him publicly. Many players loved to compete in South Africa's lucrative winter league, the so-called Sugar Circuit. Any player who offered public support for Ashe risked having his or her own visa revoked. A large number of players also competed with professional tour groups, their contracts requiring them to participate in the Sugar Circuit. Despite these factors, some players clearly sided with Ashe. Charlie Pasarell, Stan Smith, and Bob Lutz, three of Ashe's Davis Cup teammates, seemed to favor a boycott of South Africa.[28]

The day after his interview appeared in the *London Times*, South African officials denied receiving an application from Ashe. Louis Janssens, secretary of SALTU, and Jan Botha, South Africa's secretary of sport and recreation, both claimed they had no knowledge of his visa request. Ben Keet, a press secretary for Botha's department, "dared Ashe to produce a letter of refusal to back up his claims." "That would be the best evidence, surely," he told the press. Keet had called Ashe's bluff. The same day, Ashe admitted that he had not formally filed for a visa. After inviting him to play in the South African Open, SALTU failed to get his application approved by the government. "Personally I did not apply for a visa," he informed the *Washington Post*. "What was the good when I was told that I wouldn't get one anyway." Ashe had made a tactical mistake. By not filing a formal visa request, he had allowed South African officials to (correctly) assert that they had done nothing wrong. His interview with the *Times* also called into question his credibility. South Africa had forced his hand, pushing him to file a formal visa request with the press in tow. "This time I won't be silent," he vowed. "I'll go right to the South African embassy in New York. If they want to turn me down, they'll have to do it right there in front of all of you."[29]

While the mainstream press ran informative stories on Ashe's visa status, the black press demanded action. An editorial in the *Amsterdam News* called on players and administrators to bar South Africa from international competition. "Any true sportsman must say South Africa must get out of the National Lawn Tennis Association, because they and their apartheid laws have no right to compete in any kind of sports," it argued. "If the Americans on the tennis tour don't defend Arthur Ashe," the paper stated emphatically, "to a man then, he has to take a stand—and it can't be compromising, or weak." A second editorial the same day found it odd that Sweden would take a stronger stand against injustice than the United States. "They have no racial problem," it pointed out. Ashe's teammates should lead the charge against apartheid, yet based on past experience, the black daily knew not to count on the Americans. Gertrude Wilson of the *Amsterdam News* concurred with her colleagues. "Tennis players," she told her readers, "are a special breed of men. They have one arm of tremendous muscular strength, legs of steel, but, it seems, rather wobbly backbones." In baseball, soccer, boxing, or any other sport, teammates "would have risen up in indignation" if a top-ranked American player had been barred from an athletic contest. "It would seem that the USLTA doesn't give a hoot if it loses its soul, just as long as it doesn't lose the cup," she wrote. Tennis differed from baseball, soccer, basketball, and other sports in one significant respect: tennis players mostly competed as individuals, and not as members of a team. If Major League Baseball, for instance, barred Bob Gibson from pitching for the St. Louis Cardinals, then the entire team suffered. Removing Ashe from the South African Open, by contrast, had no impact on the performances of individual players, aside from increasing their chances of winning the tournament.[30]

Ashe's most vocal defender was Sam Lacy, the black journalist who had criticized him five years earlier. Ashe's public stand did not impress Lacy, but the fact that he confronted the ILTF alone did. When the IOC met in Genoa to decide the fate of South Africa, a group of nations and international organizations had already mobilized against South Africa's participation in the 1968 Games. Scandinavia, Russia, a number of Asian countries, and all of Africa pledged to stay away from Mexico City if the IOC did not bar South Africa. In London, Ashe pleaded for South Africa's removal from the Davis Cup on his own. "Ashe's performance," Lacy argued, "was more courageous than the gloved-fist salute by Tommy [sic] Smith and John Carlos in last October's Olympics . . . not as dramatic, perhaps, but more gutsy." Ashe's testimony came in the middle of Wimbledon, proving to Lacy that Ashe's fight against injustice trumped his need for rest prior to his big tennis match. "Further evidence of his courage," Lacy wrote, "is to be found in the revelation that Ashe didn't pick the stage for his fight. . . . England is still Churchillean, a country where social reforms are even slower than in Arthur's American homeland. . . . And it was the British who held with Uncle Sam the longest in opposition to scratching South Africa from the Olympic picture."[31]

In the months following his informal visa denial, a number of South African tennis stars and officials came to Ashe's defense. His friend Ray Moore called the government's decision a "tragedy" for South African sports. Moore knew Ashe personally and understood that contrary to government claims, his friend was no militant agitator. During several private conversations between the two men, Ashe agonized about the South African Open. Ashe and Moore discussed apartheid at length and often disagreed about how to confront the government. While watching the 1968 Democratic Convention, they discussed the concept of fighting apartheid from the inside. They drew inspiration from musician Frank Zappa, who suggested that the way to quell the violence in Chicago was for the protesters to clean up and join the police force. If Ashe traveled to South Africa, he could meet with local and national leaders, tour Soweto and other townships, and engage in meaningful dialogue with black and white South Africans.[32]

Cliff Drysdale and Alf Chalmers also spoke on Ashe's behalf. Drysdale, president of the ITPA, argued that barring Ashe from South Africa would result in retaliation from international sports bodies such as the IOC, ending in a "catastrophic outcome" for South African players. Drysdale based his argument on South Africa's national interest and not on Ashe's plea for civil and human rights. Reiterating that the ITPA did not intend "to agitate on political matters," Drysdale avoided focusing specifically on Ashe's situation and instead advocated fairness for all athletes. He assured everyone that SALTU backed Ashe's tournament entry. Chalmers, the head of SALTU, made a public appeal to the international community. "We would be delighted to see Arthur Ashe competing in the South African national tennis championships," he told the Associated Press. The decision, however, remained Vorster's. "All I can say," Chalmers noted, "is that we would do our very best to assist him." The previous day, Chalmers had announced that South Africa planned to remove the color ban from the nation's Davis Cup team. "I would be more than happy to see colored Africans or Indian players included on South African Davis Cup teams provided the players were up to standard," he declared. Opponents took his "up to standard" quote as a disqualifying caveat, allowing South African officials to deny blacks a chance based on "performance." The government stood silent on Chalmers's concessions, leading many to doubt his credibility.[33]

A number of tennis fans and ordinary men and women publicly reacted to Ashe's visa denial. While many unconditionally supported him, others believed that politics and sports should remain separate. In a letter to the *New York Times*, one woman assailed the ITPA for backing Ashe with a tepid formal statement. Only athletic sanctions, she argued, would deter South Africa from committing future civil rights violations. "While we of the United States," she wrote, "champions of 'fair play,' especially on July 4 sing of the home of the brave and the land of the free, Poland and Czechoslovakia *acted* by refusing to play against South Africa this year." In her mind, actions mattered more than words. Ashe also received some hate mail. One letter from "a white Englishman" read: "Nigger Ashe, South Africans will never bend. They will never allow you to play there. Before long we shall ban all of your kind from England." Thankfully for Ashe, this type of letter was rare.[34]

All of the letters, statements, hearings, and debates about his visa status distracted Ashe from tennis, he admitted in an interview with the *Los Angeles Times*. In addition to meeting with the ITPA at Wimbledon, he had to answer questions and criticisms from reporters. At the U.S. Open, where he was the defending champion, he met for hours with black protesters who threatened to disrupt the Open because Owen Williams, a South African, was promoting the tournament for the USLTA. Although Ashe negotiated a détente, he later appeared in a photograph with Williams, setting off criticism in the black press. These off-the-court issues, it seemed, contributed to a dramatic decline in his athletic performance. He did not win a major championship in 1969, failing to make the finals of Wimbledon, the French Open, the Australian Open, or the U.S. Open. He finished 1969 ranked eighth in the world, a far cry from his rank of second overall in 1968. "I must try as far as possible," he told McIlvanney, "to shut out everything but tennis. But, of course, I can't shut out the color issue. I think about it all the time." He wondered, "Is it possible to be a tennis player first and a black man second. It has to be. If I put the priorities the other way round I'll be a poor tennis player and therefore a less effective black man." Ashe recognized that his power as an activist was directly related to his athletic performance. To be a successful activist, he had to remain a world-class tennis player.[35]

The Ashe controversy threatened to disrupt the upcoming Davis Cup Challenge Round. In the summer of 1969 many oddsmakers predicted that South Africa would make it through to the Challenge Round and face off against the United States for the cup. South Africa's collection of stars, which included Bob Hewitt, Frew McMillan, and Bob Maud, had already defeated Iran in Cape Town, and Poland and Czechoslovakia subsequently withdrew from their matches in protest of apartheid, resulting in two forfeit wins for South Africa. On July 17 South Africa prepared to square off against Great Britain for the European Zone B title. If South Africa reached the Challenge Round, Ashe faced another difficult decision: withdraw in protest and risk hurting his team or play and risk condemnation from antiapartheid activists. It was a no-win situation. "Either way I guess I'm a target," he told Neil Amdur. "If I play in the Davis Cup, some people might protest. If I don't play as a sign of protest, that may only help South Africa win the cup, which would be twice as bad for everyone." The scenario involving a match between the United States and South Africa never materialized, however, because Great Britain upset the South Africans 3-2 in the Zone B final.[36]

But another development regarding the visa issue soon followed the Davis Cup controversy. On December 7 Ashe met in Paris with William Rogers, Richard

Nixon's secretary of state. Ashe announced his intention to apply for another visa, this time in person at the South African Consulate in New York. Rogers pledged to support him, dispatching Assistant Secretary of State for African Affairs David Newsome to meet with South African officials on his behalf. He also ordered Ambassador William M. Roundtree to meet directly with Vorster. In both the United States and South Africa, officials at the highest levels of government negotiated Ashe's visa application. As promised, Ashe and Donald Dell, with a press contingent, delivered the tennis star's application in New York on December 15. At a press conference organized by Dell, Ashe relayed his desire "to play tennis and only to play tennis." "I come not to expound my political beliefs about South Africa, but simply to play my best possible tennis," he explained. He even offered to sign an affidavit saying that he would not make political pronouncements while on South African soil. He expressed interest in visiting Soweto and the South African countryside but promised not to cause any problems for the government. He explained that his previous statements about apartheid and South Africa specifically had been in reference to his visa case. Ashe bent the truth. In a number of interviews over the years his criticism of the South African government had had nothing to do with his status as a tennis player. Ashe, despite these concessions, demanded that South Africa admit him as an American citizen and not as an "honorary white."[37]

Ashe would not learn his fate until early in 1970. South African officials had other pressing issues to deal with. As Christmas approached, South Africa found itself alone in the international community, a sole dissenter facing a barrage of pressure to adjust its racial policies. International sports bodies had barred its athletes from consecutive Olympic Games, international soccer, and amateur table tennis and boxing. A Davis Cup ban would surely follow if they rejected Ashe's visa application. "Scarcely a month seems to go past without an attempt to keep South Africa out of one sport or another," commented a *New York Times* reporter. By the end of 1969 South Africa was the black sheep of the sports world.[38]

—☙ ❧—

The visa controversy threatened to dominate Ashe's life. The interviews, phone calls, and meetings with activists and tennis officials all took a toll on his tennis and his social life. Rod Laver, Clark Graebner, and others had a singular focus: winning tennis matches. Ashe had much more to worry about. In 1969 he signed a number of endorsement contracts and became the face of American tennis in magazines, on billboards, and on television. He inked deals with the racquet company Head and Catalina clothing, and his endorsements for Coca-Cola and Philip Morris carried into 1969. Dell, ever the astute businessman, convinced Ashe (and a number of companies) that his race was a benefit, a feature that made him stand out from all other tennis players. Dell marketed Ashe as an athletic gentleman, a patriotic American, and a Davis Cup champion. "My experience," Ashe later wrote, "indicated I was acceptable to white Americans, who bought the racquets, shoes, and tennis clothes I hoped to sell." As a child playing with a Jack Kramer wooden racquet, Ashe dreamed of having his own name written across the side of a racquet. Head made his dream a reality. To potential companies, he did not come cheap. "I deserved a good price—six figures—because I was black, good, had an admirable reputation, and was American," he explained. In South Africa, his race kept him from competing. In the United States, he was becoming a hot commodity, in large part because of his race. He had graced the covers of *Life*, *Sports Illustrated*, and the *New Yorker* and represented black athletes on *Face the Nation*, and he drew thousands wherever he played. In the endorsement world, he was quickly coming to resemble Arnold Palmer, the white golfer, than he did Jackie Robinson or Willie Mays.[39]

As promised, he became more active with civil rights groups as well. As a "ghetto worker" for Coca-Cola, he hosted tennis clinics in the inner city, working with underprivileged black youths on makeshift tennis courts. Despite his good intentions, he struggled to persuade some teens that he was one of them. He did not speak or dress like them, and he seemed to have an overly optimistic view of their situation. Ashe admitted that he was unfamiliar with the ghetto environment. "I didn't live in a so-called ghetto situation," Ashe told John McPhee in 1968. "I never saw rat-infested houses, never hung out on corners, never saw anyone knifed." During a trip to Richmond, Ashe and members of a national service program known as Volunteers in Service to America (VISTA) visited a ghetto where he had never been. The group approached a local youth hangout. Garbage was scattered across the ground, and a jukebox inside blared soul music. The teens looked at Ashe and his entourage with disdain, wondering why they bothered to disrupt their fun. A pair of adolescent girls laughed at him. His tennis trophies and international prestige meant nothing to them. "I'll never forget that experience as long as I live," he told the *Washington Post*. "It was terrible." Ashe felt disconnected, powerless to help these kids.[40]

In addition to his inner-city programs, he gave a number of speeches in 1969 to civil rights groups, at athletic gatherings, and at local events. In November he addressed the Women's National Democratic Club and urged its members to befriend and engage with black women. After years of mistreatment and condescension, black women had become defensive, viewing white women with suspicion. Ashe told the audience that it was up to them to bring black women into their organization and into the Democratic Party. He suggested that as a sign of respect they begin addressing their maids as "Mrs." or "Miss" rather than by their first name. Ethel Payne, a reporter covering the event for the Chicago Defender, described the atmosphere in the room as "uncomfortable," a sign that some of the women were reluctant to take Ashe's advice. Ashe described how he felt when a former white girlfriend told her mother about their relationship. Angered that her daughter would date a black man, she had called her a "bitch" and a "slut," ordering her to terminate the relationship at once. The theme of the speech was open-mindedness. Black and white women had to look past stereotypes and preconceived notions to achieve racial progress. Payne was sure that Ashe offended a number of women, especially when he attacked the Reverend Billy Graham for preaching but not acting.[41]

To some, Ashe was simply too busy for his own good. In an interview with Jeff Prugh of the Los Angeles Times he admitted that within a span of two or three hours preceding the interview he had auditioned for a small movie role, handled some business with Dell, and visited his UCLA girlfriend. "That's how life is with Arthur Ashe nowadays," Prugh revealed, "a non-stop, dizzying spin through the world of high finance, bright lights and civil rights." Like other sportswriters, Prugh worried about Ashe's tennis, openly questioning his priorities. Was he spending too much time seeking fame and fortune at the expense of his tennis? Robert Lipsyte certainly thought so. Tennis needed a hero in 1969, and the mantle was Ashe's to claim. Instead of focusing on his game, however, he was giving civil rights speeches, starring in commercials, and negotiating with South African officials. "If only Arthur wasn't so busy calling off demonstrations, he could be a hero," Lipsyte remarked. With his new racquet deal, his new clothing line, and his gentlemanly demeanor, Ashe was ready to become America's star—if he kept his priorities straight. Jim Murray thought he was already there. Ashe was the face of American tennis, a black man who had taken the game by storm and never looked back. Tennis had changed to suit him. In the beginning, Ashe's task was especially difficult. "You can prizefight without becoming a part of prizefighting. You can play baseball merely for a living. But tennis is a way-of-life. The line between social, athletic and private life is blurred. It's its own cruise through life, the world's tightest key club," Murray wrote. The game had adjusted to Ashe just as he had adjusted to the game.[42]

# CHAPTER 5

# Tennis Wars

The early 1970s were frustrating years for an embattled Arthur Ashe. Anger and disappointment over his visa denials had spread beyond the tennis world. Within South Africa, Prime Minister Vorster touted his rejection of Ashe in speeches and interviews throughout the country, hoping to convince the racial hard-liners that he deserved reelection. Around the world, South African athletes faced antiapartheid protests in arenas, on tennis courts, and on the links. In August 1971 the Boston chapter of the NAACP infiltrated the grandstands at the Longwood Cricket Club during a tennis match between Australia's John Newcombe and South Africa's Frew McMillan. As Newcombe and McMillan volleyed back and forth, unaware of the scene about to confront them, the black protesters prepared to act. All at once the NAACP members stood up and in unity chanted, "Paint Him Black and Send Him Back." Back home, that is, to South Africa.[1]

Although Ashe gave numerous interviews, appeared on television shows, issued public statements, and even testified before Congress on the topic of apartheid, he continued to battle politicians, activists, officials, and reporters who appropriated his name to reinforce their own political agendas. Protesters disrupted athletic events, and the black press harangued Vorster and the Afrikaners, often invoking Ashe's name. Democratic congressman Charles Diggs Jr. of Michigan called for a full-scale investigation of the United States' involvement with South Africa. Gary Player, he argued, had no business making money in America. From 1970 to 1973, politicians, activists, and the press used Ashe's visa status to satisfy their own social and political agendas. Ashe, however, pushed back against those who attempted to appropriate his image and his public statements. Increasingly, he sought out the press, aiming to clear up misconceptions and "set the record straight." In March 1970 the ILTF's Davis Cup

Committee barred South Africa from the annual tournament because of its exclusionary policies. Those tennis purists who abhorred the intrusion of politics into the sport instantly blamed Ashe. He was now under attack from fans and players alike.

The sport of tennis was also in a state of disarray in the early 1970s. The International Lawn Tennis Federation and World Championship Tennis (WCT), a professional tour group, fought over players and television deals. Billie Jean King and other women's tennis stars, citing gender discrimination, threatened to form their own circuit if they did not receive the same treatment and prizes as their male counterparts. Independent professionals established a union to protect their interests, and for the first time a Grand Prix linked together tournaments. Promoters battled one another for profits. The "Tennis Wars," as journalist Jim Murray labeled the competition, had begun. And as the bombs landed on Cambodia and students took over college campuses, Ashe faced his own crisis of sorts. And like President Richard Nixon in Vietnam, Ashe chose the offensive.

South Africans heard the news in the streets of Cape Town and Johannesburg, in the slums of Soweto, and on the beaches of Sun City. The government made sure that everyone knew. On January 28, 1970, South Africa announced the rejection of Ashe's second visa application. The story received front-page coverage in every local newspaper, and radio broadcasts led with the news. The minister of sport, Frank Waring, cited Ashe's "general antagonism toward South Africa" as the primary reason for the government's decision. Ashe's antiapartheid statements to the press, his demand that he enter South Africa as an individual and not as a member of the Davis Cup team, and his support for African liberation movements had ultimately doomed his application. The press even quoted him as saying that his South Africa visit would be an "attempt to put a crack in the racist wall down there." Aside from the reasons given in Waring's public statement, though, Vorster had an ulterior motive for rejecting Ashe. As the New Year came and went, the prime minister faced growing opposition from his political right. Upset by some of his "liberal" concessions, his opponents planned to challenge Vorster in the 1970 parliamentary elections. Barring Ashe, then, was a way for Vorster to beef up his apartheid credentials without significantly altering his domestic policies.[2]

Ashe's visa denial made front-page headlines all across the United States. Columnist Robert Lipsyte of the *New York Times* divided the public reaction into three camps. Those on the far left, including Congressman Diggs and a number of liberal journalists, demanded swift government action. The United States should break off relations with South Africa, expel all South African athletes from the country, and push for economic sanctions. The far right insisted that South Africa had the proper authority to reject Ashe. This faction argued that politics corrupted tennis and Ashe was wrong for trying to force his way into South Africa. A third camp, made up of "tokenists," urged the U.S. government to retaliate against Vorster, perhaps by revoking Gary Player's visa. The majority of tennis players, Lipsyte found, favored the removal of South Africa from the Davis Cup rather than the expulsion of South African athletes from the United States. Lipsyte himself drew a distinction between general apartheid policies and sports apartheid. He argued that when apartheid directly affected international sports, as it did with Ashe, the United States had an obligation to discontinue athletic competition with South Africa. "South Africa should be barred from the Olympics not because it herds its blacks on to reservations," he concluded, "but because blacks are not afforded a fair channel into national class sports teams."[3]

The mainstream press predicted that Vorster's decision would result in South Africa's complete banishment from world sports. Omar Kureishi of the *Guardian* suggested that Vorster found "masochistic pleasure in committing suicide in the world of international sport." He could think of no other reason for the visa denial. Moreover, Vorster had contradicted himself. When he had barred Basil D'Oliveira from playing cricket in South Africa, his reason was that D'Oliveira was a nonwhite South African citizen. Thus, the cricketer's rejection had been based on his nationality and not his race. Ashe was a different story. He was not a South African national, and therefore the government had to justify his visa denial on nonracial grounds. His antiapartheid statements proved to be a convenient backup. Kureishi assailed Vorster for destroying one of the positive elements of South Africa's culture, its sports teams. "Often in Vietnam," he wrote, "the Americans have had to destroy a town in order to save it! Mr. Vorster seems set on some similar course . . . This is a heart transplant in reverse. Replacing a perfectly good heart with a damaged one." Ashe would certainly overcome Vorster's "stupidity," but would Cliff Drysdale, Frew McMillan, or Gary Player?[4]

To veteran columnist Shirley Povich of the *Washington Post*, Vorster was grasping at straws, wildly searching for reasons to reject Ashe. The South African embassy in Washington claimed to have an entire file on the tennis star filled with his antiapartheid comments, a fact Povich disputed and found laughable. The embassy's most outlandish public argument was that Ashe had jeopardized the progress of his own race by supporting South Africa's exclusion from the 1968 Olympic Games. Vorster and Waring had planned to send South African blacks to Mexico City, officials argued, yet because of Ashe and other black radicals they were never allowed to compete. Of course this was not true. Vorster's teams would have remained all white. Povich reminded the South Africans that tennis was not an Olympic sport and that Ashe had no influence on the IOC. "Avery Brundage would swoon if Arthur Ashe tried to muscle in on an International Olympic Committee vote," he quipped. Apparently, it was Ashe's race, not his mouth, that had caused him all this trouble.[5]

As expected, the black press leveled the harshest criticism against South Africa. *Amsterdam News* columnist Dick Edwards had firsthand knowledge of apartheid, having traveled to South Africa himself. He had witnessed the inhumane treatment of blacks and watched as black workers lugged their passbooks with them to and from work. One trip was enough for him. In his attack on apartheid, Edwards questioned Ashe's logic and wondered why the American star was so eager to visit one of the world's most racist nations. Even *if* South Africa granted him a visa, where would he stay? The Afrikaners barred blacks and coloreds from living in Cape Town and Johannesburg. Soweto would be his only option. Edwards recommended that Ashe stay home. In a second column, Edwards attacked Ashe for his moderate stance and his naive way of thinking. Before applying for a visa, Ashe had agreed to sign an affidavit stating that he would not criticize Vorster's government while on South African soil. Edwards called this a "glaring error," suggesting that Ashe was wholly unaware of the black experience in South Africa. Edwards further criticized Ashe for defending South African Owen Williams's selection as director of the U.S. Open. If he was truly opposed to apartheid, why did he not call for Williams's resignation? Edwards mocked Ashe's comment that he had "bent over backwards to be nice to" the South African government. "It is dangerous," Edwards mused, "for a man of Arthur's color to ever bend over to or around South Africans. His only reward will be a swift boot in the rear."[6]

Unlike Edwards, Sam Lacy and Doc Young directed their animus at South Africa, not Ashe. Lacy believed that Ashe was the right man to take on Vorster and lead the antiapartheid movement in sports. "He is intelligent, articulate, quietly militant and well liked," Lacy explained, a rare combination of qualities. Lacy reminded Ashe that his extraordinary talents and athletic accomplishments allowed him to speak in a way that would make people listen. He should never forget that tennis had given him a platform to fight the apartheid battle. Lacy hinted that if his tennis work habits diminished, so would his platform for activism. Young, for his part, praised Ashe for pushing back against radicals who championed the removal of South African athletes from the United States. Ashe considered the expulsion of Gary Player and others a knee-jerk reaction, a move designed to appease the far left rather than bring about real change. The removal of Player and Drysdale would not undo his visa denial; it would only punish two innocent men, both of whom were progressives, at least at heart. Young applauded Ashe's boldness. He chose to stick up for his colleagues, a decision that was unpopular with the black press. Yet a third columnist, Pete Fritchie of the *Atlanta Daily World*, found the cup half full. Although Ashe had not obtained a visa, he had forced Vorster to make a difficult decision. By denying him entry, South Africa had shown its true colors as a nation of extremists who had barred a model citizen despite pleas from white South African athletes. More tangibly, South Africa's act of defiance was sure to result in the expulsion of South Africa from the Davis Cup competition.[7]

While the press mostly defended Ashe, a number of athletes publicly joined the chorus of boos directed at South Africa. Cliff Drysdale and Abe Segal criticized the decision, telling the *New York Times* that South Africa had effectively removed itself from the Davis Cup. Past demonstrations against South Africa, including protests opposing the tour of a South African rugby team in England, had been a "Sunday school picnic" compared with likely future protests, Drysdale warned. Gary Player, who tried to stay out of politics, called the ruling a "great, great pity." Tom Okker agreed that international politics had no place in tennis, yet in his opinion it was Vorster, not Ashe, who had injected controversy into the sport. Okker believed that South Africa was finished in world tennis. Ashe's manager and lawyer, Donald Dell, claimed that the South African Lawn Tennis Union had lied to his client in 1968. He said that SALTU had engaged in talks with Ashe and assured the American star that the association would fight for his entry into South Africa. In 1969, though, SALTU denied any discussion between Ashe and its officials. "We were too simple," Dell concluded. "We acted in good faith. We should have let everyone know from the beginning exactly what we intended to do." Among Ashe's tennis colleagues there was clear support for Ashe as an individual. Most in the tennis world knew him to be reasonable, levelheaded, contemplative, and a genuinely nice guy. He would not pick a fight based purely on emotion. On the other hand, many tennis players viewed politics and sports as apples and oranges, which should not be lumped together. This controversy involving Ashe put many players in a difficult position.[8]

At the same time that Drysdale, Okker, and Dell expressed support for Ashe, the international community widely condemned South Africa's decision. This pressure, in large part, forced the ILTF to act. On January 19, more than a week before the Ashe announcement, the ILTF called a special session to discuss South Africa's standing in world tennis. ILTF spokesman Robert B. Colwell said that South Africa had forced the organization's hand by bungling Ashe's visa application. He reported that a dozen European nations had pledged to withdraw from the Davis Cup if Ashe did not receive a visa. South Africa's participation would make a mockery of the cup and turn the competition into a circus. The ILTF had to act, Colwell argued, to protect the integrity of the Davis Cup. Nowhere in his statement did he mention apartheid or human rights abuses, as his focus was on the sanctity of the cup. In other words, the ILTF would expel South Africa because it had caused trouble, not because of the particular trouble it had caused. The ITPA also placed the topic of South Africa on its agenda. A year earlier at Wimbledon, the players' union had voted against public censure of South Africa, hoping that the Afrikaners would rethink their sports policies. ITPA President John Newcombe of Australia announced that the players disagreed on the Ashe issue. "Some of the players," he explained, "seem to feel that it's Arthur's personal business, some feel that it's political and some think that the Government's action was a dirty deed." Personally, Newcombe sympathized with SALTU, believing that it had done everything possible to help Ashe. Nonetheless, the ITPA, of which Ashe was an officer, agreed to take up the matter.[9]

While world tennis bodies prepared to confront South Africa, Ashe traveled to Washington, DC, to testify before a House Foreign Affairs subcommittee investigating South Africa. He appeared calm and confident in his tailored suit, never off balance and mostly on the offensive. The majority of the congressmen present were friendly and sympathetic to his position, although he had a few tense exchanges with Charles Diggs and J. Herbert Burke, a Republican from Florida. In response to a question about retaliation, Ashe said that his "gut reaction" had been to support the prohibition of South African athletes from competing in the United States. Upon further reflection, however, his "moral conscience" had told him that this would solve nothing. "I wouldn't want them to suffer the same indignities from my government," he testified, "that I have from theirs." Diggs, the subcommittee's chairman, disagreed. To him, an eye for an eye was the only appropriate course. His prime target was Gary Player, one of South Africa's wealthiest and most successful athletes. Diggs concluded that because Player represented South Africa without condemning apartheid, he should not earn prize money from U.S. tournaments. The other tense moment came when Burke asked Ashe if he regretted any of his inflammatory comments about South Africa. Burke referred specifically to a statement in which

Ashe had expressed his desire to have an atomic bomb dropped on Johannesburg. Somewhat amused, Ashe replied that he had not been speaking literally, and he stood by his message. Near the end of the hearing, Benjamin Rosenthal, a Democrat from New York, said that athletes had an obligation to speak out against injustice, and Ashe agreed. "Athletes," Ashe argued, "especially black athletes, must use every resource at their command to right things that are wrong. . . . To have a potential to do a lot of good and not exercise this is the worst cowardice, especially in the United States."[10]

Ashe was not the only professional athlete to testify before the subcommittee. Four days later, Jim Bouton faced Diggs and the other House members. Bouton, a relief pitcher for the Houston Astros, was white and had no direct connection to South Africa. Like Ashe, he was an emerging activist, a man who felt morally obligated to oppose South Africa. A member of the American Committee on Africa, Bouton understood the inner workings of amateur sports bodies. He argued that U.S. sports officials had tried to sweep the South Africa issue under the rug, allowing the Soviet Union and other communist nations to assume the moral high ground. In Mexico City in 1968, Bouton and other American athletes had tried in vain to get a majority of world nations to support a censure of South Africa. He argued that today's athletes represented a new generation of sportsmen, a bolder, politically aware collection of men and women who favored sanctions against South Africa. He said the gray-haired dinosaurs who ran amateur sports did not understand this.[11]

Ashe had an easier time convincing Congress than he did convincing his tennis colleagues. Parton Keese of the *New York Times* discussed Ashe's predicament with a number of players, many of whom blamed Ashe himself for the trouble. A Voice of America poll of players from around the world found that a majority of tennis players believed Ashe's problems were self-inflicted. Most expressed little to no desire to become involved in political activism. Mexico's Joaquin Loyo-Mayo concluded that South Africa was an autonomous nation that could reject anyone it wanted to for any reason. Manuel Santana of Spain insisted that racism was nonexistent in his country, and for this reason he felt no need to involve himself in political debates. Many players disagreed with South Africa's decision, yet they were sure that retaliation or political protest would be futile. American Marty Riessen accused Ashe of being selfish, wondering why the black star ignored tennis players who faced more pressing troubles. Egypt's Ismail El Shafei might have to travel to Israel with the Davis Cup team, a far more dangerous proposition than Ashe's visit to South Africa, Riessen argued. Cliff Richey was succinct: "Ashe should be a tennis player, not a politician."[12]

Some players, however, vowed to back Ashe regardless of the consequences. Tom Koch of Brazil pledged not to travel to South Africa until Ashe received a visa, declaring in solidarity, "Arthur Ashe is my brother." West Germany's Ingo Buding wanted a formal censure from the players and promised to follow Ashe's lead. Koch and Buding, though, were more the exception than the rule. Ashe expressed disappointment but not surprise over the players' views, understanding that historically, tennis players had been "apolitical, independent, even egotistical." Most believed that the situation was none of their business. "We're on a first-name basis and will probably be friends for life," he noted, "but when all is said and done, each of us will go back to his own country after we finish playing." Even those who privately supported Ashe had to consider their business deals, endorsement contracts, and the apolitical culture of tennis before they acted. Anyone who spoke out in favor of or opposed to Ashe risked losing an endorsement or being shunned by officials and fellow players. Ashe understood the business of tennis, so he did not expect players to rush to his aid. What he wanted was South Africa's expulsion from the ILTF and the Davis Cup. Keese asked Ashe if the South Africa controversy had placed a heavy burden on him. "Problems such as these hurt tennis," he answered, "but I enjoy my role. Like Martin Luther King's role gave him pleasure, so does my struggle for equality. If it does good in the world, it is not a burden." Through activism, then, Ashe was filling a void in his life. Years later, he admitted that his antiapartheid activism in the 1970s had been fueled in part by his regret over political inactivity during the 1960s. As white racists had battered the Freedom Riders, harassed marchers, and firebombed black churches, Ashe had been safely holed up at UCLA, playing poker with his roommates and focusing on tennis. His crusade against apartheid was about more than Vorster, the Afrikaners, and discrimination in sports. It was *his* contribution to the civil rights movement.[13]

―◌ ◌―

Apartheid, visas, and political protests were far from Ashe's mind on January 26, 1970. He had more immediate concerns. He was in the final of the Australian Open, a Grand Slam event, opposite Dick Crealy, Australia's native underdog. Crealy, however, was not Ashe's biggest problem, as Mother Nature proved to be more of an opponent than the streaky Australian. Throughout the match, wind and rain pelted the two men, forcing each to abandon the power game in favor of a less aggressive approach. They slid, fell, and committed unforced errors. It was not the prettiest of matches.[14]

Overall, Ashe's road to the final was a relatively easy one. Three months before the tournament began, Rod Laver, Roy Emerson, Pancho Gonzalez, and other professionals had backed out of the event after their professional circuit failed to reach an agreement with tournament officials. This left the field wide open. Frank Sedgman, now forty-two years old, represented one of Australia's few hopes for a lucrative gate. The experts agreed on three favorites: Ashe, John Newcombe, and Tom Okker. In addition to the withdrawals, tournament officials had financial concerns. The Open had cost £16,333 to put on, and as of January 21 ticket sales had accounted for a mere £209 profit. The ominous weather forecast also threatened to keep fans at home. The president of the New South Wales Lawn Tennis Association called the situation "disastrous."[15]

After the first few rounds, Australian officials added injuries and upsets to their growing list of headaches. In short order, the first, second, and third seeds fell, each in the quarterfinal round. Dennis Ralston defeated Newcombe, the second seed, in four agonizing sets, marking the longest singles match in the history of the Australian championship. Plagued with a sprained elbow, top-seeded Tony Roche lost to England's Roger Taylor in straight sets, and Crealy surprised Okker with a five-set victory. Ashe eked out a five-set win over Ray Ruffels, advancing to the semifinals to play former USC rival Ralston. The semifinals began in bizarre fashion when Ralston walked onto the court carrying one of Ashe's racquets instead of his own. Ralston had forgotten some of his equipment when he packed for Australia and had to ask Ashe to spare an extra racquet. Ashe was slow out of the gate. His normally dominating serve lacked punch, and his backhand was rather ordinary. It did not matter. Early in the match Ralston's back flared up, and what was diagnosed as a pulled muscle quickly turned into a potential pinched nerve. The pain in his left side prevented him from moving to the right. Ashe noticed the injury and altered his strategy. In the middle of the fourth set the pain proved too much for Ralston, and he forfeited the match, catapulting Ashe into the final.[16]

The final match-up was not what officials had hoped for. Ashe was an exciting player and a sure gate draw, but Crealy was a relatively obscure player, an underdog without the underdog appeal. The "giant killer" had knocked off a far from elite player in Roger Taylor for the right to face Ashe, who had entered the tournament as the overwhelming favorite. In outdoor sports, however, weather sometimes has a way of leveling the playing field. Ashe and Crealy both took the court in swirling winds that transformed the day's light drizzle into a barrage of watery missiles. Both men struggled. Ashe had to ask for time on numerous occasions to wipe the rain from his glasses, and as Crealy served, Ashe shielded his glasses from the rain with his left hand. He slipped and fell twice during the match. In the end, though, neither the weather nor the underdog Crealy could stop him. He defeated Crealy in straight sets, winning £1,500 and the first leg of the 1970 Grand Slam. Two down, two to go. Only Wimbledon and the French Open stood between him and a career grand slam.[17]

The victory was a significant achievement for Ashe and the United States. He became the first American since 1959, and the first African American, to win the Australian Open. Only three non-Australians had captured the title in the last thirty years, and Ashe was one of them. With the victory he earned $3,808 in prize money, far less, however, than the professionals made on tour. At the press conference following his win over Crealy, Ashe announced plans for a vacation. His public crusade against South Africa, his dizzying tennis schedule, his endorsement obligations, and his expanding role with the ATP had left him mentally and physically exhausted. The location of his getaway, Sun Valley, Idaho, seemed like heaven. He anticipated several days of light winter sports and relaxation, a time to rest his aching body and settle his mind, promising his fans that he would only ski on "the little slopes." He also pledged to remain an "independent professional" rather than sign with a professional circuit as many players had done. "I value my independence much too much to be told where and when I have to play," he told reporters.[18]

When Ashe and others used terms like *professional, independent professional,* and *amateur,* many fans simply threw up their hands in confusion. In the early 1970s, tennis was a complicated spectator sport, marked by competing professional circuits, new player classifications, and a blurred division between professional and amateur status. Even seasoned sportswriters like Jim Murray struggled to keep it all straight. The confusion began with the advent of the open era in 1968. A number of factors precipitated the move toward open tournaments. By the mid- to late 1960s American tennis had reached a low point in terms of public interest and marketability. While Jack Kramer and Pancho Gonzalez toured the country with other professionals, American amateurs had not won the title at Forest Hills since 1954, which many viewed as a national embarrassment. The U.S. Davis Cup team had also suffered early-round losses to Spain, Brazil, and Ecuador between 1965 and 1967. Many argued that the sport needed a facelift. Sportswriters also were quick to point out how corrupt tennis had become. For years, so-called amateurs had received illegal payments under the table, leading purists to question the legitimacy of amateurism. Finally, proponents of open tennis argued that if amateurs and professionals competed at Wimbledon, Forest Hills, and other places, the sport would surely experience a revival that included lucrative television deals.[19]

Beginning in the early 1970s, public interest in tennis picked up. A youthful, misbehaving, and supremely talented Jimmy Connors became an American icon, eschewing traditional etiquette by cursing out referees and throwing his racquet in anger. Fans flocked to the grandstands to see what he might do next. Stan Smith and Ashe helped place American tennis back on the map, winning a number of tournaments and taking home gobs of prize money. Stars such as Chris Evert and Billie Jean King drew interest to the women's game with their dominating performances. Smith, for one, credited the infusion of money with the sport's rebirth. "The big purses," he observed, "made people watch who didn't know a lob from a volley, and suddenly a lot of people realized tennis was good for spectators, and good to play." From 1970 to 1973 television networks tripled their coverage of tennis. In 1975 CBS paid more for a match between Connors and John Newcombe than it did to televise a National Football League game.[20]

The open era also brought an end to the ILTF's monopolization of the sport, and Lamar Hunt helped to make this happen. Hunt was an astute businessman with an eye for a good investment who ventured into deals that appeared crazy to his friends and business associates. Tennis, he wisely predicted in the late 1960s, had the potential to grow. In 1970 the wealthy owner of the Kansas City Chiefs football team invested in World Championship Tennis, a circuit of professionals who would compete anywhere in the United States for the right price. Later that year an aging Jack Kramer formed the Grand Prix, a circuit under the auspices of the ILTF that awarded points for top tournament finishes, effectively linking these events together. Ashe, for instance, placed second in the 1970 Grand Prix, earning $17,000 in prizes for his impressive finish. In 1971 WCT announced the creation of its own Grand Prix, promising fans and players a "million dollar circuit." The ILTF and WCT were now at war, and the players, Ashe included, benefited financially from the competition. Player salaries increased exponentially as the ILTF's Grand Prix and WCT competed to sign the best and most exciting players.[21]

And Ashe stood at the center of this tennis war. The battle between the ILTF and WCT forced Ashe to make a difficult decision. He could accept Hunt's six-figure offer to join WCT and earn millions of dollars in salary and prizes. His contract, however, would require him to quit the Davis Cup team and travel with the professional circuit, severely restricting his much-valued independence. In fact it was because of his multiple endorsement contracts that he remained an independent professional. In the 1970s Ashe was the chief endorser of Head racquets. Unlike Don Budge and other former players who had their own racquet deals, Ashe worked as a consultant as well as a celebrity endorser, testing and evaluating several aluminum and fiberglass racquets before the final Arthur Ashe model went into production. And almost by happenstance, he became an endorser for Catalina, an athletic clothing line. He created a stir during the 1969 U.S. Open by wearing a yellow tennis shirt instead of a traditional white one. During warm-ups the director of the event ordered him to remove the Catalina shirt, citing USTA rules, which prohibited colorful attire on the court. After learning that Ashe had initially defied the USTA, the president of Catalina signed him to an endorsement deal. Head and Catalina, in addition to Philip Morris and Coca-Cola, kept him busy and wealthy. For a few store appearances and autograph sessions, his employers paid him a hefty sum. He could more than afford to reject Hunt's offer and retain his independent status.[22]

This autonomy allowed him to speak freely with the media. To sportswriters, journalists, and television reporters Ashe was a man who usually kept his promises, met frequently with the press, and answered questions with seemingly intelligent candor. Sportswriter D. D. Eisenberg believed that Ashe's travels to Europe, Vietnam, and other Third World nations had helped him grapple with complex issues like race, poverty, and social justice. An interview with Ashe was nothing like a session with Bobby Clarke or Dave "The Hammer" Schultz, two hockey stars of the 1970s who seemed more concerned with their false teeth than with any political or social topic. In his spare time Ashe poured through books on world affairs, race relations, and general philosophy, and he was always prepared for an interview. "He was a speed reader with a photographic memory who had a tremendously high IQ, and he just wasn't going to indulge in the screaming and shouting with all the ranting and raving," explained Donald Dell. Dell's description of Ashe was also a not-so-thinly veiled attack on black radicals such as Stokely Carmichael, Huey Newton, and Eldridge Cleaver, men whom the mainstream media portrayed as violent and angry—the screamers and shouters, so to speak. Ashe, according to Dell, although no less an activist, represented another path, one that relied on dialogue and negotiation. Ashe also knew how to work a reporter. He remembered the names of wives, husbands, and children, putting journalists at ease before an interview began. Ashe was also polite and well mannered, rarely offering snarky commentary. "It was hard to get mad at Arthur Ashe," noted his friend the *Sports Illustrated* columnist Frank Deford. Ashe did, however, express frustration with unprepared reporters. He knew the issues and believed they should as well.[23]

—◦) ◦‿—

While in Switzerland on business, the conservative columnist and founder of the *National Review* William F. Buckley encountered an angry Swiss man. The man had recently learned of Ashe's visa denial and demanded to know Buckley's opinion on the matter. "I do not make it a habit to defend South Africa," Buckley wrote, "and therefore told my friend to take his quite legitimate complaints elsewhere." This brief exchange with the Swiss man, though, made him wonder if South Africa had barred Ashe simply because of his race. Buckley suspected that it might be more complicated than that. His curiosity led him to contact an official at the South Africa Foundation and request paperwork explaining the government's justification for the visa denial. Shortly thereafter, he received a document that detailed the reasons for the government's decision. Ashe, it claimed, was a black militant, a man who actively supported South Africa's banishment from the 1968 Olympics and the 1970 Davis Cup. Further, his participation in the crusade against South African Airways proved his desire to economically cripple South Africa. Buckley then blasted the mainstream media for focusing too heavily on Ashe's race and too little on his incendiary actions. In Buckley's opinion, South Africa's position was much more nuanced than the mainstream media had let on.[24]

William F. Buckley attached meaning to Ashe's visa denial, using the controversy as a vehicle to criticize the mainstream media. It allowed him to reinforce his sustained argument that the mainstream press was an arm of the New Left, a radical movement, in his opinion, that exacerbated racial tensions. Like Buckley, Elliott Skinner had his own ax to grind. He used Ashe's visa denial to articulate his position on diplomatic procedure. Skinner was the former U.S. ambassador to Upper Volta, a semi-autonomous nation in West Africa loosely under the control of France. As a pragmatic administrator, he was particularly concerned with back-channel negotiations and quiet diplomacy. He was annoyed that Vorster's public campaign against Ashe had foiled the hard work of his colleagues in South Africa. In a letter to the *New York Times* Skinner argued, "South Africa shows its supreme contempt for the United States and the efforts of its agencies to secure a visa for an outstanding citizen, one who has gallantly served in this country's armed forces." U.S. government officials, he believed, had to "localize this cancerous growth" by issuing a strong statement in support of Ashe. Otherwise, he feared, nations around the world might defy the United States with greater regularity. Yet another participant in the public debate, tennis fan Linda Rosenberg, viewed Ashe's visa denial as a human rights issue. She assailed the tennis players who hid behind the notion that tennis was apolitical, contending that athletes had a moral obligation to rise above sports and defend a fellow player against bigotry and discrimination. "The main question," she wrote, "is quite simple and has nothing to do with sports. The question is: Is it important to support human rights?" Whether through an attack on the mainstream media, a defense of diplomatic procedure, or a call to confront human rights violations, each of these individuals appropriated Ashe's international dilemma to offer a personal commentary and satisfy his or her own political or social agenda.[25]

In addition to political columnists, diplomats, and ordinary tennis fans, the mainstream and black presses also appropriated Ashe. The mainstream media usually portrayed him as a model American citizen, a symbol for all that was right with the United States. He was patriotic, soft-spoken, highly intelligent, and polite. He was an innocent bystander caught in the middle of a political fight between warring factions in South Africa. Jim Murray viewed Ashe as an active agent, an athlete with the ability to directly affect change in South Africa. Ashe, and sports by extension, would force Vorster and his countrymen to shape up. Murray compared Ashe's fight with South Africa to Joe Louis's own symbolic bout some thirty years earlier. In 1938 the eyes of the world had been on Yankee Stadium as Louis faced Max Schmeling of Germany for boxing's heavyweight championship. To the press Louis represented capitalism, freedom, democracy, and the American Dream, while Schmeling was a symbol of Nazi Germany, Adolf Hitler, and totalitarianism. Many worried that a Schmeling victory would further legitimize Nazi Germany and Hitler's belief in Aryan supremacy. Yet Louis was determined not to let that happen. He was aggressive from the opening bell, pounding the German with strong blows to the side. The German was no match for America's Brown Bomber; he fell in the first round and never got up. The fight was over. Murray argued that Louis had done more than defeat Schmeling: he had reaffirmed the American way of life. "Landmark decisions of the Supreme Court, federal troop escorts, omnibus house bills could not have the crushing effect on white supremacists that the sight of Max Schmeling thudding to the floor did," he wrote. Louis had won round one, and Ashe would win round two. Like Louis's gloves in the lead-up to World War II, Ashe's "tennis racquet [was] afflicting apartheid half a world away."[26]

Unlike Jim Murray, Marion Jackson of the *Atlanta Daily World*, a black newspaper, focused on Ashe as an individual. Jackson remembered Ashe as a quiet and unassuming youth when he covered the Richmond phenom on the ATA circuit in the 1950s. Jackson argued that Ashe had plans to topple South Africa, but his victory would occur on center court at Ellis Park and resonate in the slums of Soweto. He was simply a competitive tennis player who wanted to demonstrate his superiority between the lines, not destabilize Vorster, Parliament, or any other South African official. Unlike Murray, Jackson avoided a comparison to Joe Louis, Jack Johnson, Jesse Owens, or any other racial trailblazer, preferring to discuss Ashe in the context of this particular case.[27]

Not everyone praised Ashe or took pity on him. The *Chicago Daily Defender* insisted that Ashe had been too quiet and calculating, sounding more like a prim and proper tennis snob than a black activist. The paper's criticism derived principally from Ashe's testimony before the U.N. Apartheid Committee, an eleven-member panel investigating South Africa for human rights violations. On April 14, 1970, he urged the United Nations to exert "pressure from the top" on the ILTF and other world tennis bodies in an effort to remove South Africa from international tennis. "If we isolate South Africa completely—athletically, legally, culturally, physically—will they change?" Ashe asked. "Maybe they will say the world really hates us. Maybe they will change." The editors of the *Defender* did not object to Ashe's message. In editorial after editorial they too argued for South Africa's complete isolation from the world community. Their critique of Ashe, then, centered on his public-relations strategy. The *Defender* believed that Ashe had not made his case frequently enough. One writer complained, "It is too bad that Capt. Arthur Ashe . . . did not avail himself of the previous occasions he had to denounce South Africa's insufferable racial policy. Instead, he waited until he received an invitation to testify before [a] United Nations committee considering the effects of South Africa's policy of apartheid, to call for the expulsion of the African country from the International Lawn Tennis Federation." The *Defender* argued that Ashe was selecting his speaking opportunities too carefully and passing on other opportunities to demand change in South Africa.[28]

For the remainder of 1970 three topics dominated the coverage of Ashe and South Africa: South Africa's formal exclusion from the Davis Cup in March, the continued harassment of Gary Player in print and on the golf course, and Ashe's symbolic role in South Africa's parliamentary elections. On March 23 seven committee members representing thirty-four nations met in London to discuss South Africa's participation in the 1970 Davis Cup competition. During the closed-door meeting, several delegates argued that South Africa's participation in the tournament would prompt other nations to withdraw in protest. In fact, angry protesters had hurled flour bombs at South African players in the middle of a match with Great Britain the previous year. Emerging from the session, representatives from the committee claimed that they were left with little choice. If the South African team was allowed to compete, demonstrations, boycotts, and defaults would almost certainly plague the Davis Cup, transforming one of the world's most prestigious events into a circus. Convinced that trouble lay ahead, the committee acted to appease member nations and preserve the sanctity of the cup, not to make an ethical or a moral statement about apartheid. "It was felt that South African participation would endanger the carrying out of the competition," explained the committee's chairman, Robert B. Colwell of the United States. He pointed out that South Africa had ignored repeated warnings from the ILTF and the Davis Cup Committee that it should allow the inclusion of nonwhites in its local tournaments and integrate its teams. Curiously, Colwell insisted that Ashe's visa denial played a minimal role in the committee's decision. He told the press, "We are not indulging in politics, but with the reality of the situation which jeopardizes the Davis Cup." Colwell's explanation was peculiar given that Ashe's rejection was the primary reason for the committee's special session. In all likelihood, had there been no Arthur Ashe, South Africa would have remained in the competition. The committee's official response was a way to maintain an apolitical facade while rendering an overtly political decision.[29]

Ashe and Donald Dell expressed mixed feelings about the committee's decision. In an interview with the *New York Times*, Dell confessed that Ashe had applied for a visa to trap Vorster, forcing the prime minister to either accept him as an individual or face expulsion from the Davis Cup and the ILTF. Ashe preferred to compete in the South African Open, Dell claimed, rather than have world tennis bodies bar his South African friends from tournaments. Ideally, Ashe would win the Open as thousands of white spectators looked on from the grandstands of Ellis Park, an ultimate affront to Vorster and his countrymen. "Personally," Ashe said, "I feel that I have gained an empty victory from which I will get about five minutes' emotional satisfaction." His goal was to reform South Africa, not isolate its sports teams. Dell's comments in particular suggest that Ashe sought more than a spot in the Open. Despite earlier interviews in which Ashe had said that his sole desire was to play tennis in South Africa, he now revealed an ulterior motive for his visa application. He knew that Vorster would deny his request once more, which would likely lead to South Africa's expulsion from the Davis Cup. Ashe knew that he had no chance to compete in

South Africa, but he applied anyway. His carefully considered action was decidedly political.[30]

Three days after the committee's announcement, Red Smith of the *Washington Post* criticized Colwell for confusing politics with human rights. In his view, Vorster had refused Ashe's visa request solely because of his race, not based on the tennis star's inflammatory statements to the press. Colwell's explanation of the committee's decision was misleading, Smith contended, saying that Colwell had ignored facts that were well known to the general public. Most Americans understood that Ashe alone had "forced the issue in front of" the committee, prompting members to place the topic on the meeting's agenda. Smith surmised that Colwell might have adopted this public-relations strategy from his counterparts in the IOC. Like the Davis Cup Committee, IOC officials had cited the potential for boycotts, forfeitures, political demonstrations, and violence in announcing their decision to bar South Africa from the 1968 Olympic Games. Although both the Olympic and Davis Cup charters expressly prohibited racial discrimination, both organizations focused on "breaches of decorum" in rendering their verdicts. "In other words," Smith explained, "the Afrikaners weren't booted out because their statutory bigotry was more than the tennis fathers could stomach. They got the brush because letting them in might invite a display of bad manners whenever they tried to play." Smith concluded that Colwell and his colleagues were "poor spokesmen for the game," always willing to bend the truth to preserve the "purity" of tennis.[31]

Although Ashe publicly supported the movement to drive South Africa from the Davis Cup, he sent mixed messages on the protests directed at Gary Player. Following South Africa's expulsion from the 1968 Olympic Games, Player became the target of antiapartheid demonstrators, who were angry that the star golfer made thousands of dollars in America, while racial and ethnic minorities could not compete in South Africa. In August 1969 a group of black men, described as civil rights workers by one paper, antipoverty protesters by another, and antiapartheid activists by a third, physically assaulted Player during a tournament in the United States. Three months later, protesters scaled a fence in New Zealand attempting to disrupt the South African's play. A local policeman wrestled one of the men to the ground, injuring himself in the process. After the round, Player tried to assure the press and the antiapartheid activists by declaring, "I'm not a racist, I love everybody." This statement echoed his earlier comments. Despite the constant threat of physical violence, Player initially refused to criticize Vorster or apartheid in general. He often avoided political questions, telling reporters that he would not pass judgment on his country while on foreign soil. His consistent refrain was that he wished "there were some way in which people all over the world could persuade politicians and protesters that sports should be above politics."[32]

Ashe objected to Player's tepid approach, arguing that Player was naive if he thought he could dismiss the apartheid debate. Ashe wanted Player to take a stand, any stand, even if his position was to defend the government. Ashe believed that the press had an obligation to ask tough political questions, forcing athletes to offer opinions. Initially, he favored political demonstrations against Player, writing, "I believe Gary Player and other South Africans should be queried on their position toward apartheid. If they publicly renounce apartheid, they can play. If they support apartheid, then I would say the public can harass the hell out of them." In March 1970 Ashe told reporters that Player's life might be in danger if he tried to play golf in the United States. He also offered a solution for the embattled golfer. "All that Player has to do to avoid trouble," Ashe advised, "is to say he is against apartheid. If Player does not come out against apartheid I think something is going to happen to him." Ashe later amended his comments and explained that he was not condoning physical violence. He was, however, expressing his dissatisfaction with Player's relative silence. "Anyone," he contended, "who says sport and politics do not mix is silly and vicious. They can no longer be kept apart."[33]

As a whole, black activists, athletes, reporters, politicians, and columnists were highly critical of Player's take on sports and apartheid. To combat the negative publicity, in early March 1970 Player announced his intention to host an exhibition golf match that would benefit the United Negro College Fund. He invited Lee Elder and Charlie Sifford, two of America's most prominent and talented black golfers, to play alongside him. Player hoped that this unsolicited gesture would help distance him from his own government, proving once and for all that he was no racist. Some black athletes did not view his move in those terms. Ashe accused Player of attempting to buy off his critics with a tokenist measure. Sifford suggested that Player invite him and Elder to the Masters, a Grand Slam event that remained off limits to racial minorities. According to the *Defender*, most black militants saw "no neutral ground"; if Player was not against apartheid, then he was the enemy.[34]

In June Player finally relented and offered his views on apartheid. Clearly agitated and fed up with the persistent questioning, he lashed out at American hypocrites and contended that blacks in South Africa lived better and happier lives than African Americans in the United States. "I think we have a greater love for and understanding of the non-white people in [South Africa] than they have in America for their Negroes," he remarked. Further, he saw inner-city riots and widespread campus disruptions as proof that the racial situation in America was much worse than that in South Africa. Brad Pye Jr., the sports editor of the *Los Angeles Sentinel*, fired back. "The worst hell hole in Mississippi," he wrote, "would seem like paradise compared to the conditions under which the most affluent blacks in South Africa are forced to live." In South Africa the Afrikaner government had passed a law prohibiting blacks from working as telephone operators, countermen, or receptionists, jobs that were open to African Americans. If you wanted to become a dog catcher, then South Africa was the right place to live. Otherwise the choice was clear. Pye concluded that the United States should revoke Player's visa because of his false and malicious statements directed at Americans.[35]

The contemplative Sam Lacy offered a much more nuanced take on Player. On the one hand, he applauded the golfer for defending Papwa Sewgolum's right to compete in South Africa. "I have said in the past," Player had told the press, "that Papwa should be allowed to play in the South African Open and I still firmly believe that." Player had taken direct aim at the government, complaining to reporters that South African officials were "slowly putting our head in the noose for world sport." Despite these comments, Lacy wondered why it had taken Player almost ten years to criticize his countrymen. Lacy concluded that Player was protecting his own self-interest, fearing reprisals from black activists, American politicians, and fellow golfers if he did not back Sewgolum. Player tried to avoid embarrassing Professional Golf Association (PGA) officials and members, who would have to contend with the antiapartheid demonstrations. He had made thousands of dollars by winning American tournaments and wanted to keep the prize money flowing. "So," Lacy guessed, "Gary became magnanimous."[36]

Mainstream American and British newspapers adopted a softer position on Player. Peter Dobereiner of the *Observer* defended Player's right to ignore political activists and argued that Player's views were "immaterial" to the apartheid debate. Dobereiner's column was a direct response to letters sent by members of the Stop the Seventy Tour Committee, an organization that opposed the tour of a South African cricket team in Great Britain. The committee mailed correspondence to Player, Eric Brown, and Dai Rees—all South African golfers—demanding their stance on apartheid. Chairman Peter Hain subtly threatened the men with political demonstrations if they did not give the "right" answer. In his column, Dobereiner likened Hain to former Republican senator and communist witch hunter Joseph McCarthy, suggesting that Hain's crusade against South African golfers was no different than McCarthy's plot to destroy the reputations of innocent State Department and U.S. Army employees in the early 1950s.[37]

Although less of an apologist than Dobereiner, Alistair Cooke of the *Guardian* praised Player's recent philosophical transformation. His popular refrain that sports and politics did not mix had given way to a more humanistic argument, namely, that Ashe and Sewgolum, among others, were talented men of high moral standing who deserved a chance to compete in South Africa. Cooke reminded his readers that Player's change of heart was particularly bold given that the "cast of characters" in professional golf was "still overwhelmingly white and gentile." By speaking in support of Ashe and others, however tepidly, Player had defied his race, his class, and his sport. The *Chicago Tribune*'s John Husar agreed, defending Player's plans for a match benefiting the United Negro College Fund. "Who can blame him," Husar asked, "particularly when he has criticized his country's position?"[38]

Within South Africa, the Davis Cup ban and Gary Player's troubles were secondary concerns for Vorster and his ruling Nationalist Party. In the spring of 1970 the Nationalists faced serious opposition from the right-wing Herstigte Nasionale Party. Led by former Nationalist cabinet member Dr. Albert Hertzog, the Herstigtes, or Reconstituted Nationalists, believed that Vorster's policies threatened apartheid and diluted Afrikaner culture. Vorster, for instance, had increased trade with African nations, promised to field an integrated team at the 1968 Olympics, and agreed to the tour of a New Zealand rugby club, a squad that would include several Maoris. In response to the Herstigte backlash, the prime minister cited his bold handling of Ashe's visa request as evidence that he was a hardliner, a leader committed to the rigid enforcement and expansion of apartheid. Vorster declared at a campaign rally, "We are building a nation for whites only. We have a right to our own identity." He promised that if reelected, he would keep whites and nonwhites separate.[39]

Vorster also encountered opposition from his left in the form of the "more educated, sophisticated and affluent" verligtes, which translates as "the Enlightened Ones." The verligtes were pragmatic internationalists who adhered to the concept of separate but equal. They supported the establishment of black and colored homelands, yet insisted that these Bantustans, as they were called, would eventually become autonomous districts under the rule of local black and colored leaders. The problem with the verligtes, explained Stanley Meisler of the *Los Angeles Times*, was their passive approach and their acceptance of tokenist measures such as the government's entertainment of African American diplomats, which was more cosmetic than substantive. Vorster's primary challenge, then, came from Hertzog. At Nationalist Party rallies, Hertzog's backers infiltrated the friendly crowds, hurling rotten eggs and spoiled fruit at Nationalist speakers. The right-wing *Die Afrikaner*, mouthpiece of the Herstigtes, published a parody of one of Vorster's campaign letters that included the prime minister's copied signature. The South African High Court ruled that the newspaper had defamed Vorster and ordered the press to cease distribution of the issue.[40]

On April 22, white South Africans went to the polls and delivered a landslide victory for the Nationalists. Vorster's party retained 117 of the 119 seats it had held in the old parliament, and the Herstigtes finished with a mere fifty thousand votes. The results, noted the *Rand Daily Mail*, represented "a trend towards moderation." The *Observer*'s Anthony Sampson viewed the returns as a sign that South Africa was ready "to come to terms with the world." He credited sports, in particular, for Hertzog's defeat. "The sports boycott," Sampson argued, "has a significance well beyond the game itself; for sport is a kind of metaphor for broader politics, and if the fallacies are revealed on the sports ground, they will reverberate in the fields of diplomacy and trade." Sampson did not specifically mention how Vorster had used Ashe to present himself as a hardliner. But by personally rejecting Ashe's visa application, the prime minister had turned away a dangerous black militant, a rabble-rouser intent on destroying apartheid and fomenting unrest among nonwhites. In speeches and public statements, Vorster had made Ashe a centerpiece of his reelection campaign, which allowed him to sidestep some of his more moderate concessions.[41]

─౿ Ꭶ─

Stan Smith was frustrated and felt unappreciated. A member of the U.S. Davis Cup team and one of America's top-ranked players, he had won the 1968 U.S. Open doubles championship with Bob Lutz and had led the 1970 Davis Cup team to a victory over West Germany. He had finished 1969 and 1970 ranked *ahead* of his friend and teammate Arthur Ashe. Yet in Africa nobody cared about Smith. It was Ashe who was the talk of the town. During a 1970 tour of Africa sponsored by the U.S. State Department, a Zambian reporter interviewed Ashe for ten minutes, asking him questions about tennis, politics, human rights, and poverty in Africa. The reporter then turned to Smith with a single inquiry, "Mr. Smith, how do you like our country?" "It's fine," replied the ticked-off Smith. Once the interviews had concluded, Smith, Ashe, and Frank Deford sat down for a bit of relaxation. Smith used the break to let off some steam. "Jesus Christ, Arthur," he complained, "I mean, you're like God here, and they don't even recognize that I'm here." Deford, listening closely, had had enough of Smith's whining. "You don't get it, Stan, do you?," he interjected. "Have you looked around at the people? You know, they're kind of a different color. . . . You are the *opponent*. Joe Louis used to have a Bum of the Month Club, and that's who you are." Ashe tried to console his upset friend, promising Smith that if the two men ever toured the American South, Smith could play the role of the Great White Hope.[42]

In the summer of 1970, Ashe, Smith, and Deford, along with reporters Bud Collins and Richard Evans, participated in a State Department goodwill tour of Kenya, Tanzania, Uganda, Zambia, Nigeria, and Ghana. Ashe and Smith played a series of exhibition matches for local Africans, met with reporters, and tried some of the local cuisine. Ashe quickly learned that he was a symbol of America— good and bad. He represented not only racial progress and the antiapartheid movement but also American greed and Western colonialism. To some he was just another wealthy African American, spending money in East Africa on expensive food, the finest hotels, and vacation attractions. "The African people look upon American Blacks as outsiders," he told Howie Evans of *Black Sports*. "It's easy for American Blacks to lay back in their easy chairs and say what their Black brothers should do in Africa." During his trip, Ashe became a source of information and news for native Africans. At the University of Dar es Salaam in Tanzania, black students demanded reports from America, including news about Vietnam, Martin Luther King Jr., the civil rights and Black Power movements, and the situation of blacks in urban America. One student wanted to know what he and other black athletes were doing to aid the black cause. "As an American," Ashe wrote in a memoir, "I was blamed for the ills of Africa. Never mind that the United States never had colonies there: we were the whipping boy."[43]

Africa in the 1970s was a continent in transition, marred by bloody coups, political factionalism, and ethnic strife. Many of Africa's leaders were under house arrest, in jail, or dead, the victims of political assassinations. Corrupt dictators like Idi Amin of Uganda used violence to keep their opponents in line, ordering executions without trial. Africa was not the black paradise that Marcus Garvey had advertised in the 1920s. Ashe left Africa more confused than ever. Even though Muhammad Ali had had a similar experience in the early 1960s, Ashe was unprepared for the anti-American sentiment across the continent. He also worried about Africa's political system, wherein one-party rule often quashed healthy dissent.[44]

Ashe did not return home to a quiet and stable tennis circuit. Instead, he came face to face with the women's liberation movement. Beginning in the mid-1960s, many women activists who had participated in various protest movements left liberal organizations such as Students for a Democratic Society and SNCC, citing institutional gender bias in these male-dominated groups as the reason for their departure. Despite differing strategies and goals, the newly formed women's organizations, such as the National Organization for Women (NOW), all advocated female self-empowerment, consciousness-raising, and an end to gender discrimination in the workplace. In the early 1970s, Billie Jean King became the voice of the women's liberation movement on the professional tennis circuit. Born Billie Jean Moffitt on November 22, 1943, King was an outspoken and fierce competitor, dominating opponents with an unmatched serve-and-volley game. The winner of twenty Wimbledon singles and doubles championships, a record until 2003, she became the first woman tennis player to earn more than $100,000 in a single year. King was a clutch performer who elevated her game in big matches. On the court and off, she always rose to the occasion.[45]

In September 1970 King and other women threatened to boycott upcoming tournaments unless officials evened the disparity between men's and women's prize money. The Pacific Southwest Championships, for example, offered $12,500 to the male winner and a mere $1,500 to the top female finisher. At the U.S. Open, a man who lost in the first round walked away with $300, double the amount given to a woman who exited on the same day. At a meeting of the Lawn Tennis Writers Association in Forest Hills, New York, representatives of women's tennis demanded that officials close the gap between men's and women's prize money, feature an equal number of men's and women's matches on center court, and force the media to devote more time and page space to women's tennis. "It's discrimination," remarked Rosemary Casals. "We expend the same amount of energy. . . . We practice as much, we play just as hard. We contribute our share to the success of the tournament."[46]

The U.S. and foreign newspapers often portrayed Ashe as a defender of human rights and equality. Yet when he had the chance to support his female colleagues in their fight for fair wages, he chose to stand in the doorway. To a *Time* magazine reporter, he said that women like King and Evert needed to play alongside men, who were the real tennis stars. The women's game, he concluded, could not survive on its own. "Men," he noted, "are doing this [playing tennis] for a living now. They have families, and they don't want to give up money just for girls to play." In other words, because men were the primary breadwinners, women athletes should defer to them and not demand better pay. Lastly, Ashe explained that tennis fans bought tickets to see the men, not the women. In his opinion, the women's game was slower, uneventful, and boring. "Only three or four women draw fans to a tourney, anyhow, so why do we have to split our money with them?" he asked. For a man who consistently championed notions of fairness and equality, these were shocking statements. A close reading of his memoirs and diary, however, reveals a man who held traditional views on the role of women inside and outside the home. Undoubtedly, his mother's untimely death and his subsequent reliance on male mentors (his father, Ronald Charity, Dr. Johnson, and J. D. Morgan) had led him to see men as natural-born leaders and thinkers. He had never had a strong female role model in his life. In tennis, he had idolized Pancho Gonzalez, not Althea Gibson. "I guess a boy needs 'man heroes,'" he told the *New York Times* in 1966. "Althea didn't set alight any fire inside me." In his diary, Ashe struggled to clarify his position on women, writing, "Women's Lib has been very trying. People should understand that most men had no preparation for it. I grew up with a father as the head of the house. I don't know if, all of a sudden, I could psychologically handle a fifty-fifty split in my house. . . . I do want to be up-to-date and fair and all that, but the truth is that I also don't want any woman telling me what to do with my life (and vice versa too)." Ashe changed his view in the 1980s, crediting his wife Jeanne for altering his perspective. In the early 1970s, though, Ashe was clearly at odds with King and other women on the tour. A confrontation was looming.[47]

—☙ ❧—

Nineteen seventy ended on a positive note for a worn-out Ashe. In October the president of the Doral Hotel and Country Club announced that Ashe had agreed to become the tennis director at the resort, an envied position that included a free suite, unlimited golf, and complete access to the club. In exchange for a few tennis lessons offered to wealthy patrons, he traded the cold New York winters for the sunny beaches of Miami. To Howie Evans of the *New York Amsterdam News*, the appointment of a black man at a wealthy white country club was evidence that white society had fully accepted Arthur Ashe. In a speech at the Doral Hotel, Ashe explained the irony of his new job. "It's rather novel becoming associated with a southern organization in this capacity," he noted, "when I can't even play at the country club in my hometown of Gum Spring, Virginia."[48]

# CHAPTER 6

# Defeat and Victory in South Africa

In late November 1973 Ashe was a long way from the beaches of Miami and the tennis courts of the Doral Country Club. And he was mentally and physically exhausted. He had just spent thirteen days in South Africa competing in the South African Open, touring the slums of Soweto, debating professors and students at Stellenbosch University on the merits of racial integration, and meeting with local reporters, black leaders, and government officials. His historic trip had been an overwhelming success, argued the *Cape Herald*. "He was not the fire-spitting revolutionary some people expected," a local writer declared. "On and off the court his courtesy and sportsmanship won the respect and friendship of people from the dusty streets of Soweto to the rich White homes of Rondebosch." Antiapartheid activist and former political prisoner Dennis Brutus disagreed. In his view, Ashe's visit had done more to legitimize apartheid than to dismantle it. In the past two weeks Ashe had posed for photographs with a Nationalist cabinet member, boarded with a wealthy white family, signed autographs for white South African children, and attended formal dinner parties. Not once had he publicly criticized apartheid. As Ashe stepped onto the plane heading back to the United States, the meaning and significance of his trip was already a contested topic.[1]

Two black South Africans, one a poet, the other the wife of a prominent political prisoner, drew little ambiguity from the tennis star's stay. Ashe had inspired the youths of Soweto and forced the government to integrate the grandstands at Ellis Park. Neither the poet nor the woman could relay their messages to Ashe in person, however. Instead they relied on Carole Dell, a member of Ashe's delegation, to smuggle their handwritten notes to the American tennis player. Enclosed in a folded-up newspaper was a poem by the banned writer Don Mattera titled "An Anguished Spirit: Ashe." Behind it was the photograph of a woman with an inscription thanking Ashe for his visit to South Africa. She urged him to assist in empowering black and colored South Africans and advised him that the "best thing you can do is ask the South Africans what you can do to help in their struggle." The author was Winnie Mandela.[2]

On October 31, 1973, following months of back-channel negotiations between U.S. and South African officials, Ashe finally received his visa. Some argued that the boycotts, protests, and athletic bans had worked. The South Africans had agreed to hold some form of integrated athletic trials, invited an American baseball team with black players to compete in their nation, and approved the visa request of Evonne Goolagong, a black Australian tennis player who belonged to the Wiradjuri aborigine tribe. While antiapartheid activists cried tokenism, the ILTF viewed the racial concessions as sincere progress, voting in 1972 to readmit South Africa to the Davis Cup competitions. Those who disagreed on everything else, however, agreed that Ashe had served as the catalyst for most of these developments. *He* was the one who had forced South Africa from the Davis Cup, publicly supported the boycotts, protests, and bans, and backed South Africa's isolation from world sports. Only when *he* had signed a professional tennis contract that rendered him ineligible to play in the Davis Cup had the ILTF revoked South Africa's ban. His words and actions between 1969 and 1973 had resulted in tangible action. By the summer of 1973 Prime Minister Vorster and the Afrikaners were back at the bargaining table, ready to discuss Ashe's visa status once more.

A close examination of the public and private discourse relating to Ashe's visa status between 1971 and 1973, his trip to South Africa in 1973, and the role of activists, State Department officials, officers of international sports organizations, reporters in both nations, and South African politicians reveals the symbolic and material participation of athletes in the policymaking process. Ashe's dogged persistence and determination drove policymakers on both sides of the Atlantic to consider new racial policies. Once Ashe entered South Africa, the American mainstream and black presses, the international press, and the South African press each appropriated his image to reinforce their preconceived views of race, nationalism, and apartheid. His travels across South Africa also exposed a division in the worldwide black freedom movement along the lines of philosophy and strategy; specifically, black leaders fiercely debated the value of engaging in talks with white South African officials.

—◦ ◦—

In January 1971 South Africa finally granted a visa to one of the world's best black tennis players. "I am only interested in playing tennis," the athlete announced. "I am not looking for any trouble. . . . It is a little bit frightening but I hope South Africans like me." The government promised to treat the tennis star as a first-class citizen, offering a visit free of racism and discrimination. The athlete in question, however, was not Arthur Ashe. The invitation instead went to Evonne Goolagong, a nineteen-year-old Australian aborigine. A *New York Times* reporter described her as "an uncomplicated, innocent, very happy girl who is still unaware that problems of race and politics do intrude into sport." Like Ashe, she grew up under a cloud of racism and relied on mentors to help her navigate the racial landscape. One of her coaches was Vic Edwards, a burly six-foot-one former army major who protected and sheltered the young phenom. Before a press conference, Edwards often announced that Goolagong would take no questions on race. Whereas Ashe eventually empowered himself to make his own decisions, Edwards spoke for Goolagong and kept the focus squarely on tennis. Despite Edwards's attempts to control the public discourse, Goolagong did understand her role as a racial pioneer and symbol. In fact, her comments on race mirrored Ashe's own statements made ten years earlier. She complained, "I'd much rather people knew me as a good tennis player than as an aboriginal who happens to play good tennis. Of course I'm proud of my race, but I don't want to be thinking about it all the time."[3]

By inviting Goolagong and not Ashe, South African officials believed they had invited a naive competitor who would not dare speak out against apartheid or challenge the racial status quo. Goolagong's visit would also back the government's claim that South Africa did not object to the presence of black athletes but instead opposed any sportsman, black or white, who was a political agitator. In their estimation, Ashe fit that category. The Nationalists could easily control Goolagong's itinerary, keeping her away from Soweto and black activists. Some political experts viewed the move as an ideological shift to the center following the Nationalists' victory in the 1970 parliamentary elections. If they had any hope of making things right with world sports bodies, South Africa had to show racial progress. A visit from Goolagong was more likely to make that happen than a visit from Ashe.[4]

Ashe's visa rejections in 1969 and 1970 showed that he was unlikely to bully his way into South Africa. In every confrontation with the Afrikaners up to 1971, the louder and more aggressive he became, the more determined the South African government was to keep him out. If he wanted to compete in South Africa, he had to alter his strategy. In February 1971 Ashe traded the press conferences and pointed public statements for back-channel diplomacy. He re-iterated his earlier claim that he sought entry into South Africa to play tennis, not to inflame political tensions. He explained, "If secrecy can get me in, I will concede that—the first time. I don't want them to think I'm trying to embar-rass them. I'm trying to play tennis, period." The *Los Angeles Sentinel* suggested that Ashe had a large financial stake in playing in South Africa, which could bring him $10,000 a match. In addition to professional tournaments such as the Tennis Champions Classic, the South African Open promised the winner be-tween $6,000 and $8,000. In the past ten years, the South African circuit had become lucrative, drawing the world's best players with the allure of cash prizes. Although Ashe insisted that money was not his primary reason for want-ing into South Africa, he conceded that the large purses enticed him.[5]

Ashe's attempt to keep his visa negotiations a secret proved impossible, and on February 11, mainstream U.S. and British newspapers reported that the American had filled out another application to play in the South African Open. Faced with irrefutable evidence, Ashe confirmed the details of the story. He would not, however, explain why he chose to apply again after the two previous rejections. "You weigh everything," he told the *New York Times*. "The less I say about it until I get an answer, the better." Reporters speculated that Ashe viewed Goolagong's visa as more than tokenism; perhaps it represented the hope of racial progress, a sign that the government would soon welcome him as well. The press also cited leaks from officials in the Nixon administration indicating that the secretary of state had quietly increased the pressure on Vorster. The *Chicago Defender* reported that Secretary Rogers had not ruled out a personal meeting between him and South African officials, attesting to the significance of Ashe's visa status for both nations. David Gray of the *Guardian* doubted that Ashe would get in. Experts in Great Britain agreed that Goolagong's visa was a political concession designed to improve relations between South African and Australian rugby teams and officials. It did not represent South Africa's inten-tion to integrate tennis. Gray predicted that Ashe's permission to play in South Africa would be preceded by the visit of another black player, such as Richard Russell or Lance Lumsden, both Jamaican athletes with little star power and no connection to the antiapartheid movement. The government would reject Ashe for a third time based on his politics and not his race.[6]

Gray was correct. On February 24 Minister of the Interior Theo Gerdener emerged from a cabinet meeting and announced that after careful consider-ation the government had denied Ashe's third visa request. Gerdener's official statement was brief and vague, noting that the cabinet had refused Ashe's visa because "he is still persona non grata." A number of confidential sources with ties to the government expressed less ambiguity. Ashe himself, they claimed, had sabotaged his visa application during a visit to Zambia in October, when he had expressed his solidarity with black liberation movements. He had also criticized South Africa on a number of occasions during his State Department tour of Africa. One source "quot[ed] chapter and verse" from Ashe, including comments he had made about dropping a bomb on Johannesburg. The sources confirmed Gray's suspicion that Goolagong's invitation was simply a political concession. South African officials believed Goolagong's visit was a precursor to South Africa's rejoining the Davis Cup. Immediately following the decision, Ashe released a statement in which he expressed "pity" for the South Africans. "Maybe it's over for me," he said, "but to South Africa, I say, there will be more after me and more after them."[7]

In the opinion of a *Washington Post* columnist, the United States shared the blame for Ashe's predicament. Even after the Sharpeville massacre of 1960, the American business community had ignored human rights violations and expanded the lucrative diamond trade with South Africa. Investors had poured money into South Africa, arguing that the United States could not abandon its Cold War ally. William Raspberry of the *Post* compared this relationship to that of a family who lived across the street from neighbors "of uncertain morals." Some would contend that the "upstanding" family had a duty to engage the immoral one in an attempt to pass on to them proper values and behaviors. "But," he countered, "when it turns out that the folk across the street are running a whorehouse, you're smart to cut them loose. Your continued association is less likely to improve their reputation than to ruin yours." Raspberry advocated strong economic sanctions against South Africa directed at the gold and diamond industries, severing some ties with South African diplomats, and barring athletes like Gary Player from competing in the United States. He called on the African American community to support the antiapartheid movement, scolding fellow blacks for their "detachment" from South Africa's sixteen million nonwhites. America had turned a blind eye to apartheid, and so it remained complicit in Ashe's visa rejection.[8]

Although the Nixon administration publicly supported Ashe, the United States continued to trade with South Africa. This steady exchange of diamonds, gold, cobalt, and uranium for U.S. dollars trumped Ashe's visa application specifically and civil and human rights more generally. Policymakers argued that America needed a capitalist ally in Africa, a strong nation that would quash communist dissenters. The Cold War demanded that America keep the money flowing and ignore South Africa's domestic agenda. Ashe understood Cold War politics better than some politicians, yet he could not hide his disappointment with the American and South African governments. He pledged a renewed fight, both public and private, that would target policymakers and public officials in both nations. "I imagine," he said, "a larger struggle for me is just beginning, for it is only because I am non-white and I told the truth that I was denied a visa." He would not reapply for admission until 1973, by which time much had changed.[9]

_ℭ℥_

In the late 1960s Ashe and two Romanian tennis friends, Ion Tiriac and Ilie Nastase, hit downtown Paris for a night of drinking and fun. Nastase would soon become one of the world's top five players, but on this night he remained a promising talent. After they patronized several bars and nightclubs, the antics began. Ever the daredevil, Tiriac broke a number of crystal glasses with his teeth, and Nastase vomited in his date's lap. It did not matter that Nastase had an important match the following day. The men stayed out until four in the morning without considering the consequences. Those were the good old days, a time before large monetary prizes, professional contracts, and television deals. "But nobody stays up till four anymore drinking before a big match," Ashe lamented in 1973, "because it's not a big match anymore—it's big money." He envisioned future tennis stars spending twelve hours a day on the practice court and all night in bed. Twenty years later tennis historian E. Digby Baltzell sadly concluded, "Today's well-behaved automatons, in the third pro generation, have apparently had little education or fun in the process of their being programmed, almost from their cradles, to make money out of tennis." For better or worse, tennis had become commercial.[10]

From 1971 to 1973 WCT and the ILTF clashed over player contracts, television deals, and the rights of players to compete in open tournaments. Financially, the feud benefited most players. In 1971, for instance, thirty-four men under contract with WCT competed in twenty tournaments in nine countries, collectively earning more than $1 million. The following year, prizes totaled $5 million, and Ashe himself took in more than $100,000. In 1971 most of the world's top players skipped the French Open in favor of less prestigious tournaments that promised larger purses. Some sportswriters and tennis officials argued that money and commercialization threatened to destroy the sport. "When two elephants fight," Donald Dell remarked, "only the grass gets hurt." A *Los Angeles Times* columnist mused, "The game is at love-40. Rival promoters are frantically trying to fight off match point while they fight off each other. The autopsy will reveal an overdose of incompatibility, death by 'double fault.'" The disagreements between WCT and the ILTF were vast and seemingly irreconcilable. Lamar Hunt insisted that his WCT players receive $20,000 in expenses for each open tournament, a figure that the ILTF could not guarantee, according to organizer Jack Kramer. Kramer accused Hunt of monopolizing tennis by outbidding the ILTF for a player's services. The game, he said, was in big trouble if players skipped Wimbledon and the U.S. Open because of prizes, contracts, or scheduling conflicts.[11]

Despite their differences, Hunt and ILTF officials worked hard to reach an agreement that benefited both sides. These public and private negotiations were based on the notion that competing circuits damaged the sport as a whole. Under the current format, most tournaments, whether WCT or ILTF events, featured some but not all of the world's top players. ILTF amateurs and independent professionals did not compete in WCT events, and WCT contract pros skipped major open tournaments because of scheduling conflicts or contract obligations. The best players in the world were rarely together for an event, a scenario that created confusion among fans. Another potential roadblock to an accord involved television contracts. If CBS and NBC were to sign a deal with WCT, the networks needed Hunt's assurance that none of his players would withdraw from televised events. The absence from a tournament of Ashe, Rod Laver, or Ken Rosewall, for example, would have a negative impact on television ratings. "Lamar has to know who he has so he can tell NBC and CBS," Ashe explained. "Otherwise NBC and CBS will tell him to go fly a kite." Hunt had good reason to favor the networks' desires over a potential agreement with the ILTF. In May 1972, 21.3 million viewers tuned in to watch Laver defeat Rosewall in the WCT Finals, greater than the number who watched the NBA or Stanley Cup playoffs.[12]

In September 1972, after years of haggling, Hunt and the ILTF struck a deal. Negotiators on both sides agreed to split the year into two segments: from mid-January to mid-May, WCT would promote twenty-two tournaments with a prize cap of $50,000 per event; the ILTF, in turn, would control the remaining eight months of the year and allow WCT pros to compete in its open tournaments. In the end, each side offered concessions. The ILTF gave up its rights to the spring season, ceding the most profitable television dates to Hunt. Without competition from the NFL, whose season lasted from September through late January, Hunt's rivals were the NBA and the NHL, two leagues he had already topped in the television ratings. Conversely, Hunt freed his contract pros to participate in ILTF-sanctioned events, ensuring that the best players in the world faced one another on a regular basis. But just as WCT and the ILTF agreed to a détente, a new organization threatened to disrupt the peace. Tennis players were set to unionize, with Ashe leading the charge.[13]

While many top players basked in the allure of big paydays, Ashe worried about his independence in a sport dominated by two warring giants. In his view, tennis players had no more freedom than factory workers or day laborers, being bound by their employer and exploited for their services. "The fight," he told the *Pittsburgh Courier*, "is over control of the players. . . . The fight will continue as long as the players refuse to get together themselves." He proposed a union made up of fifteen officers, eight from WCT and seven from the USLTA. Top players such as Laver, Rosewall, John Newcombe, Nastase, and Stan Smith had to join if the union was to wield any power. If they banded together, the players could dictate the distribution of prizes, tournament schedules, and allocation of pensions and insurance. Ashe expressed doubt, however, about the union's eventual formation. "All [the players] want to do is play and get paid," he noted. "Tennis players are a very docile group. They say they've got it good now, why rock the boat?"[14]

Nine months later a number of players had reevaluated the idea of a union. Ashe, Cliff Drysdale, and others persuaded more than fifty players that they could earn large salaries *and* control the terms of their employment. A professional did not have to sacrifice one for the other. Further, the ongoing dispute between WCT and the ILTF proved to many players that both organizations viewed them as pawns in a moneymaking game. "The way they had done it," Ashe noted, "was simply by divvying up the whole tennis world. Nobody had even consulted the players, of course; they just went ahead and acted as if tennis tournaments didn't need tennis players." Just before the U.S. Open, then, fifty-six players gathered in Forest Hills, New York, to discuss the formation of a players' union. Ed Hickey, tournament director of the U.S. pro championships, chaired the meeting, and the attendees included Ashe, Drysdale, Stan Smith, Mark Cox, Newcombe, Jaime Fillol, and Nikki Pilic, among others. The players drafted a constitution and agreed to a series of bylaws. Ashe left the meeting pleased with the organization's progress. One week later the group officially formed the Association of Tennis Professionals, a union composed of twenty-eight independent professionals and all thirty-two of WCT's contract players. The goal of the ATP, Ashe told reporters, was to "unite, promote and protect" its members from the arbitrary decisions of WCT and the ILTF. Members selected Jack Kramer to serve as executive director, elected Drysdale president, and named Ashe one of the organization's officers. As a founding member of the ATP, Ashe became a tennis pioneer for reasons other than his race. Reporters now rarely described him as "the first Negro" to accomplish this or that. Instead, they portrayed him as an eloquent, well-prepared leader, a man whom other players looked to in difficult times. His leadership skills, nurtured in civil rights and antiapartheid activism, had blossomed in the drive for player unionization.[15]

In addition to his work with the ATP, Ashe remained a formidable opponent on the tennis court in the early 1970s. In 1972 he won WCT tournaments in Louisville, Montreal, Rome, and Rotterdam. Sportswriters considered him a leading candidate to steal the U.S. Open crown from his friend and former Davis Cup teammate Stan Smith. On September 7 at Forest Hills the two Americans faced off in the quarterfinal round, with Smith as the heavy favorite. From the onset, however, Smith was slow and sluggish, laboring to reach the net following his serve. He was visibly fatigued, having played more matches than Ashe throughout the year. By contrast, Ashe appeared fresh and rested, rarely breaking a sweat during the contest. "Midway through the second set," he recalled, "I could see Stan was mentally tired. . . . The pressure was too much." Ashe's backhand drew him comparisons to the Ashe of 1968, then America's number-one player. He cruised to a surprising straight-set victory, 7-6, 6-4, 7-5. Two days later he defeated fellow American Cliff Richey, again in straight sets, to reach the final against his sometimes friend, sometimes foe Ilie Nastase.[16]

Ashe and Nastase came from different backgrounds, had distinct playing styles, and exhibited opposite personalities. Born to a Romanian banker, Nastase grew up behind the iron curtain, later serving as a lieutenant in the Romanian army. Short-tempered and aggressive, he frequently defied tennis etiquette by barking at officials and verbally harassing his opponents. During a match in December 1971 Nastase taunted the equally temperamental Clark Graebner. After a brief exchange of words, Graebner jumped over the net and attacked the Romanian. To Nastase, mind games were as important as his forehand stroke. Scholar E. Digby Baltzell argued that Nastase had learned bad manners from his friend and Davis Cup teammate Ion Tiriac. "Tiriac," he concluded, "simply had no sense of that alien, Anglo-Saxon ethic of sportsmanship. Instead, he seemed to have the attitude that one must do anything and pay any price to win." Like other sportswriters, this scholar viewed Nastase and Tiriac through an ethnic lens, suggesting that because of their Eastern European background and citizenship in a communist country they were unable to absorb genteel tradition. *Time* magazine labeled Nastase "an intruder from the socialist East" and described how he moved "about the grass courts like an impassioned Gypsy dancer." He did not understand democracy, contended some writers.[17]

On September 10 a record U.S. Open crowd of 14,690 spectators filled the grandstands at Forest Hills to watch Ashe take on fourth-seeded Nastase in the final. Columnists focused on Ashe's gentlemanly demeanor and support of traditional tennis etiquette. He represented tennis during the amateur era, a time when proper behavior mattered more than winning. The press depicted Nastase as an immature and selfish player, a prime example of the me-first generation. Writers hinted that the open era and commercialization of tennis were responsible for creating men like Nastase. Columnists also used nationalistic rhetoric to compare the two athletes. They portrayed Ashe as a symbol of American democracy and capitalism, a man who did things the right way. Nastase represented communism and government repression. He, like the Soviets, would do anything to conquer an opponent.[18]

During the match, the partisan crowd cheered loudly for Ashe and booed Nastase when he argued with the referee or shook his racquet. Ashe started strong and consistently landed his powerful serve en route to a 6-3 win in the first set. After losing the second set by an identical 6-3 score, he captured the third set 7-6 and cruised to a 3-1 lead in the fourth. He was one point from a 4-1 advantage when Nastase began his comeback. The Romanian evened the game at deuce, then aced Ashe with an unreturnable serve. Less than a minute later he muscled a volley past the former U.S. Open champ, stealing the game and the momentum. Ashe never recovered. Displaying "some of the most amazing reflexes and counter-hitting ever seen on a tennis court," the light-footed Nastase returned almost all of Ashe's serves with unusual precision. Nastase also disrupted the game's tempo with his "flamboyant and temperamental" antics. He barked and stared at the referee, threw down his racquet in disgust, and placed his head in his hands to protest a call. Later, a visibly irritated Ashe quipped, "If [Nastase] brushes up on some of his court manners he would be even better." The match ended when Nastase dropped a soft lob over Ashe's head. The elated Romanian tossed his racquet high into the air. He had won a difficult five-set match and was the new U.S. Open champion.[19]

The fireworks did not end with the final point. According to traditional tennis etiquette, following a championship match the loser shakes hands with the winner and offers congratulations. For the first time in his athletic career, however, Ashe abandoned the rules and criticized his opponent before a televised audience. David Gray of the *Guardian* described Ashe's postmatch comments as "the bitterest little speech that one had ever heard in public from a loser on a great lawn tennis occasion." Ashe praised Nastase's athletic prowess yet questioned his unseemly court manners and demonstrative behavior. The shocked Forest Hills crowd sat uncomfortably in their seats, some directing boos and catcalls at Ashe. Gray believed that Ashe had been frustrated with his own play and took it out on Nastase. Because he had not returned to top form after his 1968 U.S. Open victory or captured another significant major (aside from the 1970 Australian Open), some sportswriters labeled Ashe's 1968 win a fluke. The promise of his youth was gone, they contended, rendering him a second- or third-tier player. Other writers suggested that Ashe had been playing with the burden of defending traditional etiquette against a new generation of poorly behaved competitors. The match, then, had been for the future of tennis, a pressure that had been too much for him to handle.[20]

If the activism, unionization drive, and tennis obligations were not enough in the early 1970s, Ashe remained the sport's biggest endorser of products, ranging from razors to racquets. His lucrative contracts with Head, Catalina, Coca-Cola, and Philip Morris, among others, required him to travel throughout the United States and Europe signing autographs, holding tennis clinics, and selling merchandise. In March 1972, for instance, he appeared at Wieboldt's State Street clothing store in downtown Chicago to promote Catalina's new tennis clothing line. The company had chosen Ashe, a man of color, to introduce its "colorful" attire, which included shorts, sweaters, and jackets in sky blue. Less than fifteen years earlier, tennis clothes and the players who wore them had almost always been white. Now Catalina had selected the racial trailblazer Ashe to market its revolutionary new line. In her article "Courting with Color," Genevieve Buck of the *Chicago Tribune* hinted that Ashe's unique position as an African American in tennis made him the ideal person to promote blue and red tennis gear. The message was simple: if tennis purists could accept a black man, they could accept blue shorts and sweaters.[21]

On some occasions, Ashe used his endorsement obligations to advocate for civil rights. In late October 1973 he and several other Philip Morris representatives traveled to Germany to advertise the company's products. While in southwestern Germany, he visited Ramstein Air Force Base and participated in a race-relations seminar involving black and white servicemen. He witnessed a free exchange of accusations and complaints between black enlisted men and their white officers. "The horrible thing we see here," a black captain confided in Ashe, "is that when we bring officers in for five solid days of race relations, the bigot in them eventually comes out." Even before he attended the seminar, Ashe knew that blacks faced discrimination in the U.S. armed forces. Throughout the day, though, he heard from a number of black soldiers who reported that the race problem was much worse than he realized. They encouraged him to discuss their concerns with the commanding officer. That evening over dinner, Ashe relayed their grievances to two generals. He viewed himself as a "conduit," a former officer who could be stern with the generals without offending them. He wrote, "I was myself an officer in the army for two years, so I know how it works (and doesn't work), and, as always, I'm a black man who lives in a white world, and can communicate in both societies."[22]

—⚮ ⚭—

On April 23, 1971, South Africa's Vorster spoke before Parliament in Capetown and announced a shift in his country's sports policy. Beginning immediately, he said, nonwhite South Africans would compete in international athletic competitions both inside and outside South Africa. He declared that the decision enabled black athletes from around the world to participate in South Africa's track and field, tennis, and golf events. This athletic integration would also pave the way for the country's readmission to the Olympic Games. Although most Nationalist Party members praised the new policy, Vorster's critics, including Progressive Party member Helen Suzman, assailed the prime minister for what they believed was "an absurd technical maneuver to placate overseas sports administrators." Under the new system, South Africa's rugby and cricket teams remained segregated. Nonwhites could form their own teams and compete internationally, but they could not join South Africa's white teams, such as the Springboks. Essentially, Vorster articulated a "separate but equal" policy, akin to the 1896 *Plessy v. Ferguson* Supreme Court decision in the United States. Further, the new law allowed South Africa to bar an athlete from competition for "political" reasons, as it had done with Ashe.[23]

Vorster's speech was the direct result of international pressure from activists, sports bodies, world leaders, and some of South Africa's own athletes. In the past ten years the IOC had removed South Africa from the Olympics, and the ILTF had barred it from the Davis Cup. In 1970 England had canceled the tour of a South African cricket team, citing racial discrimination in the country's sports. Fans routinely booed and heckled South African athletes like Gary Player and Cliff Drysdale, sometimes throwing items onto the playing surfaces. When the minister of sport, Frank Waring, appeared at the national tennis championships, the crowd jeered the man who had announced Ashe's visa denial. The expanding protest movement also included white South African athletes. Two white cricket teams refused to compete after the government announced its decision not to allow two nonwhite cricketers to travel with the Springboks to Australia. Even the conservative South African Cricket Association made it clear that it backed the integrated team.[24]

In the United States, protests and political demonstrations against South African athletes intensified. For years, Ashe had maintained that Player, Drysdale, and others had the right to compete in American tournaments. South African sportsmen, he had argued, were not responsible for the government's apartheid laws. In June 1971, however, Ashe reversed course. Early in the month, the NAACP announced plans to picket golf and tennis events that featured South African athletes. Ashe promised the NAACP that he would not cross the picket line to participate in a WCT tournament held in Boston. "I have nothing against the South African players who I meet, travel with and play with almost every day," he told the *Baltimore Afro-American*. "This thing is bigger than tennis." He vowed to defy his contractual obligation with WCT before he broke the picket line. An editorial in the *Afro-American* defended Ashe against his critics. "Arthur Ashe has become aware that he will be a man much longer than he will be a tennis player," the piece read. "Such awareness, whether it comes early or late, also is a way of life."[25]

The NAACP planned to test Ashe's resolve. As expected, members of the organization's Boston chapter gathered at the Longwood Cricket Club for the 1971 U.S. Pro Championships, protesters taking their seats in the grandstands. Their target was Frew McMillan, a white South African tennis player set to take on Australia's John Newcombe in an opening-round match. Jack E. Robinson, president of the chapter, informed Ashe of the protest but did not reveal the exact nature of the planned demonstration. The NAACP did not wait long to act. As Newcombe and McMillan walked onto the court, Robinson and the other activists stood in unison and chanted, "Paint him black and send him back . . . paint him black and send him back. . . ." The protesters jeered and booed each time McMillan hit the ball and loudly applauded Newcombe throughout the match. "At Shea Stadium or Fenway Park the hooting and shouting would hardly have been noticed," observed the *Chicago Daily Defender*. "But the Longwood Cricket Club is not a baseball park." Ironically, the protesters disturbed Newcombe and not McMillan. "I'm aloof on the court," the South African told a reporter. "I never notice what's going on around me." Newcombe, on the other hand, struggled to maintain his focus. In the middle of the second game, he approached Robinson and the others, begging them to keep quiet. The demonstrations would continue, Robinson countered, "until such times as blacks and other non-whites can go to South Africa and South African black athletes can also compete outside South Africa."[26]

In addition to McMillan and other South African tennis players, antiapartheid protesters continued to shadow Gary Player. On June 17, chants of "Arthur Ashe, Sharpeville . . . Arthur Ashe, Sharpeville . . ." greeted the South African as he approached the seventeenth tee of the Merion Golf Club in Ardmore, Pennsylvania. A policeman promptly removed the two African American activists from the course. Like the tennis protest, the disruptions seemed to affect the South African's competitor more than him. "It was nothing, absolutely nothing," Player told reporters after the round. He was used to the demonstrations and had no interest in international politics. Bob Goalby, a former Masters winner paired with Player, was four under par when the chanting began. Although he claimed that the protest did not bother him, Goalby double-bogeyed the seventeenth hole, relinquishing the U.S. Open lead. Weeks after the tournament, the *Los Angeles Sentinel* interviewed three black golfers, all of whom defended their white colleague. "He's a gentleman," noted Charlie Sifford. "We're all like one big family out there. We don't take our politics out on the golf course." George Johnson argued that Player was undeserving of the treatment because he was not responsible for apartheid. Pete Brown urged the protesters to wait until after the round to confront the South African. These opinions were representative of most black golfers and tennis players in the early 1970s. Unlike their counterparts in baseball, football, basketball, and boxing, black athletes who competed in the "genteel" sports of tennis and golf often defended etiquette and tradition, while bemoaning the intrusion of politics into sports.[27]

Perhaps Sifford, Johnson, and Brown had a point. Maybe participation in the antiapartheid movement was too much of a distraction for black athletes. Sam Lacy agreed. In a column that appeared after Ashe's loss in the 1972 U.S. Open, the *Afro-American* reporter tried to explain the black star's drop in play following his 1968 victory at Forest Hills. He was not injured nor did he lack confidence, and he still possessed the devastating serve that concerned even his toughest opponents. The problem, Lacy concluded, was the distractions, which included the antiapartheid movement, Ashe's union duties, and his participation in inner-city outreach programs. Tennis "is not a game you can play well while carrying around in your head the weight of other people's problems," Lacy insisted. Unlike many other sports, tennis is a sport of individuals. Even in the Davis Cup competition, players must win their own matches to help their teams advance. In baseball, football, or basketball, if one player has a bad game, his teammates can pick up the slack. This is not the case in tennis. Off the court, Ashe remained in a precarious position. He criticized South African politicians, sports officials, and athletes in the press, then rode buses and airplanes with the likes of Cliff Drysdale and Bob Maud, making for sometimes uncomfortable conversation. Ashe would never blame activism for a poor athletic performance, Lacy insisted. Yet he was "convinced that Ashe has too much on his mind to permit him the kind of concentration that is vital to the playing of the kind of game that represents his true ability."[28]

Lacy's column defended Ashe against critics who believed he should focus on tennis and ignore civil rights. As a black sportswriter who had covered Jackie Robinson in 1947, Lacy felt that black athletes had a dual obligation to play well *and* fight racial discrimination. Lacy himself balanced his role as a sports editor, writer, and civil rights advocate throughout his career. In 1945 he had written to every Major League Baseball owner to propose the creation of a panel to study integration. The historian Jules Tygiel credited Lacy with helping to jumpstart the integration campaign, describing the reporter as "a persistent and perceptive critic of the baseball establishment." Lacy had the authority and experience to tackle the topic of racism in sports.[29]

Both Lacy and Ashe focused on South Africa again in July 1972, when, in a surprise move, the Davis Cup Committee voted to readmit South Africa to the 1972 competition. "This is absolutely wonderful news," remarked South African Lawn Tennis Union president Alf Chalmers. He announced that "all countries will be welcome to play in the republic to prove to the world that SALTU represents both white and non-white tennis players and that the South African Davis Cup team will always be selected on merit." The committee's split decision was based on Vorster's parliamentary address and what some members believed to be tangible signs of progress. Evonne Goolagong's low-key trip to South Africa had persuaded many ILTF officials that South Africa had become serious about integrating its sports. Chalmers pledged that the nation's non-whites were now eligible to compete in the South African championships. Perhaps most important, Ashe's contract with WCT prevented him from participating in the 1972 Davis Cup, ensuring that the South Africans would not have to deal with him in an official capacity. More than anyone else, Ashe had forced the South Africans from the Davis Cup. Now his absence let them back in.[30]

Condemnation of the Davis Cup Committee soon followed. Eve Malmquist, chair of the Swedish Lawn Tennis Association, hinted that the Swedes might withdraw their team if the committee did not reverse its decision. A number of antiapartheid groups announced plans to protest South Africa's matches. In

July the committee, on a 5-2 vote, formalized South Africa's readmission, entering it in the South American Zone instead of the European Zone to minimize the chances of a protest. In 1969, Poland and Czechoslovakia had pulled out of the competition in opposition to apartheid. Three years later, Sweden and other European nations threatened the same action. The United States was one of the five nations that voted to lift the ban. Despite the rhetorical support for Ashe, U.S. representatives sided with their economic and strategic interests over their countryman.[31]

While the Davis Cup story was playing out publicly, another equally significant development occurred privately. At the height of the 1973 Grand Slam season, Owen Williams approached Ashe on behalf of Piet Koornhof, the South African minister of mines, immigration, sports, and recreation. Born on August 2, 1925, Koornhof earned a degree in theology from Stellenbosch University and studied at Oxford as a Rhodes Scholar. Elected to Parliament in 1964, he held a number of cabinet-level positions under Vorster. Those on both the left and the right viewed Koornhof as a political moderate, a fun-loving and personable character who favored compromise over conflict. After the fall of apartheid in 1994, he left the Nationalist Party for the multiracial United Democratic Movement of Bantu Holomisa. In 2001 he joined the ANC. If anyone could persuade the Afrikaners to liberalize their sports policies, Koornhof was the best candidate. And he was no stranger to Ashe. The tennis star followed South African politics and read international newspapers, histories, monographs, and scholarly reports. Ashe believed that Koornhof was the most intelligent and pragmatic member of the cabinet. He also knew that Koornhof was the likely successor to Vorster, which would give Ashe access to the prime minister. Most importantly, Koornhof was prepared to grant Ashe a visa if the tennis player agreed to a series of preconditions. In the interim, Koornhof, via Williams, sent a clear message to Ashe: if he kept quiet in the press, a South African visa was inevitable.[32]

One year later, Williams visited Ashe at the Westbury Hotel in downtown London, where the two men openly discussed the visa question. A former top-ranked amateur, Williams was the sport's most able promoter. He had almost single-handedly transformed the South African championships from a small, low-level tournament to one of the top ten most profitable events in world tennis. In a 1967 letter to the editor of *World Tennis*, Ashe defended Williams and the South African championships. "Don't get me wrong," he began. "I deplore the 'apartheid' policies of South Africa *more* than 9 out of 10 Americans. . . . But the South African tournament is still great. Some of the readers [of *World Tennis*] have just assumed that since South Africa practices apartheid, their tournament does not deserve a Top Four ranking." The USLTA thought so highly of Williams that it hired him to run the 1969 U.S. Open. Others were not so impressed. In a scathing column directed at the USLTA, Williams, and Ashe, Dick Edwards of the *Amsterdam News* scolded American officials for hiring Williams and encouraged Ashe to boycott the event. "I say to Owen Williams, Afrikaner, take your family and go home!" he demanded. Neither Williams nor Ashe took Edwards's advice. Like his friend Cliff Drysdale, Williams remained a Progressive who favored the integration of sports in South Africa. Ashe wrote in his diary that Williams was "a man as decent as he is capable, and I believe that he wants the same things for people of South Africa that I do." Ashe empathized with Williams. South Africa would not admit him because of his race, while black radicals in the United States did not accept Williams because of his citizenship.[33]

As the two men engaged in discussion, Williams learned that Ashe had his own set of preconditions. He laid out four stipulations for the government to meet. If South African officials refused even one of his demands, he vowed not to enter the country. First, he insisted that the government attach no travel restrictions to his visa. He planned to visit the black townships, including Soweto, and meet with local black leaders who were fighting against apartheid. If the government planned to keep him in Johannesburg and parade him around as a symbol of racial harmony, he was not interested in a visit. Second, he told Williams that the grandstands at Ellis Park must be unconditionally integrated. He would not play before a segregated audience, nor would he compete in the shadows of a special "white section." Third, he insisted that Koornhof make a "conscientious effort" to set up a meeting between him and the prime minister. Traveling to Johannesburg to meet with low-level officials was futile and not worth his time. Last, the government had to recognize him as a black man and not as an "honorary white," as it had done with other blacks who traveled there. Williams quietly recorded Ashe's preconditions and assured him that his demands were fair and reasonable. The optimistic Williams did not anticipate a problem. "Then," Ashe said, "he told me not to drop any more H-bombs on Johannesburg," referring to a comment Ashe had made years earlier. Before leaving the Westbury, Williams instructed Ashe not to inquire about his visa status. His message was, "Don't call us, we'll call you." Ashe remained skeptical.[34]

By Independence Day 1973 the call had not come. Rather than spending the holiday on a golf course or at a barbeque with friends, Ashe sat down at his desk in his New York City apartment and wrote letters to black congressmen, literary figures, and activists as well as tennis colleagues, former mentors, and business associates. The topic of his correspondence was South Africa, specifically the pros and cons of a visit. "I sincerely want to go," he wrote in his diary, "if only from a selfish point of view, out of curiosity, but I also am deeply concerned with how other blacks might take such a trip." Those politicians and activists with an interest in South Africa generally could be divided into two camps. One group, led by the exiled Dennis Brutus, argued that isolation, disengagement, boycotts, and sanctions were the only ways to force meaningful change in South Africa. Vorster's "new" sports policy was merely window dressing, entirely devoid of substance. In a letter, Brutus lectured Ashe, "I believe that simply by keeping yourself informed on conditions in South Africa as things develop you will be persuaded that things are not in fact getting better." In opposing Brutus's approach to activism, Ashe offered the United States' severing of diplomatic ties with China and the Cuban embargo as examples of a failed foreign policy. In both cases the United States had opted for disengagement instead of diplomacy, and both nations remained communist. If disengagement had failed in China and Cuba, why would it succeed in South Africa? Additionally, his mentors and life experiences had taught him that constructive dialogue with an opponent was preferable to disengagement. In the second group were activists like Andrew Young, who pushed for a gradualist approach, relying on small steps to achieve a larger goal. "Surely," Ashe explained, "it is less emotionally satisfying this way, but, I'm certain, more realistic and more successful." The tone of Ashe's entry suggests that he had made up his mind long before he received any responses. It is likely, then, that he sought advice that would affirm his position rather than challenge it. There were no signs in his history or his public statements that he would move from the gradualist camp.[35]

Toward the end of July the response letters began to arrive. Most of the correspondence encouraged him to enter South Africa but advised that he take steps to protect himself from being misquoted or having his image misappropriated. Nearly all of the letters offered thoughtful advice and pragmatic suggestions. Ashe's friend Congressman Andrew Young believed he had a duty to win the South African Open, a victory that would inspire the nation's blacks and coloreds. He could do for South African blacks what Joe Louis and Jesse Owens had done for African Americans in the 1930s. "They kept the spark of dignity alive, and in many ways broadened the base of pride that made movements in later years possible," Young wrote. Ashe could not let the meetings, interviews, and travels around South Africa distract him. If he defeated the entire field, a field that included numerous white South Africans, he would put a dent in the theory of white superiority, at least on the tennis court. "Don't go,"

Young advised, "unless you are prepared to 'kick ass and take names' on the tennis court." The burden of winning outweighed all else.[36]

Young and others also offered more specific advice. An American reporter should accompany Ashe to any meeting with Vorster to ensure that the Afrikaner press did not misrepresent his views, Young advised. Any local article portraying him as sympathetic to Vorster or the Nationalists would hamper the antiapartheid movement. Young cautioned Ashe about meeting with local black leaders, because their effectiveness "in the black community depends on their being able to give leadership in secrecy." Georgia state congressman and civil rights icon Julian Bond suggested that Ashe include an African American journalist or photographer as part of his delegation, perhaps from *Jet* or *Ebony*. Philip Morris chairman Joseph Cullman counseled him to speak with Lee Elder, the world's top African American golfer. In 1971, Elder had competed in the South African PGA Championship at the request of Gary Player. Like Ashe, he had demanded integrated galleries so that local blacks could watch his performance.[37]

Several men, such as Democratic politician and activist Sargent Shriver, former U.S. Davis Cup captain Robert Kelleher, and Dennis Brutus objected to a potential South Africa trip. Shriver doubted that anything positive would result from the visit. The American mainstream press would relegate news coverage of his travels to the sports pages, depriving him of a larger audience. Shriver feared that the Afrikaner press intended to sanitize its reporting of the trip by focusing on positive interactions between Ashe and local white leaders. He asked, "Even if you have the private meeting with the Prime Minister, even if the stands and bleachers are integrated, even if you can come and go as you please and even if they accept your visa application on its face, what good does that do? For you?" In his view, Ashe should have demanded more. For instance, he advised Ashe to bring a "liberal" South African leader with him to a meeting with Vorster. Maybe he could give a speech at a white South African university like Stellenbosch, taking "hostile as well as friendly questions." If Ashe required a yes or no answer on whether he should travel, though, Shriver felt he should stay home.[38]

Dennis Brutus opposed a trip under any circumstances. As one of the leaders of the South African Non-Racial Olympic Committee, or SANROC, Brutus lobbied public officials to suspend dialogue with South Africa until its politicians dismantled apartheid. More than anyone else Ashe had reached out to, Brutus understood the violent, oppressive, and psychologically damaging nature of apartheid. In 1963 South African police had arrested the poet and activist on trumped-up charges of fomenting rebellion by meeting with more than two nonfamily members at once. During an attempted prison escape, guards shot an unarmed Brutus in the back, severely wounding him. He spent sixteen months locked away on Robben Island, five of those months in solitary confinement. A year after his release, government officials allowed him to emigrate to England if he agreed never to return to South Africa. Even in exile, Brutus fought against apartheid and those who maintained a relationship with South Africa. In 1971 he led a demonstration at Wimbledon after the ILTF permitted South African players to compete. A U.N. report published in 1971 labeled Brutus "one of the most persistent campaigners against racialism in sport" and identified him as "a special target of the South African regime."[39]

Brutus questioned Ashe's judgment, hinting that he was naive for believing his appearance would make a difference in South Africa. Brutus began by saying that he wished Ashe's letter had been longer "because I do not feel you have set out your position sufficiently fully for me to understand it." Ashe had not paid much attention if he believed that conditions were improving. Within the past year South Africa had placed a ban on Morgan Naidoo, a member of the multiracial federation known as the South African Council on Sport, or SACOS. South African officials had revoked his passport for five years to prevent him from sharing his views at a meeting of the International Swimming Federation. The poet Don Mattera was another casualty of apartheid. Raised in Sophiatown, a multiracial suburb of Johannesburg where the "rich and the poor, the exploiters and the exploited, all knitted together in a colourful fabric that ignored race or class structures." In 1973 he received a nine-year ban for engaging in antigovernment activity. "My house was raided more than 600 times, I was detained more than 200 times, for one hour, for 10 hours, for three months," he said, describing his house arrest. "I was tortured on more occasions than I can remember—electrical wires were put into my penis and anus, two ribs on both sides of my chest were broken, my fingers were smashed." The treatment of Naidoo and Mattera should have convinced Ashe to stay home, Brutus lectured. He also criticized Koornhof, arguing that the cabinet member was a proapartheid Afrikaner like everyone else. Brutus brought up the possibility of a debate between Koornhof and Ashe, perhaps before an audience. His own experiences in South Africa had convinced Brutus that the Afrikaners could not be reasoned with.[40]

Many, however, advised Ashe to follow his heart and decide what was best for him. "Of course," wrote poet Nikki Giovanni, "there will be those who will deride you should you choose to go but the history of mankind is the history of an individual doing what he thinks is right and necessary and others laughing at him." She reminded him that artists and athletes often led the fight for human rights. During his visit he could serve as an amateur journalist and report on the condition of blacks in the townships. Julian Bond encouraged him to "have fun" and focus on winning. Likewise, Ashe's former UCLA tennis coach and mentor J. D. Morgan wanted him to take home the trophy. "I would like you," he counseled, "to be in great condition, both mental and physical, to do your dead level best in the tournament, and connected with that, if you are so involved politically while you are there, you cannot do this." His friend and former Davis Cup teammate Stan Smith also worried about Ashe's mental state. As he traveled around Soweto and observed the suffering firsthand, he might become angry and emotional, leading to a slip-up in the press. "Art," wrote Smith, "I think your trip will be great, informative, but frustrating. Please try to keep this in perspective." Ashe had asked for and received some very good advice.[41]

For the next two months Ashe waited for news, pondering his friends' advice and envisioning the trip in his head. He also wondered if his tennis colleagues understood the political significance of such a visit. In his July 31 diary entry, he lamented the apolitical stance taken by players on the professional circuit. To them the South African Open was no different from a tournament held in Sweden or Tucson, Arizona. On October 17 he recorded, "No word from South Africa." Vorster's cabinet had met the previous day without publicly announcing the status of his visa. Ashe assumed the cabinet had either tabled the topic or was busy preparing the public-relations strategy for his appearance. Two weeks later he received his answer. "Let the record state," he wrote, "that it was on Halloween when they finally agreed to let Arthur Ashe into South Africa." Owen Williams phoned him early in the morning with the news, and later in the day a representative from the South African embassy contacted him with instructions to collect his visa. The following day, November 1, stories of Ashe's visa appeared in U.S. and British newspapers. According to one *New York Times* reporter, South Africa had reversed its position because Ashe had agreed "to come to South Africa solely to play tennis and to do so in a spirit of goodwill and cooperation." He had promised not to agitate on racial matters, at least not while in South Africa. The *Chicago Defender* expressed skepticism that South Africa had enough class to make up for its previous mistreatment of Ashe. "Such a happening would equal a snow storm in midsummer," contended the journalist.[42]

To Vorster and other South African officials, the visa announcement did not signal the erosion of apartheid. Instead, they saw it as a political maneuver to appease members of the Davis Cup Committee, who were yet to rule on South Africa's status for the 1974 competition. This was no secret. Parton Keese of the

*New York Times* noted the close proximity of the announcement to the Davis Cup meeting in Paris, and Ashe was similarly suspicious. "Gee, what a complete coincidence," he sarcastically commented. "The International Lawn Tennis Federation allowed South Africa back into the Davis Cup in 1973 to play in '74. A more cynical man than I might think that I was a quid pro quo." During its presentation before the committee, SALTU's head, Blen Franklin, included Ashe's visa as one of his eight arguments for South Africa's readmittance. The South Africans used Ashe to mend their relationship with the ILTF, and he allowed this to happen. Ashe viewed the developments as a "trade." In exchange for his visa and the amended sports policy, South Africa received another chance to compete in the Davis Cup, as well as some positive international press. The visa, in turn, enabled Ashe to explore South Africa and meet local black citizens. For the first time, black, colored, and white fans had the option of sitting beside one another in the grandstands of Ellis Park, a direct challenge to apartheid in his opinion. He planned to win the tournament and use his victory as a platform for activism. He remained an advocate of gradualism, explaining, "Whereas I don't see myself as Jackie Robinson or even as Rosa Parks, neither trailblazer nor pawn of history, I do think I'm just a little bit of progress. Ellis Park will be integrated, and I will be a free black man on display."[43]

Ashe spent the first half of November fixated on his historic trip. Would losing in an early round of the South African Open inhibit his ability to serve as an effective activist? What if local black leaders rejected his presence? These concerns and insecurities flooded his mind, leading to restless nights and poor performances on the tennis court. On November 9 a preoccupied Ashe lost handily to Tom Okker in Stockholm, Sweden, and his confidence began to wane. "I'm already starting to worry," he confessed, "that I'll go down to South Africa next week to make history and get wiped out in the first round." A last-minute meeting with members of SANROC further underscored the importance of the trip. In his hotel room at the Westbury in London, Ashe and his agitated guests fiercely debated the merits of traveling to South Africa. The men argued and rehashed the history of apartheid but made no progress. Ashe was going to South Africa, and SANROC could not convince him to do otherwise. Although SANROC opposed Ashe's decision, his friends and colleagues were overwhelmingly supportive, including the temperamental jokester Ilie Nastase. As a taxi approached the Westbury to take Ashe to the airport, Nastase looked on from the front of the lobby. "Hey, Brown Sugar," Nastase yelled, "don't let 'em put you in jail."[44]

After leaving the hotel in a rush, Ashe boarded his BOAC flight to Johannesburg with a number of trusted friends and associates. Over the next week and a half he would rely on all of them to help him maintain his composure, focus, and sanity. The delegation included Donald and Carole Dell, British sportswriter and ATP press secretary Richard Evans, *Sports Illustrated* reporter Frank Deford, and *Boston Globe* columnist Bud Collins. Those who traveled with him shared his belief in open dialogue and the power of positive symbolism. Early in the morning, Dell and Evans prepared Ashe for his first South African press conference. His success depended on following a carefully crafted script that emphasized cooperation, goodwill, and constructive dialogue while avoiding politically damaging statements that the press might take out of context. His strategy was to allow more progressive newspapers, such as the *Johannesburg Star* and the *Rand Daily Mail*, to criticize the government in his stead. The three men wrapped up their planning session and returned to their seats. Moments before the plane's touchdown, a diminutive white man walked toward Ashe's chair and introduced himself facetiously as "one of those horrible South Africans." He then turned serious, assuring Ashe that not all South Africans were evil racists. In fact, he claimed that the vast majority of South African whites wanted him to do well in the tournament.[45]

Ashe and his party exited the plane and moved through the international terminal, a facility that hid the nation's apartheid laws. There were no separate drinking fountains, restrooms, or seating areas, and no signs read "Here Blankes" or "Damas Blankes." The terminal could have been at LAX or O'Hare. The airport had its mask, and Ashe wore one too. He intended to remain on an even keel in his body language and expression, disappointing those who would try to agitate him. After passing through customs, Ashe and his group met Owen and Jennifer Williams, who drove them into central Johannesburg. Ashe stared out the window during the car ride, looking for evidence of apartheid. "My first impression," he observed, "was that apartheid was a much more subtle proposition than I had anticipated. If you were white, I doubt if you would even have seen anything out of the ordinary." The lack of activity was what bothered him. White drivers manned the passing cars, and the few blacks and coloreds he saw appeared to be aimlessly walking the streets. The scene was reminiscent of segregated Richmond in the 1950s. His party traveled to Sandton, a posh suburb of Johannesburg, where he was to stay at the residence of insurance and real estate mogul Brian Young for the next week and a half. The luxurious, Spanish-style house included a large swimming pool, a tennis court, lush gardens, and a collection of purple jacaranda trees. A cook and a house-keeper stood ready to wait on the guests.[46]

The decision to stay with a wealthy white man was an enormous risk that threatened Ashe's standing in the antiapartheid community. The best way to show solidarity with South Africa's blacks and coloreds, critics argued, was to stay in a shack in Soweto, alongside the real victims of apartheid. Spending the majority of his time hearing the tales of abuse, witnessing the economic struggles of ordinary families, and observing the cramped, decaying township could enlighten him. Critics also labeled Ashe a hypocrite for vocally supporting the antiapartheid movement and then failing to act when given the chance. To some, he appeared as an Uncle Tom willing to appease the white government as he traveled around South Africa. Black activists needed a sign that Ashe was for real and not some pawn of the Afrikaners. Ashe anticipated the criticism and agonized over the decision to stay in Sandton, knowing that it made him look bad in the eyes of local blacks and coloreds. Ultimately, his choice centered on tennis. To convey any sense of authority and achieve a political platform, he had to perform well in the South African Open. Residing in Soweto would only distract him and drain his mental and physical energy, energy he needed to win the tournament. "I did not come to South Africa in sackcloth and ashes to serve penance," he explained. "I know damn well how badly the Africans in this country live, but I cannot see how it would serve any useful purpose for me to live like one myself." Ashe had made his own decision, one that he believed was best for him and for the antiapartheid movement as well. He had two weeks to prove his critics wrong.[47]

On November 18 and 19, Ashe observed the physical signs of apartheid for the first time. Ellis Park was and still is a multisport complex located just east of Johannesburg's City Centre. Home to South Africa's Springboks rugby club and the national cricket team, the park mandated separate seating for whites, blacks, and coloreds. Inside the facility, tourists from around the world posed in front of the "Whites-Only" signs just as they would pose in front of the Statue of Liberty or the Eiffel Tower. South Africa's magnificent complex served as a reminder of the nation's discriminatory laws. The park also revealed the varying layers of apartheid. During his first day on the practice court, Ashe interrupted his normal routine to hit with some of South Africa's most talented black players, who were not very good by ordinary standards. Most of them lived in a black township, practiced on makeshift courts, and relied on inexperienced coaches if they had coaches at all. They did not have access to the same funding or facilities as a Drysdale or a McMillan. Their lack of proper mechanics, equipment, and experience was a product of apartheid, no less significant than the "Here Blankes" and "Damas Blankes" signs that littered the stadium.[48]

At Ellis Park Ashe had his first conversation with the poet and *Johannesburg Star* journalist Don Mattera. He met with a number of black and colored reporters following another practice session. Several of them, including Mattera, were on the government's watch list. If the government believed a black reporter was engaging in subversive behavior, it had the authority to place a ban on that individual. A banned person could not leave South Africa, travel to another city without permission, publish his or her work, or be in the company of more than one nonfamily member at a time. Many of the reporters seemed uneasy during the impromptu press conference. A government spy might emerge at any moment and arrest one or more of the men for "illegal" activity. For this very reason, one journalist begged Ashe to move the discussion to a private location. When he refused, the reporters began to ask him difficult questions. What did he think of the fact that many South African blacks and coloreds rejected his presence? In their view, his unwanted visit legitimized the Nationalist regime and sent the wrong signal to world sports bodies. Mattera disagreed. He was happy to see Ashe and optimistic that the trip would reverse some of the world's apathy toward South African blacks. Any African American who understood South African history and actively participated in the antiapartheid movement should visit the nation. Folks like Bob Foster, on the other hand, were not welcome.[49]

Foster was the other significant African American athlete to compete in South Africa in 1973. He was a world champion light heavyweight boxer who took home a silver medal from the 1959 Pan American Games in Chicago. Early in 1973, in Albuquerque, New Mexico, he defeated the white South African Pierre Fourie by judges' decision to retain his crown. Soon thereafter the two men scheduled a rematch to be held in South Africa, presenting Ashe with competition for the spotlight. Unlike the tennis star, Foster entered South Africa as an "honorary white," a classification Ashe refused to accept. Foster asked for but did not demand integrated seating for his bout. "They may open it up to blacks that night," he surmised, not appearing overly concerned. Foster had "heard" things about South Africa, whereas Ashe had read about, studied, and examined every element of the nation's history and culture. Foster seemed to view South Africa as an extension of Jim Crow America, no worse than his upbringing along the shores of the Rio Grande in southwestern New Mexico. "I might get a little harassment," he told a reporter, "but I've been fighting that so long it's not going to bother me." He hoped the fight would represent a "milestone" in race relations, creating a temporary environment in which blacks and whites might "mingle."[50]

Planning to capitalize politically on Foster's trip, South African officials rolled out the red carpet for the black boxing champion. He and his party stayed in a brand-new five-star hotel that was not yet open to the general public. Local television stations filmed the boxer as he walked the streets of Johannesburg, mobbed by black and white admirers. He declared, "This is a beautiful country and I just love the people. And these people really love me, so much that I can't even get out and enjoy the sunshine." In a statement that stunned many anti-apartheid activists, Foster announced his desire to purchase a summer home in South Africa to escape the winters of New Mexico. One *Washington Post* reporter explained the boxer's approach. "Foster is steadfastly remaining outside political debate and is letting his presence speak for itself. It is obvious he came here solely to fight, to win and to take home the most money he will ever have made for a single bout," noted the journalist. Foster's strategy of political silence and leading by example (i.e., dominating in the ring) stood to improve race relations more than agitation and protest. Some, including Ashe and Mattera, thought Foster received far too much credit for his thoughtless actions.[51]

Mattera argued that Foster had done a disservice to South African blacks. Although he had signed autographs for black fans, he had made no attempt to contact black activists or visit Soweto. His appearance signaled to the world that South Africa had liberalized its race policies and treated leading black figures with respect and dignity. The gifts, grand lodging, and positive publicity had mesmerized Foster, leading him to abandon his race for fame. Mattera, though, was in a difficult position, not wanting to chastise a fellow black man. "There'll come a day," he explained, "when we'll have the luxury to criticize, to disagree with each other in public, but right now we need solidarity above all." Ashe was equally disenchanted with Foster. In two days, Ashe planned to attend a reception for black South African journalists, where he was sure to face angry reporters who objected to his presence. Foster also received an invitation but chose not to attend. The two men represented opposite approaches practiced throughout the twentieth century by athletes like Joe Louis, Althea Gibson, Jesse Owens, Muhammad Ali, and Bill Russell. Foster was the apolitical athlete who abhorred the intrusion of political controversy into his sport. Like Owens in the 1936 Berlin Olympics, he wanted to inspire blacks by winning. Ashe, on the other hand, saw sports as a vehicle for achieving social and political change. Success on the tennis court offered him the platform he needed to advocate for the elimination of racial discrimination in sports and society. Both approaches were on display in Johannesburg in the fall of 1973.[52]

Ashe could not remain preoccupied with Foster or anything else. He had to set aside the distractions before taking on fellow American Sherwood Stewart in the first round of the South African Open. The pairing was a mismatch on many levels. Ashe took the court as one of the world's top-ranked players and a former U.S. Open and Davis Cup champion. Stewart was a phenomenal doubles player who had never finished higher than number sixty in the ATP singles ranking. He had arrived in Johannesburg the previous night and had not adjusted to the city's 6,000-foot altitude. Ironically, Stewart had traveled to South Africa in part to see Ashe make history, having no idea that Ashe's first match would be against him. At midday the two men walked to their sides of Ellis Park's cement center court. It was a gorgeous afternoon with little wind and a slight scattering of clouds. The match's first point went to Ashe on a sharp forehand that hugged the line. He won the game and the set decisively, 6-1. After capturing the second set in a tiebreaker, 7-6, Ashe's workmanlike performance gave him the third set, 6-4, and the match. The so-called *persona non grata* had advanced.[53]

While Ashe faced Stewart on center court, Owen Williams had his own problem to deal with. Prior to the match, he and his wife, Jennifer, had quietly distributed tickets to black and colored South Africans. The couple had promised Ashe integrated matches and worked diligently to honor their word. Many of the fans who received the free tickets entered the stadium and found their seats in the grandstands. Ashe remembered scanning the thousands in attendance and seeing pockets of black fans interspersed among the usual white crowd. Blacks filled one entire box just feet from the court, a first for Ellis Park. Despite Ashe's feelings of satisfaction, some stadium workers scrambled to make sense of the new arrangement. One exasperated usher called out, "Are you Mr. Williams? You must do something. The blacks and Coloreds are sitting in all the white seats." Williams promised to handle the situation. The encounter between Williams and the usher suggests a clear resistance to the integrated seating plan. Williams chose to integrate the grandstands in a quiet, almost deceptive manner. Ashe was under the impression that everyone understood and was willing to comply with the new seating policy. He was mistaken.[54]

Ashe's defeat of Stewart made him the first African American man to win a tennis match at Ellis Park. This, however, was only the beginning of his important day. Following the match, interviews, and a shower, he exited the stadium and instructed his driver to head for Soweto. Soweto, whose name was short for

Southwestern Township, was an urban settlement for blacks and coloreds located beside some of the nation's largest gold mines. Throughout the first half of the twentieth century the government passed a number of laws expelling blacks and coloreds from central Johannesburg and other big cities. In 1973 Soweto was a "suburb" of unpaved roads, few legitimate businesses, one usually crowded hospital, and many houses without indoor plumbing or electricity. Managing a general store, selling perishable goods, or working in a butcher shop were the few legal jobs open to residents. As a result, an informal economy developed in Soweto in which residents traded and bartered black-market goods. In the absence of electricity, families used fire to cook, and breathing the toxic fumes resulted in high child mortality rates. The government controlled nearly all of the mortgages and provided no public transportation other than a rail line to Johannesburg. "All of it sprawls," observed Ashe as he gazed from the safety of his car. "The best of it is endless rows of tiny little cottages; the worst, shacks of paper, of wood, of tin." The image that stuck with Ashe the most was the sight of the township's day laborers returning home from work. Before they reached their homes, the residents had to cross an open field that divided Soweto from the train station. The people looked tired, frail, and beaten down by years of oppression. Ashe's heart sank as he watched the scene unfold. He had his driver return to Johannesburg.[55]

The next day offered no rest or relief. In the afternoon, Ashe met Barry Phillips-Moore in the second round of the open. Phillips-Moore, an Australian lefty who stood five foot eight, had reached the round of sixteen in one major tournament, in the doubles of the Australian Open 1973. As a singles player he made the round of thirty-two at both the French and the Australian Open but could not advance. Ashe relied on his powerful serve to dispatch Phillips-Moore with ease, 6-4, 6-4, 6-1. He now had a date with South African Bob Hewitt in the quarterfinals. Later in the evening, Ashe attended a reception for local black journalists hosted by the U.S. Information Service. One of the organizers of the event was Don Mattera. In that morning's paper the government had announced its ban of Mattera, leading Ashe to believe that he would not attend the gathering. To Ashe's surprise, Mattera appeared outside the reception hall escorted by an employee of the South African Bureau of State Security (BOSS). On the day he received a government ban that prevented him from publishing or writing in his own name, the selfless Mattera had come to apologize to Ashe for missing the reception. "I don't want to do anything to jeopardize your visit," he said. "They have banned me, but they cannot stop me. If they put me in jail, they put me in jail. But they cannot stop me." Men like Mattera inspired Ashe to keep fighting for human rights despite the objections of his critics. This meeting was exactly what he needed before taking on the black journalists he was about to confront.[56]

The more than sixty black journalists who attended the reception presented a unique challenge to Ashe and his philosophy of patience and gradualism. These reporters, writers, and columnists suffered the indignities of apartheid every day and watched as the government banned or jailed their friends and colleagues. They would not sit quietly as Ashe lectured them on the value of taking small steps. This was also the first time that he confronted so many black critics at once. His previous debates with Maulana Karenga, Stokely Carmichael, and Dennis Brutus had been out of the public eye in a private location or via correspondence. The reception was his biggest intellectual challenge to date. The setting for the question-and-answer session was a cramped auditorium devoid of windows and filled with many anxious and frustrated men and women. Some of the attendees trembled, while others fearfully scanned the audience in search of government informants. The first journalist to address the crowd spoke of Mattera's banning and suggested that any one of them might be next. Many reporters chanted "Power, power," and a number of them uttered, "Shame, shame."[57]

The attendees directed their animus at Ashe. Many of the questioners demanded that he return to the United States and support the worldwide boycott of South Africa. They argued that his visit represented nothing more than tokenism. "The black man still has his place—cleaning toilets," quipped one man. "You stay away, all of you." One journalist acknowledged that a boycott might hurt the locals, yet he insisted that blacks were used to suffering and would sacrifice even more if it meant a better future. Many did not accept Ashe's comparisons to the United States. "We don't just want equality, as you do," a woman lectured him. "We were dispossessed. We want our land back." Underlying the comments was the assertion that Ashe was naive for believing he could help change the apartheid laws. One angry man whispered "Uncle Tom" under his breath, accusing Ashe of furthering the white man's interests.[58]

Ashe defended his appearance in South Africa and argued for the acceptance of gradual progress and patience. To those who pushed for tougher economic sanctions, he suggested that world leaders valued their financial interests over human rights. He listed a number of African countries that traded with South Africa despite its apartheid laws. If nations made up of blacks did not sever ties with South Africa, why would the rest of the world? In the United States, he contended, the civil rights struggle had begun with small steps like Rosa Parks's famous act of defiance in Montgomery, Alabama. Parks's arrest had led to the

Montgomery Bus Boycott, which galvanized the black community and resulted in actions such as the Greensboro sit-ins, the March on Washington, the Freedom Rides, and ultimately the Civil Rights Act of 1964. The guests responded that Ashe's examples were not applicable to South Africa. Both Parks and Martin Luther King Jr. would have received bans and/or long jail sentences if they had organized acts of civil disobedience in South Africa. Ashe tried to convince them that his trip was a positive development, citing an integrated Ellis Park as proof. "Maybe I'm naïve," he confessed, "but I think, when you're mapping out a plan for progress, emotion cannot be allowed to play a large role, except for drumming up support."[59]

If the journalists at the reception represented one extreme in the apartheid debate, Bob Hewitt represented the other. A native Australian who had emigrated to South Africa, Hewitt was known for his court antics and his quick temper. He argued with officials, opponents, and fans, sometimes resulting in physical confrontations. Following a particularly disgraceful performance in Los Angeles, a senior citizen had left the grandstands and attacked Hewitt for displaying poor court manners. He was as outspoken off the court as he was on it. In the press and on television, Hewitt praised South Africa's apartheid laws and insisted that blacks were "happy" with their current living situation. Three years earlier, Ashe had questioned Hewitt's views during a heated conversation. The Australian turned South African brushed aside Ashe's opinions and labeled him naive for believing the negative press. The two had not spoken since. Ashe entered the match as the clear favorite to defeat the unranked Hewitt. In his diary, Ashe remarked that he and Hewitt "dressed quite properly for the occasion: I in rebel red, he in a brown shirt." The crowd was split fifty-fifty, and the black spectators cheered loudly when Ashe registered a point or when Hewitt committed an unforced error. Despite struggling with his serve, Ashe jumped out to a 6-3 win in the first set. Hewitt rallied to force a tiebreaker in the second set, but his momentum proved illusory as Ashe battled back for a 7-6 victory. After one more uneventful set, Ashe captured the match, defeating a South African on his home turf. Before exiting the court, Ashe turned to the largest collection of nonwhites in the stands and waved to his loyal fans. Hewitt followed with a mocking salute.[60]

The Ashe-Hewitt match reignited the integrated-seating controversy. On November 19 the *Rand Daily Mail* reprinted an article Ashe had authored for the *London Times* in which he claimed that the South African government had promised him integrated grandstands at Ellis Park. Back in Pretoria, government officials and politicians unfamiliar with the arrangement began phoning Owen Williams to express their discontent. Ultimately, the officials succeeded in retaining the nonwhite section of the stands, effectively resegregating the park and breaking the verbal agreement with Ashe. Owen and Jennifer Williams once again subverted the ruling by giving away "white" tickets to interested blacks and coloreds. As the stadium filled to capacity, verbal arguments erupted as nonwhites started to claim their "white" seats. This time Ashe was aware of the problem. During an interview with CBS at Ellis Park, one nonwhite South African man approached Ashe with a ticket that read "Nonwhite," accusing the tennis star of lying to his black and colored fans. Reporters from the *Johannesburg Star*, a newspaper critical of the Nationalists, also apprised Ashe of the seating situation. He had expected the government to execute such a maneuver, but he had not anticipated Owen Williams's betrayal. He understood Williams's difficult position as an intermediary between him and government officials, yet he had hoped for the honest integration of the stadium. "To any logical, rational mind, this probably all sounds very deceitful," he explained in his diary, referring to the "white" ticket giveaways, "but remember that South Africa is neither logical nor rational. You negotiate the truth along with everything else." In this instance Ashe felt that rigidity would get him nowhere. Some blacks managed to find seats in the white sections of Ellis Park. This small step would have to do for the time being.[61]

Despite the emotion of the week, Ashe performed well on the tennis court, knocking off Stewart, Phillips-Moore, and Hewitt with relative ease. His semifinal match against veteran South African Cliff Drysdale presented much more of a challenge, though Ashe had a number of advantages heading into the match. Like him, Drysdale had faced distractions throughout the year, including the founding of the ATP, antiapartheid protests, and a prolonged illness early in the season. On the court, he relied on a long backswing to keep the ball inbounds, frustrating his opponents into making unforced errors. He seemed to tire in long matches and lose his strong serve. His backhand was the only stroke that troubled Ashe. Before the semifinal began, Ashe noticed that the "nonwhite" section of Ellis Park had filled to capacity. The blacks and coloreds stood in front of their seats and cheered Ashe to a 2-0 lead in the opening set. His serve then betrayed him as Drysdale fought back to take a 4-3 lead. Ashe's solid groundstrokes, though, made up for his inconsistent serve, and he rallied to win the first frame 6-4. In the second and third sets his serve caught up to his ground game, preventing Drysdale from returning consistently. With the crowd firmly behind him, Ashe eliminated the South African 6-3 and 6-2. He became the first African American man to reach the final of the South African Open, in which he would face twenty-year-old American Jimmy Connors for the title.[62]

Ashe had little time to celebrate. Immediately after the customary handshakes and postmatch interview, he received a message summoning him to Owen Williams's office. He arrived to find Williams and Donald Dell accompanied by Blen Franklin of the South African Lawn Tennis Union. There was also another figure, a tall, immaculately dressed individual who spoke deliberately while he finished off several cigarettes. From photographs, Ashe recognized the man as Piet Koornhof, the highest-ranking official he would meet while in South Africa. Koornhof exuded confidence and spoke in a colloquial manner. After introducing himself, Koornhof agreed to a candid conversation as long as their discussion remained private. Although Ashe never revealed the details of their meeting, he hinted that Koornhof wanted to end apartheid but not immediately. "I got the feeling that timing was vital," Ashe wrote. Integration of South Africa's Sugar Circuit before 1974 would represent a major step forward, Ashe advised. He left the meeting pleased with Koornhof. "I came away," he noted, "honestly believing that the man who is maybe the next Prime Minister of South Africa is committed to major advances for the black man." Later he told an *Argus* reporter, "We had a very frank conversation. We differ on some points, but we had an open and honest conversation and we know where we stand."[63]

In most places around the world a championship match would be held late on a Sunday afternoon. South Africa, however, was not like the rest of the world. The nation's blue laws prohibited two activities on Sundays: organized athletics and executions. Everything else was fair game. Therefore, the Sunday after his semifinal win over Drysdale, Ashe and a small delegation traveled the seventeen miles from Johannesburg to Soweto for a tennis clinic and an outdoor dinner party hosted by one of the township's few doctors. The location for the clinic was Pfefeni Park, a dusty, barren makeshift tennis court positioned between a train station and an old soccer field. A crowd of approximately fifteen hundred children and teenagers, along with some of their parents, surrounded the court and learned the sport from one of the world's greatest players. "It is one of the sadnesses of Soweto," Ashe explained, "that few people from the outside ever visit there, so my presence was special, no matter who I was or what I did. The main thing: *I came to them.*" After the clinic concluded, the young blacks rushed Ashe and clung to the African American star. Jennifer Williams "remembered getting into a situation where [Ashe] was mobbed, almost mobbed. . . .

He was a demigod. He was aspirational [sic] for them." From his jail cell on Robben Island, Nelson Mandela followed Ashe's travels in the newspapers. He believed Ashe was an inspiration to the black and colored children who clamored for him in Soweto. He had shown them that blacks could succeed if given the opportunity. Not all of the young blacks appreciated his visit, however. A small crowd of more militant blacks gathered around the tennis star, shouting phrases like, "Go home, leave us alone." His supporters yelled back at the angry youths, creating a tense environment filled with animosity and frustration. Jennifer Williams became frightened that a violent confrontation might erupt. The party, though, made it back to their car without incident.[64]

From Pfefeni Park, Ashe and his delegation traveled to the home of Dr. and Mrs. Methlane, one of Soweto's few middle-class couples. Dr. Methlane worked as a physician in Soweto's only hospital, laboring day and night to care for his long list of patients. Methlane, in fact, was unable to leave the hospital for his own dinner party and missed the entire event. Ashe's absent host spoke to the lack of resources, facilities, and qualified professionals in Soweto. Methlane's home was small compared with the middle- and upper-class white houses in Johannesburg, yet it stood out in impoverished Soweto. The one hundred or more guests crowded into the living and dining areas and relaxed in the spacious back yard. A band played in the background as the men and women discussed sports, politics, and apartheid. At the conclusion of dinner, Reggie Ngcobo, a lawyer and president of South Africa's black tennis association, asked for everyone's attention. "You can make us or break us, Arthur," he began, speaking in Ashe's general direction. "You are the pride and idol of us all. You epitomize sportsmanship, for the essence of sportsmanship is to experience happiness in the happiness of others—and to feel their pain and their suffering too." Ashe's appearance was a challenge to South Africa's black leaders, reminding them of their ultimate goals of equality and independence. They had to use him as inspiration to keep fighting. Ngcobo's speech ended with a spirited rendition of "For He's a Jolly Good Fellow." He then presented Ashe with an amulet and gave him a nickname, Sipho, which means "gift" in Xholsha.[65]

Ashe hoped that his visit to Soweto would be followed by a victory in the South African Open the next day. He believed that November 26 marked the most significant moment of his trip. On that date, before thousands of white, black, and colored fans, he was scheduled to face fellow American Jimmy Connors for the championship. Prior to his arrival in South Africa, his friends, mentors, and advisers had all expressed the importance of winning in Johannesburg. A victory in the open would be a symbolic triumph over the theory of white superiority and would embarrass the Pretoria regime. The moment had finally come. A confident Ashe entered as the slight favorite over the young phenom Connors. "I feel I am back to near my best form and could possibly take the title," he told a *New York Times* reporter. On paper, the match-up with Connors looked good for Ashe. He was experienced, seasoned, and on top of his game. Connors was young, immature, and seemingly preoccupied with his personal life. Ashe's strong backhand was an effective counter to Connors' impressive forehand. The fast-paced Connors would have trouble with Ashe's lobs and soft game.[66]

As the match got under way, the partisan mixed-race crowd cheered loudly for Ashe. Connors appeared undeterred. Although Connors's serve lacked its normal punch, Ashe won the break point in only one of three games and quickly fell behind 4-1. The two alternated games for the rest of the set, and Ashe could not catch up, losing 6-4. In the second set, Ashe used his lob to throw Connors off balance and matched his opponent's groundstrokes. Ashe held leads of 5-4 and 6-5 before Connors took over. In the twelfth game, Ashe hit what he thought was an unreturnable lob that moved away from Connors. Instead, the young star connected with a perfect backhand that just eluded Ashe's outstretched racquet. With the momentum at his back, Connors rallied to win the second set 7-6. "And after that," Ashe remembered, "you could feel that the air had gone out of the match." A disappointing third set followed. Jimmy Connors, a man with little to no interest in race relations or apartheid, had defeated Ashe for the title. The postmatch questions, though, focused on the entirety of Ashe's trip and not Connors or the championship. Reporters asked Ashe about his meeting with Koornhof, his impressions of South Africa, and whether the visit had been worth the trouble. "Up to now my time in South Africa has been the most interesting eight days I've ever spent," he told the press. He compared the visit to "eating a big meal—you've got to digest it." In retrospect, his performance in the South African Open was not the most important aspect of his appearance, a fact confirmed by the reporters' questions. The world had watched as he traveled to Soweto, met with Koornhof, played before arguably integrated audiences, and defeated white South Africans such as Hewitt and Drysdale. What mattered was that he was on South African soil.[67]

With only two days of his time in South Africa remaining, Ashe still had a number of obligations to fulfill. On November 27 he and Tom Okker defeated Bob Maud and Lew Hoad to win the doubles championship of the open. The victory was the first tournament win for a black tennis player in South Africa, albeit shared. The following day, Ashe and his delegation flew from Durban to Capetown to meet with Gatsha Buthelezi, a Zulu chieftan, who was one of the

most important black men in South Africa. Buthelezi lived in a relatively in-
accessible part of the African countryside, with one small landing strip nestled
behind a mountain. Thunderstorms on that particular day prevented the pilot
from landing, forcing the party to return to Capetown. In the afternoon, Ashe
and the others drove to Stellenbosch University, South Africa's premier institution of learning. Located near many lush vineyards, Stellenbosch had a reputation for vehemently defending apartheid. Many of its faculty members contended that blacks and coloreds preferred to live separately from whites. Upon
his arrival, Ashe met with anthropology professor Christopf Hanekom, an Afrikaner, and three of his best students. Hanekom thanked Ashe for working on
behalf of the black and white races and applauded his sensitivity. When Hanekom
argued that apartheid was the "balance" that prevented riots like the ones in
Watts, Newark, and Detroit, Ashe accused him of misinterpreting the riots.
"Tell me, professor," Ashe asked, "are you scared?" Confused by the question,
Hanekom responded, "No." "Boy, I'd be, if I were you," Ashe countered. Riots and
bloodshed had not yet reached the townships, but sooner rather than later they
would. The Soweto Uprising just three years later proved Ashe prophetic.[68]

Hanekom and his students struggled to keep up with Ashe. In making an argument against apartheid, Ashe cited the murders of activists, rapes of innocent blacks, illegal executions, and imprisonment of black reporters. "You must
try to understand, Mr. Ashe," Hanekom interjected, "that we are still struggling
with our colonial past. We are different cultures, different languages, trying to
find our way together, and that is not an easy task." Ashe argued that that was
the case in all nations, most of which were not locking up ethnic minorities
without cause. When Hanekom stated that integration would not benefit South
Africa as a whole, Ashe requested the source of his information. Had he queried
the men and women of Soweto? Ashe already knew the answer. Before depart-
ing, Ashe had one more question for Hanekom and his students: "All the sophisticated evolutionary arguments aside, all the intellectual and political position
papers forgotten—in your heart, do you think [apartheid is] right?" He paused,
then turned toward Conrad Johnson, a colored tennis official present at the
meeting. "Why can you vote and this man can't?" he inquired. "Why are you free
and this man isn't?" Hanekom glanced at Johnson, paused, then looked at Ashe:
"I cannot defend that." Although Ashe had failed to defeat Connors, he scored a
victory inside the halls of Stellenbosch. To the press, each man offered a different interpretation of the meeting. Ashe explained to an *Argus* reporter, "We
talked, we joked, we shared experiences, we differed, we agreed, we communi-
cated." Hanekom was a bit more specific. He suggested that he and his students

had enlightened Ashe about the real South Africa. "His original viewpoint," Hanekom told the Afrikaner press *Die Burger*, "was that all whites in South Africa were racists. . . . I believe that he has lost this illusion to a great extent." Hanekom and the South African press would have to wait until Ashe returned home to get his real take on the encounter.[69]

On his final evening in South Africa, Ashe visited a biracial hospital in Capetown, where he met with Christiaan Barnard, an Afrikaner surgeon whose views were critical of the government. As he and Barnard walked the halls of the hospital, he noticed several black nurses staring closely at him. It was probably the first time they had seen a black celebrity in person. Ashe had dinner with Barnard, then left for his hotel in Capetown. In the morning he would begin his trek back to the United States, evaluating the significance of his travels along the way.[70]

# CHAPTER 7

# Transitions

The reviews were in. "Ashe cut an aloof, disdainful figure on the courts. He was so dignified he was almost painful to watch," reported the *Cape Times*. The "integrated" crowds had erupted in cheers after every point and following each one of Ashe's powerful strokes. Exhibiting an uncharacteristic focus and a determination to win for himself and his race, he had been the epitome of the gentleman athlete, "detached and unresponsive to the obvious admiration of the centre court." In all of his victories and in his lone defeat, he had not argued with referees, expressed frustration, or celebrated his performance, keeping his emotions firmly in check. "As the time draws near for choosing the *Cape Herald* Sportsman of the Year," read one editorial, "we are grateful to have Arthur Ashe's example to remind us of the standards of good sportsmanship we should strive for." Sy Lerman of the *Johannesburg Star* argued that Ashe had "transcended all pettiness" and won over most of his critics.[1]

Ashe's 1973 visit to South Africa revealed both the strengths and the limitations of his increasingly well formed philosophy and political strategy. Unlike other black activists of the past, such as Muhammad Ali, Bill Russell, and Jim Brown, Ashe worked through established political channels and pushed for dialogue with white leaders. Against the advice of Dennis Brutus and other antiapartheid activists, he met personally with Piet Koornhof, traveled to Stellenbosch University, and relied on the advice and guidance of Owen Williams. This strategy of direct engagement had its drawbacks, such as forcing Ashe to accept promises from Koornhof that the government did not keep. Ashe's apparent coziness with Williams and Koornhof angered antiapartheid stalwarts and activists in Soweto, in whose view his very presence in South Africa legitimized the apartheid government and set back the freedom movement.

His silence in the media, a condition of his visit, also allowed Vorster, South African politicians and reporters, and supporters of apartheid to frame the significance of his visit for their own political purposes. *Die Burger*, an Afrikaner newspaper with ties to Vorster's Nationalist Party, claimed that the visit had corrected most of Ashe's ill-informed opinions of South Africa. Ashe's previous impression of South Africa, noted *Die Burger*, had been informed by "slanted and maliciously false propaganda," and now he understood the reasons for apartheid even if he disagreed with them. *Die Burger*'s hypothesis could not have been further from the truth. Ashe hated apartheid now more than ever. His silence, however, permitted the Nationalists to interpret the visit to serve their own political agenda.[2]

These conflicts, which resulted from Ashe's belief in gradual progress, his desire to negotiate with black and white leaders, and his insistence on working within the mainstream political system, persisted into 1974 and 1975. He continued to face criticism from both ends of the political spectrum. Militant activists in the United States and South Africa questioned his tempered approach and perceived deference to white officials. To them he was a sellout, an elitist, an Uncle Tom. "Don't tell me about Arthur Ashe," quipped Billie Jean King in September 1973. "Christ, I'm blacker than Arthur Ashe." Other activists, such as Dennis Brutus, assailed Ashe for traveling to South Africa and meeting with white government officials.[3]

While his opinions on race, civil rights, and apartheid baffled his critics, Ashe's performance on the tennis court equally perplexed sportswriters and fans. Often the "bridesmaid" but rarely the "bride," he lost fourteen of nineteen championship matches during one stretch, leading some frustrated fans to question his commitment to the sport. His uneven play hinted at a deeper internal conflict, one that he struggled with all his life. The balance between tennis and activism, patriotism and militancy, race representation and individualism— a double consciousness of sorts—tugged at his very being. Ashe's activism required that he do one thing; his sport, another.[4]

Between December 1973 and the spring of 1975, events on and off the court, at home and abroad, dominated Ashe's energies. From the fight against apartheid in South Africa and the infusion of the women's liberation movement into professional tennis to his professional commitments with the ATP, endorsement contracts, and civil rights work, Ashe was a man tugged in many directions. These events, issues, and developments spoke to Ashe's complex views on race, gender, the amateur ethic, and the generational divide in tennis. Though many would try, he became even more difficult to pin down.

_⌒_ _⌒_

On November 29, 1973, Ashe's four-year emotional journey came to an end. After three visa rejections, one Davis Cup ban of South Africa, scores of antiapartheid protests, and a "new" South African sports policy, he had finally arrived in the dusty streets of Soweto and on center court at Ellis Park. He had won, lost, experienced, and learned. Days before his departure, he, Donald Dell, and Richard Evans drafted a statement reflecting on their travels. Ashe planned to offer his most pointed criticism of South Africa since his arrival, arguing that Vorster and the Nationalists had moved too slowly in dismantling apartheid. He would demand that South Africa follow through on its promise to integrate sports both in the stands and on the fields of play.[5]

But moments from the press conference, as Ashe and his delegation gathered inside the terminal of Jan Smuts International Airport, he decided to leave out this portion of the speech. The press later speculated that Koornhof had gotten to Ashe, convincing him that racial change was on the way. In fact, before Ashe's departure Koornhof had arranged for a second meeting in which he promised Ashe an integrated Sugar Circuit in 1974 provided that all players of color were affiliated with SALTU. This gentleman's agreement apparently led Ashe to scrap his tough public criticism. Instead, he spoke of hope and progress. Echoing the clichéd words of astronaut Neil Armstrong, he said he believed that the multiracial Sugar Circuit represented "one small step for man, but, hopefully, one giant step for mankind." "I am optimistic," he told the press, "that progress can be made in the immediate future." He cited four developments that marked the erosion of apartheid. First, blacks in South Africa and throughout the continent were bolder, more independent, and unlikely to stand for injustice. Second, South African blacks also held an overwhelming popular majority, which the Afrikaners could no longer control. Third, Ashe reasoned, once the Vietnam and Middle East conflicts concluded, America's attention would shift to human rights violations in South Africa. Finally, as television had done in Selma and Birmingham, Alabama, during the civil rights movement, news reports would broadcast images of violence in South Africa that Americans would be loath to ignore. "I believe the first breezes of change may be reaching the Southern tip of Africa," he contended.[6]

To his critics, Ashe could not have been more naive. Soweto's impoverished day laborers, passbooks in hand, felt the stench of oppression, not the fresh breezes of change. Koornhof's concession represented an illusion, a bad joke. Did blacks and coloreds have a real chance to compete on the Sugar Circuit?

Few nonwhite players were affiliated with SALTU, and in general nonwhites lacked the funds, facilities, and coaching to become elite players. Ashe's take on things was influenced in part by his inner circle, men like Donald Dell, who fed him praise and reinforced his opinions. "Dr. Koornhof got the message and ACTED," Dell wrote to him after the trip, "the Sugar Circuit is really open to all. Another, in your own quiet, logical, exemplary way you have already made a real + meaningful contribution to better understanding + harmony among races in S.A." Dell declared the trip an unparalleled success, giving Ashe credit for helping to dismantle apartheid. Perhaps Ashe had surrounded himself with too many individuals who were unwilling to challenge his philosophy. While Dell, the mainstream media, and the English-language South African press heaped praise upon the American star, his opponents expressed another opinion. They thought he deserved scorn, not recognition.[7]

Ashe's disappointing public statement was not the only development that angered his American critics. Before leaving South Africa, he decided to establish a foundation for black and colored tennis players who were unable to afford equipment or coaching. He also decided to donate his used tennis items, including racquets, shirts, shorts, shoes, and balls, to nonwhite South Africans who exhibited skill and promise. This made all the sense in the world to Ashe. Those hopefuls unaffiliated with SALTU could earn their way into the association using his money and equipment, and he might silence his critics who complained of a lack of funding and resources for black players. At least one African American columnist in New York City assailed Ashe for aiding the children of Soweto instead of the children of Harlem. How could he spend one dime overseas when Harlem's blacks continued to play on makeshift courts in the middle of urban streets? This journalist argued that Ashe had an obligation to improve the lives of African American youths before he moved on to the world's problems. In Ashe's mind, however, Soweto's poor were no less worthy than Harlem's, and as an internationalist he believed that all blacks struggled as one.[8]

Ashe ignored his black and white critics and continued to fight apartheid through established political, diplomatic, and economic channels. In his view, rowdy public demonstrations and pickets drew the media's attention but rarely resulted in tangible progress. Some activists, he believed, were more interested in theatrics and spectacle than in achieving real change. "It may be emotionally satisfying," he argued, "to stand up on a soapbox and have a television camera pointed in your face for five minutes, but how often does that help anyone who follows you?" He contended that as the minority, blacks had to engage in dialogue with white political and business leaders. Meeting face to face with a CEO accomplished much more than picketing outside his office.[9]

Ashe applied this strategy to Ford and IBM, two multinational corporations with extensive business operations in South Africa. Just days after he returned to New York, he arranged to have lunch with his friend and business associate Joseph Cullman, the chairman of one of Ashe's chief endorsement partners, Philip Morris. Cullman also sat on the boards of Ford and IBM, so he was an ideal liaison to set up meetings between Ashe and executives of both companies. Later that afternoon, Cullman phoned Ashe with news that vice presidents from both Ford and IBM promised to contact him to discuss their operations in South Africa. In face-to-face meetings, Ashe planned to lay out in detail the history of apartheid in South Africa, focusing particular attention on civil and human rights violations perpetrated by the Afrikaner government. He hoped to convince Ford and IBM that civil and human rights, especially those of company workers, must be a major factor in contract negotiations with a foreign government. He expressed cautious optimism that executives might act on his concerns; at the very least, both Ford and IBM would have to explain their policies to him in person. He believed this behind-the-scenes discussion would have a larger impact than a hastily arranged press conference in which he assailed corporate officials. An event such as a press conference might play well in the black press and among black activists, but would it make a difference? To Ashe, the answer was no. It is likely that Ashe, a man who closely guarded his image, had an ulterior motive for the closed-door meetings. The balance between tennis and activism demanded that he negotiate his positions quite carefully; he was well aware that his sport's unwritten codes conflicted with his activism. The meetings with Ford and IBM, then, allowed him to appear as a statesman and an activist at the same time, satisfying the tennis purists who opposed direct action and many African Americans who insisted that he remain committed to civil rights causes.[10]

In the month following his trip, Ashe also worked on a documentary about South Africa. An exposé of sorts, the film profiled struggling black workers and identified human rights abuses in the country. Ashe and the filmmakers shot several scenes in Jamaica, where the nation's black citizens could be seen in the background during interviews. He and the film crew wanted media critics and ordinary viewers to receive the documentary in a positive way, which is why they sought to include as many people of color in the film as possible. Scenes of middle-class whites surrounding Ashe on camera might lead viewers to question the authenticity of the entire production, the filmmakers reasoned. In Jamaica he encountered young black militants just like those he had seen in South Africa and the United States. Some openly criticized his trip to South Africa, while others professed a desire to join with African freedom fighters. These adolescents, raised in poverty and often falling victim to institutionalized racism, reminded him of so many other young blacks who looked to violence to solve racial problems. To these youths, he preached diplomacy and dialogue.[11]

As fate would have it, Ashe was not the headliner of his own film. That role belonged to Muhammad Ali, the charismatic and always entertaining former heavyweight boxing champion. Soon, Ali would make his own pilgrimage to Africa and battle George Foreman in the now legendary "Rumble in the Jungle" match in Zaire. In mid-December 1973, though, Ali remained holed up in a training facility in Deer Lake, Pennsylvania, preparing for a title bout with Joe Frazier. After some prodding by the film's director, John Marshall, a former press agent, Ali agreed to welcome Ashe and the documentary crew to his lodge in the Pocono Mountains for a discussion on South Africa. Waking just after dawn, Ashe and Marshall boarded a flight from Miami to New York, then hopped in a cab for the drive to Deer Lake. Three hours later, Ashe and Ali, two men on opposite sides of the Vietnam War debate, met for the first time. "Ali spoke in his usual folksy way," Ashe recalled, "with bad grammar and the colorful idioms, but there certainly is no doubt in my mind that a very natively clever man lurks behind this façade." Ashe found Ali likable, honest, and very intelligent. Ali, in turn, deferred to Ashe's expertise on South Africa, displaying none of the self-righteousness so often ascribed to him. Ali had had little experience with South Africa save one. Years earlier, Ali's handlers had scheduled a series of boxing exhibitions in South Africa. When a number of U.N. diplomats from Islamic nations discovered the plan, they immediately paid a visit to the boxer. A Black Muslim and a member of the Nation of Islam, Ali was obliged by his faith and his race to stay away. "Me representing the whole Islamic world I had to listen to these people," Ali explained. "But you going as an individual, Arthur— I support everything you did as an individual." Ashe and Ali, long portrayed as philosophical adversaries in the popular press, had reached a common understanding on South Africa. Neither adopted the role the press imagined for him.[12]

Ashe was proving to be a versatile activist, an established leader who challenged apartheid from multiple angles. His antiapartheid crusade included an advocacy piece that he wrote for *Jet* magazine, a periodical with a middle-class African American readership. He began the article with a description of his travels that emphasized the diversity of his experiences. In his own mind, Ashe had to sell himself as an expert on South Africa by listing his many meetings and encounters. In the past, he had frequently called out activists who made controversial public statements without doing the proper research, and he was determined not to make the same mistake. He then offered a history lesson on apartheid. He painted a scene of oppression and exploitation in which twenty-two million nonwhites labored in the gold, diamond, and coal mines, while the white minority profited from their hard work. Segregation divided the buses, mandated separate hotels for whites and nonwhites, and kept nonwhites away from popular shows. Blacks used the term *master* with alarming frequency. Then he called on *Jet* readers to join the antiapartheid struggle. First, he encouraged blacks to read about Africa and educate themselves on the legacies of colonial oppression and violence that marred the continent. For that to happen, black periodicals such as *Jet* and *Ebony* had to increase their coverage of African freedom movements. He also asked readers to write letters to Congress, specifically to members of the House Sub-Committee on Africa, of which Charles Diggs was a member. He advised, "For the brothers and sisters who are informed about southern Africa, my personal opinion is to stop the rhetoric and start doing something positive and tangible. Words without appropriate action do very little to improve the situation." Black Africans, he said, were the only ones who could make the proper decisions for their nations and their future. African Americans should support their black brothers and sisters but never tell them what to do. Finally, Ashe called on U.S. multinational corporations such as Ford and IBM to raise wages, increase benefits, and improve work conditions for native employees. "These companies need to be told," he wrote, "that the equal opportunity laws that exist in the U.S. should apply equally as well in South Africa in the eyes of any decent American."[13]

The *Jet* feature story was vintage Ashe. In it, he promoted action, but only *after* the reader had studied the continent and learned the nuances of the black freedom struggle. Rather than simply railing against apartheid or world leaders, he told readers how to get involved. Offering multiple avenues of activism, his plan included the application of political, diplomatic, and economic pressure on both U.S. and South African officials. His advice relied on pragmatic and varied solutions. Some readers of *Jet* applauded Ashe's well-considered piece. One man from Los Angeles responded that he "was pleased by the fact that this type of article will prove to be very enlightening to Blacks, most of whom know very little about Africa." The man wanted more coverage of Africa in *Jet* to counter the biased reporting of the mainstream press. A reader from Houston took issue with Ashe's moderated approach, arguing that South Africa belonged to blacks and not the Afrikaners. "What's wrong with telling the white man to get out of South Africa and go back to Europe where he came from?" the man asked. Ashe had heard this opinion time and time again, and on each occasion he had dismissed the critique as outlandish, another example of how some black activists had veered away from the teachings of Martin Luther King Jr.[14]

_____

"Don't you think women are at their prettiest when they're sort of barefoot, pregnant, at home, taking care of the kiddies and doing the housework?" asked retired tennis professional Bobby Riggs. Riggs had no love for "girls'" tennis or "Women's Lob," a derogatory label used to describe Billie Jean King and other women in the sport who demanded equal rights and equal pay. For years, King in particular had fought for increased prizes and television exposure on levels comparable to those in the men's game. Critics, including Ashe, argued that women's tennis was too slow, too boring, and too uneventful to justify King's demands. Most men, they said, had no interest in watching girls in white skirts play a man's game. Even as a child, Ashe had cheered Pancho Gonzalez, a Mexican American, and ignored Althea Gibson, the trailblazing black phenom. The male players who commented on "Women's Lob" often used terms like *girls* and *broads* to describe King and others. In 1973 the two sides agreed to a symbolic settlement of their claims in the form of a winner-take-all tennis match between King and Riggs in Houston's Astrodome. The battle for gender superiority would play out in the media and on the court, and Ashe would be no innocent bystander.[15]

For decades men dominated tennis. In mixed doubles, men took on the aggressive and dominant role, leaving to women the passive sidekick role. There was pressure on women like Suzanne Lenglen, Maureen Connolly, Gibson, and Margaret Court to act in a proper, dignified fashion, competing quietly and in a reserved manner. Billie Jean King changed all of that. Sports historian Benjamin Rader has concluded that King, "more than any single person, helped erase the stiff formality and pomposity from the sport." Before King began her crusade for equal pay, women typically earned 10 percent of what men made. Both Lamar Hunt and Jack Kramer refused to offer circuits for women, assuming that crowds would not pay to see the likes of King and Chris Evert. In the early 1970s, King and others fought back. In 1971 King and *World Tennis* publisher Gladys Heldman formed the Virginia Slims Tour, a women's circuit sponsored by Philip Morris. The tour included large prizes and a lucrative television deal. King soon became "one of the most important symbols of the revived feminist movement of the early 1970s," noted Rader. The defiant King pushed back against reporters and columnists who suggested that her proper place was in the home, making dinners, sweeping floors, and caring for children. When a reporter asked why she wasn't at home, she would reply, "Why don't you go ask Rod Laver why he isn't at home?" Her "unladylike behavior" inspired women and angered traditionalist men, men like Bobby Riggs.[16]

Riggs's days as a top player had come and gone. Born on February 25, 1918, in Los Angeles, he had neither the power nor the physical stature of a Don Budge or a Jack Kramer. Instead, he relied on his court acumen to execute his soft game to perfection, often dropping incredible lob shots that baffled his opponents. Stoic and unflappable, Riggs worked his way to the number-one ranking in 1939, a year in which he won Wimbledon and the U.S. Nationals and finished with nine tournament victories. After a prosperous decade in the 1940s as both an amateur and a professional, he assumed the role of a tennis promoter in the 1950s, with limited success. His gambling habit intensified, and he lost countless dollars on bad bets. By 1973 Riggs was an obscure figure in tennis—that is, until he challenged Margaret Court to a match.[17]

In the early 1970s, Riggs emerged as the leading voice against "Women's Lob." The fifty-five-year-old former champion argued that women tennis players were genetically inferior to men and undeserving of large prizes. Even in old age Riggs believed he could defeat any woman who dared to challenge him. Court took him up on the offer. The winner of sixty-two major titles during her career, Court dominated many of her opponents thanks to her weight-training regimen and her long reach. She attacked her competitors with an aggressive serve-and-volley game, facilitated by her unmatched physical-conditioning program. For every three matches she played against King, Court won two. But Court was Riggs's second choice for a "Battle of the Sexes" match. Early in the spring, Riggs held a press conference in which he promised Billie Jean King $5,000 if she defeated him. "I contend that you, the top woman player in the world, not only cannot beat a top male player," he said, "but that you can't beat me, an old man." King immediately turned him down, insisting that the washed-up former champ was desperate to make a buck, not to prove male superiority. Court, on the other hand, promptly accepted Riggs's offer, now $10,000, setting the stage for a Mother's Day "Battle of the Sexes" event. Los Angeles Times sportswriter Jeff Prugh described the match-up as a contest between sickly and unprepared competitors. "The challenger is an outspoken little man who looks like a druggist or a small town mayor," he observed. Riggs was slow, frail, and blind without his glasses. The thirty-year-old Court had just given birth and suffered from a persistent viral infection. Severe leg cramps had forced her to remove her shoes in the middle of a recent match. "To the tennis purist," Prugh noted, "[the match] doesn't crackle with the pulse-quickening appeal of Budge vs. Vines, Kramer vs. Gonzales or Laver vs. Rosewall."[18]

Mother's Day 1973 proved forgettable for Margaret Court and the women's liberation movement. Bobby Riggs, the sport's "most outspoken senior citizen," embarrassed his female competitor in straight sets, 6-2, 6-1. Riggs "delivered the biggest blow to Virginia Slims here Sunday since cigaret [sic] ads were banned from TV," quipped Prugh. The aged former champion, wrote Mark Asher of the *Washington Post*, "destroyed [Court's] tennis game with a progression of off-speed, slow, slicing, topspinning lobs that caused the 30-year-old Court to lose her confidence, abandon her strong attacking game and make error after error after error." Sportswriters agreed that Court had beaten herself with a series of mistakes and that unlike Riggs, she had failed to rise to the occasion. Billie Jean King, away in Japan, could only read about the "Mother's Day Massacre." Disappointed in Court's performance, she would not let the match stand as a true "Battle of the Sexes." Back in the United States, she held a telephone news conference in which *she* challenged Riggs to another winner-take-all contest. "I think I can do a lot better," King told reporters. "I think I thrive on pressure more than Margaret does." Women tennis players were much more entertaining than Court had shown, and King had something to prove.[19]

In July and August of 1973 representatives for Riggs and King hammered out an agreement. Both sides agreed on a $100,000 match to be held in Houston's Astrodome and televised by ABC. Howard Cosell, ABC's veteran sports reporter, was tapped to lead the coverage. The match between "The Lib" and "The Lip" was on. In New York on August 30, reporters from ABC interviewed players, including Ashe, about the match. For years, Ashe and King had maintained an antagonistic relationship. Ashe had fought King's efforts to obtain better pay for women, concluding that the women's game was inferior, akin to the minor leagues. He had also made derogatory and sexist statements. On women's tennis, he argued, "The average fan, of whatever sex, can relate better to the girls' level of play. Even a great natural athlete like, say, O. J. Simpson, is intimidated when he comes out to watch men play, because when he sees us slugging the ball around, he knows that it is far beyond his capabilities. The girls' game is, by contrast, so nice and leisurely, though, that anyone can identify with it." No seasoned tennis writer would describe King's, Court's, or Evert's game as "nice and leisurely" or give Simpson, a running back for the Buffalo Bills, the slightest chance to defeat any of the top women. Ashe's comments were simply off-base. When reporters asked him about the Riggs-King match, he described the event as "just good clean fun," ignoring the social and historical significance of the contest. For someone who focused so heavily on racial equality, Ashe did not feel the same way about gender, at least not in tennis.[20]

Ashe was not the only black activist who considered women inferior to men in one way or another. As historian Ruth Rosen has noted, many male leaders of the civil rights and Black Power movements relegated women to clerical positions such as that of secretary or typist. Men like Martin Luther King Jr., Whitney Young, and Stokely Carmichael were the ones who gave the speeches and led the marches, not the Ella Bakers of the world. When King and two of his close advisers, Bayard Rustin and Stanley David Levison, formed the Southern Christian Leadership Conference, the men "kept Baker at arm's length and never treated her as a political or intellectual peer." A veteran of the civil rights movement, Baker had been pivotal in cultivating grass-roots networks across the South. The former NAACP field secretary had traveled to places that King and others had dared not go. Baker's biographer Barbara Ransby concluded that "it was probably King's sexist attitudes toward women, at least in part, that prevented him from having [a] collegial relationship with Baker."[21]

Sexism was just as persistent in SNCC and, later, the Black Power movement. In November 1964 two women in SNCC, Mary King and Casey Hayden, drafted a position paper detailing the mistreatment of women inside the civil rights organization. While men headed the important committees and planned events, women took meeting minutes, typed letters, and served coffee. King and Hayden discovered that "within the framework of the civil rights movement and the field of human rights and civil liberties at the time . . . women's rights had no meaning and indeed did not exist."[22]

This perception of women as secondary actors was present in tennis as well. Billie Jean King remembered that in the late 1960s Ashe and his Davis Cup teammates refused to hit with women, and she described the men as "very aloof toward us women players." "Indeed, for a long time," King wrote, "Arthur was worrying almost only about men's tennis . . . he didn't seem to care that much about women's tennis or women's sports or helping women." A reporter for *Time* magazine in 1970 observed that most men on the professional circuit viewed women as "sideshow attractions," and none were as blunt or outspoken as Ashe. "Men are playing tennis for a living now," he told the *Time* reporter. "They have families, and they don't want to give up money just for girls to play. Only three or four women draw fans anyhow, so why do we have to split our money with them?" Ashe's comments referred to a potential women's boycott of several tournaments in protest of unequal prizes. In his opinion, men were the breadwinners who supported their families with tournament winnings. Women like King had husbands to provide for them and therefore did not need or deserve the same prizes as men.[23]

Ashe also argued that men were more competitive with one another and thus more entertaining than women players. He believed that in a short set, any male player ranked in the top fifty could defeat any other ranked man, reflecting a high level of parity that attracted fans (and their dollars). By contrast, only a half-dozen women could best King, Court, or Evert. "Billie Jean can beat somebody like Marcie Louie 6-1 or 6-0 almost every day," he contended. This was the problem with World Team Tennis, a league of men and women that pitted teams of players against one another. Ashe concluded that men should receive higher pay and have more control over WTT because they were the better, more evenly matched competitors. But, he complained, "if anybody in the league tries to correct the imbalance by somehow giving the men a larger role in a game, then Billie Jean will scream sexist."[24]

This was the Ashe of the late 1960s and early 1970s, an Ashe who believed that men were the better sex. Following his marriage to Jeanne Moutoussamy in the winter of 1977, his views on women began to evolve. Moutoussamy was an intelligent New York City photographer with no patience for sexism or elitism. Just before his death in 1993, Ashe wrote extensively about women's tennis and King in his final memoir. In it, he offered a tepid apology to King and others for opposing equal pay. "While I once shared this view," he noted, "I now believe that women should receive all the prize money they can command." He placed King in the company of modern feminists such as Betty Friedan, Gloria Steinem, and Germaine Greer. "As far as I am concerned," he argued, "Billie Jean King is the most important tennis player, male or female, of the last fifty years." Not the best but the most significant. Although the evidence does show a gradual change in Ashe's views, his final memoir, *Days of Grace*, reconstructs parts of his past far more favorably than the historical record can confirm. He had not merely "shared this view" that women tennis players were inferior to men; he had helped to craft it. He never acknowledges his sexism in as many words, though it is clearly in print—in other memoirs, in newspapers, and in magazines.[25]

For someone to be so involved in international civil and human rights movements yet be so indifferent and at times opposed to the women's liberation movement appears quite puzzling. In his published diary Ashe tried to explain his opposition, arguing that men "had no preparation for" women's liberation and therefore did not know how to deal with women activists. "I don't know if, all of a sudden, I could psychologically handle a fifty-fifty split in my house," he said. "I do want to be up-to-date and fair and all that, but the truth is that I also don't want any woman telling me what to do with my life (and vice versa too)." If this opinion classified him as a male chauvinist, then so be it. His future wife would have to understand that *he* would make the major decisions, describing his ideal marriage as a 51 percent to 49 percent split.[26]

A number of circumstances and life experiences informed Ashe's views of women and gender roles. His mother, Mattie, died early in Ashe's life, leaving him without a female role model during his formative years. His stepmother, Lorene Kimbrough, and his live-in housekeeper, Otis Berry, never had the same effect on his development as did his father and male mentors such as Ronald Charity, Dr. Johnson, and J. D. Morgan. "The early death of my mother," Ashe wrote, "prevented me from forming an ideal image the way that other men do." Other factors that informed his views of women likely include the culture of chauvinism in tennis and in the black freedom movement. Few top male players, for instance, defended Billie Jean King's position on prize money. Regardless of the origins of these opinions, the fact remains that Ashe did not come to the aid of his female colleagues in their fight for equality in the sport.[27]

The "Battle of the Sexes" match highlighted Ashe's views of women and gender and offered King an opportunity to lobby for an end to gender discrimination in sports and society. As September 20 neared, sportswriters, fans, major newspapers, and tennis "experts" weighed in on the match. Grace Lichtenstein of the *New York Times* picked King as the victor in four sets. "When [King] falls behind, she does not get upset, she gets fighting mad," she wrote. "'Choke' is not part of her vocabulary." Lichtenstein's colleague Neil Amdur disagreed. "Forgetting male chauvinism," he argued, ". . . [Riggs] just happens to be the better player." The *Wall Street Journal* selected King, while David Gray of the *Guardian* announced for Riggs. Las Vegas oddsmakers had Riggs as an eight-to-five favorite. At a prematch press conference, King and Riggs traded verbal insults. "I think I've gotten to her psychologically and she'll crack under the strain when she gets out there," quipped Riggs, with King seated beside him. "I'm not here to be in a circus," she retorted. "I have to win the match." Hollywood celebrities, professional athletes, politicians, and activists all eagerly awaited the results.[28]

More than thirty thousand noisy fans greeted the two competitors as they emerged from separate dressing rooms. Some of those in attendance paid up to $100 per seat to view the match from courtside, a record-breaking price for tennis tickets. The winner of the contest stood to make $175,000, the largest prize in the history of tennis, with the loser taking home $75,000. As King approached the court she reflected not on women's liberation but on the triumph of tennis as a spectator sport. Early in her playing career, tennis had been for rich, white country club members who sat quietly in their seats as the action unfolded. By contrast, the Houston Astrodome on that night welcomed fans of all racial, ethnic, and socioeconomic backgrounds, many of whom had never seen a tennis match. "You know I believe in spectator participation so a lot of my dreams came true tonight," King remarked later in the evening.[29]

The match itself was one-sided, though this time it was Riggs who searched in vain for answers. In the first game of the second set, Riggs broke King's serve only to see her break back moments later. With the score even at fifteen, Riggs hit a backhand shot into the net, an unforced error that led him to swing his racquet in disgust. King's strategy was to bombard him with flat shots to his backhand and stay away from his forehand. She also knew that Riggs's old legs would make it difficult for him to chase lobs in the backcourt. Her plan worked to perfection, and Riggs struggled all night to keep up with the younger, more polished King. "In the end, it was as easy as sticking a pig," commented Robert Markus of the *Chicago Tribune*. King defeated "the No. 1 symbol of male chauvinism" in three quick sets, 6-4, 6-3, 6-3.[30]

From a bar in downtown Los Angeles, Ashe, like so many other Americans, stood glued to the television. The bar was crowded, filled with curious fans, a number of them placing bets. Early in the first game Ashe knew that King was on her game, as she moved with precision and ease and powered balls along the sidelines. "There was no choke there," Ashe observed, a reference to Margaret Court's loss to Riggs the previous May. A confident Ashe wagered forty dollars on King: one bet on her to win the match, another on her to win in straight sets. "When you've got one player who can't move and the other can hit the ball and isn't nervous, you have got a sure thing in tennis," he explained. On this night, the "Old Lady" made him eighty dollars richer. For Ashe, the "Battle of the Sexes" match was not a contest between women's liberation and male chauvinism but rather an entertainment event, a circus, just plain old fun. The significance of the match remained lost on him. "Girls'" tennis did not top his list of concerns.[31]

⁓

From Wimbledon 1973 to Wimbledon 1974, Ashe played tennis on five continents, boarded 129 flights, slept in seventy-one different beds, and traveled a total of 165,000 miles. He was a top American tennis player, an antiapartheid and human rights activist, a tennis pro at the Doral Country Club in Miami, an ATP union officer, and a wealthy celebrity, to name but five of his many roles. He gave civil rights speeches, gambled with celebrities such as boxer Joe Frazier, and dated a freelance commercial artist from Toronto named Kathy Benn. He seemingly had little time for himself or his tennis.

Ashe struggled with his game throughout 1974. As early as September 1973 he began to wonder if his career as a tennis player was in jeopardy. "Jesus, I feel like an old man," an exasperated Ashe complained after a difficult loss in the U.S. Open to teenager Bjorn Borg. Almost fourteen thousand fans at Forest Hills watched the seventeen-year-old Swedish phenom rally from a one-set deficit to shock Ashe, the 1972 runner-up, 6-7, 6-4, 6-4, 6-4. Borg muscled two backhand drives past Ashe in the seventh game of the fourth set, then aced him four times in succession in the eighth game. "I didn't serve well. I didn't volley well," said Ashe. "When I had the breaks in the third and fourth sets, he very calmly broke back." His entire game had come apart. "I'm thirty years old and teeny-boppers are upsetting me," the defeated former champion wrote in his diary. "It takes something like this to make you aware of how really short an athlete's life is."[32]

It was Jimmy Connors and not Ashe who dominated men's tennis in 1974. The abrasive, twenty-one-year-old showman won 99 of 103 matches, fifteen tournaments, and three legs of the Grand Slam—the U.S. Open, the Australian Open, and Wimbledon. Connors missed his chance at a personal grand slam when the French Tennis Federation barred him from the French Open for signing a contract with World Team Tennis. Only a tennis official, it seemed, could stop the young American. Fueled by the play of Connors and of Chris Evert on the women's side, tennis experienced a rise in spectatorship. A Louis Harris survey found that the percentage of sports fans "who say they 'follow' tennis has risen from 17 to 26 percent just in the last year." The Nielsen Company discovered that 33.9 million Americans played tennis "from time to time," and 23.4 million played at least three times a month. Bobby Riggs and Jimmy Connors appeared on the cover of *Time* magazine in the mid-1970s. Tennis had never been bigger.[33]

As the sport itself reached new heights, Ashe appeared to be in free-fall. His serve was no longer the game's most feared, and injuries threatened to sideline him. At the U.S. Open, he could not hold a one set lead, losing to John Newcombe in the quarterfinals. Newcombe matched Ashe serve for serve and pulled ahead in the third game of the final set when Ashe double-faulted twice. He also lost to Rod Laver for the fifteenth consecutive time at the U.S. Pro Indoor Championships. Another stinging letdown came in the WCT finals in Dallas, where Ashe, whose usually reliable serve failed him, was again topped by Borg in straight sets. "I'm very disappointed," he told reporters. "I guess I had the easy draw, too." His shots that had been winners in 1968 were now merely return shots. Borg had "just stuck his arm out there and the ball would be coming back." Youth had overtaken the game, and Ashe played the role of the old man in the clubhouse.[34]

Several factors accounted for Ashe's drop in play. From a physical standpoint, he had not adjusted his game to his aging body. His once-dominant serve and forehand drive had lost some of their punch; at times both shots were quite pedestrian. To succeed in the future, he would have to play smarter and rely on his soft game, dinking and dunking his way to wins. He would also need to spend more time in the gym and on the track. He continued to maintain a grueling schedule of appearances, speeches, and tennis clinics. His stint as an ATP officer also demanded blocks of his time. On June 19, 1973, he recorded in his diary, "I've been attending so many bloody hearings and ATP meetings that I've had almost no chance to practice." In the summer of 1973 Ashe and the ATP focused on Nikki Pilic, a Yugoslavian association member who withdrew from the Davis Cup after signing a deal with WCT. The Yugoslav Tennis Association Federation promptly suspended Pilic, and Wimbledon officials followed suit. In response, Ashe and other ATP officers voted to boycott Wimbledon if the ILTF did not reinstate Pilic. Pages upon pages of Ashe's diary are filled with observations about this ongoing controversy. He attended legal hearings, gave press conferences, and participated in emergency ATP meetings, activities that took time away from his tennis preparation.[35]

In addition to tennis, the ATP, endorsements, and appearances, Ashe remained committed to civil rights causes in the United States. On October 1, 1973, he served as the keynote speaker at an Urban League luncheon near Gulfport, Mississippi. He spoke on the topic of black empowerment, specifically voter registration and entrepreneurship. Mississippi remained an intimidating place for black activists, as white racists filled many of the state's assemblies and city councils and blacks and whites remained geographically divided. In Jackson, Mississippi, many registered blacks remained afraid to vote, fearful that bigots might attack them or their families.

At a tennis exhibition following the speech, Ashe met with James Meredith, the first African American student to attend the University of Mississippi. Backed by the Kennedy administration and the U.S. Supreme Court, Meredith's admission in 1962 had led to riots in Oxford, Mississippi, instigated by Governor Ross Barnett. The riots resulted in 2 deaths, 28 injured U.S. marshals, and 160 wounded soldiers. Above Meredith's dorm room students bounced basketballs hour after hour, determined not to let him rest, and in the cafeteria white students refused to sit with him. "He went down to Oxford town," sang Bob Dylan. "Guns and clubs followed him down / All because his face was brown / Better get away from Oxford town."[36]

Ashe and Meredith shared a distaste for radical activists. Ashe believed that the bravado and confrontational rhetoric of Carmichael and others undermined Meredith's efforts to register black voters. Meredith, for his part, moved further to the political right in the 1970s and 1980s. He later worked for conservative Republican senator Jesse Helms and opposed the creation of Martin Luther King Jr. Day as a national holiday. Ashe told Meredith that blacks would never acquire true political power unless they openly disagreed with one another and challenged the movement's louder voices.[37]

The ongoing criticism that black militants directed at Ashe seemed to bother him more as the 1970s progressed. He increasingly responded to his critics in a defensive manner, oftentimes explaining in detail his many contributions to the movement. "As people outline my life for me," he complained in his diary, "I should spend most of every day sticking rackets into young black kids' hands, as if I were some kind of recreational Johnny Appleseed." Ashe lamented that any decisions he made, however trivial in his mind, invited scrutiny. If, for instance, he chose to vacation in the south of France as so many other celebrities did, he likely faced criticism from the black press for being elitist and not supporting the African tourist industry. "Those of us who have made it," he wrote, "are not permitted to enjoy ourselves until *after* we have paid our arbitrary dues." For as much as Ashe claimed that he ignored his intellectual opponents, it is clear that he wrestled with their criticisms. He wondered aloud when the criticisms would end.[38]

___

In sports, the list of off-the-field rivalries is long and legendary—Muhammad Ali and Howard Cosell, Joe Louis and Jack Johnson, Harry Edwards and Jesse Owens, to name but three. By the early to mid-1970s, Arthur Ashe and Dennis Brutus had joined the list of intellectual and philosophical opponents. Ashe stood for patience, dialogue, and gradualism, while Brutus was for direct action, boldness, and isolating the Afrikaners. And Brutus pulled no punches. The exiled South African continued to lambaste Ashe and his decisions throughout 1974. Speaking before the Chicago Society of Writers and Editors, he accused Ashe of serving as a spokesman for South Africa's apartheid government. In his view, the tennis star had become too cozy with Piet Koornhof and naively agreed not to criticize the Vorster regime during his travels. According to Brutus, Ashe's documentary on South Africa was a disguised defense of apartheid, and in fact Blen Franklin of SALTU planned to use the film to support South Africa's sports policy at an upcoming meeting of the ILTF. One *Chicago Defender* reader who followed Brutus's speech also suggested that the South Africans had carefully manipulated Ashe. "The Union of South Africa," he wrote, "where the color of a person's skin governs where he or she lives, walks, sit, eats, goes to school, has his appendix out and nearly everything else, has apparently discovered the value of having a sports figure speak kindly of it in public." With a bullet lodged in his back and an extended stay on Robben Island under his belt, Dennis Brutus had experienced apartheid and the violence that came with it. Ashe had never been in prison or been beaten for trying to achieve freedom. *His* South Africa was a mirage of white officials rolling out the red carpet and promising to "integrate" the Sugar Circuit. "Ashe was treated as an honorary white while he was in South Africa," noted Brutus.[39]

Perhaps Brutus was right. Perhaps the government had used Ashe to fool world leaders and sports bodies. Then again, Ashe had used them too. He knew much more about apartheid and South Africa than Brutus let on. After the government informally denied his visa request in 1969, he had scoured international newspapers, scholarly works, and government papers, learning anything and everything about South Africa. "And unfortunately," he revealed of his studies, "I found everything I had heard about South Africa was true." His visit in November 1973 had only reinforced his perception of apartheid. He and Brutus actually agreed in principle, and Ashe concluded that a "violent resolution of South Africa's problems" was inevitable. The two men differed on tactics, just as Ashe had disagreed with black militants on a plan for achieving black empowerment. Brutus believed in boycotts and isolation, Ashe in engagement and open dialogue. Yes, Ashe had lived "like royalty" while in South Africa, but he had also witnessed the suffering and dehumanization of blacks and coloreds. During a speech at Michigan State University on the topic of apartheid, Ashe reminded those in attendance that he favored corporate sanctions against South Africa if nonwhite workers received unequal pay and treatment. He encouraged students and faculty to contact representatives from Ford and General Motors, two Michigan corporations, and ask them about their workforce in South Africa.[40]

Behind the scenes, some South African officials, including Minister of Information and the Interior Dr. Connie Mulder, expressed frustration with Ashe's speeches and public statements. An internal debate raged between verkramptes, such as Mulder, who favored little or no race mixing in sports, and verligtes, such as Koornhof, who supported more liberal sports policies. The South African reporter J. H. P. Serfontein learned through government sources that a "sharp confrontation" had occurred between Mulder and Koornhof on the topic of Ashe's anticipated 1974 visa request. Mulder had approached Koornhof and recommended that the government deny Ashe's second visa based on his anti-apartheid statements and activities. Koornhof was "furious," according to Nationalist members of Parliament. "Dr. Mulder and his department would have looked foolish if a visa for a second visit had been refused for no good reason," noted Serfontein. Unaware of this private clash, Ashe applied for and eventually received a visa to play in the South African Open for a second consecutive year, with Prime Minister Vorster siding with Koornhof over Mulder. Owen Williams announced the decision on October 16 in anticipation of Ashe's second stay in South Africa, to take place November 14–26.[41]

A month before the open, though, South Africa found itself once again embroiled in Davis Cup controversy. The recently reinstated South African team had won its first three ties of the 1974 competition in the South America Zone, defeating Brazil and Ecuador 5-0 and besting Chile 3-2. Ray Moore, Bob Hewitt, and Frew McMillan had then been victorious in the Americas Interzone final, 3-2 over Colombia. After knocking off Italy 4-1 in a first-round Interzone tie, South Africa prepared to face India in the Davis Cup final. The Indian team then surprised fans and observers by announcing its intent to forfeit the final rather than travel to South Africa. Davis Cup officials, led by Committee of Management chairman W. Harcourt Woods, scrambled to prevent the withdrawal. One possible solution involved moving the final matches from South Africa to another African nation where an integrated crowd could watch the tie, but Woods doubted that India would accept the compromise. Instead, India would likely campaign for South Africa's expulsion from the 1975 Davis Cup. "There's sentiment for kicking South Africa out," Woods told reporters. "There was sentiment at Wimbledon earlier this year, but there weren't enough votes." Opponents of South Africa lacked a two-thirds majority, which was required for expulsion, specifically the vote of one nation. For the first time in the seventy-four-year history of the competition, a default in the final round might decide the results.[42]

The public weighed in with a divided reaction to India's withdrawal. "India has exploded another nuclear bomb," wrote one New York City man who opposed the default. He accused the Indian government of practicing hypocrisy based on its maintenance of the caste system, a form of discrimination similar to apartheid. This racist structure, ranging from wealthy and privileged Brahmans at the top of the hierarchy to impoverished "untouchables" at the very bottom, governed every element of life in India. Untouchables engaged in menial labor and could not associate with members of higher castes. The writer concluded that India's move displayed less interest in civil rights and more desire to "woo" Third World nations, hoping to garner their support on other matters. One *New York Times* reader of Indian descent questioned the man's opinion. "We do not have the killing instinct and we despise it on a playground," he began. For Indians, competition represented an act of "brotherliness," and if South Africa did not consider its Indian opponents brothers because of their skin, there was no point in playing the matches. Americans, he added, had little room for criticism. Ongoing racism in the American South, poverty and racial inequality in the North, and riots and violence over school busing in Boston all were evidence that the United States was no racial utopia. A writer from Greenwich, Connecticut, did not object to India's withdrawal per se. In his view, India should have anticipated a tie with the South Africans and pulled out much sooner, preserving a final-round match-up. "India's default in the Davis Cup final round negates the efforts of a great many people," he concluded. Angered themselves by the default, India's top two players, brothers Vijay and Anand Amritraj, resigned from the team immediately, citing a "mismanagement of the whole situation."[43]

Ashe added himself to the list of individuals heaping criticism on the Indians. Calling the decision a "poor strategic move," he viewed the default as a lost opportunity for nonwhites (Indians) to compete equally against white South Africans in the land of apartheid. "By not playing," he argued, "normalization of tensions between black and white has been set back between two and three years." No doubt an exaggeration, Ashe's statement to the *Chicago Defender* spoke to his belief in direct engagement and his abhorrence of political gamesmanship. Further, he did not want the South Africans to claim the Davis Cup without a fight, a fight that India had backed down from.[44]

Internationally, South Africa had much bigger problems than the Davis Cup controversy. In late October 1974 the U.N. Security Council planned to act on a General Assembly recommendation that the United Nations expel South Africa for its apartheid policies. "In South Africa," read a *Washington Post* editorial, "it is a deeply human question touching the fates and fortunes of millions. Would confrontation or communication better bring about racial change?" This piece against expulsion asserted that proponents of banishment, such as the Soviet Union, were hypocrites, since their "own internal system makes South African apartheid look like Jeffersonian democracy." Engagement was the preferable course, a course that Polaroid, an American company, had taken by paying

equal wages to its nonwhite workers in South Africa. Ashe himself forced officials to integrate Ellis Park and the Sugar Circuit, actions that would not have
been possible if he had not visited.[45]

Prime Minister Vorster fought hard in the press to repair South Africa's image. In an important speech, he asked his critics, international and domestic, to
give him and his regime six months to improve race relations and dismantle aspects of apartheid. In fact, South Africa had made some progress. Larger cities
such as Johannesburg and Cape Town had dismantled some of their "petty
apartheid" laws, integrating park benches and allowing blacks and coloreds to
visit the zoos. Nonwhites in Johannesburg now used the same library reading
room as the Afrikaners, and municipal offices had eliminated separate waiting
lines. Arthur Ashe, Evonne Goolagong, and Bob Foster had all competed and
won in South Africa.[46]

In the view of Vorster's detractors, these cosmetic changes were not enough.
The government continued to displace thousands of blacks and coloreds from
their native homelands, forcing workers to travel many miles in search of employment. Critics also pointed out that Vorster's "six months" speech referred
to foreign, not domestic, policy. "I have made no promises of changes in domestic policy," he said in a speech. "I am not going to change it because our critics
here and elsewhere demand it." Laws prevented workers from taking new jobs
even if it meant better pay, and the state virtually barred black women from
urban centers. "The weight of the evidence," concluded Charles Mohr of the
*New York Times*, "is that things have been getting worse for the nonwhites . . .
for several years and that the prospects for fundamental improvement in racial
policy may be receding." This was the way things stood when Ashe was making
plans to visit South Africa in November 1974.[47]

Much less fanfare greeted Ashe's second arrival in South Africa. "The Negro
tennis star," read one South African newspaper, "is keeping a low profile and as
far as the public is concerned, the novelty of a Black man playing at Ellis Park
has worn off." His 1973 visit had been front-page news, a media event covered by
all of the nation's television stations. South Africans had tracked his every move
and followed his journey from center court to Soweto to Stellenbosch. In 1973
"he was like an exhibit in a glass display case," and now he was yesterday's news.
Again he chose to stay with a prominent white family rather than reside in Soweto,
concluding that this arrangement increased his chances of winning the open.
Just as he had the previous year, Ashe opted for criticism from black activists to
avoid the distractions of Soweto. He planned to play well in the open, launch a
new South African tennis foundation, scout South Africa for future black tennis

stars, meet with banned leader Robert Sobukwe in his home, and visit parts of the country he had not seen in 1973. He continued to face a "backlash" from Dennis Brutus and other blacks in the United States who encouraged a full boycott of South Africa. In fact, a poll taken in 1974 found that 34 percent of Americans believed the government "should take a more active role in opposing the policy of apartheid." Once again, his trip exposed a bitter division on this issue in America.[48]

Ashe's traveling party included two prominent African American men, Reverend Andrew Young and Dr. Robert Green, neither of whom had accompanied him in 1973. Young was a civil rights activist, politician, and religious leader born in New Orleans in 1932 and raised in the segregated South. His father, a dentist and a member of the black middle class, had forced him to take boxing lessons as a child in case he needed to practice self-defense. Like his father, he had earned a degree in predentistry from Howard University, in 1951, but later he had chosen the ministry, graduating from Hartford Seminary in 1955. A student of Mohandas Gandhi's nonviolent philosophy, he had allied with Martin Luther King Jr. in the late 1950s and joined SCLC in 1960. He had eventually moved to Atlanta, where he focused on voter registration drives. Throughout the 1960s he had been a principal architect of the Birmingham and Selma campaigns for civil rights, becoming one of King's key lieutenants and advisers. In 1972 he had won a seat as a Democrat in the U.S. House of Representatives, a position he still held in November 1974. Ashe applauded Young's philosophy of nonviolent resistance and admired the way he worked with black and white leaders in Birmingham. Calm, contemplative, and pragmatic, Young rarely made a rash decision. He suited Ashe's team perfectly.[49]

Robert Green was in the mold of Andrew Young. Born in 1933 in Detroit, he attended the city's public schools. Drafted into the U.S. Army in 1954 and stationed in a hospital, the overachieving and determined Green took night classes at San Francisco State, earning a bachelor's degree in psychology and a master's in educational psychology. He then enrolled in the PhD program at Michigan State, where he studied the effects of desegregation in Virginia's Prince Edward County, located just outside of Washington, DC. By the 1960s he too had joined King's SCLC, working as the organization's national education director until 1967. He returned to Michigan State in 1968, taking a job as the director of the Center for Urban Affairs. Three years later, he accepted the position of dean of the College of Urban Development. Green's research examined the effects of poverty and racism on urban communities. Ashe believed that Green was more qualified than anyone else to evaluate Soweto's living conditions and offer expert testimony on the psychology of its residents. Ashe was now surrounded by highly educated men who had studied racism, poverty, and government oppression, had played active roles in the civil rights struggle, and possessed the expertise to support their views. His 1974 team was much better suited to its task than his 1973 team had been.[50]

Unlike in 1973, Ashe did not keep a diary of his thoughts and his day-to-day activities while in South Africa the second time. Newspaper accounts and recollections in his memoirs, however, tell a much different story than that of his first visit. A year earlier, Ashe had gone to South Africa to observe and learn. Now wiser and more experienced, he traveled to South Africa with a series of goals, the first of which included the inauguration of his controversial tennis foundation. Even before he departed South Africa in 1973, he and Owen Williams had formulated a plan to develop and maintain a tennis foundation in Soweto for black and colored youths. He scheduled the launch of his foundation for November 27, one day after the conclusion of the 1974 open. He and Williams had persuaded several of tennis's top players to participate in a "Festival of Tennis" that included speeches and a clinic. Held at Ellis Park, the unveiling of the $1.5 million foundation aimed "to provide genuine opportunities for Blacks in tennis." Although South African officials had lifted the ban on nonwhites in the Davis Cup and other international events, poor blacks and coloreds lacked the means to become great players. It was hoped that this foundation would offer the resources they needed.[51]

Ashe also had plans to meet with Robert Sobukwe, a banned South African activist who chaired the Pan Africanist Congress. Born in the Cape Province in 1924, Sobukwe was a symbol of nonwhite resistance, first as a member of the African National Congress and then as editor of the *Africanist*, a pan-African newspaper in Johannesburg. Labeled "The Professor" because of his educational background and his skills as an orator, he believed that nonwhites must break alliances with white moderates and discontinue talks with white government officials. He opposed any cooperation between whites and nonwhites, arguing that his people had to "liberate themselves." In March 1960 he had helped organize the protest march in Soweto that culminated in the Sharpeville massacre. Following the bloodshed, in which sixty-nine protesters died, the government had convicted Sobukwe of inciting a riot and sentenced him to three years in prison. But instead of three years, the government had detained him for six, invoking a new law that allowed authorities to add years to a prisoner's term without trial, the so-called Sobukwe clause. Like Nelson Mandela, Sobukwe had lived in solitary confinement on Robben Island, using hand signals to communicate with other inmates. In 1969 he had finally been released to home confinement in Kimberley, a mining town in the Northern Cape known for its diamonds and lack of political activity. It was there that Ashe and his delegation paid him a visit.[52]

Because of Sobukwe's ban, Ashe, Young, and Donald Dell's assistant, Michael Cardoza, flew to Kimberley to meet with him. Sobukwe greeted the three men with a big smile and offered them a cup of coffee. He then turned to Young and thanked him for working on behalf of King and the SCLC. He informed Ashe that he had been following the tennis star's "exploits" in the newspapers and was aware of his foundation and his travels. After both sides finished their introductions, Ashe asked Sobukwe if he agreed with his decision to come to South Africa and if his travels had helped South African nonwhites. Sobukwe always had an opinion, and he let Ashe have it. Ashe, Young, and Cardoza sat quietly for more than an hour, not daring to interrupt Sobukwe as he discussed race relations and criticized international antiapartheid activists. Although there is no transcript of this meeting, Sobukwe likely made an argument similar to Dennis Brutus's, namely, that dialogue between black leaders and white government officials was a waste of time. Further, a coalition of black and white activists only diluted the power of nonwhites, the men and women who must lead the movement. Ashe's trip was not without merit, however. "We have many problems here," Sobukwe said, "and not too many black Americans really know our situation. If you could help explain our predicament to your countrymen, that in itself would be a help." Ashe took these comments as justification for his visit, yet another reason for traveling to South Africa. "He is a real leader of the African people," Ashe said of Sobukwe. "It is so evident, so obvious, after spending two hours with him. It was the most fascinating two hours I have spent in South Africa—and that includes my trip last year."[53]

However captivating Sobukwe had been, Ashe needed to refocus his attention in short order if he was to play well in the South African Open. He entered the open as the third seed, behind Ken Rosewall and the favorite, Jimmy Connors, who had defeated Ashe at Ellis Park the previous year to capture the title. Ashe and Connors breezed through the first six rounds of the open, as Ashe defeated Ray Moore in straight sets on November 21, while Connors routed John Yuill, losing only one game. After eliminating Marty Riessen, Ashe reached the semifinals, then bested the surprising Raul Ramirez of Mexico. Connors matched him with a victory over Harold Solomon, setting up a second Ashe-Connors final at Ellis Park, a contest in which Connors had made easy work of Ashe in 1973. One year later the rivalry between the two men had heated up. Connors had refused to join the ATP, of which Ashe was now president. Connors was represented by Bill Riordan, a highly unpopular manager and agent who carefully selected Connors's tournaments and matches. Ashe argued that Connors was "like an up-and-coming boxer who only gets thrown a carefully selected diet of palookas and washed-outs." Many of the top pros despised Riordan and his client. Connors also exhibited immature behavior on the court, tossing his racquet and berating officials with regularity. The two men were like water and oil.[54]

Connors played defensively early in the first set as Ashe peppered him with a barrage of aggressive serves and volleys. Determined to play his power game, Ashe seemed to have the advantage. Then the tables turned. Connors began to return Ashe's shots with equal power. Mistakes also plagued Ashe in the second and third sets. Two of his smash attempts wound up in the stands, and a number of volleys found his side of the net. He could no longer hold his serve. Connors was too young, too powerful, too much. Ashe lost in straight sets, 7-6, 6-3, 6-1.[55]

The disappointing final of the open now over, Ashe turned his attention to the tennis festival and the recently launched Black Tennis Foundation (BTF). At Ellis Park, U.S. and South African teams, with Ashe and Riessen on the American side and Moore and Frew McMillan representing South Africa, played an exhibition to benefit the BTF. Moore defeated Ashe, and Riessen bested McMillan, all in the name of fun and charity. In a deeper sense, though, the matches showed young South African blacks like Mark Mathabane that blacks and whites could compete against one another *and* come together for a worthy cause. Ashe's event was free of racism and petty apartheid, as everyone, black and white, enjoyed the afternoon. "Arthur Ashe left an enduring monument in South Africa," wrote Mathabane. He left an organization funded by large and small businesses and corporations and run by blacks, whites, and coloreds. Ashe integrated the Sugar Circuit, launched the BTF, and inspired future players like Mathabane.[56]

Before returning to the United States, Ashe, Young, and Green held a press conference in which they attempted to make sense of their travels. Young told South African nonwhites not to lose hope. "For a long time in the USA," he said, "Blacks felt just as helpless and hopeless as you probably do in South Africa. . . . Just fifteen years ago it was unthinkable for a Black American to be in a position of any political importance such as Congress." Young had fought the wars of racism and injustice and come through victorious. South Africans must remain positive. While visiting Orlando High School in Soweto, Green was shocked to learn that blacks and coloreds paid for their public education. He vowed to help promising young students attend U.S. colleges and universities. For his part,

Ashe urged South Africans to have patience, warning them that it might take ten years for a black tennis star to emerge from his foundation. "The starting point," he suggested, "should be to establish the correct environment in which to work and I see this as my main task in South Africa." Writing for *Africa Report*, William Cotter commended the three men for their visit and for their interest in Africa, yet accused them of having "displayed some wishful thinking in believing that" sports could lead to political reform. To Cotter, they were naive. Ashe believed that he and his delegation had expressed pragmatic realism. He knew that sports could be a vehicle for change.[57]

___˖૭ ૭˖___

Despite their acceptance of Ashe, Young, and Green, South African government officials continued to deny visas to other prominent African Americans. In most cases, African American applicants received no justification for their rejection. This was true in the case of Ethel Payne, a longtime columnist for the *Chicago Defender*, who applied for a visa to attend the inaugural Black Renaissance Convention in December 1974. Payne did not have a criminal record, nor was she particularly active in antiapartheid politics. She wrote, "I didn't even have the distinction of making that vintage list of White House enemies during the Nixon Administration which really pains me because there are so many distinguished black Americans on it." Although the government welcomed Ashe, Bob Foster, and black journalist Carl Rowan, it rejected Payne without an explanation. She argued that South Africa excelled more at manipulating African American visitors than at truly integrating its society. When NAACP executive secretary Roy Wilkins remarked that U.S. businesses should not pull out of South Africa, the government used his comments (out of context) to defend apartheid. While Wilkins was a victim of appropriation, Ashe and Foster had chose money over morals, according to Payne. South Africa's government remained strong in part "because some black sports figures like Arthur Ashe . . . and Bobby Foster are lured into that country . . . by fat purses even though they must close their eyes to the harm it is doing the black majority." Far from naive, Ashe knew exactly what he was doing: earning a buck. And Payne had a point. Both Foster and Ashe had resided in luxury—Foster in a brand-new hotel off limits to nonwhites and Ashe in a mansion owned by a wealthy white man. Foster had earned quite a large sum for his championship bout, and Ashe had spoken for years about the lucrative prizes that South Africa offered. Both men had generally refrained from criticizing the Afrikaners while on South African soil. Because of their silence or, in the case of Foster, praise of South Africa, the two men had walked around South Africa as blank canvases that the government filled in. Outsiders unaware of the nuances of Ashe's agreement in particular had easily arrived at the conclusion that both athletes were pawns of the Afrikaners.[58]

Ashe and Foster were not the only black athletes criticized for considering a South Africa trip. In February 1975 Congressman Charles Diggs questioned Muhammad Ali's decision to travel there. The *Chicago Defender* backed Ali and argued that Diggs's opposition was shortsighted. Ali's refusal to box before a South African audience would be akin to Jackie Robinson's walking away from the Brooklyn Dodgers because of the restrictions Branch Rickey placed on him. "Jackie did not lather Rickey with hot-buttered rhetoric; instead, understanding perfectly well that they were trying to 'do something big here,' Jackie agreed to Rickey's terms . . . and you know the result," pointed out the *Defender*. Singer Lovelace Watkins was a prime example of an African American performer who inspired South African blacks. "Through him," argued the editorial, "they could envision successful South African blacks of the future." Ali himself pledged to donate the proceeds of any bout to a black South African charity. "I'm not a politician, I'm an athlete," he declared at a press conference, "and I will fight wherever people can pay the price it takes to get me there." Despite his pledge, his plans were opposed by a number of organizations, including the American Committee on Africa and the African National Congress. One *Amsterdam News* reporter warned Ali that his visit to South Africa might cost him support in the black community.[59]

Ali's "Rumble in the Jungle" opponent, George Foreman, also planned an exhibition tour of South Africa for the spring of 1975. Unlike Ali, he reached out to black leaders like Diggs, Young, and Green for advice. Before committing to the tour, Foreman insisted on integrated seating for his matches, a demand that boxing promoter Maurice Towell agreed to. Towell then scheduled "one multinational and three all black bouts" so that blacks and whites could enjoy the exhibitions. When Foreman asked Diggs, Young, and Green if Towell's arrangement met with their approval, Diggs encouraged him to donate to a black South African charity or establish a scholarship fund for young blacks. Perhaps learning from Ashe's mistake, Young counseled Foreman to be wary of Towell's promises, as the government also had promised Ashe integrated seats only to renege after the tennis star arrived. Foreman had to understand that the government would try to manipulate his image. "The Republic of South Africa," Young advised, "has been most anxious in the past few years to use and exploit sports in its campaign to change its world image." Perhaps jabbing Ashe, Foreman assured the three men that the visit would be on *his* terms. He would not be a black athlete "who did little to use their influence for reform while in the country or after they returned to America or Europe." The experiences of Ali and Foreman, Ashe and Foster, exposed a deep division among black athletes. Some, like Ali and Foster, ignored the advice of black activists and planned travels to South Africa without their approval. Others, like Ashe and Foreman, sought out the opinions of black leaders. While Ashe seemed to brush aside the counsel of those who opposed his trip, Foreman took extra care to gain the approval of black activists. These black athletes, all of whom vehemently hated apartheid, formed no monolith. The black athletic revolution was solidly nuanced.[60]

_⟶ ☙ ❧_

Even after he returned to the United States, Ashe continued to have an impact in South Africa and around the world. In a *Los Angeles Times* piece, the actor Charlton Heston spoke of observing Ashe's contributions firsthand while filming a movie in South Africa. On his day off, Heston had attended a WCT match featuring Ashe. Scanning the seats, he saw thousands of cheering fans, both black and white. "I think the official government policy began to change when Ashe was granted his visa to play there," Heston remarked. "It might have seemed a picayune thing at the time but it signaled a change." Not only had Ashe set up the Black Tennis Foundation but he had his eye on a sixteen-year-old colored tennis player named Peter Lamb and was working to secure him a scholarship to attend college in the United States. In the view of Heston and others, Ashe's appearances in South Africa, his meetings with government officials, and his strategy of patience and engagement were helping to break down apartheid. "More than any athlete I know, in any sport," said Heston, "Arthur Ashe functions as effectively as a public citizen as he does a performer. He's remarkable."[61]

As 1974 came and went, Ashe had once again focused his energies on activism, appearances, and endorsements at the expense of tennis. He no longer had the power game to make up for a lack of training or practice, and he slipped in the rankings. Sportswriters wondered if he would ever return to form. In 1975 they would get their answer. Arthur Ashe had some fight left in him.

CHAPTER 8

# The Comeback

"The day will come when you're going to have to stand on your own two feet and make it," lectured Ashe over boos, jeers, and angry shouts. Like the black South African journalists to whom Ashe had spoken years earlier, this crowd of Howard University students refused to let Ashe hold serve. When he voiced his support for the *Bakke* decision, a 1978 U.S. Supreme Court ruling that struck down racial quotas in university admissions, the audience demanded that he clarify his remarks. When he tried to pivot away from *Bakke*, the students shouted, "Answer the question Arthur." His discussion of job planning, goal setting, and corporate employment prompted questions such as, "How can we help our brothers and sisters by working for a white corporation?" Ashe's attempts to reconnect with his script proved futile, as the audience now dictated the terms of the speech. One thing appeared abundantly clear: these students were not like the Church of the Redeemer members who had cheered and praised him in 1968, nor were they like the white audiences who listened quietly as he spoke. Children of the post–civil rights era, these young men and women had little patience with Booker T. bootstraps talk. The changing winds were forcing Ashe to confront another crossroads, and again he would look to the middle to find his answer.[1]

The years 1975–79 were a transitional period in Ashe's life. On the court, he resurrected his career and reemerged as one of the world's top players, challenging younger competitors like Jimmy Connors and Bjorn Borg. The media, fans, and the tennis establishment viewed him as both the sport's lone African American star who broke racial barriers each time he won and the lead defender of traditional tennis etiquette against misbehaving brats like Connors, who embodied the dangers of professionalism and the self-absorbed me-first generation. Ashe represented the American patriot, Connors the self-centered individualist that the silent majority loved to despise. Just as Joe Louis had dealt a blow to Nazi Germany with his knockout of Max Schmeling in 1938, Arthur Ashe would stand up to the New Left and the counterculture with his on-the-court prowess, whether he liked it or not.

In the mid- to late 1970s, both personal and professional events altered Ashe's opinions of society and his approach to activism. Late in 1976 he met the young photographer Jeanne Moutoussamy, and they married in February 1977. An intelligent and independent woman, Moutoussamy challenged Ashe's views of women and activism, becoming his equal partner and eclipsing Donald Dell as his lead adviser. Meanwhile, in South Africa in 1976 the Soweto Uprising, an urban rebellion of mostly black and colored youths against their white oppressors, altered the strategy and tactics of many antiapartheid activists, Ashe included, as it exposed the limits of open dialogue and peaceful negotiations. The Soweto Uprising led Ashe to consider, and eventually champion, forms of protest that he had previously rejected, including athletic and artistic boycotts of South Africa, as well as disinvestment. In the United States, he increasingly focused on the future of young blacks, and in a number of speeches at historically black colleges and universities (HBCUs) he encouraged black students to commit to their studies over their dreams of becoming star athletes. Some of his views, such as his support for the *Bakke* decision, placed him in direct opposition to other black leaders. This transitional period—in tennis, in his personal life, and as an activist—would culminate in a bolder, more aggressive, unapologetic Ashe in the 1980s.

—૭ ૭—

By 1975 Ashe faced the possibility that his best days in tennis might have come and gone. Five years removed from his last Grand Slam win, he heard whispers declaring him old, slow, and washed up. Since winning the U.S. Nationals and the U.S. Open and leading his team to the Davis Cup crown in 1968, he had fallen in the world tennis rankings and become an afterthought to many sportswriters. His victory in the 1970 Australian Open aside, he developed a reputation for losing the big matches. The future of tennis was represented by the electric and entertaining Jimmy Connors and the emerging Bjorn Borg, not Arthur Ashe, whom many viewed as closer to retirement than to a major championship. The many proved to be wrong. Refocusing on tennis and avoiding distractions as best he could, Ashe embarked on a grueling physical-conditioning program that included weight training and cardiovascular exercise. He practiced harder and studied his opponents more carefully, understanding that he could no longer be the powerful serve-and-volley player with a stellar backhand drive. From now on, preparation and strategy would have to supersede physical dominance and power. And the work began to pay off. At the U.S. Professional Indoor Championships in Philadelphia, he "played stylishly and effectively" in keeping his opponent Brian Gottfried off balance. The *Guardian's* David Gray observed that Ashe played with a distinct rhythm designed to deprive Gottfried of any momentum. His strategy was to lull Gottfried into a pattern of shots that prevented him from "forc[ing] a crisis."[2]

In short order, the victories started to pile up. Of the twenty-nine tournaments Ashe entered in 1975, he reached the final in fourteen and won nine, earning $338,337 in prizes for the year. In the process, he surpassed $1 million in earnings for his career, making him the sport's third millionaire. "At age 32, after nearly 15 years in the big time, Ashe finally fulfilled the promise that had been acclaimed for him in 1968," noted Bud Collins. Collins's "Man of the Year" defeated second-seeded Borg in straight sets in Barcelona to claim a WCT group tournament. Days later, in a repeat of the 1968 U.S. Open final, he knocked off Tom Okker in ninety-five minutes and three sets to capture another WCT event, breaking Okker's serve twice in the second set. On April 27 he bested Okker again in Stockholm, earning $60,000 and finishing first in the WCT point standings. To Ashe, these victories, however impressive, were stepping stones to two larger goals: winning the WCT Championship in Dallas and capturing the most coveted major title, Wimbledon. Victory in the 1975 U.S. Open was not a realistic goal given that officials had recently replaced the grass courts of Forest Hills with a synthetic clay known as Har-Tru. Ashe had a history of poor performances on clay, and he fell in the fourth round of the open to clay-court specialist Eddie Dibbs. The unsurprising loss proved to be a minor setback in an otherwise exceptional year.[3]

On May 6, Ashe arrived in Dallas as the favorite to win the WCT title. Having played five months of solid tennis, he had traveled to nine countries for a total of 28,500 miles, competed in chilly and scorching temperatures, and won at sea level and in the mountains. At a luncheon prior to the tournament, he received a most unusual prize for topping the WCT standings: a twelve-pound tennis ball made entirely of twenty-four-carat gold. Two women draped in gold dress accompanied by armed guards presented him with the trophy, valued at around $30,000. Never one to collect and display cups, trophies, and plaques, he would have preferred the cash. The most expensive tennis ball in the world, which soon found its home in a bank vault, served merely as a nice trophy. The real prize remained the WCT crown.[4]

Ashe's first opponent was Mark Cox, an Englishman and underdog known for his forehand drive and his impeccable sportsmanship. Cox, Ashe noted, "has his own set of values and sticks to them. I could never take a point off him but if some of the others get a bad call I feel they deserve it." Appearing slow and lethargic, Ashe quickly dropped the first set 6-1. Cox landed all but seven first serves in the opening set and pounded Ashe with an aggressive forehand. But Ashe found his rhythm in the second set and dispatched Cox in four sets. "There seemed to be nothing that [Ashe] could do to halt the flow of winners," the *Guardian* said of the first set. "But the spectators were wasting their pity because Ashe, never one to give up the fight, suddenly found his touch and just as suddenly Cox began to make errors." In the semifinal against John Alexander, Ashe again lost the first set only to rally back for a four-set victory. Borg defeated Ashe's longtime nemesis Rod Laver in the other semifinal match, setting up a finals contest between Ashe and Borg. The nationally televised, $50,000 match ended four months of competition on several continents. The two men had faced each other eleven times, with Borg leading the series 6-5.[5]

Just over nine thousand spectators crowded into Moody Coliseum to watch the top-seeded old man take on the teenager Borg. Slow out of the gate for a third consecutive match, Ashe committed twenty-three errors in the first set and missed a chance to put Borg away when he shanked a forehand drive. Down one set, Ashe fought off several service breaks in the second set and benefited from a foot fault by Borg in the tenth game. Then, in the third set, he took over with his serve. "Ashe, his smoking first serve on target," observed the *Washington Post*, "began to unnerve his younger foe." Early in his career, Ashe had often lost his concentration in long matches, allowing more seasoned opponents to pick away at his lead. This Ashe, a mature, more experienced, and smarter player, knew better. Down early in all three of the Dallas matches, he had not panicked. In the match against Borg, the fourth set proved to be the decisive frame, as Ashe broke Borg's serve three times, ending the match by winning six straight games. He played too explosively for Borg, who had won a long, hard-fought contest the previous day. The title of WCT champion came with prizes: $50,000, a Cadillac, $1,000 in clothing, a diamond ring, and a diamond bracelet for his stepmother. Despite his business-as-usual facade, it was clear that Ashe was happy with his performance. "Go ahead, Art," snapped Donald Dell, "come right out and say you're happy. Stop underplaying it." Yet this was Ashe, a master of moderation. One victory down, one to go. The grass courts of Wimbledon awaited him.[6]

The newly crowned WCT champion arrived in London a confident man. He entered the tournament on a roll, and Wimbledon had grass courts. At his usual digs at the Westbury Hotel, Ashe sat with *Guardian* reporter Frank Keating over eggs Benedict and coffee to discuss his life, his competitors, and his new memoir, *Portrait in Motion*. "To loll this midsummer week away at Nottingham, eaves-dropping on, and chatting with, Arthur Ashe was to be pleased to do what one was doing and to be pleased to be alive," wrote Keating. "Eavesdropping was best as the soft-drawled cool cat purred on; the claws came out but they were loving scratches." Based on Keating's description, it seemed that all of London was infatuated with Ashe, and there was good reason to be drawn to the American star. He stood at the top of his game, a hero ready to take on bratty and mis-behaving villains like Jimmy Connors and Ilie Nastase. Ashe's path to victory at Wimbledon, however, was filled with potential roadblocks. Connors, the de-fending champion and top seed, was also playing well, having recently defeated Laver and John Newcombe in Las Vegas. In addition, Connors had the easier draw, facing beatable opponents like John Lloyd, Vijay Amritraj, and Jan Kodes. Although the Vegas oddsmakers posted Ashe as the second favorite behind Connors, he began as the sixth seed in the tournament. His half of the draw in-cluded heavyweights such as Borg, Ken Rosewall, Stan Smith, and Okker. All of these factors made Connors the clear favorite to take home the $26,000 prize. Predicting a Connors-Ashe final, David Gray offered the following scouting report on Ashe: "Cool, stylish, doesn't like wind and worries deeply about his forehand volley. But he is playing well and this could be his year."[7]

As the tournament got under way, Ashe appeared more likely to punch his ticket back to the United States than to reach the Wimbledon final. South Afri-ca's Bob Hewitt and Britain's Graham Stillwell each forced a fourth set, Hewitt in the opening round and Stillwell in the fifth. In the quarterfinals, Ashe faced an injured Borg, who struggled to bend his knees as the result of a groin pull. Yet even with the injury, Borg extended the match to a fourth set. Ashe's semi-final match with Australia's Tony Roche proved even more challenging. He lost a bitterly contested fourth-set tiebreaker before eliminating Roche in the fifth set 6-4.[8]

While Ashe fought hard to reach the final, Jimmy Connors appeared unstop-pable. He defeated Lloyd, Amritraj, Mark Cox, Phil Dent, Raul Ramirez, and Roscoe Tanner with surprising ease. He became only the fourth man since 1938 to reach the final without dropping a single set. Tanner remarked that Con-nors's game was now "the best ever, I think even better than in the final last year." *Sports Illustrated*'s Joe Jares voiced the sentiments of most experts when he wrote that "Ashe had no more chance [of winning Wimbledon] than a scoop of ice cream in that fiery furnace."[9]

The Ashe-Connors final took on additional significance as the result of an off-the-court legal feud between the two men. One year earlier, Connors and his manager Bill Riordan had filed a $41 million lawsuit against Jack Kramer, Donald Dell, and Commercial Union for preventing Connors from entering the French Open, the only Grand Slam event he did not win in 1974. Then, in the spring of 1975 Connors had filed another suit, this one against Ashe for comments he had made in an unpublished article that was distributed to ATP members. In it, he had assailed Connors for insisting that American officials fire Davis Cup captain Dennis Ralston. Once a member of the team, Connors had boycotted the competition after Ralston benched him for a match. "If the U.S. Davis Cup captaincy is changed to accommodate Jimmy Connors," Ashe wrote, "then the U.S. public won't like it if a brash, cocky, talented, and seemingly unpatriotic youngster is to dictate who will be the United States Davis Cup captain." As a first lieutenant in the U.S. Army whose brother Johnnie had served in Vietnam, Ashe viewed Davis Cup membership as an honor and a privilege, reserved for the best American players. He had always maintained that his Davis Cup wins meant more to him than his U.S. Open title. While Ashe could tolerate a selfish and immature player, he would not sit idly by as America's top player refused to represent his country. Ashe blamed Riordan in part for giving Connors poor advice, yet the final decision ultimately rested with the young phenom. "I don't regret writing that letter," Ashe told a reporter at Wimbledon. "I just think Jimmy is misguided." Sportswriters wondered if this feud would manifest itself on the court, perhaps by one player's refusing to shake hands with the other.[10]

Connors had become unpopular with other players as well. "He ain't one of the boys," Ashe told a *Time* reporter. "Right now he's sorely misguided. We hardly say hello." Connors annoyed fellow professionals by refusing to join the ATP and compete on the WCT tour, opting instead to play an obscure winter circuit run by Riordan. A number of players also blamed Connors for heartbreaking Davis Cup losses to Colombia and Mexico, which would have been sure victories if Connors had been on the roster. And then there were his court antics. All too often he screamed at himself and at fans, made lewd gestures to the grandstands, and bounced the ball ten, twelve, or fifteen times before he served. "I like to have fans against me," he explained to a writer. "I want to do everything I can to get them against me more." Consensus on Connors had "been alternating between disgust at his behavior and admiration for his play." The oddsmakers may have been for Connors, but the players were clearly in Ashe's corner.[11]

On paper the Ashe-Connors final looked like a one-sided contest, an event not even worthy of a live telecast. Connors had obliterated his opponents all week, while Ashe had struggled. "Connors could not have been hungrier or more aggressive," noted the *Guardian*. Ashe, on the other hand, seemed hesitant to go on the offensive. The characters of the two men diverged as well. "Connors is impulsive, enterprising and an improviser," noted the British daily. "Ashe, like Sherlock Holmes' brother, Mycroft, 'has his rails and runs upon them.'" Ashe needed to find a rhythm; Connors did not. Most experts agreed that Ashe had little chance to win, and *Sports Illustrated* reporter Frank Deford chose not to attend the final, believing that Connors would sail to victory. *Boston Globe* columnist Bud Collins remembered being "scared to death that Arthur was going to be terribly embarrassed." The oddsmakers had Ashe as a decided underdog.[12]

Unbeknownst to the "experts," columnists, and reporters, Ashe had a plan. The night before the big match, Ashe met with Dell and several others over drinks. A strategy session then ensued. The men all agreed that Connors was too quick, too powerful, and too explosive to match serve for serve and volley for volley. In other words, Ashe could not fight fire with fire. Instead, they turned to another champion black athlete for a victory blueprint: Muhammad Ali. In his "Rumble in the Jungle" win over heavyweight title holder George Foreman, Ali used a strategy known as "rope-a-dope," a plan in which he absorbed a bevy of punches, while Foreman expended a lot of energy trying to knock him out. In the late rounds, with Foreman exhausted, Ali finally became the aggressor and pummeled the champ. For Ashe to win at Wimbledon, he would have to be patient and force Connors's aggressiveness to work against him. Dell suggested that he feed Connors junk and rely on soft lobs aimed at the corners of the court. As the men weighed in, Ashe took notes on a small white sheet of paper, and before he went to bed he placed the paper in his sock for good luck. He didn't look at it again. The plan was carefully filed away in his head.[13]

Before the match even began, sportswriters prepared their stories: Connors would easily topple Ashe, and Ashe would go down in history as the first African American man to make a Wimbledon final. Connors told one reporter that the afternoon was going to be "just another day at the office," offering little respect to his opponent. "They don't know how to play me," he told *Time*. "They have to play out of their minds to beat me." Ashe arrived on center court without a hint of nervousness, wearing white shorts and a white shirt. On each wrist he wore a red, white, and blue sweatband. If this display of patriotism was not enough, he walked out wearing his Davis Cup jacket, a clear statement, some said, directed at Connors. Former ATA champion Bob Ryland recalled, "Arthur was so cool; just the way he looked in the chair." Ryland had a good feeling.[14]

Ashe put his strategy in motion from the onset. In the first two sets he played "the way a junkball pitcher handles a baseball, softly returning serves, gently stroking his passing shots." When the time was right, with Connors lulled into a soft-game mentality, Ashe unleashed his signature backhand and topspin forehand. In what seemed like a flash, he broke Connors's serve three times in the first set, cruising to a 6-1 win. To him and others, Connors appeared frustrated and rattled. "Usually he hits everything clean," Ashe said of Connors. "But 70 per cent of his misses must have gone into the net. That could mean he was choking." Ashe peppered Connors's backhand with well-placed spinning, kick-out serves that forced Connors off the court. When he succeeded in returning a serve, Connors's ball fell softly in the middle of the court, perfectly placed for Ashe to drive it in the other corner. Ashe's precise lobs over his opponent's head and his sharp ground strokes forced Connors to mimic a yo-yo, running from one position on the court to the next. Ashe won the second set 6-1 and had a commanding lead. "I had the strangest feeling that I just could not lose," he said after the match. Connors, however, fought on. He came back with a strong performance in the third set, breaking Ashe's serve after he found himself down a break of his own. Winning the set 7-5, Connors jumped to a 3-0 lead in the fourth, moving fans to the edge of their seats. This day, though, belonged to Ashe. The "cool" WCT champion broke Connors's serve twice, taking the set and Wimbledon. The world crowned him King Arthur.[15]

What happened immediately after the final point resonated more with some fans than his actual victory. With the crowd erupting in cheers, Ashe turned slightly, held his head high, and extended his right hand, his forearm and upper arm forming a right angle. He then clenched his fist, not unlike the gesture by Tommie Smith and John Carlos seven years earlier, and pumped it once in the direction of a luxury box. The symbol and its implications were unmistakable. Arthur Ashe, the new champion of the tennis world, a man who wore an Afro in solidarity with fellow blacks, had given a Black Power salute for all to see. He chose to make his athletic victory a political one as well, proudly putting on his "black hat" in his sport's greatest venue. "After match point," writes scholar Sundiata Djata, "the thirty-two-year-old Ashe calmly raised a fist, a black power symbol, but an action that seemed 'momentous' for some whites who thought of Ashe as being quiet and shy." Thirty years later, two other journalists argued that Ashe "displayed the second most famous clenched fist ever by a black athlete." Others have written that Ashe's gesture represented a purposeful

Ashe gives a clenched-fist salute immediately following his shocking upset of Jimmy Connors in the 1975 Wimbledon final. The black press identified the salute as a symbol of Black Power, a characterization later disputed by Ashe. (AP Photo/RJP)

act of defiance, and some have suggested that he planned the action all along. In interviews and memoirs, however, Ashe and his friends offer a different explanation.[16]

Ashe claimed that his "Black Power" salute represented nothing more than an ordinary fist pump directed at his friend and manager Donald Dell. A review of the match film confirms that Ashe pumped his fist in the general direction of Dell's box. His "salute" was also brief, lasting no more than a second. By contrast, Smith and Carlos held their arms fully extended throughout the playing of the national anthem. Doug Smith of USA Today acknowledged Ashe's innocuous intent but concluded that his action *was* a symbol of Black Power nonetheless. Black activists and others ascribed meaning to his gesture that to some mattered more than his defeat of Connors. For his part, Ashe did not go out of his way to dispel the reporting of his "Black Power" salute. He understood what his victory meant to African Americans. A hemisphere away from England, at the ATA Championships in New Haven, Connecticut, officials stopped the matches in celebration after learning of the victory. Spectators poured onto the courts, cheering and dancing away the afternoon. "Among blacks," said Ashe, "I've had quite a few say [the win] was up there with Joe Louis in his prime and Jackie Robinson breaking in with the Dodgers in 1947." Perhaps it did not hurt to let the writers debate his "real" intentions.[17]

For Frank Starr of the *Chicago Tribune*, Ashe's victory under the pressure of lawsuits, high expectations, and representing his race made him the ideal hero for America as the country prepared to celebrate its bicentennial. He had defeated the "cocky, arrogant and seemingly unpatriotic" Connors with modesty and grace. "Ashe," Starr wrote, "wearing his Davis Cup Team uniform, was a picture of calm, almost surgical concentration, refusing himself the luxury of emotion while driving Connors into a fury." Ashe's compelling and smart performance mattered more to blacks and whites alike, Starr concluded, because he lived his life as "a good guy," a man who represented America at its finest. *Los Angeles Times* columnist Jim Murray believed that Ashe had done right by his race, whether the militants recognized it or not. "If the NAACP, the Urban League or Black America generally had computer-programmed an individual to be the first black male tennis champion, they couldn't have come up with a better choice than Arthur Ashe," he wrote. Like other black champions, he had overcome obstacles—nearsightedness, a thin physique, a passive demeanor, his race—to become the king of Wimbledon. And he had done it *his* way, opting for reason over rhetoric, argued Murray. Militant blacks "wanted him to spike somebody, not ace somebody," yet he had remained independent and followed his own path. Murray felt that Ashe had "done more to get prejudice at match-point than 100,000 racquet (or brick) throwers."[18]

The black press, for its part, discussed Ashe's place among the pantheon of African American heroes like Robinson, Louis, and Althea Gibson. Brad Pye Jr. of the *Los Angeles Sentinel* suggested that for Ashe to be considered one of the great black athletes, he had to match Gibson's résumé by winning at Wimbledon. It took him longer than Gibson, but his win proved his greatness as an athlete as well as an activist. The *Afro-American* discussed him as a man who had accomplished the impossible. The real winner, though, was Dr. Walter Johnson, Ashe's late mentor, who had also coached Gibson to a Wimbledon title in 1957. The victory had been Johnson's "wild dream" years before it had been Ashe's. The *Chicago Defender* looked back on Ashe's career in tennis, a career filled with one racial snub after another. "Ashe refused to allow [racism] to deter his play," read the *Defender*, and he had never held a grudge. He had not believed the critics who argued "that tennis is a white person's sport and Blacks can't excel in it," added Uslish Carter of the *Pittsburgh Courier*. Most of the editorials and columns praised Ashe as much for his character and convictions as for his game. "Ashe's victory," concluded the *Defender*, "stirred ashes in a game which used to be an all-white affair, beyond the skill and ingenuity of a black player."[19]

A smiling Ashe, dressed in his Davis Cup jacket, holds up the Wimbledon trophy on July 5, 1975. He was the first African American to win Wimbledon since Althea Gibson in 1957. (Russ Adams)

Now the world's number-one player, Ashe continued his dominance through the remainder of 1975 and into 1976. During the first half of 1976 he won five of the six tournaments he entered and twenty-nine of thirty overall matches. For the second straight year he finished first in the WCT point standings and took home a cash bonus of $50,000. He seemed poised to defend both his WCT title and his crown at Wimbledon, when rather suddenly everything fell apart. Plagued by chronic heel inflammation that would eventually require surgery, he fell in the first round of the WCT tournament to Harold Solomon in four sets, and he failed to reach the quarterfinals in any of the four major tournaments. Sportswriters concluded that he was simply too badly injured, too old, and too slow to compete with the likes of Connors, Borg, or Nastase. From the winter of 1975 to 1977 most reports on Ashe's matches mentioned something about his injured foot. In November 1976 he revealed the seriousness of his injury to the world. "This is an injury I've kept quiet about over the years," he told the *Los Angeles Times*, "but now it is getting more troublesome than ever, and I realize something has to be done about it." Days later he returned to New York for an examination and treatment, and surgery soon followed.[20]

Despite his increasingly poor play, Ashe remained a fierce competitor and a staunch defender of traditional tennis etiquette. In December 1975 and again in June 1976 he was involved in two ugly incidents with Ilie Nastase. On the first day of the Grand Prix Masters tournament in Stockholm, Sweden, the two men were tied at five games each in the second set when Ashe became the beneficiary of several close line calls. He then held firm on seven break points and turned back a frustrated Nastase, 7-5. Near the end of the set, an angered Nastase began waving his arms and barking in his native Romanian at official Horst Klosterkampfer of West Germany. Klosterkampfer responded by issuing Nastase a warning for delay of game and poor sportsmanship. In the final set, trailing 4-1, Nastase served the ball across the net, but instead of returning it Ashe caught the ball, insisting that it had grazed the net. When the referee ruled in Ashe's favor, Nastase lost it. He bounced the ball an inordinate number of times and sarcastically asked if Ashe was ready. After a fan in the stands yelled, "Get on with it," Nastase raced across the court and screamed, "Are you talking to me?" Once this confrontation passed, he returned to the baseline and bounced the ball for what seemed like an eternity. Ashe had witnessed this behavior in the past and was finally fed up. He walked off the court rather than be party to Nastase's antics. Klosterkampfer eventually disqualified both men, Nastase for his behavior and Ashe for leaving the court. One day later, officials reversed their decision and awarded the match to Ashe. Ashe, who claimed he was "mad for the first time in 10 years," encouraged tennis officials "to develop a code of ethics for the players."[21]

Ashe's second run-in with Nastase occurred six months later in the championship match of the WCT Challenge Cup tournament in Hawaii. In the second set a fuming Nastase called Ashe a "bloody nigger," a phrase heard and reported by television commentator Bud Collins. Ashe, however, did not learn of Nastase's slur until Collins spoke with him privately after the match. He was upset with Nastase but blamed the outburst on the Romanian's temper, telling reporters that he did not take the comments personally. "Nastase goes off half-cocked sometimes but he's no racist," argued Ashe. If he had heard the remark during the match he would have demanded an apology. Ashe credited Dr. Johnson for teaching him how to cope with racism. "I was specifically trained," he explained, "to ignore racism directed at me as a person. [Johnson] taught any black kid that showed talent to ignore the remarks and be above them." And rise above Nastase's slur he did. Ashe considered Nastase a friend. He had supported Ashe emotionally during his quest to enter South Africa, and the two men had shared a number of good times over the years. Ashe chose to believe that Nastase had made a terrible mistake, that his temper had gotten the best of him. Because Ashe viewed his friend as an individual who, like him, erred at times, and not as a racist, he publicly forgave his tennis mate. This was not the first time that Ashe brushed aside racist comments to diffuse a situation. His ability to check his emotions served him (and his public image) well on the court, in the press, and in the boardroom.[22]

Despite his unemotional demeanor, Ashe remained a fierce competitor on the court, even if his skills and his body had begun to deteriorate. Sam Lacy realized that Ashe's most recent matches likely marked the twilight of a pioneering career. In a June 19, 1976, column in the *Afro-American*, Lacy pondered the thought of a tennis world without Arthur Ashe and Althea Gibson. Although Lacy acknowledged a pipeline of young black talent, including Yannick Noah, Juan Farrow, and Peter Lamb, he feared that none of them would rise to Ashe's caliber either on the court or off. "What comes next for those of us who wish [Ashe] could go on forever?" asked Lacy, anticipating a period of "painful" tennis reporting once Ashe retired. Yet Ashe would not fade away. Lacy had much more Ashe copy to write. It was game, set, but not quite match.[23]

—⟡ ⟡—

Jeanne Moutoussamy was unlike any woman Ashe had ever laid eyes on. She stood out among a crowd of benefactors, journalists, and celebrities at a fundraiser for the United Negro College Fund. A photographer hired to work the event, she wore ordinary jeans, a beige sweater free of fancy designs, and almost no makeup. But Ashe remembered her as the most stunning and intriguing woman in attendance. "I always felt I would 'know' I had found THE ONE when I saw her," he wrote in a memoir. Jeanne was it. A fidgety Ashe approached the young photographer busy at work and managed to spit out the line, "Photographers are getting cuter these days." His attempt at an icebreaker came off as boring and unoriginal, and Moutoussamy responded with a polite thank-you, her tone hinting that he would have to do better. Their initial meeting was brief. Moutoussamy continued to snap away, while Ashe again mingled with the crowd, though his attention remained on her.[24]

Later the same day, Ashe sought out Moutoussamy again, and this time he channeled more confidence. He asked for her name, and she told him. She spelled out her last name, and Ashe rehearsed it several times, first out loud and then over and over again in his head. It was not immediately clear that Moutoussamy was single, and she appeared to be with a man who was a friend of Ashe's. Ashe had to know the truth. Inside the men's locker room, away from Moutoussamy, he approached his friend and in a more than obvious manner inquired whether he was *with* her. "No!" answered the friend rather decisively, and Ashe expressed delight. That evening he found Moutoussamy at a dinner party, and the two struck up a conversation. Not only was Moutoussamy beautiful but she exuded intelligence and sophistication. He had to see her again and asked her for a date. "When?" she shot back. "How about tomorrow?" he responded. She agreed.[25]

Ashe rarely became infatuated with a woman. Extremely careful and guarded about his relationships, he had never fallen head over heels for someone. His father and other relatives had taught him to value marriage and wait for the "right" woman. Divorce could never be an option. Since his emergence as a top player at UCLA in 1964, he had dated and broken up with many women—black women, Asian women, white women, older women, younger women. He had dated professionals such as Kathy Benn and celebrities that included Beverly Johnson and Diana Ross, yet none of these had been "the one." "Because I was never in any one place too long," he noted, "I sized up someone quickly if I was interested at all." One of the world's most eligible bachelors, at least according to the press, Ashe had not yet found the woman for him. That changed when he met Jeanne.[26]

Moutoussamy sought to further her career, not get married. Born in Chicago in 1951, she was the daughter of an architect and an interior designer. Her grandfather had come from India, and her background included strands of East Indian and African ancestry. She had attended the College of New Rochelle and later the prestigious and exclusive Cooper Union School of Art in New York, where she had majored in photography. During her junior year at Cooper Union, she had traveled throughout West Africa and put together three impressive photo collections. The National Broadcasting Company (NBC) loved Moutoussamy's work and her drive, hiring her before she finished her degree. In general, her photographs relied on a "classical simplicity of design" to offer "powerfully direct visual statements" of people, mostly black people. She quickly emerged as an up-and-coming photojournalist in a field dominated by men.[27]

When she first spotted Ashe at the UNCF benefit, Moutoussamy thought little of it. A number of attractive young women clung to his side, each one jockeying for his attention. Ashe held the title of international celebrity, and Moutoussamy remained an obscure yet promising artist. She was initially surprised that he approached her, though that surprise turned to disgust once he opened his mouth. She did not appreciate his "cute photographer" comment. Years later Moutoussamy recalled, "I thought that was sooooo bad. I thought it was cocky and I read it as a little sexist. It singled me out as a woman, which was totally against what I wanted to portray." She wrote him off as just another male chauvinist. His persistence, however, piqued her interest, and on their first date they both opened up. He described the date as an "enjoyable evening" filled with lively conversation, laughs, and a bit of debate. "She had strong opinions, and while we didn't agree about everything, we could argue well into the night and stay friends," he explained. What impressed Moutoussamy was not the dinner conversation but what happened after they left the restaurant. She took him to her cubicle at NBC, and he asked to see her portfolio. "He genuinely liked my photographs and the stories behind them," she told *Ebony*. "He got big points for that."[28]

In some ways their relationship progressed rapidly. They saw each other often when Ashe was in town and spoke frequently on the phone when he wasn't. After they had dated for just over a month, she invited him to spend Thanksgiving with her family in Chicago. He was a hit with the Moutoussamys. Jeanne quickly realized that Ashe's cool and unemotional public demeanor masked his complex and caring personality. Most of her previous boyfriends and dates had had a "line" or a series of "lines" they used on her. They had been no more than one-trick ponies lacking analytical sophistication and depth. Ashe was worldly, educated, and inquisitive, and he loved a deep conversation. He, in turn, admired her independence and her adamant desire to remain Jeanne Moutoussamy and not be labeled as Arthur Ashe's girlfriend. They took some things slow. They rarely kissed, hugged, held hands, or showed any signs of affection, especially in public. Instead, they engaged in "extensive conversations" about their pasts, their families, and their dreams. After the New Year, Ashe made two life-changing decisions: he would have surgery to repair his heel, and he would ask Jeanne to marry him. He purchased a diamond engagement ring and placed it in an envelope, which he hid in Moutoussamy's medicine cabinet. There would be no clichéd dinner, wine, or getting down on one knee. Days later she discovered the ring and said yes. He had surgery on February 10, 1977, and married Moutoussamy ten days later.[29]

_—<> <>—_

In the mid- to late 1970s Ashe dedicated his time to staying in shape, playing solid tennis, enjoying his new marriage, and contributing to social causes in the United States. He remained concerned about South African apartheid, even from afar. His trips there in 1973 and 1974 had offered him the hope of racial and economic reform. Since December 1973 Piet Koornhof had persuaded Prime Minister Vorster to integrate the Sugar Circuit and allow multiracial athletic competitions. The ILTF had readmitted South Africa to the Davis Cup, and Ashe himself had established the Black Tennis Foundation with the help of Owen Williams and South African players such as Ray Moore. Yet, below the surface tensions between whites and nonwhites continued to mount. Multiracial sports were nearly insignificant to blacks and coloreds who had their homes raided without a warrant and their family members tossed in jail. The Black Tennis Foundation did not bring jobs to Soweto or ease the suffering of the urban poor. Soweto stood ready to explode.

Internationally, some nations continued to boycott matches with South African players. In March 1975 the Colombian Tennis Federation announced plans to withdraw Colombia from the North America Zone final rather than play South Africa. Colombia's forfeit followed Mexico's similar decision to forbid its athletes from competing against South Africa. One year earlier, the ILTF had moved South Africa to the South America Zone to avoid boycotts from European nations, and now it seemed their move had backfired. Colombia based its decision in part on a U.N. resolution condemning apartheid and encouraging sanctions against South Africa. A month later, Mexico barred Frew McMillan and Bob Hewitt from playing a WCT doubles event, and they did it in dramatic fashion. McMillan, the defending champion of the event, flew with his family to Mexico City expecting a relaxed evening of dinner and lounging in the hotel. To McMillan's surprise, the Mexican authorities stopped his party and explained that the government had instructed them to detain everyone in the group. McMillan's doubles partner, Hewitt, was relaxing in his hotel room around the same time, when a knock on the door disrupted his night as well. In a statement, the Mexican government insisted that both men were in the country illegally on tourist visas, which prevented them from competing professionally. The official acknowledged that the U.N. resolution had also informed their decision. Tournament organizers, WCT officials, and Ashe were livid. "Nobody hates apartheid more than I do," commented Ashe, "but this is ridiculous." The Mexicans argued that McMillan and Hewitt were fools if they expected anything other than a rejection. "The Mexican Government had stated clearly that Mexico will not have contact, culturally or in sport, with the South African regime," read a press release.[30]

As president of the ATP, Ashe found himself in a precarious position. His job as the head of the union required him to defend fellow ATP members against political decisions rendered by foreign governments. The ATP opposed in principle the ban of a player based purely on his nationality. But as a black activist and leading figure in the antiapartheid movement, Ashe felt an obligation to support the cause. For his part, he saw no contradiction in his view that white South Africans should be allowed to play anywhere and everywhere. Like Owen Williams, he looked at McMillan, Hewitt, Moore, and Drysdale as individuals and not as representatives of apartheid. Speaking in Kingston, Jamaica, where the Jamaican government announced its ban of South African players from the Nations Cup tournament, Ashe begged officials to reverse their decision. "I know each of [the players] well and they are all good friends of mine," he assured them.[31]

Ashe made an additional trip to South Africa in November 1975 to compete in the South African Open and supervise the construction of a new tennis complex. This time, the open's number-one seed came without a traveling party, and his visit remained decidedly low-key. His play was similarly uneventful. After knocking off Andre Zietsman and David Schneider in the opening two rounds, his erratic play in the third round cost him the chance to advance, losing in three sets to unseeded Pat Cramer. His elimination was disappointing, but he soon perked up when he traveled to Soweto to oversee his new project. *Jet* observed, "Memories of a younger, brasher Arthur Ashe suggesting that Johannesburg, South Africa, become a nuclear bomb testing site were unearthed recently as the slim Virginian dug up the first sod of a $570,000 tennis court complex for Blacks in Soweto." Ashe and other black South Africans chose the site, because by law whites could not enter that section of Soweto without permission from the government. This new complex, comprising twenty courts and other recreational facilities, would be for blacks and coloreds only.[32]

Ashe understood that his new sports complex, the Black Tennis Foundation, and meetings with local leaders in South Africa could not bring jobs to Soweto or change the nation's draconian laws. Blacks and coloreds remained without work, and students continued to attend overcrowded schools that received no government aid. Despite his hope for the contrary, Ashe predicted that a violent confrontation between white officials and black youths was inevitable. The events of June 16, 1976, proved him right. As the morning broke, an estimated fifteen thousand students of junior-high to high-school age gathered at two local high schools, Isaacson and Naledi. The two large groups planned a march to Orlando Stadium for a peaceful rally protesting a government law that required students to learn in both English and Afrikaans. Most South African nonwhites considered Afrikaans "the language of the oppressor," as Desmond Tutu put it. This language law was only the latest in a series of government measures designed to deprive people of color of their civil and human rights. In 1953 the Bantu Education Act had stripped black mission schools of their government funding and forced Soweto's tax base to absorb the cost of the township's education system. Because most of Soweto's residents lived in dire poverty, that tax base remained virtually nonexistent. Another law ten years later prevented nonwhite students from attending white schools. Between 1962 and 1971 the government built a number of new schools in Bantustans but neglected Soweto entirely. At the time of the march, only 20 percent of Soweto's children attended classes.[33]

A month and a half before the march, students from Orlando West Junior School and other schools declared a strike and refused to attend classes. Teboho "Tsietsi" Mashinini assumed the most prominent leadership role. A student at Isaacson, Mashinini was president of both the school's debate team and the Methodist Youth Guild. Smart and well liked by his peers, Mashinini, who, like many other young blacks, had been inspired by the continent's Black Consciousness movement, called a meeting for June 13 to discuss a plan of action. At the meeting, the students decided to form an action committee, later known as the Soweto Students' Representative Council, and planned a march and rally for June 16. They intended to engage in peaceful acts of civil disobedience.[34]

The South African police had other ideas. As the marchers from both schools moved along, the police, in riot gear and carrying guns, clubs, and tear gas, blocked the path to the stadium. Mashinini instructed the marchers not to interfere with the barricade and rerouted the group to Orlando High School. The police followed. When the marchers arrived on the school grounds they began to sing and chant slogans, some holding signs that read, "Down With Afrikaans" and "Vorster Must Do Zulu." What happened next remains unclear. Police witnesses claimed that students initiated the violence by hurling rocks at the officers. The marchers countered that the police opened fire without warning, spraying the peaceful crowd with bullets and tear gas. The demonstrators quickly dispersed into the township, where they set up barricades, attacked police with bricks and rocks, and set fire to government buildings. By late evening twenty-three people had died, and hundreds more were injured. Political scientist Robert M. Price noted, "This series of events touched off a rebellion against the apartheid system that was unprecedented in its scope and endurance." The Soweto Uprising had just begun.[35]

The break of a new day did not quell the violence or weaken the students' resolve. On the morning of June 17 demonstrators laid siege to a government building whose occupants, the West Rand Administration Board, oversaw Soweto. The building, like the schools, stood as a symbol of government oppression and apartheid. With the WRAB headquarters under attack and the schools engulfed in flames, an estimated fifteen hundred police officers descended on the chaos, this time with stun guns, automatic rifles, and small-caliber machine guns. They confronted scores of black and colored youths nestled behind well-fortified barricades who refused to disperse. What followed looked more like a war than like a protest and police action. Throughout the night of the second day, armored police vehicles patrolled the neighborhoods, resembling tanks in search of opposition forces. The protesters stood behind buildings and disappeared into the darkness, hurling stones, bricks, and other large objects at the convoys as they passed. A sports complex behind an Orlando police station had been converted into a helicopter launching and landing site. The sounds of gunfire could be heard from dusk to dawn.[36]

Over the next days and weeks the uprising spread geographically and generationally. On June 18, the third day, the media reported disturbances throughout Transvaal and at the University of Zululand in Natal. The police disrupted each demonstration, "setting off the pattern of hit-and-run battles and burning of government property that had characterized the uprising in Soweto." At the end of day three, estimates of the number of dead ranged from 97 to more than 500. The casualty figures included few whites, a fact that Ashe took note of while following the events from London. Unlike civil rights demonstrations in the American South, where scores of whites marched alongside blacks, the

Soweto Uprising was not multiracial. "The Africans," Ashe mused, "talk in symbolic terms of destroying the system they hate, yet almost no white South Africans were killed." This undeniable fact led him to believe that white South Africans, including the so-called progressives, were more concerned about saying the right thing for international consumption than they were about doing the right thing. As the protest spread from Soweto, the average age of the demonstrators also changed. Parents, workers, and antiapartheid veterans began to join their sons and daughters on the front lines. The adults introduced new strategies and tactics, such as transportation and consumer boycotts, general strikes, and political "stayaways." Despite the presence of older members, young people were the main victims of state violence. One study concluded that more than 1,000 mostly young protesters were killed and another 5,000 were injured in clashes with police between June and December 1976. Another 21,534 people were tried "for offenses related to creating public disturbances."[37]

If most Americans, black or white, ignored or were unaware of apartheid prior to the Soweto Uprising, the violence of those summer days grabbed their attention. In the United States and across the globe, the uprising received front-page coverage in mainstream newspapers like the *New York Times*, the *Los Angeles Times*, the *Washington Post*, and the *Times* of London. Just days after the uprising began, the United Nations adopted a resolution condemning state violence and demanding that South Africa end apartheid. After the United Nations issued a mandatory arms embargo against South Africa in 1977, President Jimmy Carter barred U.S. manufacturers from exporting any products or technology to South Africa's military or police. The Carter administration even hinted that the United States might not defend South Africa in the event of a direct military confrontation with the Soviet Union. In the geopolitical context of the Cold War, this marked a major shift in U.S. policy. Multinational corporations followed the example of their governments. Whereas in the years 1974–76 South Africa took in more than $6 billion in foreign investments, by 1977 that number had sunk to less than $1 billion. Banks in the United States, Great Britain, and the Netherlands either canceled all loans to South Africa or greatly restricted them. From 1976 to 1980 South Africa's GDP grew at an average of 2.8 percent, a figure that mirrored the nation's population growth. For the first time in many years South Africa's economy teetered on the brink of collapse.[38]

On the morning of June 17, more than five thousand miles northwest of Soweto, Ashe awoke in his room in the Westbury Hotel and grabbed a copy of the *International Herald Tribune*. What he read on the front page did not shock him. The first time he had set foot in Soweto in 1973, he could feel the tension and sense the anger buried beneath the surface. Black and colored youths, inspired by the Black Power, Black Consciousness, and African liberation movements, were already challenging authority with greater regularity. Several young militants had nearly shouted him down after his tennis clinic. "You could not tell by looking around at the streets," he said of Soweto in 1975. "You had to talk to people. Black people were bolder about the things they didn't like; they were more vocally open." During his meetings with black journalists and reporters, they repeatedly warned him that riots were inevitable. Now, as he combed through the paper, reality had set in, the predictions of violence had come true. Just before 8:00 a.m. London time, Ashe phoned his friend and fellow tennis player Ray Moore, a South African. Ashe's message: "I told you so."[39]

The Soweto Uprising represented a watershed moment for Ashe and other international antiapartheid activists. Up to 1976 he had mostly relied on quiet diplomacy, including meetings with Piet Koornhof and representatives from corporations that did business in South Africa. He had written letters to members of Congress asking them to join the cause. In the past he had tried to avoid confrontation, a strategy that the uprising rendered impossible. "Outsiders like me also had to change our approach," he realized. "We too had to raise our ante. I had to get bolder just to keep up." In the coming years, Ashe would cofound an organization with actor Harry Belafonte, Artists and Athletes Against Apartheid, that lobbied individuals, teams, and groups not to compete or perform in South Africa. Ashe himself would persuade tennis star John McEnroe not to play there. He also became an active member of TransAfrica, a lobby and think tank created in response to the events in Soweto. The organization pressured Congress to take decisive action against the South African government for its apartheid policies. Further, Ashe urged U.S. stockholders to hold corporations accountable. "People who have a point to make," he advised, "could buy some stock in a multinational company doing business [in South Africa] and then go to a stockholders' meeting, demand to be heard, and make their point." The uprising forced Ashe and many others to change their strategies and their tactics.[40]

—◌ ◌—

At the end of his playing career, from 1976 to 1979, Ashe broadened his activism beyond South Africa to include mentoring and advising young blacks in the United States. On more than one occasion his moderate views placed him in opposition to other leading black figures. On February 6, 1977, just days before his wedding, he authored "An Open Letter to Black Parents," which appeared first in the *New York Times* and later in other national and local newspapers. "Since my sophomore year at University of California, Los Angeles," the letter began, "I have become convinced that we blacks spend too much time on the playing fields and too little time in the libraries." From an early age, he contended, television, magazines, movies, and some parents taught black children to idolize and emulate athletes, stars like O. J. Simpson, Kareem Abdul-Jabbar, Reggie Jackson, and Muhammad Ali. As a result, too many young blacks grew up believing that they would become a professional athlete and earn six figures a year. Children focused on "runnin' and jumpin' and singin' and dancin'" rather than on reading, writing, and learning. Citing statistics, Ashe argued that the odds were 999 to 1 against anyone's becoming a professional athlete. More discouraging was the fact that blacks made up 60 percent of the NBA but less than 4 percent of doctors and lawyers. Blacks made up 35 percent of Major League Baseball and 40 percent of the National Football League but only 2 percent of engineers and 11 percent of construction workers. "We have been on the same roads—sports and entertainment—too long," he wrote. "We need to pull over, fill up at the library and speed away to Congress and the Supreme Court, the unions and the business world." He encouraged black parents to place education above athletics and urged school administrators to invite black athletes to speak before young audiences—not the stars but the benchwarmers or the players whose careers had ended as the result of an injury. Parents should "ask [the failed athlete] if he sleeps every night. Ask him whether he was graduated. Ask him what he would do if he became disabled tomorrow. Ask him where his old high school athletic buddies are."[41]

In many ways, Ashe echoed the opinions of Harry Edwards and others who had argued for years that high schools and universities exploited black youths for their athletic talent. As in his first civil rights address in 1968, Ashe advised blacks, specifically black parents, to take ownership of their own lives and the lives of their children. He did not believe that blacks could blame whites for not achieving an education. His advice was based in part on his own experiences with his father and grandmother and his time spent at Maggie Walker and Sumner high schools. Ashe Sr. had demanded that he be the best reader in his class and had made sure that he completed his homework immediately after school. To Ashe's grandmother, his greatest achievement was graduating from UCLA, not his U.S. Open, Davis Cup, or Wimbledon titles. His teachers at Maggie Walker and Sumner, some of whom had graduate degrees, had pushed their students to work hard and aspire to do great things. In 1984 a journalist for the *Richmond Times-Dispatch* wrote of Ashe's 1961 Maggie Walker graduating class: "They set out from the other side of the color line to make it in a white world, put the lie to all the hoary racial stereotypes as they succeeded, and made the unthinkable of 1954 the commonplace of 1984."[42]

A number of columnists and ordinary Americans applauded Ashe's position on sports and education. Doc Young of the *Los Angeles Sentinel* likened Ashe's views in the *Times* to his own opinion of the recently aired television miniseries *Roots*, a highly acclaimed program that depicted a group of Africans brought to America via the slave trade. If Ashe encouraged young blacks to spend more time in the library and less time on the playing field, Young urged black adults to focus more on succeeding as Americans than on digging up their African ancestry. "I believe," he argued, "that the black American culture expends too much time, energy, and effort teasing our black children AND adults as to the dubious glories of African heritage, slavery, poverty, and ghetto life." Instead, blacks should emulate the paths taken by black "heroes" and start valuing their American citizenship. "You are Americans . . . not Africans," reminded Young, quoting former African activist Tom Mboya. Although it is likely that Ashe did not agree with Young, both men were lashing out at black radicals who disavowed the "white" education system and eschewed patriotism. Both Ashe and Young concurred that blacks had to work within the system, in education and employment, to make it in the United States.[43]

On February 27, 1977, the *New York Times* published a forum on Ashe's controversial article in which readers offered their opinions. In general, most agreed with Ashe that black leaders and parents ought to invest more time, energy, and money into education. One reader from New York asked how black children could spend more time in the library if the library was often closed. Because of its budget troubles and massive debt, New York City had decided to close or reduce the hours of most of its libraries in 1977. The writer hinted that the battle had already been lost when the city itself prioritized malls and arenas over institutions of learning. Another man suggested that ABC replace its *Wide World of Sports* programming with shows that focused on science and technology. To Larry Hawkins, the director of the Office of Special Programs at the University of Chicago, the real problem was "convincing coaches on the elementary and high school level that their first duty is not the winning of games, but the utilization of athletics as an educational tool." The forum's participants expressed doubt that parents were solely to blame for elevating sports above academics, instead concluding that civic and government leaders as well as coaches had to make education a higher priority.[44]

Others took issue with Ashe's condescending tone and seemingly hypocritical advice. In his "Open Letter to Arthur Ashe," City University of New

York tennis coach Marvin S. Dent Jr., an African American, argued that many young blacks had to excel in sports *in order* to receive a college scholarship. Ashe of all people should have known this given that athletics and not academics had facilitated his own education at UCLA. "Even though you do not mention it very often," Dent lectured, "you [became an elite player] on the aid of black money first and black sacrifice." Moreover, Dent contended, an education would never end racism or prevent discrimination in society. He reminded Ashe that by his own admission he had not grown up in the ghetto or endured harsh poverty. "Your livelihood involved playing a game," he wrote. "People have the option of getting interested in your game or turning away, but they cannot turn away from the game of life. You either play or get manipulated by those who play." All of the books and libraries in the world could not eliminate the racial and economic barriers that Ashe seemed to ignore, said Dent.[45]

Dent's criticism aside, Ashe echoed the content of his open letter in a series of paid speeches across the United States, many of them at HBCUs and black cultural centers. At Atlanta's University Center in April 1978 an assembly of students, educators, and reporters sat in disbelief as Ashe criticized blacks for their poor choices and feelings of entitlement. "Your older brothers and sisters got their heads busted in [during the sit-ins and Freedom Rides]," he told them, "but you're not utilizing the tools it took a lot of people a lot of time to get." He assailed young blacks for showing up late to work and school and spending an estimated $7.5 billion on alcohol. He accused them of "expecting easy work for high pay without trying to prove yourself." Ashe repeated his consistent refrain that professional sports were not the answer for black youths looking to avoid poverty. Although he acknowledged that institutionalized racism was a major impediment to black success, he refused to blame outside forces for the failure of an individual. Black leaders had worked too hard for too long for the younger generation to throw away gains by being "apathetic." He reminded the audience that he was a wealthy man because of his financial investments and business ventures, not as the result of his tennis career—a statement that was half-true at best.[46]

One *Jet* reader supported Ashe's position and labeled the problem of young blacks and education a "crisis." The reader wrote, "His warning to Blacks, 'we've got to prepare and do some homework,' is a very timely message. Right on to brother Ashe." Praise for Ashe in the pages of *Jet* is not entirely surprising given the magazine's decidedly black middle-class readership. *Jet* subscribers tended to be middle-aged African Americans who were veterans of the civil rights movement and disciples of King, John Lewis, and Ralph Abernathy. They were much more likely to favor a message of self-help and economic empowerment than were younger, working-class blacks. Although Black Power culture (including musicians like James Brown and Diana Ross, for example) filled the pages of *Jet*, the magazine expressed skepticism of Black Power politics and black nationalism.[47]

Ashe found a welcoming audience at Morehouse College, a historically black college in Atlanta that had produced some of the nation's best black leaders. At the school's convocation on December 21, 1978, he encouraged students to engage in long-term planning by visiting guidance counselors and writing to companies. He advised them to "make at least a four year preparation for your entrance into the world of work." Graduate school should also be an important consideration. On another occasion, he questioned the academic focus of some blacks. "We have Black sociology majors coming out of our ears. No one wants to be an engineer or a physicist," he lamented. At Fisk University in Nashville, he told 350 students, mostly black, to take control of their academic and professional future by relegating sports to a hobby. He instructed them to be assertive and sit in the front of the class rather than in the back. "When you sit in the front of the class," he argued, "you can't help but stay awake, you can't avoid the professor and, as a consequence, you will learn more."[48]

In addition to the topic of education, Ashe chimed in on a host of controversial issues between 1976 and 1979. On October 22, 1978, he authored a nuanced, sophisticated editorial for the *Washington Post* in which he argued against athletic boycotts generally and a U.S. boycott of the 1980 Moscow Olympics specifically. In it, he questioned the logic of U.S. congressman Robert Drinan, a Catholic priest, human rights activist, and Democrat from Massachusetts who was campaigning for the Olympic boycott. Drinan contended that the Soviets would jail dissidents before and during the Games, not allow Israel to participate, and violate the Helsinki Agreement, an accord in which the Soviets had agreed to respect human rights and follow international law with regard to international sporting events. Ashe accused Drinan of having a selective memory. He suggested that it was common practice for nondemocracies to lock up political opponents and undesirables on the eve of a major world event. Why had the United States not boycotted other tournaments and competitions where this occurred? On Drinan's second point, concerning Israel, Ashe argued that every Olympics had its share of withdrawals and uninvited nations. Invoking Abraham Lincoln, he reasoned, "You can please some of the countries all of the time and all of the countries some of the time, but you can't please all of the countries all of the time." As to the Helsinki Agreement, he concluded that the

Soviets had had no intention of honoring what they signed; they had agreed to the accord simply to improve their image in the international press. He conceded that an athletic boycott remained preferable to war but countered that boycotts crushed the morale of athletes, who trained so hard to compete at the highest level, leading them to question the value of sports in society. "A boycott," he wrote, "represents to the athlete the almost total negation of the competitive ethos."[49]

Historically, Ashe had always been reluctant to use the athletic boycott as a negotiating tool. He had opposed Harry Edwards's plan for black athletes to boycott the 1968 Games, placing him in direct opposition to stars like Lew Alcindor. He had also assailed India for forfeiting a Davis Cup final to South Africa. Although he understood better than most that nations frequently politicized sports, he believed that athletes themselves, not nations, advisers, or their associations, should decide whether to boycott. The editorial included a fusion of Ashe's two leading philosophies: a belief in direct engagement with one's opponents and a deep appreciation of individual self-determination.[50]

He advocated another one of his philosophies, personal uplift, during a speech and tense question-and-answer session at Howard University. On March 23, 1979, he spoke before a predominately black audience as a representative of Aetna Life and Casualty, a company that had hired him to recruit black workers. A number of attendees became emotional when one audience member asked for Ashe's thoughts on the *Bakke* decision. In 1973 and again in 1974 Allan Bakke, a white student, had applied for admission to the University of California, Davis School of Medicine. The university had rejected his applications but admitted African American and Latino students whose test scores were not as high as Bakke's. The court ultimately ruled that racial quotas were unconstitutional, though it did permit admissions committees to consider a candidate's race in making a final determination. In response to a question, Ashe said that he supported the *Bakke* decision, a statement that stunned the audience. "You have to come to the realization," he said over boos and jeers, "you're going to go through the door because you're fully qualified not because you're part of a quota." When asked to clarify his position, he said that he favored affirmative action, just not quotas. His views were under attack, and the crowd could sense his reluctance to discuss *Bakke* at any length. Those in the audience who truly knew Ashe, however, understood that his stance on *Bakke* was not out of character. He believed that all people—men, women, whites, blacks, Latinos—had to *earn* university admission and employment through hard work and dedication, not through a quota. He felt that blacks were entitled to nothing more than a fair chance.[51]

Although he had always advocated for direct engagement with opponents, valuing the individual, and self-help, Ashe spread his philosophy with increased vigor between 1976 and 1979. In focusing on black youths, he attempted to help correct black America's main problems as he saw them: too much focus on athletics and entertainment and not enough on education, the tendency to give up on society rather than engage with it, and the growing sense of entitlement among young blacks. Unlike in the past, he pushed his views in speeches at major universities and in editorials in mainstream and African American newspapers. This period was yet another phase in his evolution from an athlete to an activist. But the activist was still an athlete.

—◌ ◌—

On most days in 1977 and 1978 Ashe could be found at New York's Nautilus Sports Medical Institute rehabilitating his damaged heel and preparing for a comeback, or the "resumption of his career," as he put it. He worked tirelessly with a therapist, who stretched his foot in every conceivable direction and led him through long workouts. Unable to run, he lifted weights, swam laps and treaded water, and rode an exercise bike. During his long absence from tennis he had fallen in the world rankings from number 1 after his 1975 Wimbledon win to number 257. He managed to keep busy by serving as tennis pro at the Doral Country Club, endorsing Head racquets, working as a tennis commentator for ABC, and giving talks and speeches on a host of issues. His goal, however, was always to return to the game he loved as a player and not as a coach or administrator.[52]

The hard work and physical therapy paid off. He won three tournaments after his comeback and earned $84,000 for his performance in the first two events of 1979. He defeated Guillermo Vilas, Brian Gottfried, and Vitas Gerulaitis before eventually losing to Connors at the Philadelphia Indoor championships. *Tennis Magazine* selected him as its "Comeback Player of the Year," and he eventually achieved the rank of number fourteen in the world. "The return of Arthur Ashe to top competitive tennis has been called the game's most exciting development of the year," declared Louie Robinson of *Ebony*. "Not just because a great champion has gained extended life . . . but he is a respected celebrity in a sport which now seems to have more prima donnas than an Italian opera company." Away from the television cameras and photographers, however, Ashe still struggled with his injury. Prior to each match, he had to stretch for twenty minutes and wrap his left ankle and heel "extensively." The pain had left him, but the foot would never be 100 percent. In his piece on Ashe's comeback, Robinson reminded readers that "no player alive is yet safe from the screaming serve and the incredible backhand of the man who remains the finest tactician in the game today." Ashe, he believed, could play for another two or three years.[53]

Robinson's prediction was not to be. On a warm and humid afternoon late in July 1979, Ashe and his friend Butch Seewagen played an eight-game exhibition match before hosting a tennis clinic in New York City. At the conclusion of the match, Ashe signed a few autographs and then ducked under a large umbrella to avoid the scorching heat. Then, all of a sudden, the pain hit. His chest tightened up, and he felt as if his entire upper torso were caught in a vice. He couldn't breath. This was not the first time that he had experienced these symptoms. Twice the previous evening, severe chest pain had awoken him, but he had brushed it off. He was a healthy man in his mid-thirties; it wasn't as if he were having a heart attack, Ashe told himself. Moments after the most recent pain set in, Seewagen noticed Ashe's discomfort and brought over Dr. Lee Wallace, a physician at New York Hospital, who happened to be at the club. The two immediately rushed Ashe to the hospital. As soon as they arrived, Wallace flagged down the resident on duty and said, "I want Mr. Ashe admitted very quickly as a heart attack patient." Before long, he was rushed to the intensive-care unit, fitted with an IV, and attached to an electrocardiogram machine. His tennis career and his life hung in the balance.[54]

# CHAPTER 9

# Triumph and Tragedy

"The game desperately needs the Arthur Ashes," wrote one Richmond columnist, "the men with his vision, his voice of reason, his eloquence, his demeanor." In August 1979, however, an ailing Ashe remained in no position to take the court. While Bjorn Borg, Jimmy Connors, and John McEnroe thrilled spectators on the circuit in the prime of their careers, Ashe rested for ten days in a New York hospital room, first in intensive care and then in the coronary unit. As he waited for test results on his heart, Ashe could not help but feel sorry for himself and ask, why me? He never smoked or used drugs and did not engage in risky or dangerous behaviors. His blood pressure and cholesterol readings were always normal. He was healthier than 99 percent of men his age, or at least he thought he was. "The answer to my big question—why me?" he wrote in the *Washington Post*, "seemed to boil down to family history and random chance." His father had suffered a heart attack at the age of fifty-five and a second one just days before Ashe checked into the hospital. Ashe's doctors, Mike Collins and Virginia Bouchard Smith, also suggested that he might have a congenital birth defect that over time had weakened the left ventricle of his heart.

After his release from the hospital in late August, Ashe showed signs of progress and even agreed to participate in a United Negro College Fund exhibition match. "The UNCF benefit will probably be one of my first postrecuperative tennis engagements, and I'm looking forward to it," he announced in the *Pittsburgh Courier*. He never got the chance. In early December he checked himself back into the hospital after again suffering chest pains. Doctors informed him that unless he underwent quadruple bypass surgery, his tennis career was over and his life would be in jeopardy. On December 13, 1979, he went ahead with the procedure. Just hours after the operation, he began plotting a comeback.[1]

"In earnest, it is this writer's belief that Ashe and tennis should part," argued *Amsterdam News* columnist Michael C. Givens II just days before Christmas. He reasoned that most healthy athletes retired around the age of thirty-five, and Ashe was by no means healthy. Heart-attack victims Dave Stallworth and John Hiller had returned to the basketball court and the pitcher's mound, respectively, after their own setbacks, but both men had been under the age of thirty. Promoters and fans, though they tried, could not persuade Muhammad Ali, at thirty-seven, and Wilt Chamberlain, at forty-one, to return to professional athletics. Ashe had the enthusiasm, the drive, and the focus to launch a comeback, but did he (literally) have the heart for it? He had returned to the court after enduring left heel and Achilles tendon injuries in 1975, but he had never regained his form. "Fear should rear its ugly head for Ashe," contended Givens. "It may be the only proper medicine for an enthusiastic professional sport's figure. Arthur Ashe should not volley with enthusiasm or heart conditions." Givens wanted fans to remember Ashe as the U.S. Open and Wimbledon champion, not as a sad former star who had hung on too long. By contrast, Brad Pye Jr. of the *Los Angeles Sentinel* opted for hope over realism. In his final column of 1979 the veteran African American sportswriter wished for Ashe's good health and "one more victory at Wimbledon."[2]

Pye would have been happy to know that Ashe had his sights set on both. At a press conference eight days after undergoing a quadruple bypass, he surprised the press by announcing a comeback. "I think you'll see me playing Wimbledon in June," he confidently told reporters. His doctor, John Hutchinson, said a return to the court would be challenging but not impossible. If Ashe's repaired heart reacted well to exercise and stress, he might make a full recovery. The fact that he was a well-conditioned athlete likely had saved his life, according to Hutchinson.[3]

Two months later his comeback appeared to be right on track, as he maintained a light workout routine that included the frequent use of a stationary bicycle to elevate his heart rate. He planned to resume on-court training in three weeks. At an ATP meeting in Palm Springs, California, the *Guardian*'s Richard Evans shadowed Ashe and observed him as he joked with his friends and participated in the activities. When he spotted player Nick Saviano, Ashe immediately inquired about Saviano's own foot injury. "It is this consideration for others," wrote Evans, "coupled recently with his undeniable courage, that has made Ashe one of the most respected sportsmen of his era. Now, when fate has dealt him a cruel and unfair blow, he remains as much an inspiration to his peers as he was during his triumphant, title-winning years."[4]

One month later, on March 9, 1980, Ashe's comeback faced an overwhelming setback. Early in the month, he, Jeanne, and several friends had traveled to Cairo, Egypt, to take part in Ismail El Shafei's tennis tournament. Three months after his bypass operation, Ashe left his hotel room one afternoon for a light jog near the ancient pyramids. Just minutes into his run he experienced a soft yet jarring chest pain, a clear case of angina. Returning to his room, he telephoned Doug Stein, a doctor and close friend of his and Jeanne's who had traveled with them to Egypt. Stein immediately examined Ashe, asking him to do a few jumping jacks. The angina returned. Stein recommended that Ashe fly to New York as soon as possible. "As we flew out of Cairo," Ashe recalled in his final memoir, "I knew one thing for sure: My career as a competitive tennis player was over."[5]

If Ashe knew that his playing career had reached its end, he never told the public. On March 26 the *Washington Post* published an account of Ashe's latest setback in which he made it seem as if he might return to the court. "While his latest episode dims the prospects of a comeback on the courts," reported the *Post*, "Ashe has not yet ruled out the possibility." He would have a better idea of his comeback chances once doctors released the results of two heart tests. He informed the *Post* that his "usual crazy schedule" would resume immediately, with travels to Omaha, Raleigh-Durham, Tallahassee, and New York in the coming days. Perhaps Ashe kept busy to put off a decision that he knew was imminent, but to most his choice should have been crystal clear. He was past his prime, he had suffered a heart attack, endured a quadruple bypass operation, and continued to face physical complications. It was time to let go, and he knew it. On April 11, in a letter to his friends and business associates, Ashe formally announced his retirement from competitive tennis. "Long ago in my Sunday School classes," he wrote, "I learned that 'for everything there is a season.' . . . After many hours of hard thought and soul-searching, I have decided from today on, to end my nonstop globetrotting odyssey in search of the perfect serve and retire from competitive tennis. In its place, I hope to begin another exciting season of writing, talking, listening, reading and assisting."[6]

With Ashe officially retired, sportswriters and columnists raced to assess his legacy and reflect on his brilliant career. Peter Harris of the *Baltimore Afro-American* applauded Ashe's wise decision. "I would have hated to see him slide into pitiful mediocrity, becoming ripe old fruit fine for picking by the newcomers," he wrote. The world would much prefer to remember him as the "consummate thinker" who strategized his way past Jimmy Connors at Wimbledon or as the serve-and-volleyer who powered himself to the 1968 U.S. Open title. Perhaps most importantly, Ashe "proved that a supremely articulate human-athlete (whether you've agreed with his controversial career or not) can compete successfully and still have a social conscience." It was his independence and thoughtfulness that endeared him to fans, and Harris recognized that Ashe had much more to accomplish. He suggested that Ashe use his talents and public platform to recruit, train, fund, and publicize young black tennis players.[7]

*Washington Post* sportswriter Barry Lorge agreed that Ashe's legacy had been shaped less by his victories, his trophies, and his athletic accomplishments than by his stoic demeanor, his good sportsmanship, and his social conscience. "In a sport overpopulated with crybabies and greedy opportunists," commented Lorge, "he became a millionaire without ever forgetting his sense of responsibility to the public and the game." Ashe was sure to remain occupied as a television commentator for ABC, a syndicated columnist for the *Washington Post*, a product endorser for racquet and clothing companies, and a board member of Aetna Insurance. But the tennis world would miss him. "On the hard courts, he was a terror," recalled one Richmond sportswriter. Once he reached the age of thirty, he had adapted and "learned to play the finesse shots, the service twists, the backcourt ground strokes and he prevailed over change." And when Nastase, Connors, and McEnroe had threatened the sanctity of the game with their "vulgar court antics," Ashe had defended the gentleman's code, becoming the ideal sportsman.[8]

The end of Ashe's tennis career meant that he had to find other activities, goals, and causes to occupy his time and energies. Although he looked forward to the 1980s, he faced an uncertain future and began to second-guess his life choices. "I felt a subtle but pervasive dissatisfaction with my life . . . and a deep confusion about what the rest of it would, and should, look like," he revealed in a memoir. Despite his antiapartheid activism, his speeches across the globe, and his youth programs, he was not convinced that he had done enough to help others. He could not escape the thought that many Americans had ignored his ideas and opinions because he was "just an athlete." "For many years," he explained, "even as I built my career in tennis, I had guiltily nursed the suspicion that I had not done as much as I should have in the arena of protest and politics, civil rights, and social reform. On the other hand, another part of me did not need a cue from other athletes, no matter how militant, about my duties as a citizen." He resolved to become a more active leader, specifically as an advocate for the black community.[9]

Ashe identified four goals for his postretirement years. First, he hoped to remain active in amateur and professional tennis, possibly as captain of the U.S. Davis Cup team. It would be an honor for him to lead the American squad back to the top of world tennis and work with the likes of Jimmy Connors and John McEnroe. Second, he wanted to give public speeches that targeted young blacks in particular. Third, he aimed to put his thoughts and opinions on paper, possibly in a newspaper or magazine column, and maybe even write a book. He wanted to write for a broader, nonsporting audience and focus on politics, civil rights, and society. Finally, he thought he might like to teach a course on sports and society at a community college or small university. In retirement, he "wanted to indulge and explore my love of humanity, and especially my concern for persons less fortunate than myself."[10]

—◌ ◌—

The Davis Cup competition, according to Ashe, was tennis's premier championship tournament because it featured a battle of nations, not men. As a player exited the locker room en route to a Davis Cup match, he wore the colors of his nation and for several hours ceased to be an individual. Through the first three quarters of the twentieth century, selection to the Davis Cup team was the ultimate honor for any young player. In 1963, U.S. captain Bob Kelleher had invited Ashe, then a sophomore at UCLA, to join the squad and represent the United States on the world stage. "Even as race relations in America became increasingly stormy," Ashe remembered, "and I started to feel the attraction of more militant approaches to segregation and racism, I nevertheless saw my Davis Cup appointment as the outstanding honor of my life to that point." He had gone on to have a stellar career as a member of the U.S. team, winning twenty-seven of thirty-two matches between 1963 and 1978, a U.S. record at the time of his retirement. The Davis Cup had taken him all over the world—to Australia for the squad's memorable 1968 victory and to Vietnam and Africa as part of the U.S. State Department's goodwill tours. The Davis Cup had been good to Ashe, and he wanted to give back.[11]

He got his chance in September 1980. While attending the U.S. Open in New York, Ashe received word that USTA president Marvin Richmond wished to speak with him. He left his seat for Richmond's luxury box and found the USTA boss chatting with the association's former head, Joseph Carrico. Richmond cut right to the chase: Tony Trabert, the sitting U.S. captain, was preparing to tender his resignation. He could no longer handle his roster of volatile and emotionally unstable players, a list that included McEnroe, Connors, Peter Fleming, and Vitas Gerulaitis. Though supremely talented, the team had brought shame and embarrassment on Trabert in the late 1970s with public feuds, constant complaints, and immature court antics. Enough was enough. A smiling Richmond explained that he had summoned Ashe to his suite to offer him the job. "I felt so happy and proud I could have jumped into the air," Ashe recalled, "the job meant that much to me." He planned to take the job but asked for twenty-four hours to speak with Trabert and prepare for media interviews. Like Ashe, Trabert believed in discipline, hard work, and sportsmanship, and he "had the deserved reputation of being a law-and-order man." Ashe needed to know why he wanted to relinquish the captaincy. Trabert congratulated Ashe as the new captain but warned him that the new crop of players was different: they were irresponsible and money hungry, and they did not respect authority. Trabert and Ashe had been raised in another world. Ashe hoped, however, that "friendly persuasion" might work on the players.[12]

In September 1980 the USTA formally hired Ashe as the new captain. "When I was a kid in Richmond, Virginia," Ashe told the press, "the three entities in tennis that meant the most to me were the names Forest Hills, Davis Cup, and Pancho Gonzalez . . . there was a lot of emotion in those words." When a reporter asked how it felt to be the United States' first black captain, he replied that the "novelty" of race had worn off. Fans wanted to see the team win, not a black man coach. Soon the congratulatory letters poured in. "Since you have lived through so many firsts, I am sure you will come out on top with this one as you have with the others," wrote Roscoe Brown Jr., the president of Bronx Community College. Bob Brown, president of the Black Gospel Collection, framed his words of congratulations in racial terms. Brown said that Ashe had inspired many young blacks with his athletic talent and sound character. But it was his interaction with white America that most impressed Brown. He wrote, "Your influence on our white brothers as well will hasten our elusive goal of equality for all people." The president of Mattel Toys promised to create an Arthur Ashe action figure if he led the United States to win the cup. Perhaps the most significant letter arrived from Ashe's manager, lawyer, agent, and friend Donald Dell. He advised Ashe not to forget the most important aspect of being captain: "As Davis Cup Captain you and your Teammates represent 220,000,000 Americans above all else. Davis Cup is the Olympics of Tennis and therefore everyone on the Team must act accordingly or he shouldn't be on the Team." As a former captain in the late 1960s, Dell understood the difficulty of managing a team of individual personalities. His squads, however, had included men like Ashe, Charlie Pasarell, Stan Smith, and Clark Graebner, none of whom even remotely resembled Jimmy Connors or John McEnroe. Working with the players who would make up Ashe's squads was likely to be a challenging prospect.[13]

Ashe assumed the captaincy during a pivotal moment in American tennis. With the advent of the open era in 1968 and the baby boomers' growing interest in the sport, tennis's popularity soared in the 1970s. Yet to Ashe the commercialization of tennis represented both a positive and a negative development. Increasing interest led to packed grandstands, high television ratings, more lucrative sponsorships, and hundreds of thousands of dollars in prizes. While players and fans flocked to the professional tournaments, however, Davis Cup matches began to lose their luster. Once an honor, participation on the U.S. team became a burden for players like Jimmy Connors. Given the choice between potentially earning thousands in a professional event and representing America for free, many players opted for cash over country. "For many of us," Ashe lamented, "the deluge of money led to confusion and an unholy scrambling after dollars. Certain values and standards that had bonded players in my earlier years as a professional—certain codes of honor and a spirit of cooperation and camaraderie—disappeared." Rule changes also deterred players from competing in the Davis Cup. Prior to 1972 the defending champion had only been required to participate in the final set of matches, known as the Challenge Round. This had allowed players from the champion nation to pursue their individual interests while other nations vied to unseat them. Beginning in 1972, however, the Davis Cup Committee began requiring the defending champion to participate in all rounds of the tournament. These factors made the captain's job all the more difficult.[14]

And then there were the American players, none as talented or controversial as John McEnroe. "Right from the start, in his 1977 introduction to pro tennis," writes Bud Collins, "John Patrick McEnroe, Jr., was a hit." Born an Air Force brat on February 16, 1959, in Wiesbaden, Germany, McEnroe grew up a short, lanky left-hander in a Long Island suburb. Known for his quick temper and his energetic demeanor, he was equally skilled as a singles and a doubles player. Throughout his career, his precise shotmaking and competitiveness were unmatched, the latter frequently to his detriment, as he became one of the most frequently fined and suspended players of all time. Despite his distasteful court antics, McEnroe, unlike Connors, loved to represent his country, even if it left him lighter in the wallet. In 1979 he and Vitas Gerulaitis led the U.S. squad to defeat Italy and capture the Davis Cup for the Americans. McEnroe finished the year the winner of 27 singles and doubles tournaments and 175 matches (of 193) overall. Ashe wrote of McEnroe, "Several other players also had his amazing array of shots, but no one else could consistently select each shot at precisely the right moment under intense match pressure, execute the shot, and make it look as easy as John routinely did."[15]

In addition to McEnroe, the U.S. team included, at various times, Stan Smith, Roscoe Tanner, Bob Lutz, Marty Riessen, Sherwood Stewart, Gene Mayer, Sandy Mayer, Peter Fleming, Gerulaitis, and Connors. The squad represented a mixture of young and veteran players, some with years of Davis Cup experience and others with none. Ashe had a natural doubles pairing in McEnroe and Fleming. Labeled "Flam," the six foot five, right-handed Fleming was the perfect complement to the five foot eleven, left-handed McEnroe. Fleming featured one of the game's most powerful serves and returns, and the two had won the doubles title at Wimbledon and the U.S. Open in 1979. Another incumbent star of Ashe's new team was Vitas Gerulaitis, born in Brooklyn, New York, in 1954 to Lithuanian immigrants. Fast and quick, Gerulaitis, who wore his blond hair long, dominated in the front court and had a keen ability to track down balls in the corners. This was the team of talented yet temperamental players whom Ashe would have to coach, control, and manage.[16]

The primary job of a Davis Cup captain is to set the team's lineup. For each tie, Ashe had to identify who was available, willing, and prepared to compete. Then, he had to select two singles players and two doubles players to represent the United State in five individual matches. The nation that won three or more of those matches won the tie. On paper, his task seemed simple enough; in practice, selecting a lineup involved balancing personalities, egos, and player expectations. In the spring of 1981, for instance, Ashe benched Bob Lutz in favor of another player, Sandy Mayer, and Lutz did not take the news well. "Arthur, what is this shit?" he scribbled in a handwritten letter. "Do we have to prove ourselves this year to have a chance to play the third match when we were already told by you last year that we were playing all the matches." After questioning Ashe's logic and judgment, Lutz announced that he would not participate in another Davis Cup match for the remainder of the year. "The squad," Ashe remembered, "was a collection of individuals, each of whom was something of a star in his own right."[17]

The opening tie of the 1981 Davis Cup campaign pitted the United States against Mexico from March 6 to March 8 in Carlsbad, California. With Connors unavailable, Ashe selected the left-handed Roscoe Tanner for the second singles spot opposite McEnroe. He had initially chosen veterans Stan Smith and Lutz to play the doubles match but had replaced them with Marty Riessen and Sherwood Stewart after an arm injury sidelined Smith. After McEnroe led the Americans to a 1-0 advantage, Tanner lost unexpectedly to Raul Ramirez. In the doubles match, Ashe's strategy of using fresh players, Riessen and Stewart, instead of his best doubles player, McEnroe, backfired, as the Americans fell for a second straight match. "What was supposed to be a breeze was now a cliff-hanger," Ashe recalled. His squad was in serious danger of losing in the first round. In the final two matches, though, Tanner and McEnroe stepped up and guided the team to a narrow 3-2 win.[18]

Despite escaping with a victory, Ashe's debut was far from impressive. His mentor and former U.S. captain Pancho Gonzalez criticized his decision to play Riessen and Stewart while leaving McEnroe on the bench. He contended that Ashe should have penciled in his best lineup even if it meant that McEnroe played three matches. He also accused Ashe of being aloof and uninvolved in the matches. These comments were not surprising coming from Gonzalez, a fierce competitor who had screamed at himself, referees, opponents, and fans in his heyday. "Well, we don't want your heart to thump too much, Arthur," advised Gonzalez. "But you have to *look* more involved, I guess." Yet despite being more involved, Ashe struggled to control McEnroe's behavior in the final match. He left his captain's chair on several occasions to keep his star player from arguing with the referees. Interviewed after the match, an annoyed Ramirez suggested that McEnroe "complains too much . . . and I think he does it on purpose. He's a good player, but he thinks every ball is in." Ramirez was not the only one upset by McEnroe's antics. Bernard Loomis, a division president of General Mills, wrote to Ashe on March 10 to express his disappointment with McEnroe's behavior. It was the first of many such letters to come.[19]

As expected, the second-round tie featured the United States and Czecho-slovakia, which had defeated Switzerland 3-2 in its opening-round match-up. The surprise of the tie came just after the Mexico matches, when Jimmy Con-nors announced plans to join the U.S. team for the first time since 1976. Ashe remained quietly skeptical about Connors's newfound patriotism. In practical terms, however, the addition of Connors gave the United States the best chance to win. The team's other star, John McEnroe, arrived in New York after embar-rassing himself yet again, this time at Wimbledon. Despite winning the tourna-ment, his behavior at Wimbledon had cost him $2,250 in fines, and the tourna-ment committee threatened to fine him another $12,500 and/or disqualify him from future tournaments. Weeks after his big win, the Wimbledon committee denied him honorary membership at the club, a first. "He was an unhappy young man," Ashe remembered of McEnroe, "hardly ready now to launch him-self against powerful Czechoslovakia."[20]

In the opening match against Ivan Lendl of Czechoslovakia, it was clear that McEnroe had not recovered from his emotional hangover after Wimbledon.

His serve was off target, and he seemed to second-guess his volleys. Lendl, by contrast, was on his game, knocking off McEnroe in three sets. Down 1-0, Ashe turned to Connors to even things up. He was as impressive as McEnroe had been disappointing, defeating Tomas Smid in three easy sets and launching a streak of American victories. Smith and Lutz won their doubles match, and McEnroe redeemed himself with a dominating performance over an over-matched Smid. With Connors's dead rubber victory added for good measure, the United States moved on to the next round.

Controversy soon followed the impressive win. Almost from the start, it was evident to Ashe and others that Connors did not fit with the rest of the team. Connors was used to being the center of attention, the individual champion, the star of the show, not the second draw behind "Junior" John McEnroe, as Fleming put it. It appeared that Connors was not cut out for the Davis Cup after all. "Connors envied the fame that accrued to McEnroe with his combination of bad behavior and astonishing play," Ashe surmised. "But while Connors could put on a memorable tantrum, he lacked McEnroe's edge of genius in this department, too. He simply didn't have McEnroe's awful gift of rage." In July 1981 Connors left his teammates in the middle of their run, not to return for another three years.[21]

Even without one of its top players, in October the U.S. team easily dispatched a declining Australian team 5-0 and moved on to the finals against Argentina. But all was not well with the Americans. As captain and as a player, Ashe believed in proper sportsmanship, deference to coaches and officials, and following tennis's written and unwritten rules. He expected his players to behave on the court and treat him with respect. McEnroe and Fleming had a much different perspective. On a number of occasions, McEnroe arrived just minutes before the starting time, threatening to delay the television coverage. Once, when Ashe attempted to coach Fleming and McEnroe, Fleming responded, "John and I have played a million doubles matches. . . . We don't need advice or coaching." During their doubles match against Australia, the two men hurled insults at their opponents, swore like angry truck drivers, and made a huge scene, leaving Ashe "embarrassed, enraged, and bitter." When Ashe confronted them, McEnroe and Fleming ignored him. Letters poured in from fans who were angry with the two men. "I could take no pride nor pleasure in our winning the Davis Cup if McEnroe and Fleming acted as they did in that match against the Australian team," wrote one man. "I would rather see them defaulted." Stan Malless, the tournament director of the Indianapolis Sports Center, vowed not to attend the finals because of McEnroe. Richard Evans of

*World Tennis* argued that Ashe and McEnroe were poles apart because of their distinct upbringings. Whereas Ashe had been taught to control his emotions, McEnroe's mentors and coaches had taught him to express his emotions, not bottle them up. Ashe and McEnroe could not understand each other, often to the detriment of both.[22]

The finals of the 1981 Davis Cup took place in December at Cincinnati's Riverfront Stadium. The Americans faced a tough and competitive squad from Argentina led by Guillermo Vilas and Jose Luis Clerc. McEnroe arrived in Cincinnati a determined man, having lost to both Vilas and Clerc in Buenos Aires in the 1980 Davis Cup. Days before the championship matches, Ashe warned McEnroe and Fleming that he would default their matches if either misbehaved. The men called Ashe's bluff. After McEnroe and Roscoe Tanner split the opening two matches, it was up to the U.S. doubles team of McEnroe and Fleming to put the Americans back ahead. The two men led the United States to a 2-1 advantage after the third set, but everyone knew that McEnroe was about to lose his temper. Throughout the match, Vilas and Clerc had preyed on McEnroe's emotions with unnecessary delays and annoying comments. A small contingent of Argentinian fans also screamed obscenities at the Americans, and eventually McEnroe exploded. Earlier in the match, the grounds crew had delayed the action to fix a damaged section of the court, resulting in the cancellation of a later ten-minute break between the third and fourth sets. Just as McEnroe prepared to serve to begin the fourth set, Vilas and Clerc acted as if they planned to take the canceled break. McEnroe yelled a pointed comment at his opponents, and all four players converged at the net. Ashe immediately sprung from his seat and demanded that McEnroe knock off his antics and return to the service line. "This is a disgrace," he said to McEnroe and Fleming. "You cannot continue like this. I do not want to hear another obscenity out here. You are playing for the United States. Remember that!" Ashe thought that he had the situation under control, but he was wrong. After another comment from Clerc, McEnroe yelled, "Go fuck yourself!" Ashe returned to the court and confronted his star player. He was the angriest he had ever been at another player. McEnroe and Fleming went on to win the match, but victory was far from Ashe's mind. He had seemingly lost control of his team.[23]

That McEnroe and Fleming had played some of the best tennis of their careers mattered little to Ashe. That night he tried to sleep, but he could not shake the images of *his* players acting like immature brats while wearing the American uniform. At dawn he telephoned Marvin Richmond and Gordon Jorgensen, explaining that he wanted to forfeit the team's next match if McEnroe acted up.

Both U.S. officials pledged their full support. Later that morning, Ashe sat face to face with his emotional star and lectured McEnroe on the consequences of his behavior. McEnroe realized that the best way to end the scolding as quickly as possible was to remain silent. At the conclusion of their one-way "meeting," McEnroe glanced at Ashe, clearly annoyed, and asked, "Is that all?" In his final memoir, Ashe admitted that he had hoped for poor sportsmanship from McEnroe so that he could disqualify or suspend him. "No one had ever stood up to McEnroe," Ashe wrote, "and I was sure that his behavior would have been different if someone had done so when he was younger." In this confrontation, Ashe had played the role of an old-guard tennis purist, an unexpected role for an African American southerner born of working-class parents. He had become like boxer Joe Louis in 1938, defending American morality from an outside invader, in this case, a new generation of poorly behaved, egocentric players.[24]

Luckily for Ashe, and for everyone else involved, McEnroe behaved as a near-perfect citizen in the fourth match against Clerc. After they split the first four sets, McEnroe took control in the decisive fifth, assuming the offensive when Clerc served. He was even more dominant when he served, allowing only four points in the final frame. "McEnroe saved his best shots for last, as champions do," observed Ted Green of the *Los Angeles Times*. A winner in five sets, McEnroe jumped into Ashe's arms in celebration of the U.S. victory. The image told the story of two men who had kissed and made up, not the true tale of their strained relationship based on seemingly irreconcilable differences. At the postmatch press conference, McEnroe said of his captain, "I know it's a tough situation. Obviously, Arthur has a well-deserved reputation. Everyone is comparing him to me. We have different ways of going about things. But when you win the Davis Cup, everything is forgotten." McEnroe may have forgotten, but Ashe had not. The battle of wills had just begun.[25]

Some sportswriters and fans remembered the 1981 Davis Cup more for McEnroe's behavior than for the U.S. team's victory. Others openly questioned Ashe's coaching abilities. "With no visible joy," noted Georg Meyers of the *Seattle Times*, "Arthur has answered one of the burning questions of the day: When victory, and profits, are paramount, do superlative skills absolve outrageous, unforgivable conduct? Obviously, yes." Ashe had no business playing McEnroe after his ugly tantrum, argued Meyers. A fan, Stuart Butler, appealed to Ashe's nationalistic sensibilities, contending that McEnroe had failed to represent the best of America. He wrote, "I cannot stand quietly by and watch the repulsive actions of one of our representatives ridicule the game." Donald Dell begged Ashe to engage with McEnroe, just as he had with the leaders of South Africa. If,

As Davis Cup captain, Ashe celebrates with the 1981 championship team. From left to right are Ashe, Peter Fleming, John McEnroe, Roscoe Tanner, and Eliot Teltscher. (Russ Adams)

Dell wrote, "you can communicate more with McEnroe where he will learn to respect and listen to you, that is a step forward for everyone, and pro tennis as well." A winner so many times before, Ashe was clearly losing his fight with McEnroe.[26]

Unlike the 1981 competition, the 1982 and 1983 U.S. Davis Cup runs remained free of disgraceful behavior and infighting. Jimmy Connors, ever the controversial figure, did not participate in either campaign, resulting in a better show of team unity. And John McEnroe behaved himself. Before the 1982 season, Connors aside, the United States had fielded one of the most impressive rosters ever assembled. If Ashe kept his players in line and focused on a single goal, the team could not lose. After crushing India in the opening round, the United States faced an upstart Swedish team and jumped to a 2-1 lead. Brian Gottfried, a last-minute injury replacement, then fell to Sweden's Anders Jarryd, setting up a winner-take-all match between McEnroe and Mats Wilander. In a match lasting more than six and a half hours McEnroe and Wilander slugged it out for five long sets. In the fifth, Ashe called over his star and suggested that he remain patient and stay in the backcourt, and McEnroe listened to his captain. In the fourteenth game, he broke Wilander's serve and the United States walked away victorious. "John, that's the greatest match you have ever played in the Davis Cup," a proud Ashe told his best player. The United States went on to rout Australia 5-0 in the semifinals and France 4-1 in the finals. For a second straight year, Ashe and McEnroe had led the U.S. squad to Davis Cup glory, this time without the distractions.[27]

The 1983 campaign did not have quite the storybook ending for Ashe and his players. Just after the United States won the 1982 cup, officials announced that Ashe's squad would defend their title against a formidable Argentinian team in Buenos Aires on clay. Because Argentina had fallen to France the previous year in the first round, officials seeded Argentina high in the tournament, setting up a rather difficult match-up for the tired Americans. McEnroe entered the tie cranky and back to his 1981 tricks. During the doubles match he called the referee a "jerk" and a "moron" and even entered the grandstands to confront one Argentinian fan. He played tired and emotionally spent, and the United States lost in the first round, 3-2. This loss, as it turned out, would be the least of Ashe's worries in 1983.[28]

After attending a business meeting in April, Ashe began to suffer from chest pains again. His doctor, John Hutchinson, ordered a series of tests and determined that Ashe needed an additional bypass operation, which he scheduled for June 21 in New York City. When the *Afro-American* asked Ashe about his prognosis, he replied, "Well, I'm standing here. My doctor said I'm in no danger of keeling over now, but I'm not allowed to wander too far from home." Given his health concerns, he would not commit to coaching the 1984 Davis Cup team. On June 22 the press announced that Ashe had undergone double-bypass surgery and was resting comfortably in "satisfactory and stable" condition. Despite the operation's success, Ashe experienced much more soreness and discomfort than after his previous surgery. Scar tissue had built up around his sternum, resulting in a more invasive procedure. He also felt much weaker than in 1979, and his blood levels hovered at low levels. To correct the anemia, doctors decided to give Ashe a blood transfusion, a procedure that no one thought anything of at the time. Patients in Ashe's condition who suffered from anemia received blood, no debate. Before 1985, however, hospitals did not test donated blood for the human immunodeficiency virus, or HIV, the virus that caused acquired immunodeficiency syndrome, or AIDS. "This transfusion," Ashe wrote, "indeed picked me up and sent me on the road to recovery from my surgery; it also, unwittingly, set in motion my descent into AIDS." Unfortunately for everyone involved, it took doctors five years to properly diagnose him. By then it would be too late.[29]

Now forty years old, Ashe had to make a difficult decision. Should he remain with the Davis Cup team and possibly risk his health or resign and focus on other, less stressful activities such as writing, speaking, and running his many charities? As the mental and physical aspects of his recovery weighed on him, he sunk into a mild depression. "More than ever," he realized, "I became aware of my mortality." Time, though, remained on Ashe's side, at least in the short term. As a result of the United States' early loss, he had until the fall to recover and make a decision. With July fading into August, and August into September, resigning became less and less of an option. The thought of guiding a well-rested and hungry U.S. team became too much to resist. The 1984 campaign also brought the return of Jimmy Connors, a development that could not have helped Ashe's heart.[30]

Before the opening-round tie against Romania in Bucharest, Connors insisted on a chat with his captain. In the three years that he had been absent from the Davis Cup team, Connors had observed Ashe's coaching style from afar, read the press accounts of internal disputes, and heard rumors from other professionals. He wanted to make his position clear. He did not want Ashe to coach him as if he were a young amateur, but he did expect his captain to be more active on the sidelines. If Connors felt inclined to argue a call, he demanded Ashe's full support. "I'm on your side. I'm going to be working for you," Ashe assured him. And he *was* more involved, at least for a while. During Connors's opening match, Ashe repeatedly stood up and barked encouragement at his star. Connors and McEnroe both played well, guiding the United States to a 5-0 shutout of Romania. The U.S. then made easy work of Argentina (5-0) and Australia (4-1) en route to a final against Sweden. It was in Göteborg that things fell apart.[31]

Connors and McEnroe both arrived in Sweden with other things on their minds. McEnroe had just completed a twenty-one-day suspension for breaking his racquet (and whatever else he could find) and screaming at officials at a tournament in Stockholm. The video of his tantrum had played over and over again on news and sports shows throughout Europe and the United States. When Ashe arrived at the stadium a bit late after sitting in a traffic jam, he was greeted by a succinct message carved into the court that read "FUCK YOU." Its author, Jimmy Connors, did not appreciate Ashe's tardiness. Rather than disciplining his star, he let the circus continue. On the court, Connors was sluggish and frustrated during his match with Mats Wilander, falling in three quick sets. He also managed to curse out referee Alan Mills, resulting in a two-thousand-dollar fine and a near default. McEnroe also struggled on the slow clay court in both singles and doubles. In just a day and a half the United States had lost the cup.[32]

Once again, the behavior of the American players overshadowed the results. First, the outgoing president of the USTA, Hunter Delatour, formally apologized to Sweden for Connors's inappropriate language. Then the new president, J. Randolph Gregson, vowed to investigate the U.S. team. America's corporate sponsor, the Louisiana Pacific Corporation, also discussed the possibility of ending its partnership with the U.S. squad. Speaking on the chairman's behalf, the director of staging, Brian Parrott, said, "Mr. Merlo felt that the American team should be a positive reflection of skills and a minimum of behavior. It was embarrassing to be an American in Sweden." For their part, Connors and McEnroe remained defiant. "McEnroe and I are big boys," quipped Connors in reference to Merlo's letter. "If someone had something to say they could say it to our face." McEnroe commented, "I think the whole thing is one big joke." Fearing the loss of their corporate sponsor, Gregson and the USTA devised a plan. Beginning with the 1985 Davis Cup, each U.S. player who wished to join the team would have to sign a code-of-conduct contract in which they pledged to behave properly. "It is a reinforcement of the rules," said USTA spokesman Ed Fabricius. "We want the players alerted to what's expected of them. We want to remind them of the specific Davis Cup rules."[33]

Ashe stopped short of endorsing the personal-conduct contract. Instead, he argued that referees and the USTA should do a better job of enforcing the rules already on the books. "All athletes in all sports curse," he said. "But you hear it on a tennis court. The players have been allowed to go from the juniors to point B without any action being taken." He suggested that the star quality of players like Connors made it difficult—and unpopular—for referees to disqualify them. It was not his job, or the job of the USTA, to police athletes' behavior. "If I feel a player is wrong, I'll let the umpire nail him," explained Ashe. He told the press that fans had sent him scores of letters complaining about players' behavior and demanding action. Everyone could tell that Ashe was at the end of his rope. For almost four years he had tried in vain to discipline his players through persuasion, reason, and appealing to their sense of nationalism. None of these seemed to work.[34]

The 1985 campaign ended Ashe's Davis Cup captaincy. After defeating Japan 5-0 in Kyoto in March, a disappointing U.S. squad lost to West Germany in the quarterfinals in Hamburg, 3-2. In the end, the United States was unable to overcome the sparkling play of young phenom Boris Becker or to perform at a high

level without John McEnroe, who had chosen to skip the tie. In October Ashe
met with Gregson and Jorgensen, who informed him that the USTA would not
renew his contract, ending his five-year stint as captain. In a press release announcing his resignation, Ashe said that a change was necessary, reiterating
that his health was not a factor in the decision. Reportedly, his bosses had replaced him "for a perceived lack of discipline and organization on the team."
Ashe, though, had his own ideas. He told *Jet* magazine that his antiapartheid
activism had likely played a role in his dismissal. "I sincerely believe," he later
wrote, "that Gregson and others in the USTA saw me as someone far more concerned with politics than a Davis Cup captain should be. And by politics, I'm
sure they meant 'radical' politics." The truth aside, Ashe's departure meant
that he would have more time for South Africa. And by 1985 things were heat-
ing up.[35]

_ფ ფ_

In the winter of 1980 the eyes of the sports world were focused squarely on two
extraordinary tennis players, Bjorn Borg and John McEnroe. July had brought
Borg a narrow five-set victory over McEnroe at Wimbledon, and McEnroe had
followed suit in September with an equally close five-set win over Borg to take
home the U.S. Open title. The two men needed a third match to break the tie,
and promoter Sol Kerzner of the Southern Sun hotel chain knew just the place:
Bophuthatswana, a South African state that government officials claimed was
independent. Kerzner reached out to representatives for Borg and McEnroe
and negotiated a $1 million, five-set match slated for December 6 in a brand-
new 14,000-seat stadium in Sun City. Within hours of the formal announcement, however, civil rights leaders and organizations around the world were
asking the two men to reconsider. Sweden's leading newspaper, *Express*, ran a
story imploring Borg, "Don't Do It."[36]

In the United States, Ashe himself led the charge against McEnroe's participation. In his *Washington Post* column, Ashe argued that Bophuthatswana was
a "phony ministate" established by the Afrikaner government to rid South
Africa of its black population. "The country's 22 million black citizens," he contended, "are to be stripped of their native-born citizenship and granted new
passports from new governments that no one recognizes." Participation in the
match propped up a racist white regime that repressed the black majority. Yet
Kerzner offered Borg and McEnroe the most money ever paid for a single day's
work in the history of sports. Ashe contacted McEnroe's manager, his father,
John Sr., and laid out the consequences of a match in South Africa. Morality

aside, Ashe assured McEnroe Sr. that his son would take a huge public-relations hit if he played in Bophuthatswana. In the end, McEnroe took Ashe's advice and walked away. "Being only 21," McEnroe Sr. explained, "he tried to figure out other ways of doing it but finally agreed that in this instance morality meant more than money. Even a million dollars."[37]

In keeping McEnroe away from South Africa, Ashe had unwittingly ignited more controversy. In a *Washington Post* editorial, Ngqondi L. Masimini, a black South African, criticized Ashe for characterizing his home of Transkei as a "phony state." Far from phony, he said, Transkei functioned as a nominally independent state governed by native Transkeians with a constitution written by blacks. Did Ashe believe "that Black people are not capable of taking care of themselves?" Masimini sarcastically asked. "To call Transkei a 'phony mini-state,'" he continued, "is either an eloquent mimicry of United Nations policy that has failed to solve the South African situation during its 34 years of existence or sheer ignorance on the part of Mr. Ashe." He accused Ashe of focusing on South Africa's 3.5 million urban blacks at the expense of the country's 18.5 million rural blacks. "Those are the people who have borne the yoke of apartheid and none of the superstars noticed," lamented Masimini. Once again, Ashe had positioned himself between two poles, one that urged him to keep sports separate from politics and another that accused him of being uninformed, detached, and naive about the plight of South African nonwhites.[38]

As Ashe continued his crusade against the government of South Africa, the antiapartheid movement in sports also picked up. In March 1981 the United Nations announced its intent to publish a list of 185 athletes who had competed in South Africa, including Guillermo Vilas, Stan Smith, WBA heavyweight champ Mike Weaver, and former heavyweight boxer Floyd Patterson. If a player's name appeared on the list, he or she would be barred from competing in one hundred mostly Third World nations. Just the mention of a blacklist had an immediate effect. A number of prominent tennis players withdrew from a lucrative tournament in Johannesburg to avoid making the list. Speaking in support of the blacklist, Ashe told reporters in an interview, "The ante has been raised considerably. The level of militancy by black Africa and black South Africa is much higher than five years ago. In a way, they've accepted that some things will be sacrificed to make sure South Africa is ostracized."[39]

Ashe and actor Harry Belafonte also launched an official boycott campaign, Artists and Athletes Against Apartheid (AAAA), in September 1983. Ashe explained that the "primary goal of the very large commitment by so many people . . . is to show that there are many people who would have the opportunity to perform in South Africa but chose not to do so on moral grounds." The new campaign, already backed by thirty national and international organizations, sought ten to fifteen thousand members. Ashe and Belafonte understood that persuading musicians and athletes to reject hundreds of thousands of dollars would not be easy. For instance, the press had reported that Frank Sinatra received $1.6 million to perform in Sun City. "Word needs to get out loud and clear," Ashe said, "that [Bophuthatswana] is only a phony homeland. . . . Nobody should be fooled." He and Belafonte believed that artists and athletes had a moral obligation to refuse to perform in South Africa. By contrast, Daniel Ben Av, a member of the Conference of Personal Managers, argued that Bophuthatswana was indeed an independent nation without any form of apartheid. Before performing in Sun City, Sinatra had sent his attorney, Mickey Rudin, to Bophuthatswana to make sure it was relatively free of institutionalized racism. Rudin told the press that he had witnessed "more interracial harmony than can even be found in some of our American cities." Ben Av suggested that Ashe and Belafonte visit Sun City and see for themselves.[40]

Ashe and other celebrities hold a press conference at the United Nations to announce the founding of Artists and Athletes Against Apartheid. Seated from left to right are Gregory Hines, Tony Randall, Ashe, Ruby Dee, Randall Robinson, Ossie Davis, and Harry Belafonte. (Copyright Bettmann / Corbis / AP Images)

Criticism from Ben Av and others failed to deter Ashe and Belafonte. In October 1983 they joined forces with the United Nations in Los Angeles to initiate a nationwide cultural boycott of South Africa. The United Nations and AAAA planned an educational symposium to teach members about "the evils of apartheid." In addition to Ashe and Belafonte, the program included the participation of Randall Robinson, the executive director of TransAfrica, and performers Ossie Davis, Ruby Dee, and Gregory Hines. In lieu of formal economic sanctions against South Africa, which the United States had vetoed in the U.N. General Assembly for geopolitical reasons, the antiapartheid lobby resorted to a cultural boycott. Ashe explained at the October 8 press conference announcing the boycott that AAAA intended to focus on "gentle persuasion with those in need of conversion." He reminded reporters that AAAA was simply following a 1968 U.N. resolution that encouraged a cultural boycott. Despite a number of educational forums and newspaper articles, Ashe's organization was not able to persuade all athletes to stay away from South Africa. In November, Calvin Peete, an African American golfer, joined Lee Trevino, Craig Stadler, Nick Faldo, Fuzzy Zoeller, and others in announcing plans to compete in the 1983 Sun City Golf Challenge. For these men, the $1 million in prizes was too much to pass up. Ashe's message resonated with others, however, including singer and evangelist Brook Benton, who promised "not to return to racist South Africa until majority rule is achieved."[41]

In addition to his work on behalf of AAAA, Ashe participated in a number of public forums and interviews on the topic of South Africa in 1983 and 1984. He told *Inside Sports*, "I am convinced that South Africa's recent progress toward integration of sport is deceptive in that it was never meant to lead an advance toward a normal life for that country's blacks." In support of Ashe's position, the *Chicago Tribune* quoted U.S. Olympian and South African expatriate Sydney Maree as stating that South African Olympic officials would "always pick one black in order to fool the international community" but that they had no intention of fielding a truly integrated team. Yet some in the United States believed that South Africa had made an honest effort. American IOC representative Julian Roosevelt argued that the South African team lacked black swimmers because "blacks generally don't like to swim. They don't like the water." In October 1984 Ashe and AAAA also announced plans for a celebrity tennis tournament, the South Africa Freedom Classic, with the proceeds supporting AAAA. The list of players included Gene Mayer, Elliot Teltscher, Andrew Young, Althea Gibson, and New York City mayor David Dinkins, among others.[42]

Ashe's boldest step against apartheid occurred in late fall 1984 and early 1985, when he and scores of other protesters engaged in direct action. In December, he, Belafonte, Coretta Scott King, and others participated in a number of rallies along Embassy Row in Washington, DC, demanding the release of thirteen black labor leaders arrested for political agitation. *Time* magazine described a gathering that "could have been a scene from the civil rights movement of the 1960s: a large crowd of demonstrators, most of them black, marching in peaceful protest down an avenue in Washington, chanting slogans and carrying signs." Police arrested 15 protesters, including congressmen Ronald Dellums of California and John Conyers of Michigan. One month later, police arrested Ashe and 46 other demonstrators for campaigning against human rights violations in South Africa. Ashe, who wore a large sign that read "FREEDOM YES! APARTHEID NO!," told the press, "I speak with a great deal of personal experience. . . . I went through a segregated school system and a segregated society." Nationwide, police in a dozen cities had arrested 608 protesters within a week. "By 1985," Ashe wrote in his memoir, "I was at last satisfied that the anti-apartheid movement, once exotic, was blossoming in America." In February, a municipal prosecutor declined to pursue charges against Ashe and 11 others, disappointing those defendants, including Ashe, who wanted to testify about the plight of South Africa's blacks.[43]

Also in the early 1980s, Ashe found himself in yet another uniform: dark dress slacks, a short sleeve white dress shirt, and a fashionable tie with chalk caked on his left hand. His court was now a college classroom, and Professor Ashe held serve. His foray into teaching began early in 1982, when Yale University named him the recipient of the Kiphuth Fellowship and invited him to lecture on the topic of college athletics. After his public lecture before an audience of five hundred, he talked with Henry Louis Gates Jr., then a junior faculty member at Yale and now an eminent scholar at Harvard. Impressed with Ashe's performance, Gates offered him a teaching job at Yale, a proposal that he seriously considered. But Ashe also had other offers, the most tempting of which was a position at Florida Memorial College, a historically black college serving twelve hundred students. His old friend Jefferson Rogers, a professor at Florida Memorial, proposed that he teach a small honors course on black athletes and society. Tossing aside the more obvious choice, Ashe joined the faculty at Florida Memorial, opting to work with African American students rather than the "best and brightest" in the Ivy League. "We believe that we, with Mr. Ashe," noted FMC's president, Dr. Willie Robinson, "are pioneers in an academic pursuit that other institutions will see fit to follow." Ashe's course, Education and the Black Athlete, was one of the first of its kind.[44]

"In the classroom," observed *Ebony*, "he is a tough, no-nonsense kind of instructor who tries to impress upon students the importance of understanding and dealing with their academic responsibilities." Teaching had its difficulties and frustrations, however. Like most professors, he struggled with unmotivated students who arrived late to class and failed to turn in assignments. Their lack of basic writing skills also surprised him and was one reason that he later opposed lowering academic standards for admission into college. "I don't think it's the teaching per se that excites me," he explained, "but the teaching of Black students." More problematic than student performance, Ashe had difficulty finding and gathering academic materials for his class. He found only two books on black athletes, one published in 1939 and another, published in 1963, that was more anecdotal than comprehensive. Historians had virtually ignored athletes in their discussion of black popular culture, a serious omission that Ashe wanted to rectify.[45]

He immediately put together a book proposal explaining that he "want[ed] to write THE authoritative history of the black American athlete." He estimated that a completed manuscript would take at least two years to research, write, and revise. In March 1983 he hired Kip Branch, a professor at Wilson College, as a research assistant and editor, as well as Sandra Jamison, a librarian, as a researcher. He set up an official office in New York City, purchased a number of books, and held a press conference in which he announced a publication contract with Howard University Press. Ashe and his new team began conducting oral interviews with former and current black athletes, sportswriters, and others involved in the sports world. They reached out to universities, archives, and the public for assistance in recovering the stories of black athletes. Ashe even appeared on the radio show *Night Talk* to ask the public for help. "It did more than energize him," Ashe's brother, Johnnie, said of the book. "It gave him a new purpose, a means by which he could make contributions. . . . He'd say, 'The same problems I went through, Jack Johnson went through, Joe Louis went through.'" The book became an emotional journey into his past, allowing him to revisit segregation, institutionalized racism, and bigotry and to remember how he had overcome them. He pieced together the web that bonded all black athletes, himself included.[46]

In September 1983 Ashe and his team began drafting chapters, and soon thereafter they sent portions of the unfinished manuscript to outside reviewers. One of those reviewers was Gates, who wrote, "I *love* your manuscript and your narrative style and believe that you have in hand a book that will make a major and definitive contribution to the literature on sports and to Afro-American culture." Another reviewer, Professor Benjamin Quarles of Morgan State University, had a much different take, concluding, rather abrasively, that the manuscript lacked cohesion and transition from one paragraph to the next. "The manuscript's year by year approach," he noted, "makes it read more like a chronicle than like a history, more like a yearbook than a synthesis." Further, portions of the manuscript had little to do with black athletes. Quarles requested that Ashe remove his name from the list of outside readers. Perhaps Quarles, a professional academic trained in traditional historical methods, was unhappy that an amateur like Ashe might shape the academic discussion of blacks in sports. More likely, Quarles believed that Ashe's manuscript did not meet scholarly standards.[47]

Despite Quarles's tough criticism, Ashe and his staff forged ahead. Before the book's eventual publication in 1988, the team hit the airwaves and gave numerous interviews to draw the public's interest. To the *Chicago Tribune*'s Skip Myslenski, for instance, Ashe spoke about the FBI folder on Jesse Owens, the African American Olympic sprinter who won gold in 1936. Investigation of the file had led Ashe to conclude that Owens had incredible "clout" in the 1940 U.S. presidential election, a fact that showed the intersection of sports and politics. Ashe argued, "For the average American who is not black, his perceptions of black America come from the black athlete . . . within the black community, the position of the black athlete is much more important and much more influential than the position of any white athlete within the white community." He wanted to tell the stories of America's most visible and important African Americans, the athletes who had overcome discrimination and racism. He aimed to introduce America's teenagers, black and white, to Jack Johnson, Joe Louis, and Jackie Robinson.[48]

In November 1988, after five years of hard work, two book deals, and nearly $300,000 of his own money, Ashe announced the publication of his three-volume masterpiece, *A Hard Road to Glory: A History of the African-American Athlete*. Totaling twelve hundred pages and published by Warner/Amistad Books, the three volumes sold for between thirty and forty dollars each. By late November eleven thousand copies of the three volumes had been sold, and as of February

10, 1989, Amistad Press had received twenty thousand orders for the third volume alone. An Amistad press release declared, "Arthur Ashe is in tremendous demand for interviews and appearances by the media, booksellers and universities throughout the country. The publicity surrounding the publication of A Hard Road To Glory has been awesome." A *New York Times* advertisement for the book read: "These are some of the Best Athletes in American History. Name one. . . . They toiled in virtual obscurity for little or no money, under conditions today's lowliest minor leaguer wouldn't tolerate." In an internal memorandum, Amistad instructed its employees and press agents to frame Ashe's book as a meticulously researched, authoritative history containing exclusive interviews and newly uncovered information.[49]

In promoting his eventual book, Ashe received help from a number of sportswriters, including Jim Murray and Michael Wilbon. In his column, Murray profiled several of the black athletes that Ashe had focused on, such as nineteenth-century pugilist and former slave Tom Molineaux, baseball player Rube Foster, football star turned activist Paul Robeson, and members of the New York Cuban Giants baseball club. "The point Ashe makes is," explained Murray, "the black athlete didn't just roll out of bed with his ability. He really came from a long line of champions, people who had really worked to perfect and refine natural skill but were lost to history because they took the slave owner's name." Although Ashe certainly disagreed with Murray's suggestion that blacks might be genetically superior to whites, he undoubtedly appreciated the positive press.[50]

Most reviewers applauded the depth and significance of Ashe's work. Author David Halberstam, a popular historian and biographer, called the three-volume history "monumental." "The book," he wrote in the *New York Times*, "is a compelling history of prejudice and meanness, of honor and dishonor, a book both about sports and not about sports." Ashe had pieced together an intricate puzzle and examined the lives of so many long-forgotten athletes of color. More than a detached history, Halberstam argued, *A Hard Road to Glory* was "a cry of protest in which ancient sins are revealed." No one was more qualified to tell this story than Ashe, himself an athlete who had faced endless discrimination in his sport and in society. Sports are important, Halberstam wrote, "and for any reader trying to understand the relationship between sports and society and why there are so many blacks on the field but so few coaching and in the front offices and in the news media, I cannot commend 'A Hard Road to Glory' too highly." A review in the *Atlanta Daily World* praised Ashe for taking on "the psychological aspect of integration in sports," including a discussion of drug use among black athletes. "Many Black historians already consider it to be the Black encyclopedia of Black sports," read the review.[51]

Ashe also participated in a national book tour and gave a number of interviews promoting his work. He told reporters that *A Hard Road to Glory* was the most challenging and rewarding endeavor he had ever undertaken. "There were so many things involving the black athlete that had sociological implications for all of black America," he told the *Richmond Times-Dispatch*. After he announced the book project, archivists, librarians, amateur sports historians, and ordinary Americans, black and white, had sent him old articles, clippings, and photographs. He told the *San Diego Union* that he had taken a hands-on approach, writing "every word" of the manuscript and selecting all of the photographs. "I would think this is more important than any tennis titles," he said. *A Hard Road to Glory*, although since criticized by historians for its lack of analytical depth and encyclopedic narrative, was the first published synthesis of African American sports history. It also marked Ashe's debut as a solo author, as ghostwriters and coauthors had assisted him with his previous memoirs. With the publication of this multivolume work, Ashe became a part of history as both an athlete and an author.[52]

_⌐◦ ◦⌐_

Arthur Ashe—the coach, antiapartheid activist, teacher, and historian—wore a number of hats in the 1980s. He worked as a guest columnist for the *Washington Post* and *Tennis* magazine and a consultant on "racial issues" for Aetna Life and Casualty Company, became a cofounder of the Ashe-Bollettieri Cities Program and founder of the Athletes Career Connection, and served as a product endorser for Head USA, to name just a few of his activities. "In the last seven years," reported *Gentlemen's Quarterly*, "he's addressed 10,000 black college students, speaking on any subject concerning the black community—from the high divorce rate to the importance of taking speech and writing courses." He offered his opinions and wisdom at Princeton and the College of William & Mary, as well as at Kalamazoo College and the Dayton Street Elementary School in Newark, New Jersey. Also in Newark, Ashe established the Safe Passage Foundation, a nonprofit organization that aimed to mentor inner-city children as they transitioned from childhood to adulthood. By the end of the 1990s the foundation counted a thousand participants from Newark. Ashe dedicated himself to the formal and informal education of black youths, explaining, "I tried to speak out of my own experience, practically; I avoided hectoring young people, but sought to teach them something important about life as I had learned from it." In working with the "poor and unfortunate," Ashe realized that he derived great joy from helping others.[53]

As much as he enjoyed giving of his time and talents, Ashe also found pleasure in watching his bank account grow. In the late 1970s and throughout the 1980s he invested in the stock market and participated in a number of business ventures, including several that did not work out. In 1979 he and an old friend from Richmond formed a business named International Commercial Resources, a trading company that provided goods and services to West Africa. The company fell apart, however, when civil war erupted in Liberia, resulting in Ashe's losing thousands of dollars. In the late 1980s he and his brother, Johnnie, announced plans to construct an apartment complex in Jacksonville, North Carolina, to house U.S. Marines stationed at the nearby Parris Island Marine base. Johnnie supervised most of the construction, and Ashe funded most of the investment. By the early 1990s the Gulf War had relocated most of the marines to Saudi Arabia and Kuwait, leaving many apartments vacant. In addition, the low rents did not cover the overhead costs of operating the complex, and Ashe lost hundreds of thousands of dollars. Thanks to his overall frugality and savvy business acumen, he managed to absorb the losses.[54]

Ashe was also blessed with a wonderful marriage and, in 1986, an adopted daughter whom he and Jeanne named Camera. Describing herself as "madly in love," Jeanne told a reporter that her relationship with Ashe was "highly organized, very efficient." Each day, the two set aside one hour to discuss their lives, schedules, and anything else that was on their minds. "We're almost even," Jeanne said. "But my husband still has the edge. If there's a compromise to be made, I make it." When asked what she admired about her husband, she replied, "I love his energy and stoicism. He has qualities I'd love to have. And he'd like to be more emotional, more open, more outgoing." In his memoirs, Ashe spoke of Jeanne in reverent terms. She was the love of his life and his most trusted adviser. Theirs was a true partnership.[55]

Ashe's warm and loving marriage contrasted with his stressful public life. In January 1989 he unintentionally took on Georgetown men's basketball coach, John Thompson. In 1983 the NCAA had passed Proposition 48, a bylaw that required student athletes to have both a 2.0 GPA and a score of 700 on the standardized SAT test in order to receive athletic scholarships at Division I or Division II schools. Arguing that the new law disproportionately affected African American athletes because of the SAT's cultural bias, Grambling State University president Joseph Johnson had worked publicly and privately to have Proposition 48 repealed. The NCAA eventually compromised with Johnson and others, agreeing to let schools offer scholarships to underperforming student athletes if they had a 2.0 GPA *or* a 700 SAT score *and* sat out a year or "demonstrated satisfactory progress towards a degree." Critics of the amendment accused the NCAA of creating a loophole that allowed schools to admit woefully unqualified students who then would become eligible sometime during their freshman year. In an attempt to address this problem, the NCAA introduced Proposition 42, a proposed bylaw that would restore Proposition 48 in its original form. By a vote of 163 to 154, Proposition 42 passed with almost no support from historically black colleges and universities.[56]

Thompson, who had been a college standout in basketball at Providence University, attacked Proposition 42 as culturally biased, unfair, and "a tremendous tragedy." He contended that inner-city and underprivileged blacks "must be given every opportunity to succeed," and he concluded that the new measure threatened this principle. In response, he organized a walkout just minutes before Georgetown's game with Boston College. Ashe could not have disagreed more. At an event in West Hartford, Connecticut, he said, "If you want to play basketball or football or run track, you've got to hit the books." He pointed out that 700 on the SAT translated to a D average, making him wonder "how cultural bias plays any part." If a high-school student, black or white, could not score a 700, he or she should attend a community or junior college. He argued that "colleges do a disservice when they accept these youngsters who can't meet academic demands. I've seen what they do to these athletes and it makes me want to cry." At another public appearance, Ashe admitted that some in the black community had given him "a lot of heat" for his stance, but he reiterated his position. "Young black athletes develop an 'entitlement' philosophy in the eighth and ninth grades," he contended. "They think they're entitled to a college scholarship and don't have to study, simply because the ones before them didn't have to." His opponents in sports and the press countered that Ashe himself had attended UCLA because he was a talented athlete, *not* because of his academic prowess. He remained adamant, however, that "Black America stands to lose another generation of our young men unless they are helped to learn as well as play ball."[57]

—◌ ◌—

On a cold, rainy afternoon in late November 1985 Ashe and six hundred other protesters marched along Massachusetts Avenue NW in Washington, DC, on their way to the South African embassy. "If you think it's a nasty day out here today," Ashe told a *Washington Post* reporter, "just think about what a nasty day it is every day in South Africa." This campaign aimed to stop U.S. corporations

A handcuffed Ashe is arrested outside the South African embassy in Washington, DC, on January 12, 1985. He and forty-six other antiapartheid protesters were jailed for demonstrating against policies of the South African government. (AP Photo/Lana Harris)

that did business in South Africa. Reverend Jesse Jackson, who also joined the march, attacked U.S. president Ronald Reagan and British prime minister Margaret Thatcher for bolstering the South African regime with their investments and their unwillingness to pass sanctions. The protesters demanded the release of Nelson Mandela and applauded the work of Nobel laureate Bishop Desmond Tutu. The largest American antiapartheid demonstration to date, which began on Thanksgiving Eve 1984, had resulted in 2,918 arrests. Among those arrested was Ashe. Throughout the 1960s and into the 1970s he had frowned on this type of protest, opting instead for personal dialogue with South African leaders and patience. Yet he, like many others, could sense that the time had come for a new strategy. The Cold War and South Africa's strategic value were fading, and the nation of apartheid found itself increasingly isolated from the world. Gentle persuasion and diligent negotiation, a strategy that Ashe had employed in the 1970s, no longer represented the most effective plan. The movement was now strong enough to exert direct pressure.[58]

In June 1986 Ashe spoke at another mass demonstration, on the Great Lawn of Central Park in New York City. Anywhere from 35,000 to 90,000 antiapartheid protesters—black, white, old, young, blind, and disabled—came together and chanted "Free Mandela" and "Death to Apartheid." Participants held photos of Martin Luther King Jr., Malcolm X, and Mandela, and they heard from a number of speakers, famous and otherwise. Jesse Jackson equated apartheid to fascism, and Desmond Tutu's daughter said that South Africa was "a whisper away" from civil war. Harry Belafonte argued for Western divestment and blamed the West for apartheid's longevity. "We believe," he said, "the United States and Great Britain hold the key to whether South Africa will become a massive pool of blood." Ashe agreed with his friend. "It's a moment of moral truth," he exclaimed. "The issues are so crystal clear there is no room for equivocation. What Thatcher and Reagan do can sway the world." Ashe and others encouraged Americans to support a bill, HR 997, sponsored by Representative Ronald Dellums of California. The bill made it illegal for the U.S. government or U.S. corporations to loan money to, invest in, or trade with South Africa. It also prohibited some South African aircraft from landing in the United States. W. J. Weatherby of the *Guardian* observed that the rally reminded him of the American civil rights movement. Through the antiapartheid movement, he contended, protesters "seized on [the South Africa issue] as a way of reviving the fight against racism at home." When Ashe targeted Reagan and Thatcher, Weatherby argued, "the crowd took it that he meant not only in South Africa but also in their own country." Ashe, the self-proclaimed "Citizen of the World," was pleading for an end to racism and discrimination, not just in South Africa but everywhere.[59]

One protester, however, accused Ashe of hypocrisy for his position on South African athletes. Jerome Bibuld, the international representative of the South African Chess Association, objected to the entry of thirteen South Africans in the U.S. Open tennis tournament. He wore a placard that read, "U.S. Open Supports Apartheid." He said that when asked by star player Martina Navratilova what his statement meant, "I told her that she was playing tennis with 13 blood suckers from South Africa while millions of Blacks in that country are denied their human rights." He said that Ashe and AAAA were hypocrites for condoning the participation of these athletes. Ashe rejected Bibuld's reasoning and concluded that South African athletes were not direct agents of apartheid. "If you would publicly disavow apartheid," he said, "you are welcome in my country." He argued that each player should be evaluated individually and not lumped in with those who supported apartheid.[60]

_࿐ ࿐_

In September 1988, while in Lake George, New York, Ashe tried to make a phone call but had difficulty gripping the receiver with his right hand. He shook and stretched his tingling hand, assuming that it had just fallen asleep. When his circulation did not return, he asked Jeanne for her opinion. They both agreed to return to their home in Mount Kisco, New York, and scheduled an emergency appointment with Ashe's doctor, William Russell. Russell ordered a brain scan that revealed a large patch, possibly a tumor. Ashe then underwent a round of blood tests followed by exploratory brain surgery in which doctors performed a biopsy of the patch. While Jeanne and family friend Dr. Doug Stein waited for the results, he said to her, "Jeanne, I hope this isn't something really bad, if you know what I mean." She knew exactly what he meant. The biopsy eventually revealed that Ashe was infected with toxoplasmosis, a parasite of the brain that was curable. But the blood tests also disclosed a starker diagnosis: Ashe was infected with HIV, the virus that caused AIDS. And not only was he HIV-positive but the disease had progressed to full-blown AIDS. "Arthur and I had no words to each other," Jeanne remembered, as the two gripped each other tight. In 1988 a diagnosis of full-blown AIDS was a death sentence, and they knew it.[61]

From the beginning, Ashe and Jeanne decided to keep the illness private. They worried that publicly disclosing Ashe's condition might negatively affect their daughter. They did not want others to shape her view of the disease or make her feel bad or confused. Ashe also realized, according to friend Frank Deford, "that once word got out, this was going to define him." The Arthur Ashe he wanted to project was a tireless humanitarian, activist, lecturer, and writer, not a man dying of AIDS. He feared that an AIDS announcement might jeopardize his many charitable foundations and projects. He also knew that persons with AIDS were not allowed to enter South Africa. "We didn't consider ourselves hiding," Jeanne said. "We wanted to lead as normal a life as possible. There were lots of things we wanted to do, individually and as a family, that we felt being public would not allow us to do." For four years, many friends, family members, athletes, and journalists kept their secret. "What I came to feel about a year ago," Ashe said in 1992, "was that there was a silent and unspoken conspiracy and complicity to assist me in maintaining my privacy." In a very personal letter to his friend, Deford told Ashe that he loved him and expressed his deepest sorrow. As early as 1989 Deford advised him to draft a plan in the event that the press learned of his condition. He wrote, "What occurred to me is that it really doesn't make a lot of difference who and how the news is broken if you can then jump in and control things." He agreed, upon reflection, with Ashe's decision to keep his illness private.[62]

From 1988 to 1992 Ashe maintained an intense public schedule, giving speeches and lectures, participating in charitable events, doing media interviews, and working with young blacks. In those years, he and others around the world finally saw apartheid come apart, a development that he had sought for decades. In 1978 P. W. Botha had replaced B. J. Vorster as prime minister of South Africa. For ten years beginning in 1980 the South African military had waged a war against antiapartheid rebels in Angola and other states that the South Africans claimed were terrorist havens. The wars led to 1.5 million deaths and the displacement of more than 7 million people. By the late 1980s, thanks in large part to an international arms embargo against South Africa, the South Africans had lost the upper hand over the Cuban-backed Angolans. Also in the 1980s, pressure from within, including countrywide protests and the emergence of armed resistance movements, had combined with international sanctions, both cultural and economic, to force change. In 1983 Botha had created a tricameral parliament that included houses for colored and Indian representatives. Botha's successor, F. W. deKlerk, had then lifted the ban on the African National Congress and the Pan Africanist Congress. And on February 2, 1990, he released Nelson Mandela from prison.

In 1992, four years after Ashe's initial diagnosis, the news of his illness finally broke. On April 5 Ashe received a visit from Doug Smith, a longtime friend who was then a sportswriter for USA Today. Earlier that day Smith had taken a telephone call from a source who claimed that Ashe was infected with HIV. The caller asked to remain anonymous. The editor of USA Today, Gene Policinski, immediately dispatched Smith to Ashe's apartment in Manhattan to confirm the story, something Smith described as "the most difficult assignment I ever had as a journalist." When Smith arrived, Ashe assumed that he was there to discuss updates to A Hard Road to Glory. When his friend suddenly confronted him with the AIDS rumor, he was shocked and then became angry. Refusing to confirm the story, he instructed Smith to have Policinski telephone him early that evening. Policinski called around 4:30 p.m., and the two talked for about thirty minutes. Ashe pleaded with him to respect his privacy, arguing that his illness was a personal matter. Policinski insisted that because Ashe was a celebrity and a public figure, his illness was a legitimate news story. Fortunately for Ashe, however, USA Today policy prohibited the publication of such a story without confirmation from Ashe or another source. But it was only a matter of time before the story would make its way to the newsstands. Ashe had to act, and fast.[63]

Over the next few days he made plans to publicly disclose his illness—on his terms. He reached out to his friends at HBO and asked Frank Deford to help him with the press conference. On April 8 at 3:30 p.m. he and Jeanne sat before reporters as he read a prepared statement. "Rumors and half-truths," he began, "have been floating about concerning my medical condition since my heart attack on July 31, 1979." After disclosing his condition, he explained that he had kept his AIDS diagnosis private in order to protect his family. "Just as I am sure everyone in this room has some personal matter he or she would like to keep private, so did we," he said. He thanked the many doctors, reporters, and friends who had kept his secret for so long. Ashe lashed out at *USA Today* for even considering running the story. "I am not running for some office of public trust," he noted, "nor do I have stockholders to account to. It is only that I fall under the dubious umbrella of 'public figure.'" He became so emotional at one point during the press conference that Jeanne had to read a portion of the statement. But as usual, Ashe found a silver lining in an otherwise sad day. The global AIDS crisis, he said, was simply one more cause for him to take up, and he pledged to work with another AIDS victim, basketball MVP Earvin "Magic" Johnson.[64]

In the days and weeks following Ashe's press conference, most columnists, sportswriters, and fans defended his position that *USA Today* had violated his privacy and practiced questionable journalism. Lance Morrow of *Time* wondered if *USA Today* would have reported on Ashe's illness if he were suffering from leukemia instead of AIDS. "AIDS made it different," concluded Morrow. "Irresistible. Juicy gossip. Red meat." He argued that Ashe's daughter, Camera, should have learned of his illness on the family's terms, not on the terms of a newspaper editor. "There was no public need to know, or right to know," Morrow contended. In a passionate column, veteran sportswriter Robert Lipsyte, a cancer survivor, criticized the new era of tabloid journalism and those who practiced it. He wrote, "In return for being able to market his causes, his books, his TV appearances, his newspaper columns, he cannot secure the most intimate secrets of his life, ones that such professionals as lawyers and doctors are sworn to keep, from being cast out between ads and commercials to be clucked and commented over by you and me." "Public figure" or not, Ashe had the right to keep from the world that he suffered from AIDS. Mark Tran of the *Guardian* argued that AIDS was different than cancer and other diseases because of its association with sexual promiscuity, especially in the gay community. AIDS was an affliction that visited drug users and gay men, not straight, wealthy tennis stars. "By having to admit publicly that he has Aids," Tran wrote, "he will now become pigeonholed." Mark Gray of the *Atlanta Daily World* reminded readers, "For all he has done for this society he deserved, if nothing else, an opportunity to keep something as personal as this private."[65]

Despite being burdened with AIDS, Ashe continued to do what he did best: he kept busy and stayed positive. In May 1992 he returned to Richmond's Byrd Park, a facility and a town that had rejected him in his youth. This visit was a time for him to reconcile with Richmond and forgive his hometown once and for all. He told a reporter, "I started here, got my values and attitudes right here, and I think they have stood me in good stead." As he led a tennis clinic for black and white children in the old Confederate capital, he must have reflected on how far the city had come. Blacks and whites hit tennis balls to one another, and Virginia had even elected an African American governor. A smiling Ashe remarked, "It's nice to be home." Even as his health deteriorated, he continued to give speeches, speak at commencement exercises, host tennis clinics, and travel across the country. At an event in Atlanta honoring high-school athletes, he discussed all of the letters and support that he had received since his AIDS disclosure. "I don't feel as much like a leper as I thought I would," he told the audience. "People don't treat me that way." In late August he organized a tennis exhibition to benefit his newly established Arthur Ashe AIDS Foundation. The event featured some of the biggest names in tennis, past and present. Ashe believed that he and Magic Johnson had paved the way for corporate sponsors to financially support AIDS-related research. The two sports celebrities were helping to redefine the disease as a mainstream illness that threatened all Americans. Ashe wanted to be "a surrogate" for all who were infected with HIV.[66]

In December 1992 *Sports Illustrated* honored Ashe's life and his example by naming him its "Sportsman of the Year." Writer Kenny Moore praised Ashe as a man who always opted for reason over impulse, even at the risk of angering those around him. From an early age he had learned "to allow rebuke to slide by his ears as if it were birdsong." He had been "summoned" to serve others by his father, his coaches, and his community, accepting what he labeled "the Colored catechism." His charitable causes were too many to mention. "Ashe always embodied good sportsmanship on the playing field," noted Moore. "But if sportsmanship is also an athlete's ability to shift from being a selfish competitor to being a useful member of society, then Ashe's sportsmanship is unequaled." And among all of his causes and commitments, his heart remained with the South African people. His "one eye, one pining eye" never left South Africa. "So," Moore continued, "we celebrate Arthur Ashe as our Sportsman of the Year, not because he is a good victim but because of his good works and because of the redefining constancy with which he has pursued them. We rejoice in his battered-from-both-sides balance, his scholarly civility and his sense, even now, especially now, of perspective." Moore reminded readers that his article was no eulogy, that the final chapter of Ashe's life had yet to be written. Ashe aimed to play out his match with life, concluding that he had to "pound away as hard as you can at what you care about until it's over." After all, he had "signed his contract with the whole society of man."[67]

On February 6, 1993, Ashe's final match came to an end. Two weeks earlier, he had canceled a planned trip to Boston to receive an award, instead sending a video acceptance in which he struggled to catch his breath. Soon thereafter, he checked into a New York City hospital, where doctors diagnosed him with pneumocystis pneumonia, a complication of AIDS. Although his health was rapidly failing him, he continued to work tirelessly on his new memoir, *Days of Grace*, and to look forward to a Valentine's Day father-daughter dinner dance that he planned to attend with Camera. In his darkest days, with hope fading, he still looked to the future. On February 6 at 3:13 p.m. Arthur Robert Ashe Jr. died.[68]

# Conclusion

Virginia state flags flew at half-staff on February 9, 1993, on the orders of Douglas Wilder, the state's first African American governor. Hours before sunset on a cold and rainy winter day, white and black, rich and poor, men and women, liberals and conservatives all lined the streets of downtown Richmond to pay their final respects to Ashe, a man they remembered as an international activist, world-champion tennis player, humanitarian, teacher, writer, husband, and father. Many who attended the wake and funeral services had no interest in sports and had never played tennis. One Richmond woman braved the winter cold to honor Ashe as a crusader against South African apartheid, someone who had risked his own career and reputation to help others. Future South African president Nelson Mandela agreed. Following his release from prison on Robben Island after almost thirty years in captivity, a reporter asked Mandela who in the United States he most wanted to see. "Arthur Ashe," was his unequivocal reply. One African American professional standing in line described Ashe as a role model for black youths. "I owe him at least this," the man told the *Richmond Times-Dispatch*. "He showed me it's OK to aspire. It's OK to be articulate. I never had an older brother. Instead, I had a hero." A Richmond city councilman compared the loss to those of John F. Kennedy and Martin Luther King Jr. "The sea of faces in the line to pay respects to Arthur Ashe Jr. last night represented a melding of races and ethnic groups that observers said demonstrated the universality of Ashe's message," wrote one local reporter.[1]

At 5:00 in the evening, the first of more than five thousand mourners passed by Ashe's mahogany coffin, which was surrounded by large floral displays, palms, and dim rose lamps. Ashe, dressed in a navy blue blazer, a blue shirt, and a tropical-colored tie, appeared peaceful and at rest. Visitors left behind an old tennis ball, an inscribed American flag, two flower bouquets, and many cards.

"So long, Arthur," whispered one guest. "The struggle continues." Just after nine, 150 members of Kappa Alpha Psi, Ashe's college fraternity, walked by the casket in pairs. Bob Lipper of the *Times-Dispatch* wrote, "He was black, I was white. He was a world-class celebrity; I was just a guy from his hometown paper. But there were no barriers, no gaps, no veneer to separate us. I have a feeling that's how he dealt with anyone who was fortunate enough to know him." Lipper was right.[2]

The next day, a line began to form outside of the Arthur Ashe Jr. Athletic Center, in North Richmond, six hours before Ashe's funeral. "They waited," wrote one reporter, "dotting the sidewalks like the bright chrysanthemums, pansies and geraniums arranged outside the Ashe Center. They leaned against rental trucks, sat on flatbeds, stood against the crowd ropes. They carried cameras and babies, videocameras and puppies. They took annual leave from state jobs . . . or shut down their businesses." Former tennis players Stan Smith, Charlie Pasarell, and Rod Laver joined U.S. senators Charles Robb and Bill Bradley, New York City mayor David Dinkins, and Reverend Jesse Jackson at the front of the gymnasium. They sang "We Shall Overcome," the anthem of the civil rights movement, along with thousands of mourners and listened to a stirring rendition of "When the Saints Go Marching In." The eulogies were powerful. "Arthur Ashe was just plain better than most of us," said Dinkins. "Most athletes," Jackson explained, "limit themselves to achievements and contributions within the lines, but Arthur found greatness beyond the lines." Governor Wilder noted how Ashe "used every fiber of his strength." When the service concluded, eight pallbearers guided Ashe's casket into a hearse destined for Woodland Cemetery. He would rest for eternity in a plot beside his mother, Mattie.[3]

In the years since his death, Americans and people throughout the world have continued to honor Ashe. In 1996 Richmond placed a statue of Ashe along the city's famed Monument Row, right beside statues of Confederate heroes Stonewall Jackson and Robert E. Lee. One year later, the USTA unveiled the new home of the U.S. Open, named in honor of the tournament's first champion. Every September, the best in the world gather in Flushing, New York, and compete in the Arthur Ashe Stadium. And just after Ashe's passing, ESPN established the Arthur Ashe Courage Award, since presented to the likes of Muhammad Ali, Pat Tillman, Tommie Smith, John Carlos, and Nelson Mandela.

In life, Ashe touched many lives. To sportswriters, former and current tennis players, and fans, Ashe represented the ideal gentleman athlete, one of the greatest sportsmen the tennis courts had ever known. Humble in victories at the U.S. Open in 1968 and Wimbledon in 1975, he proved that a black man born of working-class roots could not only excel at tennis but embody what was great about the sport. To many black South Africans, Ashe was an inspiration, a living example of the possibilities of freedom. He used his celebrity status as an international platform to fight against racism, classism, discrimination, and those who violated the rights of others. He spoke softly, his words full of ideas, intelligence, and compassion, not hate and vengeance. His critics called him Uncle Tom and nigger, an accommodationist and a militant. He negotiated life from the middle, standing as a statesman at center court. "He wasn't Martin Luther King, and he wasn't Malcolm X," explained one mourner at Ashe's funeral. "But when you saw him, he stood for something. He wasn't always talking, but he always had something to say."[4]

# Notes

## Introduction

1. David Wolf, "Arthur—the New King of the Courts," *Life*, 20 Sept. 1968, 34. There is no scholarly biography of Ashe. For more on his life, see Arthur Ashe, *Days of Grace: A Memoir*, with Arnold Rampersad (New York: Knopf, 1993); Ashe, *Off the Court*, with Neil Amdur (New York: New American Library, 1981); Ashe, *Arthur Ashe: Portrait in Motion*, with Frank Deford (Boston: Houghton Mifflin, 1975); Ashe, *Advantage Ashe*, as told to Clifford George Gewecke Jr. (New York: Coward-McCann, 1967); Louie Robinson Jr., *Arthur Ashe: Tennis Champion* (Garden City, NY: Doubleday, 1967); John McPhee, *Levels of the Game* (New York: Farrar, Straus & Giroux, 1969); Mike Towle, ed., *I Remember Arthur Ashe: Memories of a True Tennis Pioneer and Champion of Social Causes by the People Who Knew Him* (Nashville: Cumberland House, 2001); Sundiata Djata, *Blacks at the Net: Black Achievement in the History of Tennis*, 2 vols. (Syracuse, NY: Syracuse University Press, 2006–8), 1:42–68; *Arthur Ashe: Citizen of the World*, produced and directed by Julie Anderson (New York: Home Box Office, 1994), videocassette, 59 min.; and Damion L. Thomas, "'Don't Tell Me How to Think': Arthur Ashe and the Burden of 'Being Black,'" *International Journal of the History of Sport* 27, no. 8 (May 2010): 1313–29.

2. Mark Asher, "Ashe Wins U.S. Open Tennis," *Washington Post* (hereafter *WP*), 10 Sept. 1968, D1, D3; Wolf, "Arthur"; Jim Murray, "Ashe Goes Big League," *Los Angeles Times* (hereafter *LAT*), 10 Sept. 1968, E1.

3. Wolf, "Arthur."

4. Examples of these studies include Theresa Runstedtler, *Jack Johnson, Rebel Sojourner: Boxing in the Shadow of the Global Color Line* (Berkeley and Los Angeles: University of California Press, 2012); Geoffrey C. Ward, *Unforgivable Blackness: The Rise and Fall of Jack Johnson* (New York: Vintage Books, 2006); Randy Roberts, *Papa Jack: Jack Johnson and the Era of White Hopes* (New York: Free Press, 1985); William J. Baker, *Jesse Owens: An American Life* (Urbana: University of Illinois Press, 2006); Randy Roberts, *Joe Louis: Hard Times Man* (New Haven, CT: Yale University Press, 2010); David Margolick, *Beyond Glory: Joe Louis vs. Max Schmeling, and a World on the Brink* (New York: Vintage Books, 2005); Lewis A. Erenberg, *The Greatest Fight of Our Generation: Louis vs. Schmeling* (New York: Oxford University Press, 2007); Jules Tygiel, *Baseball's Great Experiment: Jackie Robinson and His Legacy* (New York: Oxford University Press, 1983); Arnold Rampersad, *Jackie Robinson: A Biography* (1997; reprint, New York: Ballantine, 1998); Aram Goudsouzian, *King of the Court: Bill Russell and the Basketball Revolution* (Berkeley and Los Angeles: University of California Press, 2011); Mike Freeman, *Jim Brown: The Fierce Life of an American Hero* (New York: HarperCollins, 2006); Thomas Hauser, *Muhammad Ali: His Life and Times* (New York: Simon & Schuster, 1991); and

David Remnick, *King of the World: Muhammad Ali and the Rise of an American Hero* (New York: Vintage Books, 1999).

5. Althea Gibson, *I Always Wanted to Be Somebody* (New York: Harper, 1958), 124. See also David K. Wiggins, *Glory Bound: Black Athletes in a White America* (Syracuse, NY: Syracuse University Press, 1997), 200–220; David K. Wiggins and Patrick B. Miller, eds., *Sport and the Color Line: Black Athletes and Race Relations in Twentieth Century America* (New York: Routledge, 2003); Wiggins, ed., *Out of the Shadows: A Biographical History of African American Athletes* (Fayetteville: University of Arkansas Press, 2006); and Gerald Early, *A Level Playing Field: African American Athletes and the Republic of Sports* (Cambridge, MA: Harvard University Press, 2011).

6. Wiggins, *Glory Bound*, 200–220; Wiggins and Miller, *Sport and the Color Line*; Wiggins, *Out of the Shadows*; Early, *Level Playing Field*.

7. Murray, "Ashe Goes Big League."

8. Kenny Moore, "The Eternal Example," *Sports Illustrated* (hereafter *SI*), 21 Dec. 1992, 16–27.

9. Ashe, *Days of Grace*, 113–14.

10. Martin Luther King Jr. to Ashe, 7 Feb. 1968, Manuscripts, Archives, and Rare Books Division, Schomburg Center for Research in Black Culture, New York Public Library, New York (hereafter SCRBC), box 2, folder 1.

### CHAPTER 1: RICHMOND

1. Louie Robinson Jr., *Arthur Ashe: Tennis Champion* (Garden City, NY: Doubleday, 1967), 76; Ashe, *Off the Court*, with Neil Amdur (New York: New American Library, 1981), 33.

2. Steve Clark, "Heroes Are Not Made Overnight," *Richmond Times-Dispatch* (hereafter *RTD*), 11 Feb. 1993 (quotation); Richard Steins, *Arthur Ashe: A Biography* (Westport, CT: Greenwood, 2005), 6; John McPhee, *Levels of the Game* (New York: Farrar, Straus & Giroux, 1969), 64–65; Robinson, *Arthur Ashe*, 11.

3. I use the term *moderate integrationism* to refer to those individuals, activists, and organizations that favored desegregation yet were willing to accept gradual progress. The NAACP, a civil rights organization that focused on litigation, is an example of a moderate integrationist organization. I use the term *militant integrationism* to refer to those who demanded integration immediately, such as A. Philip Randolph and Martin Luther King Jr. Militant integrationists often engaged in direct action, including boycotts, marches, and demonstrations. For a discussion of both types of integrationists, see, for instance, Dennis C. Dickerson, *Militant Mediator: Whitney M. Young, Jr.* (Lexington: University Press of Kentucky, 1998), 1–7, 318–19; William W. Sales Jr., *From Civil Rights to Black Liberation: Malcolm X and the Organization of Afro-American Unity* (Boston: South End, 1994), 195; and Timothy B. Tyson, *Radio Free Dixie: Robert F. Williams and the Roots of Black Power* (Chapel Hill: University of North Carolina Press, 1999), 197, 200, 204, 210.

4. Steins, *Arthur Ashe*, 3; Arthur Ashe, *Arthur Ashe: Portrait in Motion*, with Frank Deford (Boston: Houghton Mifflin, 1975), 27; McPhee, *Levels of the Game*, 62; Ashe, *Off the Court*, 19; Walter Johnson, *Soul by Soul: Life inside the Antebellum Slave Market* (Cambridge, MA: Harvard University Press, 1999), 138–39. For more on skin color as an indicator of character and intelligence, see William M. Evans, "From the Land of Canaan to the Land of Guinea: The Strange Odyssey of the Sons of Ham," *American Historical Review* 85 (Feb. 1980): 15–43;

Michael Hughes and Bradley R. Hertel, "The Significance of Color Remains: A Study of Life Chances, Mate Selection, and Ethnic Consciousness among Black Americans," *Social Forces* 69 (June 1990): 1105–19; and Kathy Russell, Midge Wilson, and Ronald Hall, *The Color Complex: The Politics of Skin Color among African Americans* (New York: Harcourt Brace Jovanovich, 1992).

5. Christopher Silver and John V. Moeser, *The Separate City: Black Communities in the Urban South, 1940–1968* (Lexington: University Press of Kentucky, 1995), x, 6, 12, 24, 26, 42–43; Megan Taylor Shockley, *"We, Too, Are Americans": African American Women in Detroit and Richmond, 1940–1954* (Urbana: University of Illinois Press, 2004), 18; Steve Clark, "Waiter Who Became a Writer Came Home to Be Buried This Week," *RTD*, transcript in the hand of Arthur Ashe, SCRBC, box 1, folder 1. For more on race in Richmond, see Maurice Duke and Daniel P. Jordan, eds., *A Richmond Reader, 1733–1983* (Chapel Hill: University of North Carolina Press, 1983); and Elsa Barkley Brown and Gregg D. Kimball, "Mapping the Terrain of Black Richmond," in *The New African American Urban History* (Thousand Oaks, CA: Sage, 1996), 66–115.

6. Arthur Ashe, *Advantage Ashe*, as told to Clifford George Gewecke Jr. (New York: Coward-McCann, 1967), 20; Clarke Bustard, "Assurance Class in the Walker Class of '61," *RTD*, 6 Apr. 1984, SCRBC, box 1, folder 3; Cindy Morris, "ATP Honors Tennis' Stately Statesman—Ashe," *Cincinnati Enquirer*, 11 May 1984, B8, SCRBC, box 35, folder 3; Arthur Ashe Jr., "My Most Unforgettable Character," *Reader's Digest*, Sept. 1972, 152, SCRBC, box 26, folder 9.

7. "Appeal Planned for Two Fined for Sitting in Front of Whites," *Richmond Afro-American* (hereafter *RAA*), 6 Mar. 1943; "Ingram to Study Segregation Case," *RAA*, 27 Sept. 1947; Shockley, *"We, Too, Are Americans,"* 170, 182. For more on Richmond bus desegregation, see ibid., 170–204; and Lewis A. Randolph and Gayle T. Tate, *Rights for a Season: The Politics of Race, Class, and Gender in Richmond, Virginia* (Knoxville: University of Tennessee Press, 2003), 165–66.

8. Ashe, *Portrait in Motion*, 56; Silver and Moeser, *Separate City*, 42–43; *Arthur Ashe: Citizen of the World*, produced and directed by Julie Anderson (New York: Home Box Office, 1994), videocassette, 59 min.

9. McPhee, *Levels of the Game*, 53–54.

10. "Genealogical and Historical Sketch: The Name and Family of Ash(e)," SCRBC, box 1, folder 1; McPhee, *Levels of the Game*, 11–12; funeral program for Arthur Ashe Sr., 22 Mar. 1989, ibid.

11. McPhee, *Levels of the Game*, 61; Frank Deford, "Service, But First a Smile," *SI*, 29 Aug. 1966.

12. Ashe, *Advantage Ashe*, 110; Steins, *Arthur Ashe*, 4; Deford, "Service, But First a Smile."

13. Ashe, *Advantage Ashe*, 110; Phil Casey, "Ashe: On Being Black," *WP*, 7 Nov. 1969, D1; funeral program for Arthur Ashe Sr.

14. Ashe, *Advantage Ashe*, 110; Ashe, *Off the Court*, 13.

15. McPhee, *Levels of the Game*, 12, 62; Ashe, *Off the Court*, 25; Ashe, *Advantage Ashe*, 109.

16. Steins, *Arthur Ashe*, 4; Ashe, *Advantage Ashe*, 109; Ashe, *Off the Court*, 19.

17. Ashe, *Advantage Ashe*, 17; Chauncey Durden, "One View of Ashe," *RTD*, 14 Feb. 1975; McPhee, *Levels of the Game*, 109; Neil Amdur, "Conversations with Lt. Arthur Ashe: Part II," *World Tennis* (hereafter *WT*), May 1968, 28–29.

18. Ashe, *Off the Court*, 19; Ashe, *Advantage Ashe*, 12; Mike Towle, ed., *I Remember Arthur Ashe: Memories of a True Tennis Pioneer and Champion of Social Causes by the People Who Knew Him* (Nashville: Cumberland House, 2001), 5, 8, 16; McPhee, *Levels of the Game*, 79; funeral program for Arthur Ashe Sr.

19. McPhee, *Levels of the Game*, 64–65; Robinson, *Arthur Ashe*, 9–10.

20. Ashe, *Advantage Ashe*, 15–16; Robinson, *Arthur Ashe*, 13, 16; Steins, *Arthur Ashe*, 9–10; McPhee, *Levels of the Game*, 62–63; Ashe, *Portrait in Motion*, 206–7; Ashe, *Off the Court*, 7, 19; Arthur Ashe, *Days of Grace: A Memoir*, with Arnold Rampersad (New York: Knopf, 1993), 3, 49–50.

21. McPhee, *Levels of the Game*, 63; Ashe, *Off the Court*, 19–20.

22. Ashe, *Off the Court*, 22; Ashe, *Advantage Ashe*, 16.

23. Ashe, *Days of Grace*, 3, 50, 186; Mike Zitz, "Arthur Ashe: Career Has Come Full Circle," *Freelance Star* (Fredericksburg, VA), 17 July 1982, SCRBC, box 35, folder 3.

24. Doug Smith, *Whirlwind: The Godfather of Black Tennis; The Life and Times of Dr. Robert Walter Johnson* (Washington, DC: Blue Eagle, 2004), 73; McPhee, *Levels of the Game*, 36; Ashe, *Off the Court*, 34–35; Ashe, *Advantage Ashe*, 14.

25. Parke Cummings, *American Tennis: The Story of a Game and Its People* (Boston: Little, Brown, 1957), 18; "Comment on Bunche," *New York Times* (hereafter *NYT*), 14 July 1959, 15.

26. Ashe, *Portrait in Motion*, 148; Ashe, *Days of Grace*, 224–25; Hal Higdon, "Plays Tennis Like a Man, Speaks Out Like," *NYT*, 27 Aug. 1967, SM115; *Tea and Sympathy*, directed by Vincente Minnelli (Beverly Hills, CA: MGM, 1998), videocassette, 122 min.; Roscoe Harrison, "'I'm a Crusader,' Tennis Champ Ashe Reveals in Jet Interview," *Jet*, 19. Dec. 1968, SCRBC, box 37, Scrapbooks; *Dial M for Murder*, directed by Alfred Hitchcock (Burbank, CA: Warner Home Video, 1996), videocassette, 109 min.

27. Harry Gordon, "Arthur Ashe Has to Be Aware That He Is a Pioneer in Short White Pants," *NYT*, 2 Jan. 1966, 164; "Negroes in Davis Cup Play, Expert Predicts," *Chicago Daily Defender* (hereafter *CDD*), 5 June 1962, 23; Robinson, *Arthur Ashe*, 79; "Davis Cupper Arthur Ashe Threatens Aussie Net Domination," *Chicago Defender* (hereafter *CD*), 9 Apr. 1966, 17.

28. Clark, "Heroes Are Not Made Overnight"; Sundiata Djata, *Blacks at the Net: Black Achievement in the History of Tennis*, 2 vols. (Syracuse, NY: Syracuse University Press, 2006–8), 1:43; Ashe, *Off the Court*, 34, 37; Ashe, *Portrait in Motion*, 148.

29. Ashe, *Off the Court*, 34–35.

30. McPhee, *Levels of the Game*, 37–38, 130; Robinson, *Arthur Ashe*, 37–38.

31. McPhee, *Levels of the Game*, 37.

32. Robinson, *Arthur Ashe*, 40–44.

33. "Southmayd Says Ashe's Entry Not Rejected," *WP*, 12 July 1959, C6; Robert Walter Johnson to William Riordau, 10 July 1959, SCRBC, box 1, folder 1.

34. Ashe, *Off the Court*, 33; "Throw the Rascals Out: A Proposal to Stop the Approving of Tournaments That Practice Discrimination," *WT*, Oct. 1968, 14.

35. James Jackson Kilpatrick, *The Southern Case for School Segregation* (New York: Cromwell-Collier, 1962). For more on Hill, see Oliver W. Hill Sr., *The Autobiography of Oliver Hill, Sr.* (Winter Park, FL: Four-G, 2000). A good biography of Byrd is Ronald L. Heinemann, *Harry F. Byrd of Virginia* (Charlottesville: University Press of Virginia, 1996). For more on the *Brown* decision, see James T. Patterson, *Brown v. Board of Education: A Civil Rights Milestone and its Troubled Legacy* (New York: Oxford University Press, 2002); and Peter F. Lau,

ed., *From the Grassroots to the Supreme Court: "Brown v. Board of Education" and American Democracy* (Durham, NC: Duke University Press, 2004).

36. Silver and Moeser, *Separate City*, 69, 71; Randolph and Tate, *Rights for a Season*, 79, 137. For a good overview of desegregation and MR in Richmond, see Mildred Davis Bruce, "The Richmond School Board and the Desegregation of Richmond Public Schools, 1954–1971" (EdD diss., College of William & Mary, 1988).

37. Silver and Moeser, *Separate City*, 123, 136; Randolph and Tate, *Rights for a Season*, 180. Randolph and Tate echo Silver and Moeser when they write: "The factors that contributed directly to Richmond's CRM and the rise of the [Richmond Crusade for Voters], were the two *Brown* decisions, the rise of massive resistance in 1955, and the decline of the [Richmond Civic Council]" (136).

38. Ashe, *Days of Grace*, 116.

39. Ibid. For more on the murder of Till and the trial of Bryant and Milam, see Ruth Feldstein, "'I wanted the whole world to see': Race, Gender, and Constructions of Motherhood in the Death of Emmett Till," in *Not June Cleaver: Women and Gender in Postwar America, 1945–1960*, edited by Joanne Meyerowitz (Philadelphia: Temple University Press, 1994), 263–303.

40. Ashe, *Advantage Ashe*, 17; McPhee, *Levels of the Game*, 63; Bustard, "Assurance Class in the Walker Class of '61."

41. Ashe, *Off the Court*, 24; *Arthur Ashe: Citizen of the World*.

42. Ashe, *Off the Court*, 26–27; McPhee, *Levels of the Game*, 63.

43. Ashe, *Off the Court*, 14, 25; Steins, *Arthur Ashe*, 16; McPhee, *Levels of the Game*, 14, 55, 58.

44. Jennings Culley, "Native Son Comes Home—and Wins Davis Cup Match," *Richmond News Leader*, 4 May 1968; Ashe, *Advantage Ashe*, 111–12.

45. Ashe, *Portrait in Motion*, 44; Ashe, *Off the Court*, 22, 162–63.

46. D. Smith, *Whirlwind*, 73.

47. Ibid., 74; McPhee, *Levels of the Game*, 30.

48. D. Smith, *Whirlwind*, 103; *Arthur Ashe: Citizen of the World*; McPhee, *Levels of the Game*, 41, 43; Ashe, "My Most Unforgettable Character."

49. D. Smith, *Whirlwind*, 9–18.

50. Ibid., 19–43. For more on African Americans and the National Football League, see Thomas G. Smith, "Outside the Pale: The Exclusion of Blacks from the National Football League, 1934–1946," *Journal of Sport History* 15, no. 3 (Winter 1988): 255–81; and Michael Lomax, "The African American Experience in Professional Football," *Journal of Social History* 33, no. 1 (1999): 163–78.

51. D. Smith, *Whirlwind*, 43–44, 48.

52. Ibid., 3, 83; McPhee, *Levels of the Game*, 23; "Arthur Ashe New Interscholastic Champ of ATA," *CD*, 7 June 1958, 24.

53. D. Smith, *Whirlwind*, 3, 72; Ashe, *Portrait in Motion*, 148; Robinson, *Arthur Ashe*, 63; Higdon, "Plays Tennis Like a Man, Speaks Out Like."

54. D. Smith, *Whirlwind*, 74; Ashe, *Off the Court*, 40–41; Ashe, "My Most Unforgettable Character."

55. McPhee, *Levels of the Game*, 28–29; Ashe, *Advantage Ashe*, 24, 26; D. Smith, *Whirlwind*, 91.

56. D. Smith, *Whirlwind*, 91, 99.

57. McPhee, *Levels of the Game*, 29; Ashe, *Portrait in Motion*, 225; George Minot, "Across the Net," *WP*, 19 July 1959, C5.

58. D. Smith, *Whirlwind*, 99–100; Damion Thomas, "'The Quiet Militant': Arthur Ashe and Black Athletic Activism," in *Out of the Shadows: A Biographical History of African American Athletes*, edited by David K. Wiggins (Fayetteville: University of Arkansas Press, 2006), 279.

59. Ashe, *Advantage Ashe*, 29–30, 33; "Arthur Ashe New Interscholastic Champ of ATA."

60. Ashe, *Advantage Ashe*, 34; Minot, "Across the Net"; McPhee, *Levels of the Game*, 44–45; Djata, *Blacks at the Net*, 1:168; Towle, *I Remember Arthur Ashe*, 11–12; Ashe, *Off the Court*, 42; *Arthur Ashe: Citizen of the World*; Bill Parillo, "Arthur Ashe Earned His Place in History," *Providence Journal*, 14 July 1985, D1, SCRBC, box 35, folder 4.

61. Ashe, *Advantage Ashe*, 32–33.

62. Ibid., 41–42, 45; Ashe, *Portrait in Motion*, 70; D. Smith, *Whirlwind*, 100.

63. Ashe, *Advantage Ashe*, 45.

64. Ashe, *Off the Court*, 52.

## CHAPTER 2: UCLA

1. Ashe, *Off the Court*, with Neil Amdur (New York: New American Library, 1981), 55–56.

2. Julian Bond, "SNCC: What We Did," *Monthly Review* 52, no. 5 (Oct. 2000). For a good overview of SNCC, see Manning Marable, *Race, Reform, and Rebellion: The Second Reconstruction in Black America, 1945–1990* (Jackson: University of Mississippi Press, 1991).

3. For a good overview of the civil rights movement, see Steven F. Lawson, *Running for Freedom: Civil Rights and Black Politics in America since 1941* (Philadelphia: Temple University Press, 1991); Raymond Arsenault, *Freedom Riders: 1961 and the Struggle for Racial Justice* (New York: Oxford University Press, 2006); and Manning Marable, *Race, Reform, and Rebellion: The Second Reconstruction and Beyond in Black America, 1945–2006* (Starkville: University Press of Mississippi, 2007).

4. Ashe, *Off the Court*, 52, 61; David K. Wiggins, *Glory Bound: Black Athletes in a White America* (Syracuse, NY: Syracuse University Press, 1997), 200. In *The Souls of Black Folk* (New York: Vintage Books, 1990) black activist W. E. B. Du Bois argued that double consciousness was "this sense of always looking at one's self through the eyes of others, of measuring one's soul by the tape of a world that looks on in amused contempt and pity. One ever feels his two-ness—an American, a Negro; two souls, two thoughts, two unreconciled strivings; two warring ideals in one dark body, whose dogged strength alone keeps it from being torn asunder" (8).

5. Lawrence H. Larsen, *A History of Missouri, 1953–2003* (Columbia: University of Missouri Press, 2004), 6, 43–44, 61–62, 100; Ann Morris, ed., *Lift Every Voice and Sing: St. Louis African Americans in the Twentieth Century* (Columbia: University of Missouri Press, 1999), 14; John A. Wright, *Discovering African American St. Louis: A Guide to Historic Sites* (Columbia: Missouri Historical Society Press, 2002), 19, 30, 103.

6. A. Morris, *Lift Every Voice*, 4, 163, 165; Ashe, *Advantage Ashe*, as told to Clifford George Gewecke Jr. (New York: Coward-McCann, 1967), 48–49; Carolyn Hewes Toft, *The Ville: The Ethnic Heritage of an Urban Neighborhood* (St. Louis: Landmarks Association of St. Louis, 1975), 9–10, 15.

7. Ashe, *Advantage Ashe*, 46, 48–49.

8. H. Llewellyn Harris, "Dick Hudlin Helped Make 'Nationals'—Harris," *Atlanta Daily World* (hereafter *ADW*), 2 Aug. 1934, 5. For more on Hudlin, see A. S. "Doc" Young, "Tennis Is

Not a Stranger to Blacks," *LAT*, 22 July 1972, B4; "Race Problem Up for Discussion between University Students," *CD*, 19 Apr. 1924, 4; and "Richard Hudlin Wins Saint Louis Net Play," *CD*, 7 Aug. 1926, 10.

9. Ashe, *Advantage Ashe*, 46–47; "Ashe Wins Tennis Title," *NYT*, 28 Nov. 1960, 45; "Ashe Wins Tennis," *WP*, 28 Nov. 1960, A18; Faces in the Crowd, *SI*, 12 Dec. 1960; Les Matthews, "Negro Wages Uphill Fight in Sports," *New York Amsterdam News* (hereafter *NYAN*), 17 Dec. 1960, A7; Ashe, "My Most Unforgettable Character," *Reader's Digest*, Sept. 1972, SCRBC, box 26, folder 9.

10. "Tennis the Menace," *SI*, 3 July 1961; "An Unfair Rap," newspaper clipping, 1961, SCRBC, box 35, folder 1. Tebell answered his critics with the fact that blacks had attended UVA for eleven years prior to 1961, proof that the university was not a racist institution.

11. Ibid.

12. "Ashe Takes Tennis Title," *NYT*, 23 June 1961, 23; "Ashe Captures School Tennis," *WP*, 23 June 1961, C13; Marion E. Jackson, "Sports of the World," *ADW*, 6 Aug. 1961, 8; Ashe, *Off the Court*, 51. For other examples emphasizing Ashe as the first African American to accomplish something in particular see Fred Tupper, "11 U.S. Players Reach 2D Round," *NYT*, 26 June 1963, 45; Allison Danzig, "Ashe, McKinley, Ralston and Riessen Are Named to U.S. Davis Cup Team," *NYT*, 2 Aug. 1963, 20; and Harry Gordon, "Arthur Ashe Has to Be Aware That He Is a Pioneer in Short White Pants," *NYT*, 2 January 1966, 164.

13. Doug Smith, *Whirlwind: The Godfather of Black Tennis; The Life and Times of Dr. Robert Walter Johnson* (Washington, DC: Blue Eagle, 2004), 105; *Arthur Ashe: Citizen of the World*, produced and directed by Julie Anderson (New York: Home Box Office, 1994), videocassette, 59 min.; Gordon, "Arthur Ashe Has to Be Aware"; Louie Robinson Jr., *Arthur Ashe: Tennis Champion* (Garden City, NY: Doubleday, 1967), 70–71.

14. Ashe, *Off the Court*, 51; Ashe, *Advantage Ashe*, 50; D. Smith, *Whirlwind*, 106; Al Wolf, "Ashe's Victories Not Surprising," *LAT*, 5 Aug. 1965, B2; Mike Towle, ed., *I Remember Arthur Ashe: Memories of a True Tennis Pioneer and Champion of Social Causes by the People Who Knew Him* (Nashville: Cumberland House, 2001), 5; Ashe, "New Competition for the California Tennis Factories," *Tennis*, July 1980, SCRBC, box 40, Scrapbooks; Ashe, "My Most Unforgettable Character."

15. "An Open Letter," *UCLA Daily Bruin* (hereafter *DB*), 3 Oct. 1962, 4; Kurt Edward Kemper, "Reformers in the Marketplace of Ideas: Student Activism and American Democracy in Cold War Los Angeles" (PhD diss., Louisiana State University, 2000), 100, 153; Ashe, *Advantage Ashe*, 50; Marty Kasindorf, "The Emancipator Hasn't Won Yet," *DB*, 12 Feb. 1960, 1, 11; Damion L. Thomas, *Globetrotting: African American Athletes and Cold War Politics* (Urbana: University of Illinois Press, 2012); Thomas Borstelmann, *The Cold War and the Color Line: American Race Relations in the Global Arena* (Cambridge, MA: Harvard University Press, 2003). On his decision to become a Bruin, Ashe said, "I chose to attend UCLA because it had a tradition of fairness to black athletes dating back to the time of Jackie Robinson, who broke major-league baseball's color line." Ashe, "My Most Unforgettable Character."

16. Ashe, *Off the Court*, 53–54, 68; "Arthur Ashe Hits Tennis Stride," *Los Angeles Sentinel* (hereafter *LAS*), 22 Apr. 1965, B4. For more on Graebner, see Neil Amdur, "The Graebner Few People Know," *NYT*, 21 July 1968, S7; and Roy Blount Jr., "A Paper Tiger Wins with Steel," *SI*, 5 Aug. 1968. See also Robert Fischer, interviews by David Rose, 9, 24 Mar. 1982, transcript 1984, in "The Right Man at the Right Time: J. D. Morgan," UCLA Oral History Program, Department of Special Collections, Young Research Library, UCLA, 54.

17. Harry Edwards, *The Revolt of the Black Athlete* (New York: Free Press, 1969); Edwards, *The Struggle That Must Be: An Autobiography* (New York: Macmillan, 1980); "RAP on Blacks and Sports $$$," interview with Jesse Jackson, *Black Sports*, May 1975, 22-25, 61-62; Kenneth L. Shropshire, *In Black and White: Race and Sports in America* (New York: New York University Press, 1996), 72-73, 85-86, 153.

18. William C. Ackerman, interview by David Rose, 19 Feb. 1982, transcript 1984, in "Right Man at the Right Time," 1-2, 4, 10, 16; Fischer interview, 25-26, 32-34, 45-54; John Wooden, interview by David Rose, 12 Mar. 1982, transcript 1984, in "Right Man at the Right Time," 357.

19. Ashe, *Off the Court*, 89-90; Ackerman interview, 16; Byron K. Atkinson, interviews by David Rose, 18 Feb., 23 Mar. 1982, transcript 1984, in "Right Man at the Right Time," 185.

20. Ashe, *Advantage Ashe*, 53, 55; Ashe, *Off the Court*, 66.

21. Bill Brower, "Ashe Shoots for Greatness," *LAS*, 14 December 1961, B11; "Arthur Ashe Jr. on Way to Net Greatness," *Pittsburgh Courier* (hereafter *PC*), 28 Apr. 1962, A18; A. Wolf, "Ashe's Victories Not Surprising."

22. Wendell Smith, "Ashe a Player with Too Many Strokes," *PC*, 5 Sept. 1964, 22; John McPhee, *Levels of the Game* (New York: Farrar, Straus & Giroux, 1969), 88, 93. At least one writer disagreed that Ashe lacked concentration at critical moments. A writer for *World Tennis* argued that the problem was Ashe's "looseness," not his wandering mind. J.D.H., "The Ashe Game: Part I," *WT*, Dec. 1968, 34-37. See also Allison Danzig and Peter Schwed, eds., *The Fireside Book of Tennis: A Complete History of the Game and Its Great Players and Matches* (New York: Simon & Schuster, 1972), 452-53; and Gordon, "Arthur Ashe Has to Be Aware."

23. Gertrude Wilson, "Ashe Grows of Age," *NYAN*, 21 Aug. 1965, 15; W. Smith, "Ashe a Player with Too Many Strokes."

24. Ashe, *Off the Court*, 67; Frank Deford, "Trojan Triumph over Troy," *SI*, 1 July 1963.

25. "Ashe Takes Southland College Tennis Crown," *DB*, 18 Mar. 1963, 6; Frank Deford, "Service, But First a Smile," *SI*, 29 Aug. 1966; Arnold Lester, "Tennis Squad Opens NCAA Play," *DB*, 14 June 1963, 13; Frank Stewart, "UCLA's Ashe Looms as Davis Cupper," *LAS*, 11 Apr. 1963, B8.

26. Bill Becker, "Ashe Is Approaching Stardom in Tennis," *NYT*, 15 Aug. 1965, S7; Arnold Lester, "It's Ashe's Tourney," *DB*, 18 June 1965, 9; Lester, "Netters Heavy Favorites over SC," *DB*, 9 Apr. 1965, 7; Jamie Curran, "Belkin Overcome by Ashe's Attack," *LAT*, 20 June 1965, F3; "Ashe's Next Goal: Davis Cup Title," *LAS*, 24 June 1965, B1; Ashe, *Advantage Ashe*, 65.

27. Ashe, *Off the Court*, 53-54.

28. For more on Carmichael, see Kwame Ture and Mumia Abu-Jamal, *Stokely Speaks: From Black Power to Pan-Africanism* (Chicago: Chicago Review Press, 2007); and Carmichael, *Ready for Revolution: The Life and Struggles of Stokely Carmichael (Kwame Ture)*, with Ekwueme Michael Thelwell (New York: Scribner, 2005).

29. Peniel Joseph, *Waiting 'Til the Midnight Hour: A Narrative History of Black Power in America* (New York: Henry Holt, 2006), 132-40; Manning Marable, *Race, Reform, and Rebellion: The Second Reconstruction in Black America, 1945-1990* (Jackson: University Press of Mississippi, 1991), 94; Jeffrey O. G. Ogbar, *Black Power: Radical Politics and African American Identity* (Baltimore: Johns Hopkins University Press, 2004), 60-63.

30. Joseph, *Waiting 'Til the Midnight Hour*, 141-42; Jack Nelson, "Three Mississippi Marchers Jailed, Released on Bond," *LAT*, 17 June 1966, 1; Gene Roberts, "Mississippi Reduces Police Protection for Marchers," *NYT*, 17 June 1966, 1; Nicholas von Hoffman, "3 Marchers Arrested in Greenwood," *WP*, 17 June 1966, A1.

31. Joseph, *Waiting 'Til the Midnight Hour*, xiii. Works that explicitly or implicitly divide the civil rights and Black Power movements include Lawson, *Running for Freedom*; and Clayborne Carson, *In Struggle: SNCC and the Black Awakening of the 1960s* (Cambridge, MA: Harvard University Press, 1981). Examples of the new Black Power historiography include Jeanne F. Theoharis and Komozi Woodard, eds., *Freedom North: Black Freedom Struggles outside the South, 1940–1980* (New York: Palgrave Macmillan, 2003); Woodard, *A Nation within a Nation: Amiri Baraka (LeRoi Jones) and Black Power Politics* (Chapel Hill: University of North Carolina Press, 1999); Jama Lazerow and Yohuru Williams, eds., *In Search of the Black Panther Party: New Perspectives on a Revolutionary Movement* (Durham, NC: Duke University Press, 2006); Peniel Joseph, *The Black Power Movement: Rethinking the Civil Rights–Black Power Era* (New York: Routledge, 2006); Timothy B. Tyson, *Radio Free Dixie: Robert F. Williams and the Roots of Black Power* (Chapel Hill: University of North Carolina Press, 1999); William Van Deburg, *New Day in Babylon: The Black Power Movement and American Culture, 1965–1975* (Chicago: University of Chicago Press, 1992); Ogbar, *Black Power*; and Simon Wendt, *The Spirit and the Shotgun: Armed Resistance and the Struggle for Civil Rights* (Gainesville: University Press of Florida, 2007).

32. Arthur Ashe, *Days of Grace: A Memoir*, with Arnold Rampersad (New York: Knopf, 1993), 113–14; Barry Lorge, "Inside the Heart & Mind of Arthur Ashe," *Tennis*, Sept. 1988, SCRBC, box 35, folder 4.

33. Van Deburg, *New Day in Babylon*, 11–28, 64–81; Ashe, *Off the Court*, 59–60.

34. Ashe, *Days of Grace*, 113–14; Susan Herrmann, "Southland Coed Caught in Rioting," *LAT*, 22 May 1961, 1; "First Alabama Rioter Arrests Made by U.S.," *LAT*, 23 May 1961, 1; "Rider Describes Brutality," *DB*, 18 Sept. 1961, 1; "Freedom Rider Tells Experience," *DB*, 3 Oct. 1961, 1; "Police Arrest UCLA CORE Demonstrators," *DB*, 4 Nov. 1963, 1; "Yes on the Riders," *DB*, 14 Feb. 1962, 1; Douglas Faigin, "Southern Brutality Fosters Protests," *DB*, 9 Mar. 1965, 1; "SCOPE Worker Tells Experiences," *DB*, 23 July 1965, 1; Dorothy Vine, clipping from *Class*, Feb. 1984, 36, SCRBC, box 35, folder 3.

35. Ashe, *Days of Grace*, 87–88, 113; Ashe, *Off the Court*, 215; Vine clipping, Feb. 1984; Joel Boxer, "Summer—Dixie Way," *DB*, 2 Feb. 1965, 4; Faigin, "Southern Brutality Fosters Protests." In *Off the Court* Ashe writes, "At UCLA, I was geographically removed from most of the major activities of the civil rights movement. The marches and sit-ins and arrests were on the front pages every day, but I was a long way from them" (61).

36. Tamara L. Brown, Gregory S. Parks, and Clarenda M. Phillips, eds., *African American Fraternities and Sororities: The Legacy and the Vision* (Lexington: University Press of Kentucky, 2005), 137–80, 211–31; Ashe, *Advantage Ashe*, 58; Kasindorf, "Emancipator Hasn't Won Yet." Originating in the early 1900s, black fraternities were an outgrowth of racial prejudice on college campuses. Even in the 1960s, fraternities at UCLA excluded blacks, prompting African American activists to demand sensitivity training for white fraternity officers.

37. Ashe, *Off the Court*, 58.

38. Ibid., 61; Joseph, *Waiting 'Til the Midnight Hour*, 217–18; "Interview with Maulana Karenga," *Emerge*, Jan. 1992, 11–12. For more on the life and philosophy of Karenga, see Scot Brown, *Fighting for US: Maulana Karenga, the US Organization, and Black Cultural Nationalism* (New York: New York University Press, 2003); Maulana Karenga, "Ideology and Struggle: Some Preliminary Notes," *Black Scholar* 6, no. 5 (Jan./Feb. 1975): 23–30; and Karenga, "A Response to Muhammad Ahmad on the Us/Panther Conflict," ibid. 9, no. 10 (July/Aug. 1978): 55–57.

39. Ashe, *Off the Court*, 61–62; Ashe, *Days of Grace*, 113.

40. Gerald Horne, *Fire This Time: The Watts Uprising and the 1960s* (Charlottesville: University Press of Virginia, 1995), 3; Don Harrison, "Reporting from Watts," *DB*, 16 Nov. 1965, 3; David O. Sears and John B. McConahay, *The Politics of Violence: The New Urban Blacks and the Watts Riot* (Boston: Houghton Mifflin, 1973), 13; "New Los Angeles Rioting," *Chicago Tribune* (hereafter *CT*), 13 Aug. 1965, 1; Jack McCurdy and Art Berman, "New Rioting," *LAT*, 13 Aug. 1965, 1; Charles Hillinger, "Burning Buildings Symbolize Spirit of Hate Underlying Violent Rioting," *LAT*, 14 Aug. 1965, 2.

41. Ashe, *Days of Grace*, 87–88, 113; Ashe, *Off the Court*, 215.

42. "Ashe Stops to Visit 'Whirlwind,'" *NYAN*, 7 July 1962, 28; Danzig and Schwed, *Fireside Book of Tennis*, 453; Ashe, *Advantage Ashe*, 55, 62.

43. Ashe, *Advantage Ashe*, 55, 75–76.

44. Chris Foster, "Walt Hazzard Dies at 69," *LAT*, 19 Nov. 2011; "Walt Hazzard, Former Star and Coach for U.C.L.A., Dies at 69," *NYT*, 18 Nov. 2011.

45. Ashe, *Advantage Ashe*, 55, 59, 61.

46. Ashe, *Off the Court*, 53–71; Ashe, *Advantage Ashe*, 52–68.

47. Ashe, *Advantage Ashe*, 74–75.

48. Ibid., 74.

49. "Tennis," *NYT*, 19 Dec. 1965, S5; Frank Litsky, "Ashe Has Come Far, Will Go Far," *NYT*, 14 May 1963, 66; Jules Tygiel, *Baseball's Great Experiment: Jackie Robinson and His Legacy* (New York: Oxford University Press, 1983), 205; *Arthur Ashe: Citizen of the World*.

50. Gordon, "Arthur Ashe Has to Be Aware"; Ashe, *Off the Court*, 56. For more on the history of intermarriage in the United States, see Maria P. Root, ed., *Love's Revolution: Racial Intermarriage* (Philadelphia: Temple University Press, 2001); and Paul Spickard, ed., *Mixed Blood: Intermarriage and Ethnic Identity in Twentieth-Century America* (Madison: University of Wisconsin Press, 1994).

51. Jack Olsen, "Pride and Prejudice," *SI*, 8 July 1968; Olsen, *The Black Athlete: A Shameful Story; The Myth of Integration in American Sport* (New York: Time-Life Books, 1968).

52. Ashe, *Advantage Ashe*, 58, 73; Towle, *I Remember Arthur Ashe*, 76.

53. Ashe, *Off the Court*, 82–83; Ashe, *Arthur Ashe: Portrait in Motion*, with Frank Deford (Boston: Houghton Mifflin, 1975), 247.

54. Ashe, *Advantage Ashe*, 76–77; "Tennis Star Fiance of Dianne Seymour," *NYT*, 19 Mar. 1966, 14.

55. Borstelmann, *Cold War and the Color Line*, 4–5, 48, 56–57, 75, 96, 112, 136, 142.

56. For more on race, human rights, and the Cold War, see Thomas, *Globetrotting*; Borstelmann, *Cold War and the Color Line*, 72–74, 95, 240–41, 265; Mary Dudziak, *Cold War Civil Rights: Race and the Image of American Democracy* (Princeton, NJ: Princeton University Press, 2002); and Penny Von Eschen, *Race against Empire: Black Americans and Anticolonialism, 1937–1957* (Ithaca, NY: Cornell University Press, 1997).

57. "No Place for Politics in Sports, Says Ashe," *LAT*, 27 June 1964, A5.

58. Sam Lacy, "A Communist without a Card," *Baltimore Afro-American* (hereafter *BAA*), 30 June 1964.

59. Clayton Moore, "The Winning Blow," *LAS*, 2 July 1964, B3.

60. Ashe, *Advantage Ashe*, 98–99.

CHAPTER 3: AN EMERGING ACTIVIST

1. William H. Chafe, *The Unfinished Journey: America since World War II* (New York: Oxford University Press, 1999), 343, 378; David K. Wiggins, *Glory Bound: Black Athletes in a White America* (Syracuse, NY: Syracuse University Press, 1997), 104. For more on 1968, see Chafe, *Unfinished Journey*, 343–80; Todd Gitlin, *The Sixties: Years of Hope, Days of Rage* (New York: Bantam Books, 1987), 285–304; Terry H. Anderson, *The Movement and the Sixties: Protest in America from Greensboro to Wounded Knee* (New York: Oxford University Press, 1995), 183–237; and Debi Unger and Irwin Unger, *The Times Were a Changin': The Sixties Reader* (New York: Three Rivers, 1998), 314–47.

2. Wiggins, *Glory Bound*, 106, 121.

3. Ibid. The Cy Young Award is given annually to the best pitchers in the American and National Leagues. In 1968 Gibson won 22 games for the St. Louis Cardinals, struck out a league-best 268 batters, had a league-leading 1.12 earned run average, and pitched 13 shutouts. For more on Gibson, see Bob Gibson, *Stranger to the Game: The Autobiography of Bob Gibson*, with Lonnie Wheeler (New York: Penguin, 1996).

4. Bud Collins, ed., *The Bud Collins History of Tennis: An Authoritative Encyclopedia and Record Book* (Washington, DC: New Chapter, 2008), 491, 698; Jim Murray, "Ashe Goes Big League," *LAT*, 10 Sept. 1968, E1.

5. Ashe, *Advantage Ashe*, as told to Clifford George Gewecke Jr. (New York: Coward-McCann, 1967), 66.

6. Arthur Ashe, *Days of Grace: A Memoir*, with Arnold Rampersad (New York: Knopf, 1993), 61; "First Negro Davis Cupper," *Ebony*, Oct. 1963, 32, 151; Allison Danzig, "Ashe, McKinley, Ralston and Riessen Are Named to U.S. Davis Cup Team," *NYT*, 2 Aug. 1963, 20; "Arthur Ashe Named to 11-Player Team for 1963 Davis Cup," *CDD*, 9 May 1963, 32; Ruth Jenkins, "Family Proud of 1st Davis Cupper," *BAA*, 13 Aug. 1963, 13; Charles Friedman, "One More Barrier Is Overcome in Tennis," *NYT*, 11 Aug. 1963, 151.

7. Collins, *Bud Collins History of Tennis*, 485–86. For more on the history of the Davis Cup competition, see Richard J. Evans, *The Davis Cup: Celebrating 100 Years of International Tennis* (New York: Universe, 1999). For more on Dwight Davis, see E. Digby Baltzell, *Sporting Gentlemen: Men's Tennis from the Age of Honor to the Cult of the Superstar* (New York: Free Press, 1995), 47, 65–68, 72, 94, 123, 128, 141, 245, 264.

8. Collins, *Bud Collins History of Tennis*, 485–86.

9. John McPhee, *Levels of the Game* (New York: Farrar, Straus & Giroux, 1969), 121; Thelma Hunt Shirley, "A New Arthur Ashe," *CDD*, 21 July 1965, 13; Bud Collins, "Arthur Ashe Sounds Off on His New Role in Tennis," *Sport*, Aug. 1969, 25; Cecilia Elizabeth O'Leary, *To Die For: The Paradox of American Patriotism* (Princeton, NJ: Princeton University Press, 1999), 210, 220, 230, 245; Lizabeth Cohen, *A Consumers' Republic: The Politics of Mass Consumption in Postwar America* (New York: Vintage Books, 2003), 83–100. For more on African Americans in the military, see, for instance, Shane A. Smith, "'The Crisis' in the Great War: W. E. B. DuBois and His Perception of African-American Participation in World War I," *Historian* 70, no. 2 (2008): 239–62; Timothy L. Schroer, *Recasting Race after World War II: Germans and African Americans in American-Occupied Germany* (Boulder: University Press of Colorado, 2007); James E. Westheider, *The African American Experience in Vietnam: Brothers in Arms* (Lanham, MD: Rowman & Littlefield, 2007); Natalie Kimbrough, *Equality or Discrimination? African Americans in the U.S. Military during the Vietnam War* (Lanham, MD: University Press of America, 2007); and Bill Harris, *The Hellfighters of Harlem:*

*African-American Soldiers Who Fought for the Right to Fight for Their Country* (New York: Carroll & Graf, 2002).

10. S. L. Price, "The Lone Wolf," *SI*, 24 June 2002; Jose M. Alamillo, "Richard 'Pancho' Gonzalez: Race and the Print Media in Postwar Tennis America," *International Journal of the History of Sport* 26, no. 7 (June 2009): 947–65.

11. Dave Anderson, "His Toughest Rival," in *The Fireside Book of Tennis: A Complete History of the Game and Its Great Players and Matches*, edited by Allison Danzig and Peter Schwed (New York: Simon & Schuster, 1972), 301; Claude Lewis, "Arthur Ashe: 'I Want to Be No. 1 Without an Asterisk,'" *Sport* (May 1966): 96.

12. Lewis, "Arthur Ashe," 97; Harry Gordon, "Arthur Ashe Has to Be Aware That He Is a Pioneer in Short White Pants," *NYT*, 2 Jan. 1966, 164; "End of Tortuous Road," *NYT*, 10 Sept. 1968, 51; McPhee, *Levels of the Game*, 147; Ashe, *Arthur Ashe: Portrait in Motion*, with Frank Deford (Boston: Houghton Mifflin, 1975), 77; Louie Robinson Jr., *Arthur Ashe: Tennis Champion* (Garden City, NY: Doubleday, 1967), 76; Frank Litsky, "Ashe Has Come Far, Will Go Far," *NYT*, 14 May 1963, 66; Arthur Daley, "A Rugged Assignment," Sports of The Times, *NYT*, 28 Aug. 1968, 55; L. I. "Brock" Brockenbury, "Tying the Score," *LAS*, 3 Mar. 1966, B2; David Wolf, "Arthur—the New King of the Courts," *Life*, 20 Sept. 1968, 34.

13. Lewis, "Arthur Ashe," 96; Robinson, *Arthur Ashe*, 99; McPhee, *Levels of the Game*, 123.

14. Price, "Lone Wolf."

15. "Arthur Ashe Easily Wins Davis Cup Match," *WP*, 16 Sept. 1963, A20; "Ralston, Ashe Finish Sweep in Davis Cup," *CT*, 16 Sept. 1963, E5; "Davis Cup Semi-Final for Ashe," *NYAN*, 21 Sept. 1963, 34; Frank Deford, "An Understudy Takes Charge," *SI*, 9 Aug. 1965; Around the World, *WT*, Apr. 1967, 62; Ashe, *Portrait in Motion*, 61–62, 66. In 1967 all of Ashe's losses were on clay courts. Allison Danzig, "Ashe Urges Stress on Clay Courts," *NYT*, 12 Feb. 1967, 187.

16. "The Ace," *Time*, 13 Aug. 1965; Deford, "Understudy Takes Charge."

17. "Ace"; Deford, "Understudy Takes Charge"; Ashe, *Advantage Ashe*, 86; Robinson, *Arthur Ashe*, 111–17. For more on scientific racism, see, for instance, Wiggins, *Glory Bound*, 177–99; and David K. Wiggins and Patrick B. Miller, *The Unlevel Playing Field: A Documentary History of the African American Experience in Sport* (Urbana: University of Illinois Press, 2005), 144, 156–63, 188–89, 444–45.

18. Deford, "Understudy Takes Charge"; Gordon, "Arthur Ashe Has to Be Aware"; Lewis, "Arthur Ashe," 96.

19. "Davis Cup for Ashe?," *LAS*, 10 Sept. 1964, B2; Deford, "Understudy Takes Charge"; Gordon, "Arthur Ashe Has to Be Aware"; McPhee, *Levels of the Game*, 143.

20. Around the World, *WT*, Aug. 1966, 87; Ashe, *Advantage Ashe*, 9–11, 15; Robinson, *Arthur Ashe*, 132; "Arthur Ashe to Be Feted," *NYT*, 23 Aug. 1966, 44; Bob Lipper, "The Grace and Grit of Arthur Ashe," *RTD*, 21 May 1989; "Philadelphia Honors Ashe," *CD*, 3 Sept. 1966, 17; Around the World, *WT*, Oct. 1966, 74; "A Visit to Richmond," *WT*, July 1968, 32–35.

21. Collins, *Bud Collins History of Tennis*, 335–36, 413, 491.

22. Lewis, "Arthur Ashe," 35, 97; Ashe, *Off the Court*, with Neil Amdur (New York: New American Library, 1981), 95; "An American Ace," *Time*, 19 Nov. 1965; Erwin Schulze, "The 1966 Men's Rankings," *WT*, Jan. 1967, 17; Ashe, *Portrait in Motion*, 188–97; Ashe, *Off the Court*, 96; Jeff Prugh, "Ashe Takes Aim on Pros in Open," *LAT*, 1 Sept. 1968, G7; Gertrude Wilson, "Arthur Ashe to Be a GI," *NYAN*, 13 Nov. 1965, 48.

23. Gordon Briscoe, "Aboriginal Australian Identity: The Historiography of Relations between Indigenous Ethnic Groups and Other Australians, 1788 to 1988," *History Workshop*, no. 36 (Autumn 1993): 148–49; Jan Pettman, *Living in the Margins: Racism, Sexism, and Feminism in Australia* (St. Leonards, Australia: Allen & Unwin, 1992), 1, 54–77; Ashe, *Off the Court*, 96–97; McPhee, *Levels of the Game*, 139; Ashe, *Advantage Ashe*, 99; Sundiata Djata, *Blacks at the Net: Black Achievement in the History of Tennis*, 2 vols. (Syracuse, NY: Syracuse University Press, 2006–8), 1:167.

24. Gordon, "Arthur Ashe Has to Be Aware"; "Ashe Makes Tennis a Gentleman's Game," *CT*, 18 Feb. 1966, 18; "Stands Tall in Defeat," *Hobbs (NM) Daily News-Sun*, 16 Feb. 1966, 4; Robert H. Bradford, "The World Is King Arthur's Court," *CT*, 1 Dec. 1968, N40.

25. Ashe, *Advantage Ashe*, 67.

26. "Athletes Face Call in Draft Step-Up," *NYT*, 20 Feb. 1966, S1; "Accelerated Calls Affecting Many Big Names," *CT*, 20 Feb. 1966, I1; "American Ace"; "Ashe Will Report to Army in June," *NYT*, 10 Nov. 1965, 10; "Ashe to Enlist, '66 Cup Play Doubtful," *CDD*, 10 Nov. 1965, 32; "Ashe to Enter Armed Forces Next Summer," *LAT*, 10 Nov. 1965, B1; Ashe, *Off the Court*, 117; Ashe, "Ali's Greatest Opponents Could Be 'The Jackals,'" *RTD*, 14 Sept. 1980, B14, SCRBC, box 40, Scrapbooks.

27. "American Ace"; "Ashe Will Report to Army in June"; "Ashe to Enlist"; "Ashe to Enter Armed Forces Next Summer"; Ashe, *Off the Court*, 117; Ashe, "Ali's Greatest Opponents."

28. Ashe, *Off the Court*, 97.

29. Ibid., 97–98.

30. Ibid., 98; Ashe, *Advantage Ashe*, 10. For more on the use of athletes as goodwill ambassadors, see, for instance, Damion L. Thomas, *Globetrotting: African American Athletes and Cold War Politics* (Urbana: University of Illinois Press, 2012); and Steve Bullock, "Playing for Their Nation: The American Military and Baseball during World War II," *Journal of Sport History* 27 (Spring 2000): 67–89.

31. Thomas, *Globetrotting*; Bullock, "Playing for Their Nation."

32. "Ashe, U.S. Swimmers Set Pace in Pan-American Games," *NYT*, 26 July 1967, 30; Frank Litsky, "The Absentees," *NYT*, 31 July 1967, 32; Daley, "Rugged Assignment"; Sam Lacy, "Ashe Wants Title More Than Reprieve," *BAA*, 19 Feb. 1966, 17.

33. Neil Amdur, "Conversations with Lt. Arthur Ashe: Part I," *WT*, Apr. 1968, 52, 54; Bradford, "World Is King Arthur's Court"; Ashe, *Advantage Ashe*, 183; McPhee, *Levels of the Game*, 101; Richard Steins, *Arthur Ashe: A Biography* (Westport, CT: Greenwood, 2005), 22; Ashe, *Off the Court*, 98. The Arthur Ashe Papers have a folder of hate mail written to Ashe; see SCRBC, box 2, folder 13.

34. Gordon, "Arthur Ashe Has to Be Aware." Ashe made similar statements to *Ebony* in 1967. He said, "I'm no militant Negro, no crusader. I want to do something for my race, but I figure I can do it best by example, by showing Negro boys the way." "Negro Youth in Sports," *Ebony*, Aug. 1967, 130–33; Lewis, "Arthur Ashe," 97.

35. Collins, *Bud Collins History of Tennis*, 698; "Ecuador Flattens U.S. Net Team," *LAT*, 20 June 1967, C1; "Hopman Is Astonished," *NYT*, 20 June 1967, 44; Bud Collins, "The Best Losers in the World," *SI*, 3 July 1967; "U.S. Davis Cup Team Upset," *CT*, 20 June 1967, C1; "U.S. Eliminated from Davis Cup as Ecuador's Guzman Beats Ashe in 5 Sets," *NYT*, 20 June 1967, 44; "Ecuador Ousts U.S. in Davis Cup," *WP*, 20 June 1967, D1; "Aussies 'Can't Believe' U.S. Davis Cup Loss," *LAT*, 21 June 1967, B2; "Americans Writhe in Defeat," *Guardian* (London), 21 June 1967, 19; "A Giant Floperoo," *LAT*, 23 June 1967, D3.

36. Walter Carlson, "Advertising: More Debate Over 'DDB Look,'" *NYT*, 6 Apr. 1966, 66; "Executive Training for Ashe," *CDD*, 6 Apr. 1966, 32; Amdur, "Conversations with Lt. Arthur Ashe: Part I"; McPhee, *Levels of the Game*, 102; Ashe, *Off the Court*, 131; Gordon, "Arthur Ashe Has to Be Aware"; Neil Amdur, "Ashe, Net Pro of Future, Prepares Civil Rights Talk," *NYT*, 28 Jan. 1968, S5; Ole Nosey, "Everybody Goes When the Wagon Comes," *CD*, 1 Apr. 1967, 32; Lewis, "Arthur Ashe," 35.

37. Shirley Povich, "'Black Power' on Victory Stand," *LAT*, 17 Oct. 1968, C1; George Strickler, "Smith and Seagren Win Gold Medals," *CT*, 17 Oct. 1968, F1; "2 Accept Medals Wearing Black Gloves," *NYT*, 17 Oct. 1968, 59; "U.S. Apologizes for Protest by Blacks," *CT*, 18 Oct. 1968, C1; "Black-Fist Display Gets Varied Reaction in Olympic Village," *LAT*, 18 Oct. 1968, D1; John G. Griffin, "Black Power Bows at the Olympics," *CDD*, 19 Oct. 1968, 1; Sam Lacy, "Lacy Hits 'Protest' at Olympics," *BAA*, 19 Oct. 1968, 1.

38. Randy Roberts and James Olson, *Winning Is the Only Thing: Sports in America since 1945* (Baltimore: Johns Hopkins University Press, 1991), 164; William Van Deburg, *New Day in Babylon: The Black Power Movement and American Culture, 1965–1975* (Chicago: University of Chicago Press, 1992), 1–10.

39. Peniel E. Joseph, "The Black Power Movement: A State of the Field," *Journal of American History* 96, no. 3 (Dec. 2009): 762; Joseph, *Waiting 'Til the Midnight Hour: A Narrative History of Black Power in America* (New York: Henry Holt, 2006), 176–77, 208, 229, 243–44; Jane Rhodes, *Framing the Black Panthers: The Spectacular Rise of a Black Power Icon* (New York: New Press, 2007). For more on the BPP, see Charles Jones, ed., *The Black Panther Party Reconsidered* (Baltimore: Black Classic, 1998); Robert O. Self, *American Babylon: Race and the Struggle for Postwar Oakland* (Princeton, NJ: Princeton University Press, 2003); Jeffrey O. G. Ogbar, *Black Power: Radical Politics and African American Identity* (Baltimore: Johns Hopkins University Press, 2004); and Jama Lazerow and Yohuru Williams, eds., *In Search of the Black Panther Party: New Perspectives on a Revolutionary Movement* (Durham, NC: Duke University Press, 2006).

40. Martin Luther King Jr., *Where Do We Go from Here: Chaos or Community?* (New York: Harper & Row, 1967), 32, 33, 36, 38, 44, 49.

41. Joseph, "Black Power Movement," 751–52; Timothy B. Tyson, *Radio Free Dixie: Robert F. Williams and the Roots of Black Power* (Chapel Hill: University of North Carolina Press, 1999); Komozi Woodard, *A Nation within a Nation: Amiri Baraka (LeRoi Jones) and Black Power Politics* (Chapel Hill: University of North Carolina Press, 1999); Jones, *Black Panther Party Reconsidered*; Ogbar, *Black Power*; Self, *American Babylon*; Matthew Countryman, *Up South: Civil Rights and Black Power in Philadelphia* (Philadelphia: University of Pennsylvania Press, 2005); Joseph, *Waiting 'Til the Midnight Hour*; Joseph, *The Black Power Movement: Rethinking the Civil Rights–Black Power Era* (New York: Routledge, 2006).

42. Ashe, *Days of Grace*, 119; Parton Keese, "Tennis Pros Hesitant on Support for Ashe on South Africa Issue," *NYT*, 22 Feb. 1970, S11.

43. Hugh McIlvanney, "Black Is Beautiful," *LAT*, 7 July 1969, B1; Around the World, *WT*, Sept. 1968, 84; "End of Tortuous Road"; Hugh McIlvanney, "Ashe Tries to Knock Down Racial Wall," *WP*, 14 July 1968, C4; Andrew Crane, "Lt. Ashe, First Black to Top Men's Tennis," *NYAN*, 7 Sept. 1968, 1; Crane, "Ashe Cops Open; Okker Grabs Dough," *NYAN*, 14 Sept. 1968, 1; Bradford, "World Is King Arthur's Court"; Dennis C. Dickerson, *Militant Mediator: Whitney M. Young, Jr.* (Lexington: University Press of Kentucky, 1998).

44. Neil Amdur, "Conversations with Lt. Arthur Ashe: Part II," *WT*, May 1968, 28–29; Bradford, "World Is King Arthur's Court"; McIlvanney, "Ashe Tries to Knock Down Racial Wall."

45. Joseph Dorinson and Joram Warmund, eds., *Jackie Robinson: Race, Sports, and the American Dream* (Armonk, NY: M. E. Sharpe, 1998), 208–9; Arnold Rampersad, *Jackie Robinson: A Biography* (New York: Knopf, 1997), 210–16.

46. Scorecard, *SI*, 19 June 1967; Bill Russell, *Go Up for Glory: Bill Russell, The Great Negro Basketball Star, Tells the Exciting Story of His Life*, with William McSweeny (New York: Coward-McCann, 1966); Aram Goudsouzian, *King of the Court: Bill Russell and the Basketball Revolution* (Berkeley and Los Angeles: University of California Press, 2011).

47. Mike Towle, ed., *I Remember Arthur Ashe: Memories of a True Tennis Pioneer and Champion of Social Causes by the People Who Knew Him* (Nashville: Cumberland House, 2001), 66; Wiggins, *Glory Bound*, 121; Ashe, *Off the Court*, 102.

48. Ashe, *Off the Court*, 101–2.

49. Mark Asher, "Ashe Becomes Activist, Plans Civil Rights Speech Here," *WP*, 6 Mar. 1968, E5.

50. Amdur, "Ashe, Net Pro of Future."

51. Ashe, *Days of Grace*, 145–46; Mark Asher, "Ashe Wants Athletes to Act," *WP*, 11 Mar. 1968, C1. For more on Booker T. Washington and racial uplift, see, for instance, Robert J. Norrell, *Up from History: The Life of Booker T. Washington* (Cambridge, MA: Belknap Press of Harvard University Press, 2009); and Jacqueline M. Moore, *Booker T. Washington, W. E. B. DuBois, and the Struggle for Racial Uplift* (Lanham, MD: Rowman & Littlefield, 2003).

52. Ashe, *Off the Court*, 102.

53. *Arthur Ashe: Citizen of the World*, produced and directed by Julie Anderson (New York: Home Box Office, 1994), videocassette, 59 min.; Lawrence Casey, "Sports Ledger," *CDD*, 21 Mar. 1968, 33; Phil Finch, "Ashe Isn't Afraid to Tell It Like It Is, Baby!," *Washington Daily News*, 18 Mar. 1968, 52, SCRBC, box 35, folder 1.

54. Bob Boozer, Oscar Robertson, and Jackie Robinson to unnamed athlete, 27 Feb. 1968, NCAA Library and Archives, Indianapolis, Charles Neinas Files, "Olympic Basketball folder"; Leonard Koppett, "Robinson Urges So. Africa Ban," *NYT*, 9 Feb. 1968, 58; Frank Litsky, "65 Athletes Support Boycott on S. Africa Issue," *NYT*, 12 Apr. 1968, 28; Amdur, "Conversations with Lt. Arthur Ashe: Part I"; "Athletes of Both Races Sign Boycott Resolution," *BAA*, 16 Apr. 1968, 13; Casey, "Sports Ledger."

55. Litsky, "65 Athletes Support Boycott"; "Athletes of Both Races Sign Boycott Resolution."

56. Memorandum, Agent "SAC" to FBI director, 3 July 1969, 1–3, www.africanafrican .com/negroartist/fbi%20files/ashe_authur.pdf.

57. Martin Luther King Jr. to Ashe, 7 Feb. 1968, SCRBC, box 2, folder 1; McIlvanney, "Ashe Tries to Knock Down Racial Wall"; Ashe, *Off the Court*, 103; King to Ashe, 7 Feb. 1968.

58. Ashe, *Off the Court*, 103; Casey Bukro, "Bobby Tells Crowd of Slaying, Calls for Compassion, Wisdom," *CT*, 5 Apr. 1968, 23; Nicholas C. Chriss and Jack Nelson, "Dr. King Slain by Sniper in Memphis," *LAT*, 5 Apr. 1968, 1; David Garrow, *Bearing the Cross: Martin Luther King, Jr., and the Southern Christian Leadership Conference* (New York: Vintage Books, 1986), 575–623.

59. McPhee, *Levels of the Game*, 143; Around the World, *WT*, Sept. 1968, 84; Crane, "Lt. Ashe, First Black to Top Men's Tennis"; Ashe, *Off the Court*, 60, 103.

60. Ashe, *Off the Court*, 91; Ashe, *Advantage Ashe*, 139.

61. Crane, "Ashe Cops Open"; "Ashe Beats Lutz, Gains Singles Title," *CT*, 26 Aug. 1968, C5; "Ashe, Down 2-1, Roars Back to Stop Lutz for U.S. Title," *LAT*, 26 Aug. 1968, E2; Neil Amdur, "Ashe Beats Lutz in 5 Sets for U.S. Amateur Tennis Title," *NYT*, 26 Aug. 1968, 51; "Ashe Beats Lutz in Final," *Guardian*, 26 Aug. 1968, 12; "Ashe Defeats Lutz for Title in Five Sets," *WP*, 26 Aug. 1968, D1; Robert Markus, "2 Facts Overlooked in Triumph of Ashe," *CT*, 27 Aug. 1968, C3; "Ashe Gets U.S. Net Title," *CDD*, 26 Aug. 1968, 31.

62. Jim Murray, "Open-Heart Surgery Is Bringing Tennis Back to Life," *LAT*, 3 Sept. 1968, E5; Murray, "Amfessional or Proteur?," *LAT*, 25 Sept. 1969, E1; British journalist quoted in Baltzell, *Sporting Gentlemen*, 341; Eugene L. Scott, "Volley for Open Tennis," *NYT*, 10 Dec. 1967, 264; Allison Danzig, "Tennis Faces Crisis," *NYT*, 15 Dec. 1967, 67; Eugene L. Scott, "No Open and Shut Case," *NYT*, 11 Feb. 1968, S6; "The Failure of Pro Tennis," *Los Angeles Herald-Examiner*, 26 Dec. 1965, E1, E6. For more on the open transition, see Baltzell, "The Great Revolution of 1968–1992: The Rise of Open (Pro) Tennis and the Decline of Civility," in Baltzell, *Sporting Gentlemen*, 341–78.

63. Collins, *Bud Collins History of Tennis*, 145–46.

64. Ibid.; Daley, "Rugged Assignment"; Prugh, "Ashe Takes Aim on Pros in Open"; Dave Anderson, "For Laver's Tennis Opponents, Forearmed Is Forewarned," *NYT*, 1 Sept. 1968, S5; "The Fountain of Youth Trickles Over," *NYT*, 1 Sept. 1968, S5.

65. Jeff Prugh, "Drysdale Shocks Laver in Tennis Upset of Year," *LAT*, 4 Sept. 1968, F2; Charles Friedman, "Laver Says He Lost His Rhythm," *NYT*, 4 Sept. 1968, 53; David Gray, "Forest Hills Resounds to Laver's Fall," *Guardian*, 4 Sept. 1968, 13; "Pancho Whips Roche, Ashe Meets Drysdale," *CDD*, 5 Sept. 1968, 33; Jeff Prugh, "The Fans Yell 'Bravo!' as Pancho Stuns Roche," *LAT*, 5 Sept. 1968, F5.

66. Steins, *Arthur Ashe*, 38; Ashe, *Portrait in Motion*, 17; Ashe, *Days of Grace*, 109; L. I. "Brock" Brockenbury, "Tying the Score," *LAS*, 4 Apr. 1968, B2; Neil Amdur, "Okker Ousts Gonzalez and Ashe Beats Drysdale in 4-Set U.S. Open Matches," *NYT*, 6 Sept. 1968, 50.

67. Arthur Daley, "Direct Confrontation," Sports of The Times, *NYT*, 10 Sept. 1968, 51.

68. Gene Scott, "Ashe-Okker Final One of Contrasts," *NYT*, 9 Sept. 1968, 60; Ashe, *Off the Court*, 110; "Ashe Defeats Okker to Win U.S. Open Net Title," *CDD*, 10 Sept. 1968, 24; "Ashe Takes U.S. Open Tennis Crown," *CT*, 10 Sept. 1968, C1; Dave Anderson, "Ashe Beats Okker to Win Tennis Open," *NYT*, 10 Sept. 1968, 1; "Arthur Ashe Completes a Fine Double," *Guardian*, 10 Sept. 1968, 15; Mark Asher, "Ashe Wins U.S. Open Tennis," *WP*, 10 Sept. 1968, D1; Crane, "Ashe Cops Open."

69. Towle, *I Remember Arthur Ashe*, 29; "End of Tortuous Road."

70. Doug Smith, *Whirlwind: The Godfather of Black Tennis; The Life and Times of Dr. Robert Walter Johnson* (Washington, DC: Blue Eagle, 2004), 124–25.

71. Telegrams, Jackie Robinson to Ashe, 10 Sept. 1968; Bill Cosby to Ashe, 9 Sept. 1968; Ralph Bunche to Ashe, 26 Aug. 1968; Edward Brooke to Ashe, 11 Sept. 1968; and J. D. Morgan to Ashe, 11 Sept. 1968, all in SCRBC, box 2, folder 1. Dave Anderson, "Gift of 100 GM Shares Worth $8,900 Keeps Arthur Ashe Smiling!," *NYT*, 20 Oct. 1968, S6. Around the World, *WT*, Dec. 1968, 62. McPhee, *Levels of the Game*, 113. Ashe, *Off the Court*, 113–14.

72. Robert Markus, "Arthur Ashe Is Going to Become Rich Man," *CT*, 11 Sept. 1968, C3; Jeff Prugh, "Ashe Win Restores U.S. Net Prestige," *LAT*, 10 Sept. 1968, E1; Dick Edwards, "Ashe Shot 'Em Up; No Blacks in Club," *NYAN*, 14 Sept. 1968, 32.

73. Murray, "Ashe Goes Big League."

CHAPTER 4: BRIGHT LIGHTS AND CIVIL RIGHTS

1. Bob Schieffer, *Face the Nation: My Favorite Stories from the First 50 Years of the Award-Winning News Broadcast* (New York: Simon & Schuster, 2004), 57–71.

2. John C. Regan to unidentified newspaper, SCRBC, box 35, folder 1; "Ashe Feels a Duty to Aid His Race," *CT*, 16 Sept. 1968, C4; "Ashe Says Negro Athletes Should Back Negro Causes," *NYT*, 16 Sept. 1968, 13; Ashe, *Off the Court*, with Neil Amdur (New York: New American Library, 1981), 113; Mike Zitz, "Arthur Ashe: Career Has Come Full Circle," *Freelance Star* (Fredericksburg, VA), 17 July 1982, SCRBC, box 35, folder 3; "World Tennis Champion Arthur Ashe Declares His Militancy, Determination to Struggle for His People," *Muhammad Speaks*, 27 Sept. 1968, 16; "Ashe to Guest on Face Nation Sunday," *LAT*, 13 Sept. 1968, D20.

3. Robert H. Bradford, "The World Is King Arthur's Court," *CT*, 1 Dec. 1968, N40. Ashe appeared on *The Tonight Show* on 10 October 1968.

4. Mike Towle, ed., *I Remember Arthur Ashe: Memories of a True Tennis Pioneer and Champion of Social Causes by the People Who Knew Him* (Nashville: Cumberland House, 2001), 31–32, 104–5; Ashe, *Arthur Ashe: Portrait in Motion*, with Frank Deford (Boston: Houghton Mifflin, 1975), 82; Bob Addie, "Dell Turns Promoter," *WP*, 17 Aug. 1966, D1; "That Special Feeling," *Time*, 3 Jan. 1969. For more on Dell, see Donald L. Dell, *Minding Other People's Business* (New York: Villard Books, 1989).

5. Doug Smith, *Whirlwind: The Godfather of Black Tennis; The Life and Times of Dr. Robert Walter Johnson* (Washington, DC: Blue Eagle, 2004), 166–67; Ashe, *Portrait in Motion*, 81; Ashe, *Off the Court*, 105–6; Ashe, *Days of Grace: A Memoir*, with Arnold Rampersad (New York: Knopf, 1993), 178–79.

6. "Ashe-Led Team Top Favorite to Return Davis Cup to U.S.," *WP*, 22 Dec. 1968, E5; "Ashe Doubtful for Cup," *CDD*, 5 Dec. 1968, 46; Don Pierson, "Ashe, Graebner Miss NU Tennis Meet with Injuries," *CT*, 5 Dec. 1968, C1; "Ashe, Graebner Called Fit for Davis Cup Meet," *CDD*, 10 Dec. 1968, 27; "Strong US Davis Cup Team," *Guardian*, 17 Dec. 1968, 15; "Australia's Reign in Jeopardy," ibid., 24 Dec. 1968, 15. Although Wimbledon and the U.S. Open were open tournaments in 1968, the Davis Cup remained an amateur competition. Any player who signed a professional contract was automatically ineligible for Davis Cup play.

7. Ashe, *Portrait in Motion*, 82; "Father to See Ashe Play," *NYT*, 15 Dec. 1968, S6; ". . . and to Complete the Report," *CT*, 14 Dec. 1968, D4; "Ashe's Father Will See His Son Play in Australia," *LAT*, 19 Dec. 1968, E10; "Ashe Sr. is VIP in Australia," *WP*, 27 Dec. 1968, C2; "Arthur Ashe, Sr. Gets Free Trip," *PC*, 28 Dec. 1968, 3.

8. Kim Chapin, "Reaching for the Davis Cup," *SI*, 18 Nov. 1968; "Aussies Plan Psycho Attack in Davis Finale," *CDD*, 26 Dec. 1968, 32.

9. Ashe, *Off the Court*, 114–15; "Bowrey Tops Ashe; U.S. Wins Cup, 4-1," *NYT*, 29 Dec. 1968, S1; "Bowrey Tops Ashe to Foil Cup Sweep," *LAT*, 29 Dec. 1968, C9; "Smith, Lutz Claim Davis Cup for U.S.," *CT*, 27 Dec. 1968, C1; "U.S. Leads, 2-0, in Davis Cup," *CT*, 26 Dec. 1968, E1; "That Special Feeling," *Time*, 3 Jan. 1969; "Ashe, Graebner Win Singles as U.S. Gets Davis Cup," *Jet*, 16 Jan. 1969, 50.

10. Towle, *I Remember Arthur Ashe*, 142; Ashe, *Off the Court*, 116–17; William H. Chafe, *The Unfinished Journey: America since World War II* (New York: Oxford University Press, 1999), 345–48. For more on Tet as a turning point in the Vietnam War, see James H. Willbanks, *The Tet Offensive: A Concise History* (New York: Columbia University Press, 2007); and Don Oberdorfer, *Tet! The Turning Point in the Vietnam War* (Baltimore: Johns Hopkins University Press, 2001).

11. Towle, *I Remember Arthur Ashe*, 143–44.

12. Ibid., 142–43; Bud Collins, "Our Good-Will Envoys to Asia," *Tennis USA*, SCRBC, box 37, Scrapbooks; Bud Collins, letter to the editor, *WT*, Apr. 1969, 2.

13. "Interview with Arthur Ashe," *Racquet*, Winter 1991, SCRBC, box 26, folder 10; Ashe, *Off the Court*, 117; Ashe, *Portrait in Motion*, 35. For more on the domino theory in American foreign policy, see Frank Ninkovich, *Modernity and Power: A History of the Domino Theory in the Twentieth Century* (Chicago: University of Chicago Press, 1994), 203–310. For a discussion of African Americans in Vietnam, see James E. Westheider, *The African American Experience in Vietnam: Brothers in Arms* (Lanham, MD: Rowman & Littlefield, 2007); and Westheider, *Fighting on Two Fronts: African Americans and the Vietnam War* (New York: New York University Press, 1997).

14. Collins, "Our Good-Will Envoys to Asia"; Collins, letter to the editor; Towle, *I Remember Arthur Ashe*, 141–42; "Davis Cup Team Arrives in Vietnam," *WP*, 25 Jan. 1969, C3; "Davis Cup Team Visits Vietnam," *CDD*, 27 Jan. 1969, 27.

15. Ashe, *Off the Court*, 103, 113, 122.

16. "Nat'l Jaycees to Cite Ashe, Starr, Ryun," *CDD*, 13 Jan. 1969, 25; Ashe, *Off the Court*, 120; "Blind Teacher, Tennis Player Named on '10 Outstanding' List," *LAT*, 13 Jan. 1969, D1; "Jaycees Salute Arthur Ashe," *LAS*, 9 Jan. 1969, B2; Neil Amdur, "Ashe, Out of Army, Stays Independent," *NYT*, 25 Feb. 1969, 49.

17. Amdur, "Ashe, Out of Army, Stays Independent"; "Ashe Turned Down $400,000," *NYT*, 27 Feb. 1969, 51; Arthur Daley, "What's in a Name?," Sports of The Times, *NYT*, 21 Mar. 1969, 56; "Ashe Spurned $400,000 Pro Tennis Contract," *Jet*, 13 Mar. 1969, 54.

18. Ashe, *Off the Court*, 145–46; Towle, *I Remember Arthur Ashe*, 71; Ashe, *Portrait in Motion*, 16; Cecil Harris and Larryette Kyle-DeBose, *Charging the Net: A History of Blacks in Tennis from Althea Gibson and Arthur Ashe to the Williams Sisters* (Chicago: Ivan R. Dee, 2007), 81; William F. Buckley Jr., "Perhaps the College Press Needs Some Competition," *LAT*, 23 Mar. 1970, A9; Bernard D. Nossiter, "Don't Retaliate for Denial of Visa, Ashe Tells Hill Unit," *WP*, 5 Feb. 1970, A2. Ashe made his "bomb on Johannesburg" comment in 1967. Eugene Scott, "No Apartheid in Kruger Park," *WT*, June 1968, 40–44.

19. Wellington W. Nyangoni, *Africa in the United Nations System* (Madison, NJ: Fairleigh Dickinson University Press, 1985), 181; Richard E. Lapchick, *The Politics of Race and International Sport: The Case of South Africa* (Westport, CT: Greenwood, 1975), 32. For more on the Sharpeville massacre, see Philip Frankel, *An Ordinary Atrocity: Sharpeville and Its Massacre* (New Haven, CT: Yale University Press, 2001).

20. Lapchick, *Politics of Race and International Sport*, 40–49; Lapchick, "South Africa: Sport and Apartheid Politics," *Annals of the American Academy of Political and Social Science* 445 (Sept. 1979): 155–65; Bruce K. Murray, "Politics and Cricket: The D'Oliveira Affair of 1968," *Journal of Southern African Studies* 27, no. 4 (Dec. 2001): 672.

21. Lapchick, *Politics of Race and International Sport*, xx–xxi, 8–11, 27–31; Douglas Booth, *The Race Game: Sport and Politics in South Africa* (New York: Routledge, 1998), 58.

22. Lapchick, *Politics of Race and International Sport*, 15–16, 65.

23. Ibid.; *New Zealand Herald*, 30 Jan. 1970.

24. Lapchick, *Politics of Race and International Sport*, 63–64; "South Africa Officially Booted out of Olympics," *CDD*, 19 Aug. 1964, 28; "Tennis Anyone?," *NYAN*, 22 Aug. 1964, 18.

25. Lapchick, *Politics of Race and International Sport*, 60–84; B. Murray, "Politics and Cricket," 667–84.

26. Advertisement, "South African Airways: Tell It Like It Is," *NYT*, 28 May 1969, 32; "Ali Among 162 Ripping Flight Plan," *CDD*, 27 May 1969, 4; "162 Black Americans Rap S. Africa Flights," *CDD*, 31 May 1969, 4; "Black Americans Protest So. African Airway Flights," *LAS*, 5 June 1969, C6.

27. "Ashe Is Refused Visa by South Africa to Compete in Nation's Tennis Open," *NYT*, 30 June 1969, 49; Ashe, *Off the Court*, 147; "Ashe Banned by S. Africa," *Guardian*, 30 June 1969, 1; "S. Africa Denies Ashe Travel Visa," *CDD*, 1 July 1969, 33; "S. Africa Denies Ashe Ban; U.S. Star Says He Was Refused Visa," *WP*, 1 July 1969, C1.

28. "Ashe Is Refused Visa by South Africa"; "Ashe Banned by S. Africa"; "S. Africa Denies Ashe Travel Visa"; "S. Africa Denies Ashe Ban."

29. "S. Africa Denies Ashe Ban"; Neil Amdur, "Ashe to Test So. Africa Policy," *NYT*, 30 July 1969, 32.

30. "Arthur Ashe Barred," *NYAN*, 5 July 1969, 37; "USA Should Lead," *NYAN*, 5 July 1969, 16; Gertrude Wilson, "Phony 'Gentlemen' in Tennis," *NYAN*, 19 July 1969, 17.

31. Sam Lacy, "Ashe Deserves a Doff of the Hat," *BAA*, 8 July 1969, 16.

32. "South Africa Star Irked by Ban on Ashe," *CT*, 1 July 1969, C5; *Arthur Ashe: Citizen of the World*, produced and directed by Julie Anderson (New York: Home Box Office, 1994), videocassette, 59 min.; Ashe, *Portrait in Motion*, 48; Ashe, *Days of Grace*, 103; Harris and Kyle-DeBose, *Charging the Net*, 81–82.

33. "South African Unit Backs Entry of Ashe," *NYT*, 4 Dec. 1969, 20; "South Africa Relaxes Color Ban in Selection of Davis Cup Team," *NYT*, 29 July 1969, 31; Amdur, "Ashe to Test So. Africa Policy"; "Government Is Silent," *NYT*, 30 July 1969, 32; "Evidence by S. Africa," *Guardian*, 28 June 1969, 15.

34. Mrs. Peter Hahn, letter to the editor, *NYT*, 13 July 1969, S5; Hugh McIlvanney, "Black Is Beautiful," *LAT*, 7 July 1969, B1. On hate mail in England, Ashe griped to McIlvanney, "Do you know Britain is the only country in Europe where I get letters like that one that addressed me as 'Nigger Ashe'? The papers here pontificate about how ridiculous the race problem in the United States is. They tell us blacks how right we are, as if we could never possibly encounter the same troubles here. But those editorials are garbage, or if they are not exactly garbage they are certainly not realistic." "Race Baiters Attack Ashe," *LAS*, 17 July 1969, B1.

35. "Arthur Ashe," *NYAN*, 6 Sept. 1969, 16; Bud Collins, ed., *The Bud Collins History of Tennis: An Authoritative Encyclopedia and Record Book* (Washington, DC: New Chapter, 2008), 698; Hugh McIlvanney, "Black Is Beautiful," *LAT*, 7 July 1969, B1.

36. "Ashe Is Refused Visa by South Africa"; Amdur, "Ashe in Quandary over So. Africa," *NYT*, 9 July 1969, 48.

37. Lapchick, *Politics of Race and International Sport*, 184–85; "Rogers Assures Ashe of Aid in Seeking South African Visa," *NYT*, 12 Dec. 1969, 43; "State Department Joins Ashe in S. African Fuss," *BAA*, 20 Dec. 1969, 8; Parton Keese, "Ashe Applies for So. Africa Visa 'Only to Play Tennis,'" *NYT*, 16 Dec. 1969, 65; "Big S.A. Furor over Arthur Ashe Visit," *CDD*, 16 Dec. 1969, 27; "Ashe Applies for Visa to Play in South Africa," *CDD*, 16 Dec. 1969, 24; "Ashe Asks Visa for South African Tennis," *CT*, 16 Dec. 1969, C1; "Ashe Applies for Visa to Play in S. Africa," *LAT*, 16 Dec. 1969, F4; "Ashe Asks S. Africa Visa," *WP*, 16 Dec. 1969, D4.

38. "Apartheid Puts South Africa in Danger of Being Barred from World Sports," *NYT*, 5 Oct. 1969, S9.

39. Ashe, *Off the Court*, 128–29.

40. Mark Asher, "Ashe Can't Afford Pro Tour," *WP*, 13 July 1969, 44; John McPhee, *Levels of the Game* (New York: Farrar, Straus & Giroux, 1969), 64; "Tennis Star Ashe Serves Coke USA," *CDD*, 21 Mar. 1970, 36; Hugh McIlvanney, "Ashe Tries to Knock Down Racial Wall," *WP*, 14 July 1968, C4.

41. Ethel L. Payne, "So This Is Washington," *CDD*, 15 Nov. 1969, 16; Ticker, *Jet*, 4 Dec. 1969, 12.

42. Jeff Prugh, "Leading Independent Life," *LAT*, 10 Aug. 1969, C3; Robert Lipsyte, "Looking for Heroes," Sports of The Times, 30 Aug. 1969, 15; Jim Murray, "Arthur Ashe: Bigger Than the Game Itself," *LAT*, 28 September 1969, C1; Roscoe Harrison, "'I'm a Crusader,' Tennis Champ Ashe Reveals in Jet Interview," *Jet*, 19 Dec. 1968, 50–51, SCRBC, box 37, Scrapbooks.

### CHAPTER 5: TENNIS WARS

1. "NAACP Protests Tennis Tourney," *CDD*, 4 Aug. 1971, 32.

2. "South Africa Denies Visa to Arthur Ashe," *NYT*, 29 Jan. 1970, 1; "South Africa Bars Ashe," *CDD*, 29 Jan. 1970, 37; "Ashe Refused Visa by South Africans," *LAT*, 29 Jan. 1970, C1; "South Africa under Fire for Refusing Ashe Visa," *LAT*, 29 Jan. 1970, B1; David Gray, "Ban on Ashe Could Mean Total Sport Boycott of S. Africa," *Guardian*, 29 Jan. 1970, 1; "S. Africa Bars Ashe, Faces Ostracism," *WP*, 29 Jan. 1970, G1; "South Africa's 'Demise' in Sports World Is Likely," *CT*, 30 Jan. 1970, C1.

3. Robert Lipsyte, "Coming Attractions," Sports of The Times, *NYT*, 2 Feb. 1970, 42; International, *Dominion-News* (Morgantown, WV), 29 Jan. 1970, 1.

4. Omar Kureishi, "Heart Transplant in Reverse," *Guardian*, 30 Jan. 1970, 21; "South Africa 'Finished,'" *Guardian*, 30 Jan. 1970, 21; "South Africa's 'Demise' in Sports World Is Likely"; "South Africa Attacked for Ashe Decision," *LAT*, 30 Jan. 1970, D6. See also "An Open and Shut Case," *Sporting News*, 21 Feb. 1970, 14; and Dick Young, Young Ideas, ibid., 28 Feb. 1970, 16.

5. Shirley Povich, This Morning . . . , *WP*, 30 Jan. 1970, E1.

6. Dick Edwards, "From Johannesburg to Tampa, Florida," *NYAN*, 10 Jan. 1970, 24; Edwards, "A Blessing for Ashe," *NYAN*, 7 Feb. 1970, 34; "Ashe Says U.S. Shouldn't Hit Back at S. Africans," *ADW*, 12 Feb. 1970, 8.

7. Sam Lacy, "Why the Furore [*sic*] over Arthur Ashe?," *BAA*, 3 Feb. 1970, 21; A. S. "Doc" Young, Good Morning Sports!, *CDD*, 11 Feb. 1970, 28; Pete Fritchie, "Comment on Sports: Tennis," *ADW*, 10 Feb. 1970, 5.

8. "South Africa Denies Visa to Arthur Ashe"; "Dell Alleges Breach of Faith by South Africa," *WP*, 30 Jan. 1970, E3.

9. "U.S. Calls Davis Cup Meeting on South Africa and Rhodesia," *NYT*, 20 Jan. 1970, 36; "Bo Returns," *CDD*, 21 Jan. 1970, 34; "South African Says Ashe Visa Unlikely; Tantamount to Refusal," *WP*, 22 Jan. 1970, F3; Datelines in Sports, *LAT*, 22 Jan. 1970, 42; Neil Amdur, "It's Players' Serve Next," *NYT*, 1 Feb. 1970, S7.

10. Bernard D. Nossiter, "Don't Retaliate for Denial of Visa, Ashe Tells Hill Unit," *WP*, 5 Feb. 1970, A2; Adam Raphael, "Liberal Ashe," *Guardian*, 5 Feb. 1970, 1; "Ashe Doesn't Want Ban of S. Africa," *LAT*, 5 Feb. 1970, B3; "Ashe, Diggs Blast South Africa Bias," *CDD*, 5 Feb. 1970, 39; "ATA Backs Arthur Ashe," *LAS*, 5 Feb. 1970, B3; "No Room on the Tennis Court," *WP*, 6 Feb. 1970, A18; "S. African Ban Urged," *BAA*, 7 Feb. 1970, 8; What Others Say, *San Antonio Express and News*, 8 Feb. 1970, 90; "End U.S.–S. Africa Sports: American Committee," *Jet*, 19 Feb. 1970, 54.

11. "Bouton Blasts Officials, Advocates S. Africa Ban," *CDD*, 9 Feb. 1970, 26; Marion E. Jackson, "Jim Bouton: Minuteman for Fair Play," *ADW*, 8 Feb. 1970, 10.

12. Parton Keese, "Tennis Pros Hesitant on Support for Ashe on South Africa Issue," *NYT*, 22 Feb. 1970, S11.

13. Ibid.; Ashe, *Days of Grace: A Memoir*, with Arnold Rampersad (New York: Knopf, 1993), 112–13. On his antiapartheid activism Ashe said, "I also wrestled with a far more perplexing question. To what extent was I trying to make up, with my anti-apartheid crusade, for my relative inaction a decade or more earlier during the civil-rights struggle?" Ibid., 112.

14. "Ashe Beats Crealy in 3 Sets for Aussie Open Tennis Title," *NYT*, 27 Jan. 1970, 50.

15. "Crisis in Sydney LT Event," *Guardian*, 22 Jan. 1970, 18.

16. "Ashe, Ralston Advance in Aussie Tennis," *LAT*, 25 Jan. 1970, B4; "Ralston Is Victor of 93-Game Match," *NYT*, 25 Jan. 1970, 169.

17. "Ashe Makes History," *Guardian*, 28 Jan. 1970, 19; "Ashe, Smith-Lutz Australia Champs," *WP*, 27 Jan. 1970, D3; "Ashe Trounces Crealy for Aussie Net Crown," *LAT*, 27 Jan. 1970, C3; "Ashe Beats Crealy."

18. "Ashe Skis after Net Title Grab," *CDD*, 28 Jan. 1970, 34; "Ashe Heads Home with Aussie Title," *NYT*, 28 Jan. 1970, 76; "Ashe Makes History."

19. For a discussion of the transition to open tennis, see E. Digby Baltzell, *Sporting Gentlemen: Men's Tennis from the Age of Honor to the Cult of the Superstar* (New York: Free Press, 1995), 341–44.

20. Judson Gooding, "The Tennis Industry," *Fortune*, June 1973, 126; William Leggett, "Serving Up Tennis to a Fault," *SI*, 24 Mar. 1975, 54. Although tennis appeared more frequently on television between 1970 and 1975, the length of the matches forced the networks to show many contests on tape delay. Television officials also encouraged tennis administrators to replace white balls with green ones, adopt sudden-death tiebreakers to speed up matches, and build slower courts to discourage the serve-and-volley game. The adoption of slower surfaces negatively affected many of America's stars, most of whom had learned to play on fast surfaces such as asphalt.

21. Rich Coster, *The Tennis Bubble: Big Money Tennis—How It Grew and Where It's Going* (New York: Quadrangle, 1976); Bud Collins, ed., *The Bud Collins History of Tennis: An Authoritative Encyclopedia and Record Book* (Washington, DC: New Chapter, 2008), 153–54.

22. Ashe, *Off the Court*, with Neil Amdur (New York: New American Library, 1981), 128–31; Mike Towle, ed., *I Remember Arthur Ashe: Memories of a True Tennis Pioneer and Champion of Social Causes by the People Who Knew Him* (Nashville: Cumberland House, 2001), 95; "Tennis Star Ashe Serves Coke USA," *CDD*, 21 Mar. 1970, 36.

23. Towle, *I Remember Arthur Ashe*, 45–46, 62, 72–73. Eisenberg was a sportswriter for the *Philadelphia Bulletin* in the 1970s.

24. William F. Buckley Jr., "Perhaps the College Press Needs Some Competition," *LAT*, 23 Mar. 1970, A9. For more on Buckley, see Buckley, *Cancel Your Own Goddam Subscription: Notes and Asides from National Review* (Philadelphia: Basic Books, 2007); Buckley, *Miles Gone By: A Literary Autobiography* (Washington, DC: Regnery, 2004); and Linda Bridges and John R. Coyne Jr., *Strictly Right: William F. Buckley Jr. and the American Conservative Movement* (Hoboken, NJ: John Wiley & Sons, 2007). Buckley founded the *National Review* in 1955 and hosted the television show *Firing Line* from 1966 to 1999. He died on 27 Feb. 2008.

25. Buckley, "Perhaps the College Press Needs Some Competition"; Elliott P. Skinner, letter to the editor, *NYT*, 3 Feb. 1970, 42; Linda Rosenberg, letter to the editor, *NYT*, 1 Mar. 1970, 204.

26. Jim Murray, "Contempt of Court," *LAT*, 6 Mar. 1970, E1; David Margolick, *Beyond Glory: Joe Louis vs. Max Schmeling, and a World on the Brink* (New York: Vintage Books, 2005), 259–309.

27. Marion E. Jackson, "Arthur Ashe, Jr., South Africa's Scorn," *ADW*, 26 Feb. 1970, 6.

28. "Ashe against S. Africa," *CDD*, 23 Apr. 1970, 19; "Ashe Asks ILTF to Expel S. Africa," *CDD*, 15 Apr. 1970, 29; "Ashe Seeks S. Africa Ban; Asks U.N. for Total Exclusion," *CDD*, 25 Apr. 1970, 33; Kathleen Teltsch, "Ashe at U.N., Urges World Tennis Union Expel South Africa," *NYT*, 15 Apr. 1970, 7; Robert H. Estabrook, "Ashe Carries Argument on S. Africa into U.N.," *WP*, 15 Apr. 1970, D3; "United Nations," Datelines in Sports, *LAT*, 15 Apr. 1970, D6; "Ashe Wants SA Expelled from Tennis," *New Mexican* (Santa Fe), 15 Apr. 1970, 43.

29. Fred Tupper, "South Africa Barred in Davis Cup Tennis," *NYT*, 24 Mar. 1970, 1; "South Africa Barred from Davis Cup Play," *CDD*, 24 Mar. 1970, 25; "South Africa Banished from Davis Cup Play," *LAT*, 24 Mar. 1970, D1; "Davis Cup Nations Bar South Africa," *WP*, 24 Mar. 1970, D1.

30. Dave Anderson, "Ashe Scores a Victory in Forcing the South African Apartheid Issue," *NYT*, 24 Mar. 1970, 76; " 'Empty Victory,' Says Ashe on Barring of South Africa," *NYT*, 25 Mar. 1970, 83; "Ashe Calls South African Ban an 'Empty Victory,' " *WP*, 25 Mar. 1970, D4.

31. Red Smith, "Right Act Follows Wrong Reasons," *WP*, 27 Mar. 1970, D3.

32. Des Wilson, "When Backlash Hits Campaigners," *Guardian*, 19 Aug. 1969, 9; "Racial Protest at Golf Match," *WP*, 7 Nov. 1969, A3; Lincoln A. Werden, "Gary Player Plans Golf Series to Aid Negroes," *NYT*, 10 Mar. 1970, 37; Sam Lacy, "Hors D'Oeuvres for the Sports Fan," *BAA*, 15 Nov. 1969, 8; Peter Dobereiner, "Down in Black and White," *Observer* (London), 21 Dec. 1969, 14.

33. Ashe, *Off the Court*, 147; Ashe, *Days of Grace*, 110; "Player's 'Life in Danger,' " *Guardian*, 21 Mar. 1970, 2; "Ashe Fears for Player's Safety on U.S. Golf Tour," *LAT*, 21 Mar. 1970, B1; "Ashe Fears Harm May Befall Player," *CDD*, 23 Mar. 1970, 24; Dwayne Hartnett, "Source of Concern," *Denton (TX) Record-Chronicle*, 30 Apr. 1970, 13; "Fears for Safety of S. African Golfer's Life in U.S.," *Jet*, 9 Apr. 1970, 52.

34. "Gary Player in Racial Bind," *CDD*, 25 Mar. 1970, 30; Werden, "Gary Player Plans Golf Series to Aid Negroes"; "Benefit Idea 'Buying Favor,' " *WP*, 21 Mar. 1970, D2; Brad Pye Jr., "A Great Love," *LAS*, 18 June 1970, B1.

35. Werden, "Gary Player Plans Golf Series to Aid Negroes"; "Benefit Idea 'Buying Favor,' "; Pye, "Great Love."

36. Sam Lacy, "South African Becomes Magnanimous," *BAA*, 24 Jan. 1970, 8. In March 1970 Lacy received a letter from a student at the University of Toledo that rebutted his column of 24 January. The man, who claimed to be a personal friend of Player's, argued that the golfer was a man of deep faith, compassion, and conviction. Player, for instance, had set up a nine-hundred-acre farm near Johannesburg for orphans, approximately a third of whom were black. Additionally, he had donated money to help American junior golfers and mailed a check for five thousand dollars to the American Cancer Society. Player, the man wrote, "loves people, both black and white, and he was extremely hurt by the demonstration against him at the PGA last summer at Dayton." Quoted in Lacy, "The Other Side of Gary Player," *BAA*, 28 Mar. 1970, 8.

37. Peter Dobereiner, "Now Why Pick on the Golfers?," *Observer*, 22 Feb. 1970, 26.

38. Alistair Cooke, "Gary Player Offers a U.S. 'Negro Tour,' " *Guardian*, 11 Mar. 1970, 4; John Husar, "The Locker Room," *CT*, 15 Mar. 1970, B9.

39. "Vorster's Rift with Extreme Rightists Widens as South African Election Nears," *NYT*, 18 Apr. 1970, 9; Stanley Meisler, "S. Africa Exaggerates Elections' Significance," *LAT*, 19 Apr. 1970, F5.

40. Ibid.

41. "South African Rightists Dealt Election Blow," *LAT*, 23 Apr. 1970, 4; "South African Voting Is Heavy as Whites Elect a Parliament," *NYT*, 23 Apr. 1970, 8; "Vorster Defeats Challenge," *Guardian*, 23 Apr. 1970, 1; Tertius Myburgh, "Nationalists' Margin Cut in South Africa," *NYT*, 24 Apr. 1970, 2; Anthony Sampson, "South Africa v. The Rest," *Observer*, 26 Apr. 1970, 6.

42. Towle, *I Remember Arthur Ashe*, 128–29; Ashe, *Off the Court*, 140; Collins, *Bud Collins History of Tennis*, 147–48, 157, 698; "Ashe Is Hero in Zambia," *Robesonian* (Lumberton, NC), 16 Aug. 1970, 2; "Tennis Star Arthur Ashe Hailed in Africa," *Jet*, 17 Dec. 1970, 14–15.

43. Towle, *I Remember Arthur Ashe*, 128; Ashe, *Off the Court*, 141–42; Howie Evans, "Arthur Ashe Stays in the Swinging Set," *Black Sports*, June 1971, 17–18, SCRBC, box 37, Scrapbooks.

44. Ashe, *Off the Court*, 141–43.

45. For more on the origins and history of the women's liberation movement, see Ruth Rosen, *The World Split Open: How the Modern Women's Movement Changed America* (New York: Penguin Books, 2000). There is no scholarly biography of Billie Jean King. Popular and autobiographical accounts of her life include King, *Pressure Is a Privilege: Lessons I've Learned From Life and the Battle of the Sexes*, with Christine Brennan (New York: LifeTime Media, 2008); King, *Billie Jean*, with Frank Deford (New York: Viking Adult, 1982); and Joanne Lannin, *Billie Jean King: Tennis Trailblazer* (New York: Lerner Books, 1999).

46. "Women Tennis Stars Threaten Boycott over Unequal Purses," *NYT*, 8 Sept. 1970, 1; "Women's Lob," *Time*, 7 Dec. 1970. Women players who attended the meeting included Margaret Court, Gail Chanfreau, Mary Ann Curtis, Francoise Durr, Kerry Harris, Ingrid Bentzer, Kathy Harter, and Esme Emanuel.

47. "Women Tennis Stars Threaten Boycott over Unequal Purses"; "Women's Lob"; Harry Gordon, "Arthur Ashe Has to Be Aware That He Is a Pioneer in Short White Pants," *NYT*, 2 Jan. 1966, 164; Ashe, *Arthur Ashe: Portrait in Motion*, with Frank Deford (Boston: Houghton Mifflin, 1975), 53.

48. Howie Evans, "Tennis Director of Doral Hotel," *NYAN*, 17 Oct. 1970, 39.

### CHAPTER 6: DEFEAT AND VICTORY IN SOUTH AFRICA

1. "A Nation of Bad Sports," *Cape Herald*, 8 Dec. 1973, SCRBC, box 1, folder 7; Ashe, *Arthur Ashe: Portrait in Motion*, with Frank Deford (Boston: Houghton Mifflin, 1975), 143–44; "Arthur Ashe Sticks to Tennis—and Wins Praise of Crowds," *Argus*, 24 Nov. 1973, SCRBC, box 1, folder 7.

2. Ashe, *Portrait in Motion*, 143; Ashe, *Days of Grace: A Memoir*, with Arnold Rampersad (New York: Knopf, 1993), 106. Carole Dell was the wife of Donald Dell, Ashe's manager, attorney, and adviser.

3. "Black Aussie Tours Africa," *CDD*, 16 Jan. 1971, 29; Harry Gordon, "How the Daughter of an Ancient Race Made It out of the Australian Outback by Hitting a Tennis Ball Sweetly and Hard," *NYT*, 29 Aug. 1971, SM10. For more on Goolagong, see Evonne Goolagong Cawley, *Home! Evonne Goolagong Story*, with Phil Jarratt (New York: Simon & Schuster, 1995); and "Aborigine Tennis Star to Play in S. Africa," *Jet*, 28 Jan. 1971, 55.

4. "So. Africa Woos Miss Goolagong," *NYT*, 12 Jan. 1971, 41.

5. "Ashe Still Wants to Play in South Africa," *LAS*, 11 Feb. 1971, B4.

6. "Ashe Applies Again to Play in South African Open," *NYT*, 11 Feb. 1971, 62; "Congress Backs Ashe," *CDD*, 11 Feb. 1971, 38; "Grand Jury N.F.L. Probe Is Recessed Till March," *CT*, 11 Feb. 1971, C4; "Ashe Tries Again for Travel Visa," *WP*, 11 Feb. 1971, K8; David Gray, "Visa Not Likely for Ashe," *Guardian*, 12 Feb. 1971, 18.

7. "So. Africa Bars Ashe 3d Time, Calls Him 'Persona Non Grata,'" *NYT*, 25 Feb. 1971, 51; "S. Africa Says No to Ashe," *WP*, 25 Feb. 1971, G1; Stanley Uys, "S. Africa Bars Ashe," *Guardian*, 25 Feb. 1971, 4; "Ashe Draws Ban by South Africa," *LAT*, 25 Feb. 1971, E3; "South Africa Upholds Ban," *CDD*, 25 Feb. 1971, 38.

8. William Raspberry, "How to Treat South Africa," *WP*, 21 Jan. 1971, A19.

9. "Ashe Declares Greater Pity for S. Africa Than for Self," *BAA*, 6 Mar. 1971, 19.

10. E. Digby Baltzell, *Sporting Gentlemen: Men's Tennis from the Age of Honor to the Cult of the Superstar* (New York: Free Press, 1995), 344–46. For more on Nastase, see Ashe, *Portrait in Motion*, 99–101; "Intruder from the East," *Time*, 25 Sept. 1972; and Ilie Nastase, *Mr. Nastase: The Autobiography* (New York: HarperCollinsWillow, 2009).

11. Bud Collins, ed., *The Bud Collins History of Tennis: An Authoritative Encyclopedia and Record Book* (Washington, DC: New Chapter, 2008), 158–66; Mark Asher, "Tennis: Struggle at Grass Roots," *WP*, 13 Aug. 1972, C5; Jeff Prugh, "Tennis War," *LAT*, 28 Oct. 1971, E1.

12. Mark Asher, "TV Key to 'Imperfect Peace' in Tennis," *WP*, 23 July 1972, D8. While WCT fulfilled its multimillion-dollar contract with the major television networks, the USLTA signed a $90,000 deal with PBS and other local educational channels to broadcast its matches. Additionally, WCT paid its players' airfare, while the USLTA insisted that players finance their own transportation to tournaments.

13. Jeff Prugh, "The War's Over: Tennis Open Again," *LAT*, 13 Sept. 1972, D10. As part of the agreement, Hunt could schedule four special events, including an eight-man, $100,000 event in Dallas, a sixteen-man televised tournament featuring the top WCT pros, a team match between the United States and Australia slated for 1975, and one televised doubles tournament during the ILTF portion of the year.

14. "Ashe Proposes Players' Association," *PC*, 29 Jan. 1972, 13.

15. Ashe, *Portrait in Motion*, 13; "Top Tennis Pros Form a Group to Have a 'Voice,'" *WP*, 1 Sept. 1972, D4; "60 Tennis Pros Unite with Kramer as Head," *NYT*, 8 Sept. 1972, 24; "Pros Pick Kramer," *WP*, 7 Sept. 1972, K4; "Kramer Backs Cup Change," *WP*, 8 Sept. 1972, D6; Charles Friedman, "Tennis Pros Organize in Move to Bar Squeeze from 2 Sides," *NYT*, 10 Sept. 1972, S5.

16. "Stan Smith Upset by Ashe in 3 Sets," *CT*, 8 Sept. 1972, C7; Jeff Prugh, "Ashe Surprises Smith by Winning in Straight Sets," *LAT*, 8 Sept. 1972, D1; Parton Keese, "Smith Toppled by Ashe in 3 Sets," *NYT*, 8 Sept. 1972, 21; David Gray, "Ashe Topples Stan Smith," *Guardian*, 8 Sept. 1972, 23; Mark Asher, "Mrs. King Keeps Title, Ashe Wins in Open," *WP*, 10 Sept. 1972, C12.

17. Baltzell, *Sporting Gentlemen*, 349; "Intruder from the East"; Jeff Prugh, "Romanian Turns into 'Capitalist' with $25,000 Win," *LAT*, 11 Sept. 1972, C1; Ashe, *Portrait in Motion*, 99–101; Ashe, *Days of Grace*, 91.

18. Prugh, "Romanian Turns into 'Capitalist.'"

19. "Nastase Beats Ashe for U.S. Open Title," *CT*, 11 Sept. 1972, C5; "Ashe to Take 2d," *CD*, 11 Sept. 1972, 26; Parton Keese, "Nastase Turns Back Ashe in U.S. Open Final," *NYT*, 11 Sept. 1972, 49; David Gray, "Temperamental Nastase Wins US Open," *Guardian*, 11 Sept.

1972, 19; Mark Asher, "Nastase Wins U.S. Open Title as Ashe's Service Falters," *WP*, 11 Sept. 1972, D3; Gray, "Ashe Bitter in Defeat," *Guardian*, 12 Sept. 1972, 23; Collins, *Bud Collins History of Tennis*, 164.

20. Gray, "Ashe Bitter in Defeat"; "A Scolding for Nastase," *NYT*, 17 Sept. 1972, S9; Fred Williams, The Tennis Beat, *LAS*, 14 Sept. 1972, B4.

21. Genevieve Buck, "Courting with Color," *CT*, 13 Mar. 1972, B12; "Arthur Ashe Is Coming," *PC*, 20 May 1972, 12; advertisement for Head Shoes, *New York Magazine*, 15 May 1972, 2; "The Week's Best Photos," *Jet*, 4 Mar. 1971, 33; advertisement for Arthur Ashe racquet, *Black Enterprise*, May 1973, 28.

22. Ashe, *Portrait in Motion*, 102–4.

23. "New Sports Policy Stirs South Africa," *NYT*, 24 Apr. 1971, 11.

24. "S. Africa Studies Change in Policy," *WP*, 20 Apr. 1971, D3.

25. "Ashe Supports S. Africa Line," *CDD*, 5 June 1971, 30; "Ashe Issues War Declaration against S. African Athletes," *BAA*, 5 June 1971, 7; "NAACP Disrupts Tennis Meet If S. Africans Play," *Jet*, 19 Aug. 1971, 47.

26. "South Africans Harassed," *CDD*, 4 Aug. 1971, 32; Michael Widmer, "Protests Hit S. Africa Stars," *BAA*, 7 Aug. 1971, 8; "Cliff Drysdale Denies Racism," *CDD*, 7 Aug. 1971, 30; "South Africa's Netters Target of Boston NAACP," *ADW*, 19 Aug. 1971, 11; "NAACP Disrupts Tennis Meet If S. Africans Play"; *Crisis*, Oct. 1971, 261.

27. "Gary Player Is Heckled over Apartheid Policy," *NYT*, 18 June 1971, 46; Lincoln A. Werden, "Harris's 67 Leads U.S. Open by Shot," *NYT*, 18 June 1971, 45; "Blacks Heckle Player," *LAS*, 8 July 1971, B6.

28. Sam Lacy, "What Is Wrong with Arthur Ashe?," *BAA*, 25 Sept. 1971, 7.

29. Lacy, "What Is Wrong with Arthur Ashe?"; Jules Tygiel, *Baseball's Great Experiment: Jackie Robinson and His Legacy* (New York: Oxford University Press, 1983), 24, 36, 41–42, 63–64. Lacy experienced the same racial discrimination as Ashe. Tygiel wrote, "The efforts of [Lacy] and other black writers to integrate sports possessed an element of irony. They too were victims of Jim Crow, who held analogous positions to the athletes they covered. Segregation hid their considerable skills from the larger white audience and severely restricted their income earning potential. Yet they rarely mentioned their own plight. Indeed, the barriers for black journalists lasted long after those for athletes disappeared" (36). Lacy's previous columns on Ashe in the *Baltimore Afro-American* include "Jackie and Floyd and 1100 Houses," 6 Aug. 1963, 13; "Ashe Weakness: His Own Daring," 14 May 1964; "A Communist without a Card," 30 June 1964; "Ashe Wants Title More Than Reprieve," 19 Feb. 1966, 17; "Arthur Ashe Grows Up, So Does NCAA," 22 Feb. 1966, 11; "Ashe Deserves a Doff of the Hat," 8 July 1969, 16; and "Why the Furore [*sic*] over Arthur Ashe?," 3 Feb. 1970, 21.

30. "South Africa Back in Davis Cup," *Guardian*, 15 Jan. 1972, 23.

31. "So. Africa Wins Davis Cup Entry," *NYT*, 13 July 1972, 41. The United States, France, Australia, Great Britain, and Argentina voted to readmit South Africa, while the Soviet Union and India voted for a continued ban.

32. Ashe, *Portrait in Motion*, 16–17; "Obituary: Piet Koornhof," *Times* (London), 19 Nov. 2007; "Apartheid-Era Minister Piet Koornhof Dead at 82," *Mail & Guardian* (Johannesburg), 13 Nov. 2007. For more on Koornhof, see John Nauright, *Sport, Cultures and Identities in South Africa* (London: Leicester University Press, 1997).

33. Lt. Arthur Ashe (West Point, NY), letter to the editor, *WT*, Aug. 1967, 8; Dick Edwards, "USLTA Insults Ashe, S. African US Open Boss," *NYAN*, 23 Aug. 1969, 34; Ashe, *Portrait in Motion*, 17. For more on the relationship between Ashe and Williams, see Neil Amdur, "Ashe to Test So. Africa Policy," *NYT*, 30 July 1969, 32; Robert Lipsyte, "The Promoter," *NYT*, 23 Aug. 1969, 22; "Ashe Forestalls Tennis Picketing," *NYT*, 29 Aug. 1969, 32; Dick Edwards, "A Blessing for Ashe," *NYAN*, 7 Feb. 1970, 34; and Frank Rostron, "Owen Williams," *WT*, Mar. 1967, 64–66.

34. Ashe, *Portrait in Motion*, 18.

35. Ibid., 22–24; Dennis Brutus to Ashe, c. July 1973, SCRBC, box 1, folder 6. Ashe wrote to activists Julian Bond and Dennis Brutus, congressmen Andrew Young, Ronald Dellums, and Barbara Jordan, poet Nikki Giovanni, Urban League chairman Vernon Jordan, politician Sargent Shriver, ambassador John G. Hurd, former mentor and coach J. D. Morgan, former USLTA head Bob Kelleher, and Philip Morris chairman Joseph Cullman. The responses to some of these letters are in Arthur Ashe Papers, SCRBC, box 1, folder 6.

36. Andrew Young to Ashe, 16 July 1973, SCRBC, box 1, folder 6.

37. Young to Ashe, 16 July 1973; Julian Bond to Ashe, 18 July 1973; and Joseph Cullman to Ashe, 16 July 1973, all in ibid.

38. Sargent Shriver to Ashe, 19 July 1973, ibid. Shriver suggested that Ashe demand the release of one or more political prisoners in exchange for his visit.

39. Douglas Martin, "Dennis Brutus Dies at 85, Fought Apartheid with Sports," *NYT*, 2 Jan. 2010; Cameron Duodu, "Dennis Brutus Obituary," *Guardian*, 23 Feb. 2010; "Dennis Brutus: South African Poet and Anti-Apartheid Campaigner," *Times* (London), 6 Jan. 2010; Richard E. Lapchick, *The Politics of Race and International Sport: The Case of South Africa* (Westport, CT: Greenwood, 1975), 24–27, 99–102. For more on Brutus's poetry and activism, see *Poetry and Protest: A Dennis Brutus Reader*, edited by Aisha Karim and Lee Sustar (Chicago: Haymarket Books, 2006).

40. Brutus to Ashe, c. July 1973; "Writer Banned," *Guardian*, 21 Nov. 1973, 2; Charles Mohr, "South African Whites Hear a Plea and a Warning," *NYT*, 16 Nov. 1972, 5; Clarence Page, "Black Rule: A Struggle for Freedom," *CT*, 30 June 1976, 1; Don Mattera, *Sophiatown: Coming of Age in South Africa* (Boston: Beacon, 1989); David Beresford, "Call to Keep Sports Bar on South Africa," *Guardian*, 10 Jan. 1980, 3; "South African Play Banned by Police," *Guardian*, 22 Aug. 1973, 3. Mattera was a journalist for the *Johannesburg Star*.

41. Nikki Giovanni to Ashe, 25 July 1973; Bond to Ashe, 18 July 1973; and J. D. Morgan to Ashe, 12 July 1973, all in SCRBC, box 1, folder 6. The U.S. ambassador to South Africa, John G. Hurd, also supported Ashe's trip to South Africa. Hurd to Ashe, 26 Nov. 1973, ibid. In Giovanni's letter Ashe underlined the sentence, "Mankind has conquered the heavens and is attempting to unravel the oceans yet the spirit must also be unlocked." For more on the poetry of Giovanni, see *The Collected Poetry of Nikki Giovanni, 1968–1998*, intro. Virginia C. Fowler (New York: William Morrow, 2003).

42. Ashe, *Portrait in Motion*, 47–49, 98, 106; Parton Keese, "South Africa Opening Door to Ashe," *NYT*, 1 Nov. 1973, 60; "South Africa Grants Visa to Ashe," *WP*, 1 Nov. 1973, D7; "S. Africa Admits Ashe," *CD*, 5 Nov. 1973, 13; "S. Africa Bends; To Let Ashe Compete in Tourney," *Jet*, 22 Nov. 1973, 68.

43. Ashe, *Portrait in Motion*, 107–8; Keese, "South Africa Opening Door to Ashe"; "South Africa Grants Visa to Ashe"; "S. Africa Admits Ashe," *PC*, 24 Nov. 1973, 6.

44. Ashe, *Portrait in Motion*, 112–13; Mike Towle, ed., *I Remember Arthur Ashe: Memories of a True Tennis Pioneer and Champion of Social Causes by the People Who Knew Him* (Nashville:

Cumberland House, 2001), 73. Brutus and the other SANROC members almost forced Ashe to miss his plane to Africa. Journalist Frank Deford explained, "Brutus had been a South African colored and had gotten out, and he didn't want Arthur to go. He was running an organization and was trying to talk him out of it. I mean, this was at the last minute with the plane on the runway and there's Brutus arguing with Arthur, not letting him out of the hotel, although I don't mean physically. Arthur finally says, 'I know they're using me, but I'm using them, too.' We did manage to make the plane" (ibid.).

45. Ashe, *Portrait in Motion*, 115–16.

46. Ibid., 116–18.

47. Ibid., 118. Ashe was uncomfortable around Young's housekeeper, Anna. After touring Young's house, Ashe asked the housekeeper for a beverage, and she responded passively, "Yes, master." The encounter transported him back to his youth in Richmond, when he had been the one lowering his eyes and answering whites in an overly polite tone. He hadn't liked it then, and he didn't like it now.

48. Ibid., 119; Nauright, *Sport, Cultures, and Identities in South Africa*, 171–72; Max Robertson, *The Encyclopedia of Tennis* (New York: Studio, 1974), 319; Eugene L. Scott, *Tennis: Game of Motion* (New York: Crown, 1973), 176–77.

49. Ashe, *Portrait in Motion*, 120–22.

50. "S.A. Labels Foster as 'Honorary White,'" *CD*, 12 Nov. 1973, 20; "S.A. Cheers Bob Foster," *CD*, 14 Nov. 1973, 25; Parton Keese, "Welcome, Bob Foster," *NYT*, 14 Nov. 1973, 55; "S. Africa Welcomes Foster," *WP*, 14 Nov. 1973, D5; John Gonzales, "No Worse Than Home," *BAA*, 17 Nov. 1973, 10.

51. Peter Younghusband, "Foster Wows South Africa," *WP*, 22 Nov. 1973, E9; "Foster Loves People; Ashe Is Guarded About S. Africa," *Jet*, 20 Dec. 1973, 86.

52. Ashe, *Portrait in Motion*, 121, 124; "Foster Loves People"; David K. Wiggins, *Glory Bound: Black Athletes in a White America* (Syracuse, NY: Syracuse University Press, 1997), 61–79, 200–220; Wiggins, ed., *Out of the Shadows: A Biographical History of African American Athletes* (Fayetteville: University of Arkansas Press, 2006), 111–31, 133–45, 187–205, 223–78.

53. "Ashe Wins 1st Round in Africa," *CD*, 21 Nov. 1973, 24; "Ashe Is Easy Winner in S. African Opener," *WP*, 21 Nov. 1973, D5; "Ashe Wins in S. African Net Debut," *NYT*, 21 Nov. 1973, 46; Ashe, *Portrait in Motion*, 122–23.

54. Ashe, *Portrait in Motion*, 122–23.

55. Ibid., 123–24; Joyce Sikakane, *A Window on Soweto* (London: International Defence and Aid Fund, 1977), 11, 78; P. L. Bonner and Lauren Segal, *Soweto: A History* (Cape Town: Maskew Miller Longman, 1998); Peter Magubane and Charlene Smith, *Soweto* (Cape Town: Struik, 2001); Baruch Hirson, *Year of Fire, Year of Ash: The Soweto Revolt, Roots of a Revolution?* (London: Zed Books, 1979).

56. "Ashe Gains Round of 8 in S. Africa," *NYT*, 22 Nov. 1973, 60; Ashe, *Portrait in Motion*, 124–25.

57. Ashe, *Portrait in Motion*, 126.

58. Ibid., 126–27.

59. Ibid., 127–28.

60. Ibid., 129–31; "Ashe Tops Hewitt in Three Sets," *NYT*, 23 Nov. 1973, 50.

61. Ashe, *Portrait in Motion*, 131–32; "Ellis Park Seating Was Segregated," *Rand Daily Mail*, 27 Nov. 1973, SCRBC, box 1, folder 7.

62. Ashe, *Portrait in Motion*, 133–34; "Ashe Makes History Books," *WP*, 25 Nov. 1973, B9; "Ashe Gains Tennis Final in S. Africa," *NYT*, 25 Nov. 1973, 268; "Ashe Reaches Final Round in South Africa," *LAT*, 25 Nov. 1973, D14.

63. Ashe, *Portrait in Motion*, 134–35; "Ashe Says He Must 'Digest' SA Visit," *Argus*, 27 Nov. 1973, SCRBC, box 1, folder 7; "Ashe Sees 'Breezes of Change' in S. Africa," *Argus*, 29 Nov. 1973, ibid.; "Secrecy on Ashe Talks with Koornhof," *Argus*, 26 Nov. 1973, ibid. Ashe and Koornhof left the meeting by separate doors.

64. Ashe, *Portrait in Motion*, 135–36; *Arthur Ashe: Citizen of the World*, produced and directed by Julie Anderson (New York: Home Box Office, 1994), videocassette, 59 min.; Ashe, *Off the Court*, 155; Cecil Harris and Larryette Kyle-DeBose, *Charging the Net: A History of Blacks in Tennis from Althea Gibson and Arthur Ashe to the Williams Sisters* (Chicago: Ivan R. Dee, 2007), 85; Bob Lipper, "Ashe's Legacy: 'Stumbling Blocks into Steppingstones,' " *RTD*, 11 Feb. 1993.

65. Ashe, *Portrait in Motion*, 136; "Arthur Ashe Sticks to Tennis—and Wins Praise of Crowds," *Argus*, 24 Nov. 1973, SCRBC, box 1, folder 7; "Ashe Loses, Will 'Digest' His Views on South Africa," *LAT*, 27 Nov. 1973, B1.

66. Ashe, *Portrait in Motion*, 137; "Ashe Favored Today in S. Africa Net Final," *NYT*, 26 Nov. 1973, 44; "Ashe Makes History Books."

67. Ashe, *Portrait in Motion*, 137–38; "Ashe Falls to Connors in S. Africa," *CT*, 27 Nov. 1973, C4; "Ashe Loses, Will 'Digest' His Views on South Africa"; "Ashe Bows in Final in So. Africa," *NYT*, 27 Nov. 1973, 89; "Connors Downs Ashe in Final," *WP*, 27 Nov. 1973, D3; "Conners [sic] Upsets Ashe in S. African Tournament," *Jet*, 13 Dec. 1973, 80.

68. Ashe, *Portrait in Motion*, 139–42; "Ashe to Meet Buthelezi for Breakfast," *Natal Mercury*, 28 Nov. 1973, 1, SCRBC, box 1, folder 7.

69. Ashe, *Portrait in Motion*, 139–42; "A Message for South Africans," *Argus*, 4 Dec. 1973; "Ashe: Insight into the Most Interesting Week of His Life," *Argus*, 29 Nov. 1973; and "Prof. Hanekom Feels Ashe Has Already Experienced Apartheid," *Die Burger*, 30 Nov. 1973, all in SCRBC, box 1, folder 7.

70. Ashe, *Portrait in Motion*, 142; "Ashe: Insight into the Most Interesting Week of His Life."

CHAPTER 7: TRANSITIONS

1. "The Importance of Being Arthur," *Cape Times*, 2 Dec. 1973; "A Nation of Bad Sports," *Cape Herald*, 8 Dec. 1973; Sy Lerman, "SA Visit a 'Duty,' " *Johannesburg Star*, 19 Nov. 1973, 40; and "Arthur Ashe Sticks to Tennis—and Wins Praise of Crowds," *Argus*, 24 Nov. 1973, all in SCRBC, box 1, folder 7.

2. "Nationalist Viewpoint: Ashe Exposure," undated clipping from *Die Burger*, in ibid.

3. Ashe, *Arthur Ashe: Portrait in Motion*, with Frank Deford (Boston: Houghton Mifflin, 1975), 86.

4. Ibid.; Bud Collins, ed., *The Bud Collins History of Tennis: An Authoritative Encyclopedia and Record Book* (Washington, DC: New Chapter, 2008), 172–73, 176. David Wiggins has argued that "to maintain an ethnic identity while actively participating in organized sport and the larger American society was not an easy task for black athletes." Wiggins, *Glory Bound: Black Athletes in a White America* (Syracuse, NY: Syracuse University Press, 1997), 220.

5. "Ashe Says S.A. 'Tried,'" *CD*, 4 Dec. 1973, 21; Sam Mirwis, "Ashe 'Censors' Attack on Apartheid," *Sunday Express*, 2 Dec. 1973, SCRBC, box 1, folder 7; "Ashe Sees 'Breezes of Change' in S. Africa," *Argus*, 29 Nov. 1973, ibid.; Ray Williams, "Ashe Censors His Own Speech," *Sunday Times*, 2 Dec. 1973, ibid.; Ashe, *Portrait in Motion*, 144.

6. Ibid. The South African Sugar Circuit included five tournaments—in Bloemfontein, Durban, East London, Port Elizabeth, and Cape Town—played in December and January. It was one of the most popular winter circuits in the 1960s and 1970s.

7. Handwritten note, Donald Dell to Ashe, 22 Jan. 1974, SCRBC, box 1, folder 6; Brutus to Ashe, c. July 1973, ibid.; Ashe, *Portrait in Motion*, 143–44.

8. Ashe, *Portrait in Motion*, 144–45; "Racquet-Wielders New Motto: Tennis Everyone!," *NYT*, 21 Aug. 1966; Neil Amdur, "Ashe to Test So. Africa Policy," *NYT*, 30 July 1969, 32; "Tennis Stars of Tomorrow Get Pointers from Tennis Stars of Today," *NYT*, 3 Sept. 1966, 25; "2 Black Players Pay Debt to Tennis with Clinic for Watts Youth," *NYT*, 12 July 1970, 145; "Tennis Star Ashe Serves Coke USA," *CDD*, 21 Mar. 1970, 36.

9. Ashe, *Portrait in Motion*, 151–52. One cannot ignore that King, John Lewis, Ella Baker, the SCLC, CORE, and SNCC used various forms of political demonstrations throughout the course of the civil rights movement. King himself joined several pickets. In short, Ashe did not object to political demonstrations per se. Rather, he opposed leaders who seemed to rely exclusively on physical protests without considering other forms of activism such as boycotts and dialogue with adversaries. For more on grass-roots activism during the civil rights movement, see Barbara Ransby, *Ella Baker and the Black Freedom Movement: A Radical Democratic Vision* (Chapel Hill: University of North Carolina Press, 2003).

10. Ashe, *Portrait in Motion*, 151–52; Barbara Metch, *The Role of IBM in South Africa: A Transcript of Hearings Sponsored by the National Council of Churches, November 20 and 21, 1974* (New York: ICCR, 1974).

11. Ashe, *Portrait in Motion*, 152.

12. Ibid., 153–54.

13. Ashe, "Ashe Advises Blacks Following Visit to S. African Cities," *Jet*, 10 Jan. 1974, 12–16.

14. Arthur McMorris and Olu Imari Chapman, letters to the editor, *Jet*, 31 Jan. 1974, 4.

15. Charles Maher, "The Selling of a Tennis Match," *LAT*, 21 Aug. 1973, B1; Mark Asher, "Bonnie and Clyde vs. Billie, Bobby," *WP*, 24 Aug. 1973, D6; "It's All Set! Riggs-King on Sept. 20," *CT*, 3 Aug. 1973, C2; Jane Leary, "Daring Decade: How Women Served and Won," *Women Sports* 5 (Jan. 1978): 22–23; Curry Kirkpatrick, "There She Is, Ms. America," *SI* 39 (1 Oct. 1973): 30–37. For more on the "Battle of the Sexes Match," see Susan Ware, *Game, Set, Match: Billie Jean King and the Revolution in Women's Sports* (Chapel Hill: University of North Carolina Press, 2011); Selena Roberts, *A Necessary Spectacle: Billie Jean King, Bobby Riggs, and the Tennis Match That Leveled the Game* (New York: Crown, 2005); and Billie Jean King, *Pressure Is a Privilege: Lessons I've Learned from Life and the Battle of the Sexes*, with Christine Brennan (New York: LifeTime Media, 2008).

16. Benjamin G. Rader, *American Sports: From the Age of Folk Games to the Age of Spectators* (Englewood Cliffs, NJ: Prentice-Hall, 1983), 342–43; Robert Lipsyte, *Sportsworld: An American Dreamland* (New York: Quadrangle, 1977), 223; Billie Jean King, *Billie Jean*, with Kim Chapin (New York: Harper & Row, 1974); Hal Higdon, "Plays Tennis Like a Man, Speaks Out Like," *NYT*, 27 Aug. 1967, SM115.

17. Collins, *Bud Collins History of Tennis*, 614–15; Tom LeCompte, *The Last Sure Thing: The Life and Times of Bobby Riggs* (Easthampton, MA: Black Squirrel, 2003). Riggs reportedly joked that he wanted his epitaph to read, "He Put Women on the Map." Ibid., iii.

18. Collins, *Bud Collins History of Tennis*, 630; Court with Barbara Oldfield, *Winning Faith: The Margaret Court Story* (Sydney: Strand, 2000); Jeff Prugh, "Riggs-Court Net Battle of Sexes Stirs Fan Interest," *LAT*, 7 May 1973, G1.

19. Jeff Prugh, "Riggs Puts His Racquet Where His Mouth Is—and Wins," *LAT*, 14 May 1973, E1; Neil Amdur, "Riggs Defeats Mrs. Court, 6-2, 6-1," *NYT*, 14 May 1973, 41; Mark Asher, "Riggs Rattles Court, 6-2, 6-1," *WP*, 14 May 1973, D1; "Riggs Upholds Men's Superiority," *CD*, 15 May 1973, 25; "King Challenges Riggs," *CT*, 15 May 1973, C1; "Billie Jean Changes Her Mind, But Now Riggs' Price $50,000," *LAT*, 15 May 1973, F1.

20. "King Meets Riggs in $100,000 Match," *CT*, 12 July 1973, C2; "King, Riggs Will Fight It Out—for $100,000: Women's Libber, Male Chauvinist to Play in Richest Winner-Take-All Tennis Match," *LAT*, 12 July 1973, D1; "Riggs-King Tennis Match Set for Astrodome Sept. 20," *LAT*, 3 Aug. 1973, B1; Ashe, *Portrait in Motion*, 72, 86.

21. Ruth Rosen, *The World Split Open: How the Modern Women's Movement Changed America* (New York: Penguin Books, 2000), 108–10, 124, 128, 140; Ransby, *Ella Baker and the Black Freedom Movement*, 173–75. Baker commented sarcastically on why King and others excluded her: "After all, who was I? I was female, I was old. I didn't have any Ph.D." (ibid., 173).

22. Rosen, *World Split Open*, 108–10.

23. Arthur Ashe, *Arthur Ashe on Tennis: Strokes, Strategy, Traditions, Players, Psychology, and Wisdom*, with Alexander McNab (New York: Knopf, 1995), xxiii; "Women's Lob," *Time*, 7 Dec. 1970; "Women Tennis Stars Threaten Boycott over Unequal Purses," *NYT*, 8 Sept. 1970, 1. For more on sexism in tennis, see Sundiata Djata, *Blacks at the Net: Black Achievement in the History of Tennis*, 2 vols. (Syracuse, NY: Syracuse University Press, 2006–8), 1:176, 179–80, 183, 199; and Rosen, *World Split Open*, 293, 301–2.

24. Ashe, *Portrait in Motion*, 266–67. Formed in 1973 by four men—Lawrence King, Dennis Murphy, Fred Barman, and Jordan Kaiser—World Team Tennis Featured sixteen teams from major U.S. cities, such as Los Angeles, Philadelphia, and New York, playing a season of forty-four matches. Each team included at least two men and two women. The singer and musician Elton John wrote the song "Philadelphia Freedom" for his friend Billie Jean King of the Philadelphia Freedoms. The league still exists today.

25. Ashe, *Days of Grace: A Memoir*, with Arnold Rampersad (New York: Knopf, 1993), 231–37; Ashe, *Arthur Ashe on Tennis*, xxiii.

26. Ashe, *Portrait in Motion*, 53; Ashe, *Off the Court*, with Neil Amdur (New York: New American Library, 1981), 184.

27. Ashe, *Off the Court*, 184; Ashe, *Portrait in Motion*, 53.

28. Grace Lichtenstein, "King Will Win in Four Sets," *NYT*, 16 Sept. 1973, 221; Neil Amdur, "Riggs Will Win in Three Sets," *NYT*, 16 Sept. 1973, 221; "Riggs Named 8-5 Favorite," *WP*, 16 Sept. 1973, D11; "One Vote for Billie Jean," *Wall Street Journal*, 18 Sept. 1973, 20; David Gray, "Cards against Mrs. King," *Guardian*, 20 Sept. 1973, 27; William Gildea, "Tennis Match Just Last Act," *WP*, 20 Sept. 1973, D1.

29. Robert Markus, ". . . Best Man Loses," *CT*, 21 Sept. 1973, 1; Charles Maher, "Barnum Would Have Loved It," *LAT*, 21 Sept. 1973, 1; Neil Amdur, "Mrs. King Defeats Riggs, 6-4, 6-3, 6-3, amid a Circus Atmosphere," *NYT*, 21 Sept. 1973, 85; Grace Lichtenstein, "Mrs. King Calls Victory 'Culmination' of Career," *NYT*, 21 Sept. 1973, 31; William Gildea, "Riggs Reels

to 4–6, 3–6, 3–6," *WP*, 21 Sept. 1973, A1; David Gray, "Joke Over for Riggs," *Guardian*, 22 Sept. 1973, 19.

30. Ibid.

31. Ashe, *Portrait in Motion*, 90.

32. Ibid., 74; Ralph Leo, "Ashe Upset by Borg," *CT*, 3 Sept. 1973, C1; "Sweden's Borg, 17, Upsets Ashe," *LAT*, 3 Sept. 1973, D1; Parton Keese, "Borg Ousts Ashe in U.S. Open," *NYT*, 3 Sept. 1973, 9; David Gray, "Age Gives Way to Youth," *Guardian*, 3 Sept. 1973, 19.

33. Collins, *Bud Collins History of Tennis*, 172–75.

34. "Tanner Upsets Smith, Faces Connors Next," *LAT*, 6 Sept. 1974, D1; Ralph Leo, "Laver Routs Ashe for Title in Pro Indoor Tennis, $15,000," *CT*, 28 Jan. 1974, C2; "Ashe Drops 16th to Laver," *CD*, 28 Jan. 1974, 21.

35. Ashe, *Portrait in Motion*, 9; "Pilic Banned by Wimbledon," *LAT*, 7 June 1973, P4; "Boycott Threatened," *WP*, 8 June 1973, D5; "ILTF will not bow to strike threats," *Guardian*, 13 June 1973, 27; "Wimbledon Is Facing Loss of Top Players," *NYT*, 14 June 1973, 99.

36. James Meredith, *Three Years in Mississippi* (Bloomington: Indiana University Press, 1966); Charles W. Eagles, *The Price of Defiance: James Meredith and the Integration of Ole Miss* (Chapel Hill: University of North Carolina Press, 2009); William Doyle, *An American Insurrection: James Meredith and the Battle of Oxford, Mississippi, 1962* (New York: Doubleday, 2001); Frank Lambert, *The Battle of Ole Miss: Civil Rights v. States' Rights* (New York: Oxford University Press, 2009); Bob Dylan, "Oxford Town," *The Freewheelin' Bob Dylan*, 1963, Warner Bros., 33⅓ rpm. Folk artist Phil Ochs also touched on southern racism in his song "Here's to the State of Mississippi": "The sweating of their souls can't wash the blood from off their hands / They smile and shrug their shoulders at the murder of a man." From Ochs, *There But for Fortune*, 1989, Elektra Records, 33⅓ rpm.

37. Ashe, *Portrait in Motion*, 93.

38. Ibid., 172–74.

39. Herbert G. McCann, "Apartheid," letter to the editor, *CD*, 12 June 1974, 15.

40. "Ashe Sees No Peaceful End to Racism in S. Africa," *NYAN*, 12 Oct. 1974, A8; "Ashe Knocks Apartheid in Speech," *BAA*, 19 Oct. 1974, 10.

41. J. H. P. Serfontein, "Bitter Visa Row on Ashe," *Johannesburg Sunday Times*, n.d., SCRBC, box 39, Scrapbooks; Al Harvin, "Ashe to Play Again in S. Africa," *NYT*, 17 Oct. 1974, 54. Experts viewed Koornhof and Mulder as the frontrunners to succeed Vorster as prime minister. For more on Mulder's views, see Mulder, "South Africa's Objectives," *NYT*, 14 May 1974, 37.

42. Collins, *Bud Collins History of Tennis*, 174, 492; Amdur, "Davis Cup Group May Renew Bid to Expel South Africa," *NYT*, 25 Oct. 1974, 44; Candace Mayeron, "India Couldn't Wait to Skip Cup Final," *LAT*, 6 Nov. 1974, E8; "South Africa, India and Untouchables," Sports Editor's Mailbox, *NYT*, 20 Oct. 1974, 228; "Declines S. Africa," *CD*, 24 Sept. 1974, 24; David Gray, "Davis Cup's Crisis Nears," *Guardian*, 4 Oct. 1974, 23; "Still Hope for Davis Cup," *CT*, 5 Oct. 1974, F2; "India Refuses to Sanction Apartheid by Playing SA," *BAA*, 12 Oct. 1974, 9.

43. "South Africa, India and Untouchables"; Sobhotosh Khan, "Indians Do Not Play to Win," letter to the editor, *NYT*, 3 Nov. 1974, D2; Mayeron, "India Couldn't Wait to Skip Cup Final"; "Attempt to Have India Expelled," *Guardian*, 30 Oct. 1974, 27; "Amritrajes Refuse Davis Participation," *WP*, 3 Nov. 1974, D11. It was Raj Kumar Khanna, secretary of the All-Indian Tennis Federation, and not the Indian government, who made the decision to forfeit the final-round tie.

44. "Art Ashe Says India Goofed on Davis Cup," *CD*, 17 Dec. 1974, 24; Ashe, *Days of Grace*, 107; Sy Lerman, "India Erred—Ashe," *Rand Daily Mail*, 19 Nov. 1974, SCRBC, box 39, Scrapbooks; Thomas Rogers, "Ashe Faulting India's Default," *NYT*, 17 Dec. 1974, 47; "India Erred in Davis Cup Boycott of S. Africa: Ashe," *BAA*, 28 Dec. 1974, 11.

45. "The Ins and Outs of the United Nations," *WP*, 29 Oct. 1974, A18.

46. Charles Mohr, "The South Africans and Apartheid Today," *NYT*, 17 Nov. 1974, 1.

47. Ibid.

48. "Crusader Ashe Has Mellowed," clipping from unnamed newspaper, c. Nov. 1974, SCRBC, box 1, folder 7; "Ashe Is Back in Spite of US 'Backlash,'" *Rand Daily Mail*, 18 Nov. 1974, 39, SCRBC, box 39, Scrapbooks; *Survey by Chicago Council on Foreign Relations and Louis Harris & Associates, Dec. 6–14, 1974*, iPOLL Databank, The Roper Center for Public Opinion Research, University of Connecticut, www2.lib.purdue.edu:4076/ipoll.html.

49. Andrew Young, *An Easy Burden: The Civil Rights Movement and the Transformation of America* (Waco, TX: Baylor University Press, 2008); Young, *A Way Out of No Way: The Spiritual Memoirs of Andrew Young* (Nashville: Thomas Nelson, 1996).

50. Robert Green, *The Urban Challenge: Poverty and Race* (Chicago: Follett, 1977); Green and Frances S. Thomas, eds., *Metropolitan Desegregation* (New York: Plenum, 1985).

51. Mike Towle, ed., *I Remember Arthur Ashe: Memories of a True Tennis Pioneer and Champion of Social Causes by the People Who Knew Him* (Nashville: Cumberland House, 2001), 124; Sy Lerman, "Ashe Has a Plan for Black Tennis," *Rand Daily Mail*, 19 Nov. 1974, SCRBC, box 39, Scrapbooks; "Ashe to Start Foundation in South Africa," *CT*, 20 Nov. 1974, C2.

52. Benjamin Pogrund, *Sobukwe and Apartheid* (New Brunswick, NJ: Rutgers University Press, 1991); Pogrund, *How Can Man Die Better? The Life of Robert Sobukwe* (Johannesburg: Jonathan Ball, 2003); S. E. M. Pheko, *The Land Is Ours: The Political Legacy of Mangaliso Sobukwe* (New York: Pheko & Associates, 1994); Elias L. Ntloedibe, *Here Is a Tree: Political Biography of Robert Mangaliso Sobukwe* (Mogoditshane, Botswana: Century-Turn, 1995); John F. Burns, "Discord Erupts at South Africa Black's Rites," *NYT*, 12 Mar. 1978, 3; Ashe, "Sobukwe Shadow Hangs over Davis Cup Tie," *Guardian*, 18 Mar. 1978, 7.

53. Ashe, *Off the Court*, 159–60; Patrick Laurence, "Sobukwe a True Leader, Say Black Americans," *Rand Daily Mail*, 30 Nov. 1974, SCRBC, box 39, Scrapbooks; William R. Cotter, "We Have Nothing to Hide," *Africa Report* 21, no. 6 (Nov./Dec. 1976): 39.

54. "Connors, Court Top Seeds in S. Africa," *WP*, 14 Nov. 1974, G4; "Connors, Ashe Gain in Tennis," *NYT*, 22 Nov. 1974, 49; "Yankees Dominant in S. African Open," *WP*, 22 Nov. 1974, D8; "Ramirez Defeats Rosewall," *NYT*, 23 Nov. 1974, 23; Sport in Brief, *Observer*, 24 Nov. 1974, 25; "Connors and Ashe in S. African Final," *WP*, 24 Nov. 1974, 54; Ashe, *Portrait in Motion*, 36–37; Sam Mirwis, "Connors and Ashe Feud Comes to Boil," *Sunday Express*, 1 Dec. 1974, SCRBC, box 39, Scrapbooks.

55. "Connors Defeats Ashe for South African Title," *LAT*, 26 Nov. 1974, D6; "Ashe Bows to Connors in S. Africa," *NYT*, 26 Nov. 1974, 49; "Connors' Title," *Guardian*, 26 Nov. 1974, 26; "Connors Tops Ashe in S. Africa," *WP*, 26 Nov. 1974, D5.

56. Bob Logan, "Apparently a Horse of a Different Name," *CT*, 28 Nov. 1974, L2; Sy Lerman, "It's SA v. US," *Rand Daily Mail*, 20 Nov. 1974, SCRBC, box 39, Scrapbooks; Mark Mathabane, *Kaffir Boy: The True Story of a Black Youth's Coming of Age in Apartheid South Africa* (New York: Macmillan, 1986), 240.

57. Eric Mani, "Don't Lose Hope—Message from Black Americans," *World*, 27 Nov. 1974, SCRBC, box 39, Scrapbooks; Nat Serache, "Pledge of US Study Help," *World*, 27 Nov. 1974,

ibid.; "Our Tennis Players Need 10 Years: Ashe," *World*, n.d., ibid.; Cotter, "We Have Nothing to Hide."

58. Ethel L. Payne, "South Africa Rejects," *CD*, 21 Dec. 1974, 8. The *Pittsburgh Courier* reprinted Payne's column on 4 January 1975, p. 6.

59. "Diggs Is Wrong About Ali's Visit," *CD*, 20 Feb. 1975, 32; Nandi Guillaume, "Ali to Share His Money," *NYAN*, 22 Feb. 1975, C16.

60. "Foreman Gets Backing from High Officials," *LAS*, 3 Apr. 1975, B2.

61. Dwight Chapin, "As Barriers Fall: Arthur Ashe Brings Two Colors to Play in Once-Restricted South African Tennis," *LAT*, 19 May 1975, D1.

### CHAPTER 8: THE COMEBACK

1. Curtis Austin, "'I support the Bakke decision,' Ashe Says," *BAA*, 24 Mar. 1979, 8.

2. David Gray, "Arthur Ashe Looks Too Good to Last," *Guardian*, 25 Jan. 1975, 21.

3. Bud Collins, ed., *The Bud Collins History of Tennis: An Authoritative Encyclopedia and Record Book* (Washington, DC: New Chapter, 2008), 176-77; "Ashe Trips Borg in Spain, 7-6, 6-3," *WP*, 24 Feb. 1975, D5; "Ashe Tops Borg in Barcelona," *BAA*, 1 Mar. 1975, 10; "Ashe Rally Whips Okker in 'Green,'" *CT*, 3 Mar. 1975, E6; "Ashe Downs Okker," *NYT*, 3 Mar. 1975, 32; "Ashe Conquers Okker in Final," *NYT*, 28 Apr. 1975, 52; "Ashe Whips Okker in WCT Final," *WP*, 28 Apr. 1975, D2.

4. "Gold Ball for Ashe," *Guardian*, 7 May 1975, 23; The Tennis Beat, *LAS*, 8 May 1975, B4; "Ashe Top Seed in WCT Finals," *BAA*, 10 May 1975, 9.

5. "Gold Ball for Ashe"; "Ashe Outlasts Cox in Dallas," *WP*, 9 May 1975, D5; "Pity Is Wasted on Ashe," *Guardian*, 10 May 1975, 21; Leonard Koppett, "Borg-Ashe Final Today," *NYT*, 11 May 1975, S3; "Borg, Ashe in Classic WCT Match," *WP*, 11 May 1975, 52.

6. "Sharp Serve Wins WCT for Ashe," *WP*, 12 May 1975, D1; "Ashe Beats Tired Borg in Four Sets, Wins $50,000," *LAT*, 12 May 1975, D1; Leonard Koppett, "Ashe Victor over Borg," *NYT*, 12 May 1975, 48; "Ashe in Charge," *Guardian*, 12 May 1975, 21; "World Championship Tennis Champion," *ADW*, 13 May 1975, 1; "Ashe Rallies for 3rd Time to Win World Tennis Crown," *BAA*, 17 May 1975, 10; "Arthur Ashe Explains His WTC Victory," *LAS*, 15 May 1975, B3; "Arthur Ashe Wins Title," *NYAN*, 21 May 1975, A2.

7. Frank Keating, "Cool Black Cat," *Guardian*, 21 June 1975, 17; "Connors Is Top Choice at Wimbledon Tourney," *NYT*, 22 June 1975, 197; "Odds Lengthen on Connors as Wimbledon Begins," *CT*, 23 June 1975, C7; "Connors Choice to Retain Title," *LAT*, 23 June 1975, D6; David Gray, "Jimmy Connors and Arthur Ashe Seem Well Set to Challenge," *Guardian*, 23 June 1975, 19.

8. Joe Jares, "A Centre Court Case," *SI*, 14 July 1975; "Moment of Truth," *Guardian*, 3 July 1975, 21; "Connors, Ashe Win, Head for Title Match," *LAT*, 3 July 1975, 1; "Connors, Ashe Win and Reach Wimbledon Tennis Final Round," *NYT*, 4 July 1975, 9.

9. Ibid.

10. Rick Talley, "Connors, Ashe in Men's Final at Wimbledon," *CT*, 4 July 1975, C1; Barry Lorge, "Ashe vs. Connors on Court, in Court," *WP*, 5 July 1975, E1; Dave Anderson, "Tennis in Cold Blood," *NYT*, 6 July 1975, 137; "Connors Sues Ashe, Seeks $5 Million," *WP*, 22 June 1975, 44; "Connors Sues Ashe for Libel," *CT*, 22 June 1975, B3. In April 1975 Kramer filed a $3 million countersuit against Connors for libel and slander. Connors insisted that Kramer was simply trying to disrupt his concentration ahead of an important match with John Newcombe.

11. "Jimmy Connors: The Hellion of Tennis," *Time*, 28 Apr. 1975.

12. "Ashe No Write Off," *Guardian*, 5 July 1975, 17; Mike Towle, ed., *I Remember Arthur Ashe: Memories of a True Tennis Pioneer and Champion of Social Causes by the People Who Knew Him* (Nashville: Cumberland House, 2001), 39–41, 75; Cecil Harris and Larryette Kyle-DeBose, *Charging the Net: A History of Blacks in Tennis from Althea Gibson and Arthur Ashe to the Williams Sisters* (Chicago: Ivan R. Dee, 2007), 88.

13. *Arthur Ashe: Citizen of the World*, produced and directed by Julie Anderson (New York: Home Box Office, 1994), videocassette, 59 min.; David K. Wiggins, *Out of the Shadows: A Biographical History of African American Athletes* (Fayetteville: University of Arkansas Press, 2006), 286.

14. Harris and Kyle-DeBose, *Charging the Net*, 91; "Upset at Wimbledon," *Time*, 14 July 1975.

15. Rick Talley, "For Wimbledon Crown," *CT*, 6 July 1975, B1; "Champion!," *LAT*, 6 July 1975, C1; "Connors Loses to Ashe at Wimbledon," *LAT*, 6 July 1975, A1; Fred Tupper, "Ashe Topples Connors for Crown at Wimbledon," *NYT*, 6 July 1975, 133; Christopher Brasher and Shirley Brasher, "King Arthur Holds Court," *Observer*, 6 July 1975, 16; "Arthur Ashe's Blow for Peace," *Guardian*, 7 July 1975, 20; Jares, "A Centre Court Case"; "Upset at Wimbledon"; Marty Bell, "Arthur Ashe vs. Jimmy Connors Is No Love Match," *Sport*, Sept. 1975, 30, 36, 38.

16. *Arthur Ashe: Citizen of the World*, videocassette; Sundiata Djata, *Blacks at the Net: Black Achievement in the History of Tennis*, 2 vols. (Syracuse, NY: Syracuse University Press, 2006–8), 1:49; Harris and Kyle-DeBose, *Charging the Net*, 92.

17. Doug Smith, *Whirlwind: The Godfather of Black Tennis; The Life and Times of Dr. Robert Walter Johnson* (Washington, DC: Blue Eagle, 2004), 166; *Arthur Ashe: Citizen of the World*; Steve Flink, The Inside View, *WT*, July 1985, 16, SCRBC, box 35, folder 4; "Upset at Wimbledon."

18. Frank Starr, "A Quiet Hero for the Bicentennial," *CT*, 9 July 1975, A2; Jim Murray, "King Arthur," *LAT*, 10 July 1975, D1.

19. Brad Pye Jr., "Ashe Writes His Own History Story," *LAS*, 10 July 1975, B1; "Wimbledon Triumph Completes Arthur's 'Impossible Dream,'" *BAA*, 12 July 1975, 9; "Ashe Didn't Let 'Snubs' Stand in His Way to Top," *CD*, 12 July 1975, 21; Uslish Carter, "What Happened at Wimbledon?," *PC*, 12 July 1975, 25; James P. Murray, "Underdog Arthur Ashe Is the World's Best," *NYAN*, 16 July 1975, A1; "We Salute You, Arthur Ashe!," *NYAN*, 16 July 1975, A4; "Wimbledon a Stage in Ashe 'Rebellion,'" *BAA*, 19 July 1975, 9; "Why Ashe Won and Connors Won, Too," *NYT*, 20 July 1975, S2.

20. Louie Robinson Jr., "Arthur Ashe: The Man Who Despite Age and an Operation Refused to Quit: He Comes Back as a Top Star," *Ebony*, Apr. 1979, SCRBC, box 40, Scrapbooks; "Ashe Plagued by Foot Injury," *LAT*, 5 Nov. 1976, C4; "Ashe Loses, Returns Home for Treatment," *WP*, 5 Nov. 1976, D2; Collins, *Bud Collins History of Tennis*, 181–85.

21. "Ashe, Nastase Disqualified," *LAT*, 1 Dec. 1975, C1; Bernard Kirsch, "Referee Disqualifies Ashe and Nastase," *NYT*, 1 Dec. 1975, 45; David Gray, "A Double Disqualification," *Guardian*, 1 Dec. 1975, 19; "Nastase, Ashe Disqualified," *WP*, 1 Dec. 1975, D2; Bernard Kirsch, "Ashe Ruled Victor in Dispute," *NYT*, 2 Dec. 1975, 51.

22. "Ashe in Car Crash after Nasty Match with Nastase," *Jet*, 10 June 1976, 14; "Ashe Ignores Slur, Defends Nastase as 'No Racist,'" *BAA*, 5 June 1976, 9.

23. Sam Lacy, "Ashe in Twilight? What Comes Next?," *BAA*, 19 June 1976, 9.

24. Ashe, *Off the Court*, with Neil Amdur (New York: New American Library, 1981), 181–82; Laura B. Randolph, "Jeanne Moutoussamy-Ashe: On Love, Loss and Life after Arthur,"

*Ebony*, Oct. 1993, 27–34; Ashe, *Days of Grace: A Memoir*, with Arnold Rampersad (New York: Knopf, 1993), 51.

25. Ashe, *Off the Court*, 181–82.

26. Ibid., 86–87, 182; Ashe, *Arthur Ashe: Portrait in Motion*, with Frank Deford (Boston: Houghton Mifflin, 1975), 2; Neil Amdur, "Ashe, Net Pro of Future, Prepares Civil Rights Talk," *NYT*, 28 Jan. 1968, S5.

27. Randolph, "Jeanne Moutoussamy-Ashe"; Ashe, *Off the Court*, 189.

28. Randolph, "Jeanne Moutoussamy-Ashe"; Ashe, *Off the Court*, 181–204.

29. Ashe, *Off the Court*, 181–204; "And So They Were Married!," *NYAN*, 26 Feb. 1977, A1; Karen Rew, People, *CT*, 20 Mar. 1977, 29.

30. "Colombia Joins Veto of S. Africa," *BAA*, 22 Mar. 1975, 10; "Mexicans Bar Hewitt and McMillan," *NYT*, 30 Apr. 1975, 64; "Mexico Bans SA Tennis Players," *Guardian*, 30 Apr. 1975, 1.

31. "Let S Africans Play, Says Ashe," *Guardian*, 6 Oct. 1975, 23.

32. "Ashe Paces Advance in S. Africa," *WP*, 20 Nov. 1975, F6; "Ashe Gains 3d Round in S. Africa," *NYT*, 21 Nov. 1975, 74; "Ashe Upset in S. Africa," *NYT*, 22 Nov. 1975, 22; "Ashe Digs in S. Africa," *Jet*, 18 Dec. 1975, 50.

33. Robert M. Price, *The Apartheid State in Crisis: Political Transformation in South Africa, 1975–1990* (New York: Oxford University Press, 1991), 46–48; Alan Brooks and Jeremy Brickhill, *Whirlwind before the Storm* (London: International Defense and Aid Fund for Southern Africa, 1980); Thomas Lodge, *Black Politics in South Africa since 1945* (London: Longman, 1983), 321–56. For more on the Soweto Uprising, see Elsabe Brink et al., *Soweto 16 June 1976: Personal Accounts of the Uprising* (Cape Town: Kwela Books, 2006); Anthony W. Marx, *Lessons of Struggle: South African Internal Opposition, 1960–1990* (New York: Oxford University Press, 1992); and Mosegomi Mosala, *Soweto Explodes: The Beginning of the End of Apartheid* (Dubuque, IA: Kendall Hunt, 2007).

34. Price, *Apartheid State in Crisis*, 46–48; Lodge, *Black Politics in South Africa since 1945*, 321–56.

35. Ibid.

36. Price, *Apartheid State in Crisis*, 47–48.

37. Ashe, *Off the Court*, 157; Price, *Apartheid State in Crisis*, 47–48.

38. Price, *Apartheid State in Crisis*, 49–68.

39. Ashe, *Off the Court*, 156–58; Ashe, *Days of Grace*, 104.

40. Ashe, *Off the Court*, 156–58; Ashe, *Days of Grace*, 104; "African Update," *Africa Report* 28, no. 6 (Nov./Dec. 1983): 41; Michael Maren, "Building a Constituency against Apartheid," *Africa Report* 29, no. 3 (May/June 1984): 59; "Marching against Apartheid," *Time*, 10 Dec. 1984.

41. Ashe, "Send Your Children to the Libraries," *NYT*, 6 Feb. 1977, S2.

42. Ibid.; Ashe, *Off the Court*, 48–49; Clarke Bustard, "Assurance Class in the Walker Class of '61," *RTD*, 6 Apr. 1984, SCRBC, box 1, folder 3.

43. A. S. "Doc" Young, "TREES Grow in America," *LAS*, 10 Feb. 1977, A7.

44. "Not for Blacks Only," Mailbox, *NYT*, 27 Feb. 1977, 152.

45. Marvin S. Dent Jr., "An Open Letter to Arthur Ashe," *NYT*, 27 Feb. 1977, 152.

46. "Ashe Raps Black Students for Sad Values, Bad Habits," *Jet*, 20 Apr. 1978, 48.

47. "Ashe on Target . . . ," *Jet*, 11 May 1978, 4.

48. "Arthur Ashe Addresses Morehouse Convocation," *ADW*, 22 Dec. 1978, 8; Words of the Week, *Jet*, 8 Feb. 1979, 32; "De-Emphasize Sports, Ashe Advises Youth," *PC*, 10 Feb. 1979, 12.

49. Ashe, "Sports Boycotts Are Against the Nature of Competition," *WP*, 22 Oct. 1978, 20.
50. Ibid.
51. Austin, "'I support the Bakke decision,' Ashe Says."
52. Louie Robinson Jr., "Arthur Ashe: The Man Who Despite Age and an Operation Refused to Quit: He Comes Back as a Top Star," *Ebony*, Apr. 1979, 74–76, 78, 80, SCRBC, box 40, Scrapbooks.
53. Ibid.
54. Ashe, *Off the Court*, 1–12; "Ashe Enters N.Y. Hospital Complaining of 'Weakness,'" *NYT*, 1 Aug. 1979, A21; "Ailing Ashe Checked for Heart Attack," *CT*, 2 Aug. 1979, C2; "Ashe Takes Heart Test," *WP*, 2 Aug. 1979, C5; "Ashe May Have Suffered Heart Attack, Tests Show," *LAT*, 4 Aug. 1979, C4; "Arthur Ashe in Hospital," *ADW*, 5 Aug. 1979, 7.

CHAPTER 9: TRIUMPH AND TRAGEDY

1. Jennings Culley, "A Champion, Retired," *RTD*, 23 Apr. 1980, SCRBC, box 40, Scrapbooks; Ashe, *Days of Grace: A Memoir*, with Arnold Rampersad (New York: Knopf, 1993), 33–35; Ashe, "Ashe Heart Attack: Why Me?," *WP*, 29 Aug. 1979, A1, A6; "Ashe Undergoes Testing," *NYT*, 2 Aug. 1979, D17; "Arthur Ashe in Hospital," *ADW*, 5 Aug. 1979, 7; Donald Beard, "Ashe, Father Plan Recuperation Together," *WP*, 9 Aug. 1979, F9; "Rest Therapy for Ashe," *BAA*, 18 Aug. 1979, 10; "Ashe to Participate in UNCF Benefit," *PC*, 6 Oct. 1979, 10; "Ashe Taken to Hospital with Chest Pains," *ADW*, 7 Dec. 1979, 5; "Heart Surgery for Arthur Ashe," *LAT*, 13 Dec. 1979, A1.
2. Michael C. Givens II, "Arthur Ashe: Can He Comeback [*sic*]?," *NYAN*, 22 Dec. 1979, 64; Brad Pye Jr., "Looking Ahead," *LAS*, 27 Dec. 1979, B1.
3. "Ashe, 8 Days after Surgery, Eyes Wimbledon," *WP*, 22 Dec. 1979, D6.
4. Richard Evans, "Ashe Prepares His Come-Back," *Guardian*, 12 Feb. 1980, 23.
5. Ashe, *Days of Grace*, 36.
6. Barry Lorge, "Ashe Suffers Setback," *WP*, 26 Mar. 1980, D1; Lorge, "Ashe Ends Career as Player," *WP*, 17 Apr. 1980, F1; "Ashe Retires from Tennis," *NYT*, 17 Apr. 1980, B27; Tom Duffy, "Sports Briefing," *CT*, 17 Apr. 1980, C3; Barry Cooper, "Ashe Pushes Books," *PC*, 19 Apr. 1980, 26.
7. Peter Harris, "Ashe Retirement: A Move for Betterment," *BAA*, 10 May 1980, 9.
8. Lorge, "Ashe Ends Career as Player"; Culley, "A Champion, Retired."
9. Ashe, *Days of Grace*, 39–40.
10. Ibid., 44.
11. Ibid., 60–62. For more on the Davis Cup, see Edward Clarkson Potter, *The Davis Cup* (New York: A. S. Barnes, 1969); Richard J. Evans, *The Davis Cup: Celebrating 100 Years of International Tennis* (New York: Universe, 1999); and Alan Trengove, *The Story of the Davis Cup* (London: S. Paul, 1985).
12. Ashe, *Days of Grace*, 62–64.
13. "Ashe Is Named U.S. Cup Captain," *BAA*, 13 Sept. 1980, 10; Les Matthews, Sport Briefs, *NYAN*, 13 Sept. 1980, 63; Fred Williams, The Tennis Beat, *LAS*, 11 Sept. 1980, B4; "Ashe to Coach Davis Cuppers," *WP*, 8 Sept. 1980, D3; "Ashe Will Coach Davis Cup Team," *NYT*, 8 Sept. 1980, C12; "Arthur Ashe Is Named U.S. Davis Cup Captain," *LAT*, 8 Sept. 1980, D8; Roscoe C. Brown Jr. to Ashe, SCRBC, box 29, folder 7; Bob Brown to Ashe, 10 Sept. 1980, ibid.; Glenn A. Hastings to Ashe, 11 Sept. 1980, ibid.; Donald Dell to Ashe, 30 Nov. 1980, ibid., box 31, folder 2.
14. Ashe, *Days of Grace*, 66.

15. Bud Collins, ed., *The Bud Collins History of Tennis: An Authoritative Encyclopedia and Record Book* (Washington, DC: New Chapter, 2008), 196–99, 592; Ashe, *Days of Grace*, 69. For more on McEnroe, see McEnroe, *You Cannot Be Serious*, with James Kaplan (New York: Berkley Books, 2002); Tim Adams, *On Being John McEnroe* (New York: Crown, 2005); Matthew Cronin, *Epic: John McEnroe, Bjorn Borg, and the Greatest Tennis Season Ever* (Hoboken, NJ: Wiley, 2011); Patrick McEnroe, *Hardcourt Confidential: Tales from Twenty Years in the Pro Tennis Trenches*, with Peter Bodo (New York: Hyperion, 2010); and Richard Evans, *John McEnroe: Taming the Talent* (New York: Bloomsbury, 1991).

16. Collins, *Bud Collins History of Tennis*, 206, 670.

17. Bob Lutz to Ashe, 13 May 1981, SCRBC, box 29, folder 7; Ashe, *Days of Grace*, 69.

18. Ashe, *Days of Grace*, 68–70; memorandum, Gordon D. Jogensen (USTA treasurer) to Ashe, 2 Jan. 1981, SCRBC, box 29, folder 7; "Ramirez, McEnroe Win for 1-1 Tie in Davis Cup," *NYT*, 7 Mar. 1981, 18; Dave Distel, "Mexico Beats U.S. in Doubles," *WP*, 8 Mar. 1981, D16; Distel, "U.S. Comes Back to Defeat Mexico," *LAT*, 9 Mar. 1981, D1.

19. Ashe, *Days of Grace*, 68–70; Dave Anderson, "U.S. Pulls Out Cup Victory, 3-2," *NYT*, 9 Mar. 1981, C3; Bernard Loomis to Ashe, 10 Mar. 1981, SCRBC, box 29, folder 10.

20. Ashe, *Days of Grace*, 73; Mike Lupica, "McEnroe Ends Toil, Trouble, and Borg's Wimbledon Reign," *CT*, 5 July 1981, B1; "McEnroe Fails to Show at Champions' Dinner," *LAT*, 5 July 1981, D8; William E. Carsley, "Terrible-Tempered Tennis Brat," *CT*, 6 July 1981, 13; "A Champion in All But Etiquette," *Guardian*, 6 July 1981, 18; "Fines and Ban Face McEnroe," *Guardian*, 6 July 1981, 18; "McEnroe Quits London amid Shower of Glass," *WP*, 6 July 1981, D2; Malcolm Moran, "McEnroe Afterglow Dimmed," *NYT*, 7 July 1981, S1.

21. Ashe, *Days of Grace*, 73–75; "McEnroe Loses—But Connors Gives U.S. Split," *LAT*, 11 July 1981, C1; "U.S. Takes Lead in Davis Cup," *CT*, 12 July 1981, C5; "McEnroe Wraps Up U.S. Victory," *LAT*, 13 July 1981, D1; "McEnroe Seals U.S. Win," *Guardian*, 13 July 1981, 16; "Connors Nixes Ashe and Cup," *BAA*, 5 Dec. 1981, 9.

22. Ashe, *Days of Grace*, 75–77; William T. Maeck to Ashe, 5 Nov. 1981, SCRBC, box 29, folder 7; Stan Malles to Paul R. Hoffman, 19 Nov. 1981, ibid.

23. Ashe, *Days of Grace*, 77–80; "Ashe Prefers Forfeit to Default If McEnroe Acts Up in Cup Final," *LAT*, 9 Dec. 1981, E5; John Feinstein, "Ashe to Warn McEnroe on Davis Tantrums," *WP*, 8 Dec. 1981, C1; Ted Green, "After McEnroe's Win, Argentina Gets Even," *LAT*, 12 Dec. 1981, E1; Green, "A Great Day for Tennis, a Bad Day for Manners," *LAT*, 13 Dec. 1981, F1; Linda Kay, "McEnroe Saves Best for Last to Give U.S. the Davis Cup," *CT*, 14 Dec. 1981, D1; "Ashe's First Captaincy a Winner," *BAA*, 19 Dec. 1981, 7C.

24. Ashe, *Days of Grace*, 77–80.

25. Ted Green, "McEnroe Settles Down and Then Settles Issue," *LAT*, 14 Dec. 1981, B1; Neil Amdur, "McEnroe's Victory Clinches Davis Cup," *NYT*, 14 Dec. 1981, C1; Richard Evans, "McEnroe Rises to Steer America Home," *Guardian*, 14 Dec. 1981, 23; John Feinstein, "McEnroe Brings Cup Back to U.S.," *WP*, 14 Dec. 1981, B1; Kay, "McEnroe Saves Best for Last to Give U.S. the Davis Cup."

26. Georg N. Meyers, "Question: What Does It Take to Absolve Outrageous Conduct?," *Seattle Times*, 14 Dec. 1981, SCRBC, box 29, folder 13; Stuart M. Butler to Ashe, 14 Dec. 1981, ibid.; Donald Dell to Ashe, 17 Dec. 1981, ibid., box 1, folder 15.

27. Ashe, *Days of Grace*, 82–85; Chris Cobbs, "McEnroe and Fleming, Quite a Pair, Clinch Win for U.S.," *LAT*, 7 Mar. 1982, E2; "It's McEnroe—in 6 Hours 32 Minutes," *LAT*, 12 July 1982, D1; Bill Jauss, "It's McEnroe in 79 Games and 6½ Hours," *CT*, 12 July 1982, D1; "U.S. Wins

Davis Cup Semifinal," *WP*, 3 Oct. 1982, G10; Neil Amdur, "U.S. Clinches Davis Cup," *NYT*, 28 Nov. 1982, S1; Bud Collins, "Noah's Ark Capsizes," *Observer*, 28 Nov. 1982, 42; David Irvine, "McEnroe and Co Look to Defence," *Guardian*, 29 Nov. 1982, 17.

28. Ashe, *Days of Grace*, 85–87; Jackson Diehl, "McEnroe Is Routed in Straight Sets," *LAT*, 7 Mar. 1983, D1; Edward Schumacher, "U.S. Out of Cup," *NYT*, 7 Mar. 1983, C1; "Vilas Has McEnroe's Number," *Guardian*, 7 Mar. 1983, 21.

29. Ashe, *Days of Grace*, 87; "Ashe Heart Problem Reappears," *BAA*, 25 June 1983, 9; "Setback for Ashe," *NYT*, 18 June 1983, 12; "Ashe Is 'Stable' after Surgery," *NYT*, 22 June 1983, B11; Fred Williams, The Tennis Beat, *LAS*, 23 June 1983, B4; Names in the News, *LAT*, 23 June 1983, G7; Sports in Brief, *Guardian*, 21 June 1983, 22.

30. Ashe, *Days of Grace*, 88.

31. Ibid., 89–90; "McEnroe, Fleming Close Out Romania," *LAT*, 26 Feb. 1984, C9; "Weary U.S. Ousts Argentina," *CT*, 15 July 1984, C14; Mike Penner, "McEnroe and Fleming Send U.S. into Davis Cup Final," *LAT*, 30 Sept. 1984, C2.

32. Ashe, *Days of Grace*, 92–94; Barnaby J. Feder, "U.S. Trails in Cup Final, 2-0," *NYT*, 17 Dec. 1984, C1; David Irvine, "Petulant Americans Lose Opening Singles," *Guardian*, 17 Dec. 1984, 25; "A Feat of Clay—Swedes Eliminate U.S. in Davis Cup," *LAT*, 18 Dec. 1984, D1; David Irvine, "Sweden Can Match the Musketeers," *Guardian*, 19 Dec. 1984, 20.

33. Peter Alfano, "U.S.T.A. to Stiffen Cup Conduct Code," *NYT*, 11 Jan. 1985, A18; John Feinstein, "Davis Cup Changes?," *WP*, 12 Jan. 1985, D5; "McEnroe: No to Davis Cup," *WP*, 13 Jan. 1985, M6; Peter Alfano, "USTA Acting on Behavior," *NYT*, 15 Jan. 1985, B12.

34. Ashe, *Days of Grace*, 94–96; Alfano, "U.S.T.A. to Stiffen Cup Conduct Code"; "Davis Cup Warning to US Team," *Guardian*, 16 Jan. 1985, 24.

35. "Ashe to Be Dropped as Davis Captain," *NYT*, 22 Oct. 1985, B5; Mark Asher, "Ashe Resigns as Captain of Davis Cup Team," *WP*, 23 Oct. 1985, B1; Ashe, *Days of Grace*, 96–103.

36. Ashe, "McEnroe: 'No' to Borg Duel," *WP*, 17 Oct. 1980, D1, D3; Ashe, *Days of Grace*, 107–9; "Ashe Thwarts S. Africa in Bid for Tennis Plum," *BAA*, 25 Oct. 1980, 10; "Ashe Slams an Ace against South Africa," *NYAN*, 25 Oct. 1980, 63; "John McEnroe Applauded," *NYAN*, 15 Nov. 1980, 16.

37. Ashe, "McEnroe: 'No' to Borg Duel"; Ashe, *Days of Grace*, 107–9.

38. Ngqondi L. Masimini, "There's Nothing Phony in Transkei," *WP*, 26 Oct. 1980, D14.

39. "U.N. Readies Blacklist against South Africa," *WP*, 13 Mar. 1981, E4; Neil Amdur, "Sports—Apartheid Moves Build," *NYT*, 26 Apr. 1981, S6; "S. Africa Ties Get Stars' Ban," *BAA*, 23 May 1981, 9.

40. Lexie Verdon, "Boycotting S. Africa," *WP*, 13 Sept. 1983, B1, B9; Judith Michaelson, "Ironies in the Fired 'Cagney,'" *LAT*, 14 Sept. 1983, G1; Clarke Taylor, "Entertainers, Athletes Join to End Apartheid," *LAT*, 15 Sept. 1983, K1; Gertrude Gipson, "Money's the Game," *LAS*, 22 Sept. 1983, B7; Daniel Ben Av, "Sun City Boycott," *LAT*, 25 Sept. 1983, W95; "Ebony Etchings," *ADW*, 29 Sept. 1983, 9.

41. Simon Anekwe, "Cultural Boycott of So. Africa Launched on Both Coasts," *NYAN*, 8 Oct. 1983, 23; Anekwe, "Set Anti-Apartheid Confab on Oct. 8–9," *NYAN*, 8 Oct. 1983, 12; Gertrude Gipson, "Media Forum at Ebell," *LAS*, 6 Oct. 1983, B7; Gipson, "Actor Mourned," *LAS*, 13 Oct. 1983, B7; "South African Report," *NYT*, 3 Nov. 1983, B21; Anekwe, "Benton: No More S. African Visits," *NYAN*, 7 Jan. 1984, 4.

42. Skip Myslenski and Linda Kay, "Odds & Ins," *CT*, 5 July 1984, C2; Simon Anekwe, "Apartheid Fight Games Benefit," *NYAN*, 6 Oct. 1984, 2; "Tennis Tournament Supports

Liberation in South Africa," *ADW*, 2 Nov. 1984, 7. A good article that outlines South Africa's position is Courtland Milloy, "Apartheid's Salesman," *WP*, 18 Oct. 1984, DC1.

43. "Marching against Apartheid," *Time*, 10 Dec. 1984; Ashe, *Days of Grace*, 110-12; "39 Are Held in Protest at South Africa Office," *NYT*, 12 Jan. 1985, 26; Karlyn Barker, "Arthur Ashe Jailed in Apartheid Protest," *WP*, 12 Jan. 1985, B1; Peter Pringle, "Moral Crusade Grows," *Observer*, 27 Jan. 1985, 14. Others arrested in January 1985 included Edward Bloustein, president of Rutgers University; Alan Karcher, Speaker of the New Jersey State Assembly; and Maxine Waters, a member of the California State Assembly. Karlyn Barker, "Apartheid Protesters' 'Show Trial' Canceled," *WP*, 26 Feb. 1985, A13.

44. "Professor Arthur Ashe: Tennis' Class Act Moves into the Classroom," *Ebony*, July 1983, 79-80, 82; Ashe, *Days of Grace*, 169-70.

45. "Professor Arthur Ashe"; Ashe, *Days of Grace*, 169-74; Edwin B. Henderson, *The Negro in Sports* (Washington, DC: Associated Publishers, 1939); A. S. Young, *Negro Firsts in Sports* (Chicago: Johnson, 1963).

46. Ashe to unknown recipient, 8 Dec. 1982, SCRBC, box 9, folder 1; "Manuscript Status Report," 1983, ibid.; Bob Lipper, "The Grace and Grit of Arthur Ashe," *RTD*, 21 May 1989.

47. Henry Louis Gates Jr. to Ashe, 20 Sept. 1984, and Benjamin Quarles to Sandra Jamison, 31 May 1984, both in SCRBC, box 9, Correspondence General, 1983-1986.

48. Skip Myslenski, "Ashe Tells Story of Glory, Shame," *CT*, 14 May 1985, C1; G. D. Clay, "A Knowledgeable Chalk Talk," *LAT*, 26 June 1987, B16.

49. Ashe, *Days of Grace*, 174; Bill Millsaps, "Ashe Is Enjoying Another Kind of Triumph," *RTD*, 14 Dec. 1988; David Halberstam, "Champions We Never Knew," *NYT*, 4 Dec. 1988, BR11; Amistad Press Fact Sheet, 1988, SCRBC, box 9, folder 2; President's Annual Report, Amistad Press, 1988, ibid.; memorandum, Sammie Jackson Harris (secretary to Amistad board of directors), 10 Feb. 1989, ibid.; book advertisement, *NYT*, 6 Nov. 1988, ibid.

50. Jim Murray, "A History That Needs to Be Told," *LAT*, 21 Apr. 1985, C1; Michael Wilbon, "'Black Champions' in Focus Again," *WP*, 14 May 1986, C12.

51. Halberstam, "Champions We Never Knew"; "Tennis Legend Arthur Ashe and New Book 'Big Smash,'" *ADW*, 12 Feb. 1989, 8; Barry Lorge, "Inside the Heart & Mind of Arthur Ashe," *Tennis*, Sept. 1988, 46, SCRBC, box 35, folder 4; Herbert Kupferberg, "Their Hard Road to Glory," *Parade*, 12 Mar. 1989, 12, 14, ibid.; Ebony Book Shelf, *Ebony*, Feb. 1989, 30.

52. Millsaps, "Ashe Is Enjoying Another Kind of Triumph"; Barry Lorge, "Ashe Book Literary Labor of Love," *San Diego Union*, 2 Nov. 1988, SCRBC, box 9, folder 2; Lipper, "Grace and Grit of Arthur Ashe."

53. Thomas Boswell, "Arthur Ashe," *Gentlemen's Quarterly*, Jan. 1985, 134, SCRBC, box 35, folder 4; Ashe, *Days of Grace*, 169, 191-94.

54. Ashe, *Days of Grace*, 180-83. For a detailed discussion of Ashe's views on financial planning, see ibid., 176-84.

55. Marian Christy, "They Are Living a Love Match," *Newport News Daily Press*, 10 Oct. 1980, SCRBC, box 40, Scrapbooks.

56. Howie Evans, "Thompson, Ashe Clash on Prop. 42," *NYAN*, 21 Jan. 1989, 52; William Sullivan, "Ashe Takes Heat for Position," *WP*, 15 Feb. 1989, F5; Ashe, *Days of Grace*, 147-51.

57. Ibid.; Ashe, "Coddling Black Athletes," *NYT*, 10 Feb. 1989, A35; Mark Asher, "Thompson Urges Input of Blacks," *WP*, 3 Apr. 1989, C9; Jaime Harris, "Sports Forum Focuses on Prop. 42," *NYAN*, 15 Apr. 1989, 56; Ken Denlinger, "Proposition 42: Thompson's Act of Conscience Leaves Us Something to Consider," *WP*, 29 Jan. 1989, B9; Ashe, "NCAA Propositions

Itself over 42," *WP*, 20 Jan. 1990, D1; Lipper, "Grace and Grit of Arthur Ashe"; Paul A. Witteman, "A Man of Fire and Grace: Arthur Ashe, 1943–1993," *Time*, 15 Feb. 1993.

58. Karlyn Barker, "Antiapartheid Activists Vow to Pressure U.S. Businesses," *WP*, 28 Nov. 1985, B1.

59. Dennis Hevesi, "Thousands in New York Rally against Apartheid," *NYT*, 15 June 1986, 1; Simon Anekwe, "Famous Pols and Stars to Join Apartheid Rally," *NYAN*, 14 June 1986, 2; "N.Y. Rally Calls for U.S. Sanctions on S. Africa," *LAT*, 15 June 1986, A7; Lyle V. Harris, "New York Rally Protests Apartheid," *WP*, 15 June 1986, A21; Cheryll Y. Greene, "Support Dellums South African Sanctions Bill," *NYAN*, 14 June 1986, 15; W. J. Weatherby, "Singing the Old Songs," *Guardian*, 27 June 1986, 17.

60. Peter Noel, "S. Africans Playing in US Open Tourney?," *NYAN*, 6 Sept. 1986, 1; Ira Berkow, "South Africans at the Open," *NYT*, 1 Sept. 1987, A21.

61. Ashe, *Days of Grace*, 16; Jacqueline Trescott, "Ashe's Steady Partner," *WP*, 29 May 1992, D1.

62. Mike Towle, ed., *I Remember Arthur Ashe: Memories of a True Tennis Pioneer and Champion of Social Causes by the People Who Knew Him* (Nashville: Cumberland House, 2001), 113–14; Trescott, "Ashe's Steady Partner"; "Press Release of Tennis Legend Arthur Ashe Jr., Announcing He Has AIDS," *Historic Documents of 1992* (Washington, DC: CQ Press, 1993), CQ Electronic Library, CQ Public Affairs Collection, http://library.cqpress.com/cqpac/hs dc92-0000090924; Frank Deford to Ashe, 22 Dec. 1989, SCRBC, box 1, folder 14.

63. Doug Smith, *Whirlwind: The Godfather of Black Tennis; The Life and Times of Dr. Robert Walter Johnson* (Washington, DC: Blue Eagle, 2004), 173–76; Ashe, *Days of Grace*, 7–17; Towle, *I Remember Arthur Ashe*, 110–14.

64. Ashe, *Days of Grace*, 10–17; "Press Release of Tennis Legend Arthur Ashe Jr., Announcing He Has AIDS."

65. Lance Morrow, "Fair Game?," *Time*, 20 Apr. 1992; Robert Lipsyte, "None of Us Needs Other People's Fears," *NYT*, 10 Apr. 1992, B13; Mark Tran, "Illness in the Public Domain," *Guardian*, 10 Apr. 1992, 23; Mark Gray, "Ashe Deserved to Keep His Privacy," *ADW*, 12 Apr. 1992, 8. Other examples of columns that defend Ashe include Richard Sandomir, "It's Easy to 'Pig Out' at This Buffet," *NYT*, 10 Apr. 1992, B16; Anna Quindlen, "Journalism 2001," *NYT*, 12 Apr. 1992, 168; "Double Anguish of Arthur Ashe," *Observer*, 12 Apr. 1992, 12; Laura Barish and Joseph Rougeau, "Public Figures, Private Lives," *WP*, 16 Apr. 1992, A22; Howie Evans, "Who Betrayed Arthur Ashe?," *NYAN*, 18 Apr. 1992, 52; A. S. "Doc" Young, "Violation of Arthur Ashe," *LAS*, 23 Apr. 1992, A7.

66. B. Drummond Ayres Jr., "Ashe Returns to the City He Disowned in Youth," *NYT*, 7 May 1992, A18; Carolyn Click, "Ashe Says Life Has Changed since AIDS Revelation," *ADW*, 12 May 1992, 5; Howie Evans, "Tennis Stars Coming Out for Arthur Ashe Foundation," *NYAN*, 29 Aug. 1992, 52; Harvey Araton, "On an Inspiring Day, Everyone Gets to Serve," *NYT*, 31 Aug. 1992, C8; Marc Hopkins, "Arthur Ashe Speaks Out on AIDS," *PC*, 17 Oct. 1992, 1.

67. Kenny Moore, "The Eternal Example," *SI*, 21 Dec. 1992, 16–27.

68. Robin Finn, "Arthur Ashe, Tennis Champion, Dies of AIDS," *NYT*, 7 Feb. 1993, 1; Martin Weil, "Tennis Legend Arthur Ashe Dies at 49," *WP*, 7 Feb. 1993, A1.

### CONCLUSION

1. Michael Paul Williams, "Arthur Ashe: A Virginia Hero for the World," *RTD*, 8 Feb. 1993; Mike Allen, "He Had to Know How Much He Meant," *RTD*, 10 Feb. 1993; Olivia Winslow, "Thousands Pay Respects to Ashe," *RTD*, 10 Feb. 1993.

2. Allen, "He Had to Know How Much He Meant"; Bob Lipper, "Friend Ashe Left Behind Felt Knowing Him Was a Fortune," *RTD*, 7 Feb. 1993.

3. "Arthur Ashe, Model Champion," *NYT*, 9 Feb. 1993, A20; Mike Allen, "Just Plain Better Than Most of Us," *RTD*, 11 Feb. 1993; Alison Muscatine, "He Never Rested with Fame," *Guardian*, 10 Feb. 1993, A3; "The Ultimate Competitor," *LAS*, 11 Feb. 1993, B1; Howie Evans, "Arthur Ashe: A Quiet Voice Leaves a Resonating Legacy," *NYAN*, 13 Feb. 1993, 1.

4. Allen, "Just Plain Better Than Most of Us."

# Essay on Sources

## ARTHUR ASHE

Scholars interested in Ashe's public life should first consult the mainstream popular press. Beginning in the mid-1960s, sportswriters such as Allison Danzig, Jim Murray, Neil Amdur, Frank Deford, and Bud Collins reported on Ashe's athletic career and social activism for the *New York Times*, the *Los Angeles Times*, the *Washington Post*, the *Chicago Tribune*, and the *Boston Globe*, as well as for popular magazines, including *Sports Illustrated*, *Sporting News*, *World Tennis*, *Life*, *Time*, and *Newsweek*. The black press, particularly the *Chicago Defender*, the *Baltimore Afro-American*, the *New York Amsterdam News*, the *Pittsburgh Courier*, and the *Atlanta Daily World*, extensively covered and commented on Ashe's civil rights and antiapartheid activities and travels to Africa. Better than any other columnist, Sam Lacy, of the *Afro-American*, led a nuanced and sustained attack on apartheid and placed sports in the context of international politics. *Ebony* and *Jet*, the two black periodicals with the largest circulation, closely followed Ashe in the 1970s and 1980s, as he transitioned from world-class tennis player to coach, motivational speaker, businessman, activist, and public intellectual. The British and South African popular presses, specifically the *Guardian*, the *London Times*, the *Rand Daily Mail*, the *Johannesburg Star*, and the *Cape Times*, provided comprehensive editorial coverage of Ashe's visa controversy and his visits to South Africa. *Die Burger* best conveyed the views of the South African government. A number of local U.S. newspapers, most notably the *Richmond Times-Dispatch*, the *Richmond News-Leader*, and the UCLA *Daily Bruin*, helped fill in the early years of Ashe's life.

Most athletes do not leave behind a collection of personal papers. Fortunately for me, Ashe was no ordinary tennis player. Shortly after his death, the Ashe family donated forty-two boxes of material to the Schomburg Center for Research in Black Culture in New York City. The collection includes private correspondence, transcribed interviews with Ashe and other important figures, speeches, handwritten notes, photographs, scrapbooks, telegrams from Martin Luther King Jr. and Jackie Robinson, hate mail, and other items. The Ashe Papers offer a window into his private life, especially after 1988, when he struggled to keep his AIDS diagnosis from the public. Three other archives—in Los Angeles, Evanston, Illinois, and Washington, DC—house useful collections. The Department of Special Collections at the Young Research Library, UCLA, holds transcribed interviews with friends and associates of J. D. Morgan. The papers of Dennis Brutus at the Northwestern University Library provided great insight into the philosophies and tactics of one of Ashe's fiercest intellectual opponents. And the Library of Congress, in Washington, DC, houses an extensive collection of newspapers and magazines.

Although Ashe went to great lengths to protect his private life and his public image, he told his story in four coauthored memoirs. *Advantage Ashe*, published in 1967 and cowritten with Clifford George Gewecke Jr., is a cursory narrative of Ashe's childhood, his time at UCLA, and his experiences as a member of the U.S. Davis Cup team. Though clearly focused on tennis, *Advantage Ashe* briefly discusses Ashe's views on race and includes a chapter of interviews with his UCLA teammates. Years later, Ashe claimed that he had had little to do with the writing of *Advantage Ashe*. His second memoir, written with *Sports Illustrated* reporter Frank Deford and titled *Arthur Ashe: Portrait in Motion* (1975), follows Ashe from Wimbledon 1973 to Wimbledon 1974 and reads like a personal diary. It details Ashe's hectic travel schedule and work on behalf of the ATP, as well as his views on race, South Africa, and women's tennis. *Portrait in Motion*'s thorough account of Ashe's controversial trip to South Africa is particularly useful to scholars. *Off the Court*, coauthored by Neil Amdur, of the *New York Times*, and published after Ashe's playing career ended in 1981, offers a more balanced narrative of Ashe's life. Each of its twelve chapters focuses on an important event or period in his life, such as his heart attack, growing up in the segregated South, attending UCLA, joining the army, winning the U.S. Open and Wimbledon, speaking out on racial matters, and marrying Jeanne Moutoussamy. *Off the Court* chronicles Ashe's intellectual transformation and his emergence as a human rights and civil rights activist. It remains his most honest memoir. *Days of Grace*, written with Princeton literature professor Arnold Rampersad and released following Ashe's death in 1993, rehashes many of the stories told in *Off the Court* but sheds new light on Ashe's postretirement activities. The book discusses his run-ins with Jimmy Connors and John McEnroe as captain of the U.S. Davis Cup team, his social activism in the United States and South Africa, and his efforts to maintain a degree of privacy in the wake of his AIDS diagnosis. Unlike his other memoirs, *Days of Grace* addresses a variety of controversial issues, including homosexuality, politics, and cutting-edge AIDS treatments. In eloquent, reflective prose, Ashe tried to (re)shape his legacy, well aware that his life was coming to an end.

Since the early 1960s a number of journalists have written about Ashe, none better than John McPhee. McPhee's masterful book *Levels of the Game* (1969), originally published as a series of articles in the *New Yorker*, narrates Ashe's match with Clark Graebner in the semifinal round of the 1968 U.S. Open. McPhee alternates between a description of the match and a deep examination of the two men doing battle. Relying on interviews with Ashe, Graebner, Ashe Sr., and other friends, mentors, and family members, McPhee skillfully examines the factors and events that brought Ashe and Graebner together at Forest Hills. *Levels of the Game* is an essential read for scholars and sports fans alike. Mike Towle's *I Remember Arthur Ashe* is a collection of interviews with tennis players, journalists, political figures, civil rights activists, and friends, who share their memories of Ashe and reflect on his legacy. Other histories and memoirs that informed my work include Cecil Harris and Larryette Kyle-DeBose, *Charging the Net: A History of Blacks in Tennis from Althea Gibson and Arthur Ashe to the Williams Sisters* (2007); Douglas Henderson Jr., *Endeavor to Persevere: A Memoir on Jimmy Connors, Arthur Ashe, Tennis and Life* (2010); Frank Deford, *Over Time: My Life as a Sportswriter* (2012); Bud Collins, *My Life with the Pros* (1990); Peter Bodo, *The Courts of Babylon: Tales of Greed and Glory in the Harsh New World of Professional Tennis* (1995); and Sam Lacy with Moses J. Newson, *Fighting for Fairness: The Life Story of Hall of Fame Sportswriter Sam Lacy* (1998).

There are no full-length scholarly studies on Arthur Ashe, but a handful of useful articles and book chapters examine various aspects of Ashe's life. My article "'I guess I'm becoming more and more militant': Arthur Ashe and the Black Freedom Movement, 1961–1968" (*Journal of African American History*, 2011) traces Ashe's intellectual journey from moderate to militant integrationist and examines his participation in the black athletic revolution. Eric Morgan's article "Black and White at Center Court: Arthur Ashe and the Confrontation of Apartheid in South Africa" (*Diplomatic History*, 2012) focuses on Ashe's visa denials and his highly publicized trip to South Africa in 1973. Morgan offers a compelling case for the importance of nongovernmental actors in the diplomatic process and argues that Ashe's willingness to directly engage South African officials further isolated South Africa from the international community. Damion Thomas has authored several pieces on Ashe. In "'Don't Tell Me How to Think': Arthur Ashe and the Burden of 'Being Black'" (*International Journal of the History of Sport*, 2010) Thomas identifies Ashe as a black conservative forced by the African American intelligentsia to navigate the politics of race. Thomas further examines Ashe's double consciousness as a black man playing a predominately white sport in his essay "'The Quiet Militant': Arthur Ashe and Black Athletic Activism" (in *Out of the Shadows: A Biographical History of African American Athletes*, edited by David K. Wiggins, 2006). Additional scholarship on Ashe includes Sundiata Djata, *Blacks at the Net: Black Achievement in the History of Tennis* (2006–8); and Kristen Elizabeth Norton, "I Am a Citizen of the World: Constructing the Public Memory of Arthur Ashe" (MA thesis, Florida State University, 2010).

## TENNIS

Few scholars have written broad histories of tennis, especially the modern game. The sociologist E. Digby Baltzell's *Sporting Gentlemen: Men's Tennis from the Age of Honor to the Cult of the Superstar* (updated 2013) remains the best starting point. Baltzell provides a comprehensive history of the game while focusing on tennis's written and unwritten rules. He is highly critical of tennis players during the Open era, believing them to be greedy egotists with little respect for the sport's "code of honor." Ashe, he notes, is an exception. Other books on the history of tennis include Heiner Gillmeister, *Tennis: A Cultural History* (1998); Allison Danzig and Peter Schwed, eds., *The Fireside Book of Tennis: A Complete History of the Game and Its Great Players and Matches* (1972); Marshall Jon Fisher, *A Terrible Splendor: Three Extraordinary Men, a World Poised for War, and the Greatest Tennis Match Ever Played* (2009); Richard Evans, *The Davis Cup: Celebrating 100 Years of International Tennis* (1999); Steve Flink, *The Greatest Tennis Matches of All Time* (2012); Caryl Phillips, *The Right Set: A Tennis Anthology* (2010); and Stephen Tignor, *High Strung: Bjorn Borg, John McEnroe, and the Last Days of Tennis's Golden Age* (2011).

There are a number of excellent biographies of other well-known tennis players, none better than Susan Ware's *Game, Set, Match: Billie Jean King and the Revolution in Women's Sports* (2011). Ware is less interested in King's playing career than in her active and symbolic role in the women's liberation movement. She argues that King's leadership in combating sexism, combined with second-wave feminism and Title IX, ushered in a new era in women's sports. Another biography with direct bearing on my work is Doug Smith's *Whirlwind: The Godfather of Black Tennis; The Life and Times of Dr. Robert Walter Johnson* (2004). Johnson, a mentor to both Ashe and Althea Gibson, established the Junior Development Program under the auspices of the ATA and pushed for the integration of junior tennis. Smith was also one of the *USA Today* reporters who broke Ashe's AIDS story, which Smith discusses in detail in *Whirlwind*. Other useful biographies and autobiographies are Jimmy Connors, *The Outsider: A Memoir* (2013); John McEnroe with James Kaplan, *You Cannot Be Serious* (2002); Billie Jean

King with Christine Brennan, *Pressure Is a Privilege: Lessons I've Learned from Life and the Battle of the Sexes* (2008); Billie Jean King with Frank Deford, *Billie Jean* (1982); Ilie Nastase, *Mr. Nastase: The Autobiography* (2009); Richard Evans, *Ilie Nastase* (1978); and Richard "Pancho" Gonzales, *Man With a Racket: The Autobiography of Pancho Gonzales*, as told by Cy Rice (1959). A great article on Pancho Gonzalez is José M. Alamillo, "Richard 'Pancho' Gonzalez: Race and the Print Media in Postwar Tennis America" (*International Journal of the History of Sport*, 2009).

## African Americans and Sports

There are many excellent historical surveys and anthologies on the black experience in American sports, an impressive number of them written or edited by David K. Wiggins. *Glory Bound: Black Athletes in a White America* (1997) is a collection of eleven essays that provide a solid foundation for the study of race and sports. Particularly helpful is Wiggins's essay on Joe Louis, in which he applies W. E. B. Du Bois's theory of double consciousness to Louis. *Out of the Shadows: A Biographical History of African American Athletes* (2006) is an accessible collection of short biographies whose subjects include Ashe and Althea Gibson. Two of his best survey readers are Wiggins and Patrick B. Miller, *The Unlevel Playing Field: A Documentary History of the African American Experience in Sport* (2005); and Wiggins and Miller, *Sport and the Color Line: Black Athletes and Race Relations in Twentieth Century America* (2003). The most comprehensive piece on African Americans and sports, though now somewhat dated, remains Jeffrey T. Sammons's article "'Race' and Sport: A Critical, Historical Examination" (*Journal of Sport History*, 1994). Other valuable works are William C. Rhoden, *Forty Million Dollar Slaves: The Rise, Fall, and Redemption of the Black Athlete* (2007); Russell T. Wigginton, *The Strange Career of the Black Athlete: African Americans and Sports* (2006); and Simon Henderson, *Sidelined: How American Sports Challenged the Black Freedom Struggle* (2013).

The "revolt of the black athlete" of the late 1960s and early 1970s has received significant scholarly attention. Amy Bass's *Not the Triumph But the Struggle: The 1968 Olympics and the Making of the Black Athlete* (2004) and Douglas Hartmann's *Race, Culture, and the Revolt of the Black Athlete: The 1968 Olympic Protests and Their Aftermath* (2004) explore the events that led to John Carlos and Tommie Smith's iconic Black Power salute, including racial discrimination in American cities and African decolonization, as well as racism in sports. Of the many athletes who participated in the black athletic revolution, Bill Russell, Jim Brown, and especially Muhammad Ali continue to dominate the literature. Aram Goudsouzian's *King of the Court: Bill Russell and the Basketball Revolution* (2011) is the definitive biography of Russell, basketball's first black superstar, who challenged racial discrimination and embraced the teachings of both Martin Luther King Jr. and Malcolm X. Mike Freeman focuses on the life and times of NFL Hall of Fame running back Jim Brown in *Jim Brown: The Fierce Life of an American Hero* (2006). The well-balanced biography examines Brown's football and acting careers, his increasing militancy, and his contributions to the black freedom movement. There are numerous studies on Ali, the most comprehensive being Elliott Gorn's edited volume *Muhammad Ali: The People's Champ* (1995). Gorn's collection of seven original essays discusses Ali as a cultural icon and explores the ways in which he influenced black and white sports fans as well as the black freedom struggle. Thomas Hauser's *Muhammad Ali: His Life and Times* (1991) relies on interviews with Ali's friends and associates. Other works are Gerald Early, *The Muhammad Ali Reader* (Ecco paperback 2013); David Remnick, *King of the World: Muhammad Ali and the Rise of an American Hero* (1999); and José Torres, *Sting Like a Bee: The*

*Muhammad Ali Story* (new ed. 2009). There remains no definitive scholarly biography of Ali. Several important studies on race and college sports helped shape my work. Charles H. Martin, in his many articles and in his book *Benching Jim Crow: The Rise and Fall of the Color Line in Southern College Sports, 1890–1980* (2010), surveys the slow and uneven process of desegregation, concentrating mostly on the Southeastern Conference, the Atlantic Coast Conference, and colleges and universities in Texas. Richard Pennington's *Breaking the Ice: The Racial Integration of Southwest Conference Football* (1987) is another informative study. Finally, John Matthew Smith's *The Sons of Westwood: John Wooden, UCLA, and the Dynasty That Changed College Basketball* (2013) and his article " 'It's Not Really My Country': Lew Alcindor and the Revolt of the Black Athlete" (*Journal of Sport History*, 2009) examine the intersection of college basketball, the black freedom movement, the antiwar movement, and the athletic revolution through the lens of the UCLA dynasty of the 1960s and 1970s.

## THE CIVIL RIGHTS MOVEMENT

The literature on the civil rights movement is quite extensive. The best overviews are Manning Marable, *Race, Reform, and Rebellion: The Second Reconstruction in Black America, 1945–1990* (1991); Steven F. Lawson, *Running for Freedom: Civil Rights and Black Politics in America since 1941* (3rd ed. 2009); Kevin Gaines, *Uplifting the Race: Black Leadership, Politics, and Culture in the Twentieth Century* (1996); Harvard Sitkoff, *The Struggle for Black Equality* (2008); Adam Fairclough, *Better Day Coming: Blacks and Equality, 1890–2000* (2002); Rhoda Lois Blumberg, *Civil Rights: The 1960s Freedom Struggle* (1991); Doug McAdam, *Political Process and the Development of Black Insurgency, 1930–1970* (1999); Pat Watters, *Down to Now: Reflections on the Southern Civil Rights Movement* (1993); Elaine Landau, *The Civil Rights Movement in America* (2003); Taylor Branch, *The King Years: Historic Moments in the Civil Rights Movement* (2013); Robert Weisbrot, *Freedom Bound: A History of America's Civil Rights Movement* (1989); Jon Meacham, *Voices in Our Blood: America's Best on the Civil Rights Movement* (2003), and Hugh Davis Graham, *The Civil Rights Era: Origins and Development of National Policy, 1960–1972* (1990).

Other, more focused works on the movement include James T. Patterson, *Brown v. Board of Education: A Civil Rights Milestone and Its Troubled Legacy* (2002); Raymond Arsenault, *Freedom Riders: 1961 and the Struggle for Racial Justice* (2006); Bruce Watson, *Freedom Summer: The Savage Season of 1964 That Made Mississippi Burn and Made America a Democracy* (2011); Charles W. Eagles, *The Price of Defiance: James Meredith and the Integration of Ole Miss* (2009); Clayborne Carson, *In Struggle: SNCC and the Black Awakening of the 1960s* (1981); August Meier and Elliot Rudwick, *CORE: A Study in the Civil Rights Movement, 1942–1968* (1973); Patricia Sullivan, *Lift Every Voice: The NAACP and the Making of the Civil Rights Movement* (2009); and Thomas Sugrue, *Sweet Land of Liberty: The Forgotten Struggle for Civil Rights in the North* (2008). For the civil rights movement and Massive Resistance in Richmond, see Lewis A. Randolph, *Rights for a Season: The Politics of Race, Class, and Gender in Richmond, Virginia* (2003); and Megan Taylor Shockley, *"We, Too, Are Americans": African American Women in Detroit and Richmond, 1940–54* (2004). Kurt Edward Kemper's "Reformers in the Marketplace of Ideas: Student Activism and American Democracy in Cold War Los Angeles" (PhD diss., Louisiana State University, 2000) provides a great examination of civil rights activism on the UCLA campus. Another fine study on the movement in California is Mark Brilliant, *The Color of America Has Changed: How Racial Diversity Shaped Civil Rights Reform in California, 1941–1978* (2012).

Several key biographies tell the story of the movement through the eyes and experiences of a single individual. Barbara Ransby's *Ella Baker and the Black Freedom Movement: A Radical Democratic Vision* (2005) follows the life and career of Ella Baker, one of the founders of SNCC, who had previously worked for the NAACP and SCLC. Like Ashe's, Baker's participation in the movement bridged the civil rights and Black Power eras. Timothy Tyson's *Radio Free Dixie: Robert F. Williams and the Roots of Black Power* (1999) examines the origins of Black Power through the lens of a former NAACP organizer and radical icon forced to flee the United States for Cuba. The best biographies of Martin Luther King Jr. are David Garrow, *Bearing the Cross: Martin Luther King, Jr., and the Southern Christian Leadership Conference* (1986); Taylor Branch, *Parting the Waters: America in the King Years, 1954–63* (1989); Branch, *Pillar of Fire: America in the King Years, 1963–65* (1999); Branch, *At Canaan's Edge: America in the King Years, 1965–68* (2007); and David Levering Lewis, *King: A Biography* (3rd ed. 2013). Dennis C. Dickerson's *Militant Mediator: Whitney M. Young, Jr.* (1998) focuses on the head of the Urban League, a leader who successfully worked with both blacks and whites, as well as conservatives, moderates, and radicals. In his later life, Ashe's philosophies most closely aligned with those of Young. The best new biography of the movement is Jeanne Theoharis, *The Rebellious Life of Mrs. Rosa Parks* (2013).

### THE BLACK POWER MOVEMENT

As Peniel E. Joseph points out in his essay "The Black Power Movement: A State of the Field" (*Journal of American History*, 2009), Black Power is often characterized by a series of iconic images: armed Black Panthers riding around the streets of Oakland, Stokely Carmichael's speech in Greenwood, Smith and Carlos's black-gloved salute, and Angela Davis's wanted poster, to name a few. Focusing largely on these images and the militant rhetoric of Black Power advocates, the early histories of the movement discussed Black Power as the "evil twin" of the civil rights movement. According to this narrative, the Black Power movement corrupted the New Left, drowned out the nonviolent voices of the civil rights movement, and offered white politicians a convenient scapegoat for racial violence. Fortunately for scholars and nonscholars alike, recent literature has corrected this perception. Joseph's own *Waiting 'Til the Midnight Hour: A Narrative History of Black Power in America* (2006) is a superbly written and comprehensive narrative of the Black Power era. Locating the origins of the movement in the black radicalism of the mid-1950s, Joseph argues that the Black Power movement "paralleled, and at times overlapped, the heroic civil rights era." Other fine works on Black Power that focus mostly on culture are William Van Deburg, *New Day in Babylon: The Black Power Movement and American Culture, 1965–1975* (1992); and James Edward Smethurst, *The Black Arts Movement: Literary Nationalism in the 1960s and 1970s* (2005). Van Deburg contends that Black Power was most enduring as a cultural movement, while Smethurst better connects politics and culture. Jeffrey O. G. Ogbar, in *Black Power: Radical Politics and African American Identity* (2004), offers a fresh perspective on the Nation of Islam, the Black Panther Party, and notable civil rights leaders while arguing convincingly that many African Americans embraced both nationalist and desegregationist political agendas.

Black Power organizations have also received significant scholarly attention in recent years. For discussions of the Black Panther Party, see Charles Jones, ed., *The Black Panther Party Reconsidered* (1998); Yohuru Williams, *Black Politics/White Power* (2000); Robert O. Self, *American Babylon: Race and the Struggle for Postwar Oakland* (2003); Curtis J. Austin, *Up Against the Wall* (2006); Paul Alkebulan, *Survival Pending Revolution* (2007); and Jane

Rhodes, *Framing the Black Panthers: The Spectacular Rise of a Black Power Icon* (2007). Most relevant to Ashe is Scot Brown's *Fighting for US: Maulana Karenga, the US Organization, and Black Cultural Nationalism* (2003), which examines the politics and cultural practices of Organization US, a black nationalist group based in Los Angeles. Other important Black Power studies are Komozi Woodard, *A Nation Within a Nation: Amiri Baraka (LeRoi Jones) and Black Power Politics* (1999); Matthew Countryman, *Up South: Civil Rights and Black Power in Philadelphia* (2005); Winston A. Grady-Willis, *Challenging U.S. Apartheid* (2006); Kent Germany, *New Orleans After the Promises* (2007); and Joseph, ed., *The Black Power Movement: Rethinking the Civil Rights–Black Power Era* (2006).

## SOUTH AFRICA, APARTHEID, AND SPORTS

The literature on South African apartheid, scholarly and otherwise, is vast. The best general histories and introductions are Leonard Thompson, *A History of South Africa* (2001); P. Eric Louw, *The Rise, Fall, and Legacy of Apartheid* (2004); T. R. H. Davenport and Christopher Saunders, *South Africa: A Modern History* (2000); Nancy L. Clark and William H. Worger, *South Africa: The Rise and Fall of Apartheid* (2011); and Robert Harvey, *The Fall of Apartheid: The Inside Story from Smuts to Mbeki* (2001). Two comparative works on black and white ideologies in the United States and South Africa are George M. Fredrickson's *Black Liberation: A Comparative History of Black Ideologies in the United States and South Africa* (1996); and Fredrickson, *White Supremacy: A Comparative Study of American and South African History* (1982). The public and private debates over engagement, divestment, and the cultural boycott are thoroughly examined in Christopher Coker, *The United States and South Africa, 1968–1985: Constructive Engagement and Its Critics* (1986) and Robert Kinloch Massie, *Loosing the Bonds: The United States and South Africa in the Apartheid Years* (1997). On American participation in the antiapartheid movement, see Francis Njubi Nesbitt, *Race for Sanctions: African Americans Against Apartheid, 1946–1994* (2004); David L. Hostetter, *Movement Matters: American Antiapartheid Activism and the Rise of Multicultural Politics* (2006); and Lewis V. Baldwin, *Toward the Beloved Community: Martin Luther King, Jr. and South Africa* (1995). Both Nesbitt's and Hostetter's studies discuss Ashe's visa controversy.

Works on sports and apartheid include Douglas Booth, *The Race Game: Sport and Politics in South Africa* (1998); John Nauright, *Sport, Cultures and Identities in South Africa* (1997); and Richard Lapchick, *The Politics of Race and International Sport: The Case of South Africa* (1975). Lapchick in particular devotes an entire chapter to what he terms the "Ashe Affair." The African National Congress, South Africa's largest antiapartheid organization, has received considerable scholarly attention. Two fine works on the ANC both inside and outside South Africa are Stephen Ellis, *External Mission: The ANC in Exile, 1960–1990* (2012); and Raymond Suttner, *The ANC Underground in South Africa, 1950–1976* (2009). No South African—black or white—has had more written about him than Nelson Mandela. The ideal starting points for a discussion of Mandela are Thomas Lodge, *Mandela: A Critical Life* (2007); and Anthony Sampson, *Mandela: The Authorised Biography* (2011). Finally, the best insight into Dennis Brutus's philosophies is Aisha Karim and Lee Sustar, eds., *Poetry and Protest: A Dennis Brutus Reader* (2006).

# Index